From Music
to
MEDICINE

From Music
to
MEDICINE

SHAWN A. ROUSSIN, PAC

KINDLE PUBLISHING DIRECT / SEATTLE, WASHINGTON

ISBN: 979-8-9923474-0-1 (Paperback)
ISBN: 979-8-9223474-1-8 (Hardcover)
ISBN: 979-8-9923474-2-5 (ebook)
Library of Congress control number: 2025903755

First printing edition 2025.
Publisher: Shawn A. Roussin. Exeter, New Hampshire 03833

Disclaimer:
I have tried to recreate events, locales, and conversations from my memories of them. In order to maintain their anonymity, in all instances I have changed the names of patients, medical personnel, and educators, including some locations where scenes may have taken place, except where written permission was provided to use real names and descriptors. I may have changed some or all identifying features and details such as physical properties, titles, genders, and occupations of characters, as well as times and dates of certain scenes. Any resemblance to persons living or dead resulting from these changes is unintentional and entirely coincidental. The content of this book is for informational and entertainment purposes only and is not intended to diagnose, treat, cure, or prevent any condition or disease.

www.SHAWNauthorROUSSIN.com

SHAWNauthorROUSSIN@yahoo.com

DEDICATION

For my son, Carter, and daughter, Cecelia.

Many supportive people along this journey have offered their congratulations, stating how amazing it must be to leave this legend behind for future generations to read. Although I humbly thank them, I know the most important legacy I leave behind are my children.

Carter and Cecelia,

Your health and happiness will always be what matters most. I hope I can pass along the same wisdom, values, and ethics that my parents instilled in me. You fill me with pride every day.

You are my greatest gifts in life.

Love,
Dad

CONTENTS

PART III: APPLYING MEDICINE

CHAPTERS

PROLOGUE

At 11:40 am, my eyes opened to the soft silent glow above me. I was alone, except for the faint rhythmic beat of my heart monitor that could be heard in the distance. *Was the cancer gone?* There were wires on my chest, IVs in my arms, and a catheter in my bladder. Through slurred speech, I began pleading with the nurses to let me go home. "I must get home right now. Please. Let me go."

When my demands were unanswered, I began pondering my existence and reflecting on my life. I thought about my children, my parents, my wife, and my remaining time on this earth.

* * *

In the mid-1990s, as I questioned my career as a musician, and began contemplating my future as either a physician assistant (PA) or medical doctor (MD), I searched for resources that could help me make that decision. Determinedly, I explored bookstores and libraries for months, but could not find any information about the experience of going through a PA program—only medical school and residency.

Among the questions I had: What challenges would a PA student face? What would a typical day look like? Might there be an impact on personal relationships? Are rotations scattered all over the country? How heavy is the financial burden? Is it possible to hold a job while attending classes?

Aggravation arose when I did not find any satisfying answers. So, it was at that time I decided if I were ever accepted into a PA program,

I'd write a book about my journey, aiming to provide answers to these questions and many more, in a candid, raw, and intimate way, so anyone considering a career in healthcare would have a personal look into the mind of a physician assistant student. What if I were to record a journal (microcassette-style) and enlist a couple of fellow classmates to secretly do the same? Post graduation, I would transcribe our observations and impressions, edit and organize those adventures, and write a "medical memoir."

Two years into the four-year PA program (at the time, master's degrees were not required), I selected four classmates who I thought could handle the task, follow through to completion, and provide book-worthy content during our final two years. The first of those two years, the didactic year, considered to be the most intense and demanding, is when a student learns the equivalent of the curriculum taught during the first two years of medical school, but consolidated into only nine months. The final year of PA school is dedicated to several clinical rotations in various mandatory specialties, but often includes one or two electives. That year most resembles a medical doctor's first year of residency, known as their internship.

Dan, Janelle, Heather, and Alex made the cut. I chose each of them for unique reasons, and provided each with a small, handheld microcassette recorder, along with all the blank cassettes they would need, and a generous supply of batteries.

Upon graduating, collectively we had filled almost fifty tapes. After purchasing a dictation machine (this was many years before Nuance Dragon software or other mainstream speech-to-text tools), I spent three years transcribing them, typing out the content word for word. It was an unremitting experience (especially when you only use two fingers and a thumb). The more I transcribed, the more overwhelmed I became by the vast amount of material that had been captured.

Eventually, boiling over with frustration and just wanting to advance the project, I hired a medical transcriptionist to finish the work. Months later, I received the Microsoft Word files of Janelle's,

Dan's, and my own entries. I printed each page, put them in three-ring binders, mailed Dan and Janelle their hard copies, and set mine aside. Alex had removed himself from the project early in the process, and Heather's recordings were irrecoverable after the transcriptionist said her computer's hard drive crashed as she was working on the final cassette. Although she told me she'd redo them for free, my growing despondency was becoming incurable. Then in May of 2006, due to flooding in our basement, Heather's actual tapes were destroyed, and this entire endeavor seemed destined to drown.

The binder containing my own transcribed entries changed locations in our home a thousand times over the next sixteen years. When inspiration would arise, I'd grab a red pen, read an entry or two, do some editing, then relocate the binder to collect another layer of dust, awaiting the next unpredictable wave of motivation that I hoped would eventually emerge. I would often pause for many months without reviewing a word. My binder contained 270 pages of crude material. Dan's was around 200 pages, Janelle's was similar, and Heather's would have been over 350. It was intimidating to stare at the nearly 700 pages of unrefined and unedited personal chronicles that would require my detailed and creative attention to make them publishable. And in fact, after thoroughly reviewing Dan's and Janelle's entries, I made the agonizing decision to eliminate their stories from contention and instead focus solely on my own. However, between that harrowing obstacle, building a career, nurturing a marriage, and raising two children, this book project never remained a significant priority.

Then came the spring of 2022, when I began experiencing an intense upper abdominal squeezing sensation that was accompanied by nausea with every meal. After about a week, I became convinced that these were gallbladder attacks. Unable to eat, I made an appointment at my doctor's office, had labs drawn, and was scheduled for an abdominal ultrasound. The labs came back perfectly normal, but an hour after the ultrasound, I received a call about an incidental finding—a solid mass on my right kidney. I figured it was not good. The subsequent CT scan completed three weeks later illuminated unfavorably. Signs pointed to a type of renal cell cancer, but at least it had been caught early, so it appeared.

On October 4th, 2022, Dr. Munoz performed a laparoscopic, robotic, partial right nephrectomy (removing a portion of the kidney). The surgery was swift and uncomplicated, and the pathology was favorable: a chromophobe, which carries a 92%, five-year survival rate for all tumor sizes. Mine was 1.3 cm: extremely small.

Within minutes, anesthesia still not worn off and my mortality in question, I couldn't understand why I had this extraordinary urge to get home, but the following day, when I arrived there, I immediately fled to our basement. My eyes gravitated toward the binder of my transcriptions sitting at the bottom of a bookshelf. I slid it out, blew off the dust, opened to page one, and began reading. Words were swirling around me like an apparition, and when creativity strikes, you harvest it, ignoring life's chores that threaten to rob you of your next adjective.

That urge to get home was because the entire book had mapped itself out for me while I was under anesthesia. The extraordinary sleep had slid scenes into my subconscious, and directed me to a place where they could begin diffusing from my fingertips. It was time to make good on that promise I had made to myself in 1996.

Every word in the first five chapters of this book erupted from me during the thirteen days I was home on medical leave. I struggled to stop typing; I couldn't type fast enough.

ADDITIONAL DISCLAIMER

At no point during the two years of my journal entries were other individuals (professors, administrators, preceptors, students, patients, providers) ever recorded. The only voice that appeared on the microcassette tapes was mine. Additionally, having read every transcribed word from the recordings of Dan and Janelle, they too did not record any voice but their own. That said, none of their entries appear in this book.

PART I

FINDING
MEDICINE

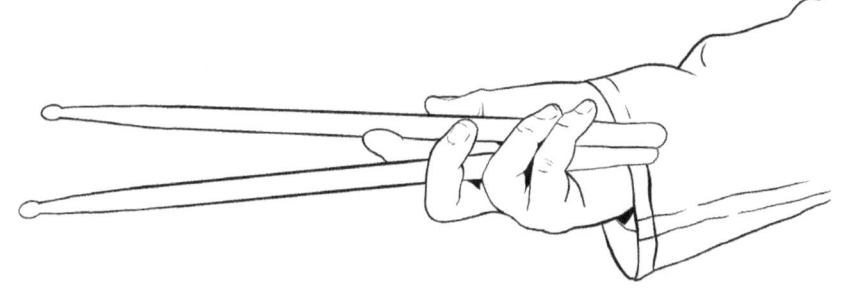

1

SO, YOU WANT TO
BE A ROCK STAR

"He's going to be on MTV!" my stepmom proudly shouted at the
newspaper reporter during my high school post-graduation celebration.
I had convinced the senior class advisor and principal to let me speak
at the convocation. They also allowed me to play a song I had co-
written and recorded with a friend. I was not a class officer, Honor
Society member, or in the top ten, but I wasn't stupid either. Out of
approximately 160 graduates, I ranked 24th in the class. Despite my
supportive guidance counselor advising me to consider college prep
and honors classes, I refused and only signed up for the minimum
credits required for graduation. Any open slots in my schedule I filled
with music program courses.

Like many musicians, I started with the flutophone in third
grade and played *Home on the Range* at the annual school concert.
The following year I was on to the alto saxophone. The music bug
didn't truly strike me until the conclusion of seventh grade. Mrs. B,

my junior high school music teacher, couldn't find any drummers to play in the following year's "stage band." That band was for kids who wanted to play more advanced, "cooler" music. Auditions were required, so she approached eight non-drummers and asked if they wanted to study the drum set over the summer.

In the end, she would select two of us. I had witnessed the popularity that the eighth-grade drummers in the stage band had garnered, and I wanted a part of it. Puberty had found its way into my head. Music had found its way into my heart.

Every day during that summer, I would practice in my room on the makeshift drum set constructed from old album covers, Tupperware bowls, and saucepans—and it paid off. I was one of the two non-drummers selected. Nothing had made me feel like I did when I was behind the drums, creating a rhythm, and basking in the attention of my peers. *I could get used to this.* But I had an enormous obstacle. I never wanted to leave school at the end of the day because that's where the real drum set was.

I'd never had a reason to go into the Music Unlimited store at the local mall until Christmas shopping one day with my family in 1982. It was a tiny store with dozens of guitars hanging on the walls, amplifiers stacked three-high in every direction, and two private lesson rooms in the back. Centrally located, rising from a platform, was a single black, seven-piece drum set, made by CB700. It stood out over the inferior musical instruments that failed to be as magnificent. It rested just far enough away that it couldn't be touched or played. It was priceless. No, really. It was utterly unaffordable on a twelve-year-old's budget.

I'd visit "my" drum set every chance I could, and each time I'd ask the same AC/DC-concert-T-shirt-wearing-salesman, "How much is the CB700?"

And each time, without any eye contact, I'd get a sarcastic, "How serious are you about buying it?"

Deflated, I'd reluctantly reply, "Well, I won't have the money until the end of the summer." I then snuck away quietly, hoping no other teens exploring the store had heard me say that I was going to be the one to buy it. I'd take one more glance before heading to Orange Julius to sulk over a virgin piña colada.

Several weeks later, I was given a gift. It couldn't be wrapped, nor could it be held, and any sensible teenager would not have interpreted it as a gift. My Uncle Mike owned a house painting business. During a holiday gathering, he asked me if I would be interested in helping him out over school vacations, and if things worked out, maybe he'd offer me a summer job. I think he was in cahoots with my parents.

At $3.25 an hour, I could make about $120 per week—a far cry from the $14 a week I'd earned the previous three years on a paper route, though it had allowed me to go in halfsies with my parents to buy my saxophone. Delivering newspapers was an hour-long, six-days-a-week responsibility, and it required me, a nine-year-old, to wake up at 5:30 am. This new painting job, however, would demand a much deeper commitment. I just kept my eyes on the prize. With each scrape of the putty knife, swipe of the sandpaper, and stroke of the brush, I envisioned that drum set nestled in my bedroom.

By summer's end, I had saved $720. I knew it would be sufficient for a set of drums, but not the CB700 from Music Unlimited. That one had sold. But Dad always had a plan, albeit covertly. He had heard of an enormous music store more than an hour away, called Ted Hebert's Music Mart. With cash in hand, he and I made the trip to Ted's in his silver '73 Ford pickup.

Upon arrival, we examined the drum kits they had arranged in their display windows, most of which were of the four- or five-piece variety, but I was looking for bigger.

As we pushed open the glass door, a set of sleigh bells attached to the inside handle alerted two gentlemen at the front desk of our arrival. One looked up from a shiny brass trumpet he was repairing and enthusiastically greeted us. The other was stringing up an acoustic guitar for a waiting customer. "I saw you checking out the drums," he said. "Head in that direction. You'll want to see Chuck. I'm sure he'll be banging on something with a pair of sticks. That's how you'll know it's him."

Following the pitter-patter of paradiddles coming from the back corner of the store, we caught the attention of Chuck, who paused occasionally to sip a coffee from a white Styrofoam cup. With a cool, confident swagger, he rose from his pale-green folding chair and effortlessly transitioned to air-drumming.

After quick introductions, my father let me do the talking, which wouldn't normally be his style. Lurking in the wings, I think he was loosening the leash a bit, allowing me, as a thirteen-year-old, to try my hand at some adulting.

Immediately drawn to the only drum set in the room (a silver Pearl seven-piece), I suffered sticker shock when I saw the $1,100 price tag—and that didn't even include cymbals. Sure, at a price I could barely afford, he attempted to sell me one of the smaller sets we saw in the display windows, but I knew that bigger was better. Oh, how Chuck tried... He could feel my admiration for this Pearl set, and he could sense my disgust with every other deal he was struggling to strike.

Once we had two deals I could stomach, my dad suggested we get lunch at the sub shop across the street and think about it. There was no fooling him. He knew I was obsessed and would not settle for a lesser drum set. I think he also saw a teachable moment. He threw around several what-ifs, which of course made perfect sense, but I wanted to leave with a drum set that day, and it had to be the silver one.

After inhaling our hoagies, we found Chuck right where we had left him, minus the coffee, plus a cigarette. "What did you gentlemen decide?"

My dad began implementing our playbook. "Chuck, my son here is thirteen. He bought a saxophone four years ago, at age nine, by delivering newspapers at five-thirty every morning. He helped my brother-in-law paint houses all summer long—usually forty hours per week, because he wanted to buy his first set of drums. I'm sure he worked more in one week than any of his friends did the entire summer." My father pulled out an envelope from his shirt pocket. "This here is every dollar he earned. Over seven hundred. He's willing to purchase a drum set without cymbals, work some weekends this fall, and come back in a few months. But he really wants this silver Pearl kit."

Chuck put out his cigarette and looked over the deeply embedded scratches on the lenses of his glasses. As he hovered, one eyebrow rose up suspiciously. "You'll come back in a few months to buy cymbals?"

I said, "I will," decisively.

He left us to walk over to a music stand where he began tapping again, but this time on a calculator. Moments later he walked over to me, extended a congratulatory hand, and said, "Well, you just bought a set of Pearl drums. But you can't play without cymbals. Since I know you're going to be a rock star one day, I'm going to want your business for a long time." He pulled four cymbals off a display rack. "Although not great, they're new and will get you started. Do you have a drum throne to sit on?"

"No. That's okay. I have a desk chair I can use."

"That may hurt your back. Take this used stool I accepted on trade last week. There's nothing wrong with it."

My dad and I were stunned.

"I'll start breaking down the drums. I hope you have a truck. You're gonna need it," Chuck said.

"We do," I told him.

"Pull it up to the front. You can back it right up to the door."

During the ride home, I focused more on my new drums in the back of the truck than on the road ahead. That one-hour drive seemed more like a cross-country trip. I longed for it to be over.

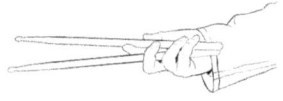

More than forty years and a couple of drum sets later, I still have one small drum from that original kit. I will always remember and appreciate what Chuck and my dad did that day. What my immediate family endured in the years to follow was an even greater feat, yet not once did they ever discourage me from practicing, despite the thunderous noise I created in our modest and poorly insulated home.

I bought a lot of stuff from Chuck over the next several years, and even took some future bandmates there to make large purchases. That drum set eventually took up 90% of my bedroom; a twin mattress on the floor and a four-drawer dresser were my only furnishings.

As it turned out, I should have worried less about the size of my kit and more about the skill of my craft. Had I invested more money into lessons, and time into practicing, maybe I'd still be a musician today. Or had I focused on my first love, baseball, instead of trying to impress girls with my tight pants, long hair, and stick-twirling, maybe I would've had a professional baseball career. But if either of those things had happened, this book would not have.

No, I don't live with regrets—at least not the kind that causes me to lose sleep, fuel angst, or cloud the perception of who I am.

I still dream of hitting the game-winning home run with two outs in the bottom of the ninth to win the seventh game of the World Series in front of the Fenway Faithful.

I still dream of touring with a band and selling out stadiums.

It's okay to hold on to those dreams, occasionally reliving them during a deep sleep...

Some dreams fade. Some dreams morph. Others come later in life, unexpectedly, and in the strangest of ways.

2

THE GOODNIGHT KISS

Music dominated my high school life. I wish I could've found more balance and continued to play high school athletics, especially baseball. Although I loved to play catcher, as a junior varsity pitcher, I was 5-1 on a team that was 8-12. As a hitter that year, my on-base-percentage was just over .700. In one seven-inning game, I struck out 18 batters, only to lose the game on a throwing error to first base.

I threw two different fastballs, and that was it. I didn't even have a true off-speed pitch or breaking ball. My arm was strong, and I threw hard. Accurate as hell, I could throw strikes at will. I also played high school basketball, but never cracked the starting line-up. I wouldn't get any college offers as an athlete. And neither sport got me the attention of girls, unlike playing drums. So after my sophomore year, I stopped playing school sports and decided to make it my goal to achieve rock star status.

Nothing extraordinary occurred during my final years of high school. I played in bands, learned piano, and dabbled in songwriting. My original plan was to move to Hollywood and study at the

Percussion Institute of Technology (now part of Musicians Institute), but to attain a more comprehensive education, I enrolled at Berklee College of Music in Boston. I didn't attend right out of high school. I worked a factory job for eighteen months, saving enough money ($20,000) to pay for my first year there. My mother and stepfather, Norm, told me that if I paid for my first year without student loans, they would pay for my second year. Mission accomplished.

When you're from East Puckabush, Maine, and everyone around you constantly sings your praises and tells you how awesome you are, you believe it. Thus, I rested on my laurels. By the end of my second week at Berklee, the rude awakening had begun.

At Berklee, there is an area known as "Drummer's Row." It's where drummers just sit around with their sticks and practice on whatever is in front of them. I renamed it "Intimidation Alley." Berklee was home to more than 400 drummers from across the world. By the end of my second week, I hadn't seen nor heard a single one of them I thought I was better than. Not one. Oh, sure, I was "King of the Kit" in East Puckabush, but here in Boston? Forget about it. I was nowhere near the most talented. I was an unknown. And to make matters worse, the male-to-female ratio of music students there was about 15:1.

I'd just dropped $20,000 (my entire savings), moved to Boston, signed a lease, and felt like I'd been punched in the face by Iron Mike Tyson. Though disheartened, I committed to Berklee and immersed myself in music for the next two years.

Ultimately, I did fine. In this field, though, just being fine often leads to failure. Sure, I'd had fun—and there was no failure in that. However, after the second year at Berklee, I was slowly becoming convinced that a career in music was not for me. The problem was, if not music, then what?

After completing two years there, I moved back home and resumed painting houses again. Once I had saved all my money for a year, I rented a very small house in the deep woods of Maine, stopped working, and began "shedding." Shedding is a term that musicians use to describe a long period of profound isolated practice. I thought, if music was all that I knew, before I give up, I might as well immerse myself as intensely as I can for as long as I can and see what my music career looks like on the other side of a year. For the next ten months, I practiced eight hours a day, six days a week.

I did more than immerse myself, I drowned myself in drumming. Once I came up for air, I was proud of the results. Something major had shifted and I was breathing new life.

When my money had run out and my lease had ended, I began looking for any musical opportunities to invest in. I did some temp agency work, painted a few homes, and drove a forklift at a factory. Then I got a call from Marty, a local singer-songwriter who I'd played in a band several years prior. His previous band had recently broken up, and he was eager to create a more mainstream project.

For me, it was perfect. Within weeks, Grover was born. The name didn't last long because of copyright problems. Our logo bore a striking resemblance to a particular Sesame Street character, and other bands on the East Coast apparently shared the name. We then picked the name Pondering Judd, the band developed a new identity, and we took off. The following four years were the very best of my life. Writing, rehearsing, recording, gigging, networking, repeat. Happily living below the poverty line, I only needed to pay the rent and feed my belly. My every breath revolved around Pondering Judd. I thought it would be my big chance at the rock star dream. But then, along came a woman.

Kendra was Roxanne's best friend and roommate, and Roxanne was Marty's girlfriend. I was immediately smitten, even though Kendra had a two-year-old daughter, Sadie. The relationship matured rapidly.

Before long, I had moved in with Kendra, Sadie, and Roxanne. To help earn the relationship, I wholeheartedly jumped into the role of father figure. It happened with no request or requirement from Kendra. In hindsight, I understand it to have been the beginning of my inherent desire to be a provider. At twenty-four, I was a struggling musician with no money, stability, or promises to offer a woman and her toddler. Going on the road, sleeping in lowly motels and only eating one meal per day made me wonder if it was the life for me.

Something had to give. I felt I was going to need a sign—or maybe two or three—in order to force a massive shift in my life.

Though tangential to me, the delivery of the first sign marked the start of my journey into medicine.

Dallas, a close friend of my father, in his late forties like Dad, suffered a heart attack. He pulled through it fine, but I began thinking, *What the hell would I do if someone I loved collapsed in front of me?* I'd have no idea, and that frightened me.

I began asking friends if they knew where I could take a CPR class. Sean, a fellow drummer, advised me to investigate an EMT-Basic course at the University of New Hampshire. It was offered two nights a week from 6:00 pm to 9:00 pm for an entire semester. That was more than I bargained for, but I decided to go for it. At that point, I couldn't even tell you what CPR stood for.

By the time that first week of classes were over, I knew there was something happening. I didn't know how, what, or where this path might take me, but medicine was calling.

About halfway through the semester, I began sorting things out when I was hired to paint the inside of the Oswell family's house. Mr. Oswell, a native Texan, overheard me talking to my business partner, Don, about the EMT course.

In his deep southern drawl, "Hey, Shawn. You ever thought about becoming a physician assistant?" Mr. Oswell asked.

"A what?"

"You know, like a nurse practitioner."

I hadn't a clue what he was talking about, but by the time I left his house that afternoon, he had already arranged for me to have lunch with a physician assistant, Theresa, from the family practice where he was the office manager. He told me to dress for success and bring lots of questions, so I did.

Only a few years removed from my high school senior pictures, I located the only shirt and tie combo from that photoshoot. I found it balled up at the bottom of a garbage bag amongst a modest pile of everything that I owned, in the basement of my mother's house.

With no one to provide me a tutorial on ironing, I recalled where Kendra kept the supplies for creating a wrinkle-free garment tucked away in our apartment's formal dining room, otherwise known as Sadie's bedroom. Emerging one sitcom episode later, having created more pleats than I removed, what remained of this smoldering masterpiece was now ready for the trash can—its final resting place. Since my arsenal of formal attire was now reduced to zero, my choices were to wear one of my band's T-shirts or a double-extra-large polo shirt bearing my stepfather's company logo. I chose the latter since it at least had a collar.

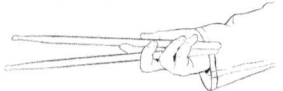

Mr. Oswell greeted me and my legal notepad in the waiting room. "Welcome, Shawn. C'mon in. Lunch just arrived. I'll show you back to our kitchen. Theresa just finished with her last patient and I think is in her office."

"Thanks again for having me. My apologies. I had a little accident this morning with an iron. My dress shirt didn't survive, but at least the fire department got to sleep in."

"No worries. This is a lunch, not the prom."

Each step towards the kitchen raised the intensity of the oregano, garlic, and Italian dressing smell. Pizza? Classic rock-band-on-a-budget food. I was relieved to be faced with a meal that would not require me to remember which piece of silverware was the salad fork, but still felt uncomfortable eating finger-food while trying to conduct an interview necessitating a frantic pace of note-taking.

Legal pad tucked under my arm, I grabbed two slices and a can of soda as Mr. Oswell showed me to Theresa's office.

"Theresa. This is Shawn. Are you ready for him?" Mr. Oswell asked.

"Yes. Absolutely. Hi, Shawn. Have a seat. Let me clear some of these charts off my desk so you can put your plate down. I see you brought questions. Excellent. Let's just dive right in. What is your background and experience?"

"In healthcare? None. Well, I'm in an EMT-Basic course right now."

"So, you haven't actually treated a patient or earned a paycheck in the medical field?"

"That's correct."

"Okay. That needs to change. You need a certificate or degree; something in the health sciences where you can acquire patient contact hours. Maybe that's paramedic, nursing? When I applied to Northeastern's PA program, the demographic trend of an average applicant was a 28-year-old female with 2,000 hours of hands-on medical experience."

"Isn't that like working full-time for an entire year?"

"Roughly, yes."

"I don't have that kind of time."

"Time? You're what, 25?"

"Almost."

"You've got time, Shawn. How are you doing in the EMT course?"

"Good, I guess. We have weekly quizzes, but no big exams yet."

"You need an A. Everything must be an A from here on out. You'll need to shoot for perfection. If you fall a bit short, pray it is still good enough."

"Good enough for…?"

"Getting an interview."

"You lost me. An interview? A job interview?"

"No. Your application to a PA program needs to be impressive enough to survive the trash heap during the first few rounds of cuts. Most programs have a minimum GPA that they are looking for. If you aren't above it, nothing else on your application matters—it'll be off to the shredder."

"So, let's say I have the GPA. What next?"

"I'm sure they'll want grade transcripts from every college course you took during the previous ten years, and maybe even your SAT scores, but let's assume yours were so good that the admissions director decided not to make a paper airplane out of them and toss them out her third-story office window. Now they'll actually start reading through the multiple essay questions you were required to submit on your application. This is the moment of truth. What separates you from the other applicants? How are your writing skills? These essays are used to determine if they want to meet you in person—the interview."

"Wait," I said, covering my mouth and signaling for a time-out. "Essay questions? Like what?"

"Like: describe a time when you faced adversity or overcame a difficult situation and what you learned from it. Or describe what you envision your first five years will be like when you are a practicing physician assistant. They may even throw you a curveball too, something quirky and philosophical, such as: Who would play you in a movie about your life and why? Or what is the title of your memoir? You're granted a day in a time machine, so what year do you choose, and where are you going? The final essay is usually a blank page where you have free rein to write about whatever you want, but every program is different."

"Ha! Memoir? Me? Write a book? Right... Anyway, how hard is it to get an interview?" I knew I was jumping way ahead of myself, but I still had one full slice of time remaining on my plate, and when would I have another opportunity like this to ask these questions of an actual PA?

Theresa continued. "I think I read some data recently that for about every four applications received, a single interview is granted, and PA programs end up accepting one out of every four interviewees. Most classes consist of twenty to twenty-five students."

I nearly choke on my Pepsi. "That can't be right." Math was not my strong suit. The 420 that I scored on the math component of my SATs as a nineteen-year-old was proof, but I could quickly estimate that it would take about four hundred applicants to fill two dozen slots. "I can't imagine how difficult it must be to get accepted into medical school."

"It's actually easier," she said, "by almost tenfold."

"What? No way. Are you kidding me?"

"No, so think about it."

"Think about what? Medical school?"

"I'm just saying, a lot of PA students previously considered it. I've spoken to a lot of docs who wished PA school had been an option when they were contemplating their careers, but it works both ways."

My wheels began churning. *Four years for undergrad. Four years of medical school. A three- to five-year residency. I would be almost forty before I land my first job as a doctor.*

Leaving that lunch, I had gained a wealth of knowledge, but also some unanticipated confusion. Why not become a doctor? Is that what I aspire to? How do I figure this out?

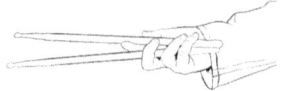

Published in 1978, *The House of God* by Samuel Shem is a satirical novel that tracks a group of medical interns. Despite being fictional, it was recommended to me by a friend considering medical school himself. Within hours, I was at the bookstore asking for its whereabouts. The clerk was inquisitive as he guided me through the aisles. "Oh, you're thinking about becoming a doctor? Why would you want a fictional account of medical school?" he said as he handed me a copy of the book. "I'd think you'd be more interested in *Learning to Play God* by Dr. Robert Marion. Let me show you where that one is."

After minimal debate, I bought both. Once I left the bookstore, I never cracked open *The House of God* again, but it was because I read *Learning to Play God* first. In this book, Dr. Marion gives honest insights into the difficulties of medical school and those inhumane years of training. As much as I despised reading (and still do), I had that book read in only a few nights. It scared the crap out of me and at the same time, intrigued me.

Approximately ten years after publishing *Learning to Play God*, Dr. Marion, as a practicing physician in New York, had three of his interns keep meticulous diaries while they navigated through their first year of residency—their internship. Published as *The Intern Blues* in 1989, this second work shows how young, exhausted, naïve doctors deal with overcoming their own fears and insecurities, the impact of AIDS, and hospital bureaucracy in the 1980s.

Marion repeated his experiment by having another group of interns record their thoughts and observations while guiding themselves through what many doctors describe as the most grueling year of their lives. The book *Rotations: The Twelve Months of Intern Life*, was released in 1997. *Rotations* was written using the same formula as his previous release, but Marion concluded it by comparing and contrasting it to *The Intern Blues*, analyzing how the healthcare system, medical schools, and technology had evolved in such a short amount of time.

As if I didn't already have enough information to help me arrive at a decision, I stumbled upon a PBS NOVA documentary called *The Making of a Doctor*. Produced by WGBH in Boston, the film followed seven Harvard medical students as they began their rigorous training: four years of medical school followed by their internship and residency. After one viewing, I bought the VHS tape for $29.95 and wore that thing out, often making friends and family watch it along with me.

If reading those books and watching this documentary doesn't change your mind about wanting to become an MD, it may just do something else—push you into the path of an oncoming physician assistant program. That's exactly what it did to me.

The moment I made that decision was the moment I began feeling overwhelmed by confusion, pressure, and anxiety: confusion about what to do next, the pressure to commit to crazy life changes, and anxiety about the challenging road ahead.

Consider again my background. Academically, I'd hardly applied myself in high school because I didn't really need to—I was going to be a rock star. I worked in factories and painted houses. Then I left music college and started playing in bands. I hadn't planned any of this, but I had been forming a close bond with my girlfriend Kendra and her daughter Sadie for a year, and our relationship was about to become more serious.

One evening, Sadie and I were snuggled on the couch while Kendra was getting ready to head out on a work assignment. I had a gig that night, and when the television show that we were watching was over, I told her it was time for me to go. She wasn't happy about that and let me know it. As I stood up, she jumped onto my back and I headed towards the stairs. "I'm sorry, Sadie. When I get home, I'll be sure to come give you a kiss goodnight, okay?" I began my descent. Halfway down the staircase, her arms clung tightly around my neck and her knees digging into my ribs, she said, "Don't go, Daddy."

I froze. Then I dropped to the step below me and cupped my hands over my face. Sadie's breath pulled away from my ear. She gently loosened her grip and slid off to my side. I heard Kendra's footsteps coming down the third-floor staircase above us.

"See you later, Daddy," she said, kissing my cheek.

Sadie was the first child to address me as "Daddy," even though I wasn't her father. That rocked me and gave me all the clarity I needed. It was spontaneous, innocent, and private. From her words, I was reborn.

3

BETTING AGAINST THE ODDS

After the worst gig ever, I returned to our apartment, delivered the kiss that I had promised, and crawled into bed. Motionless, I stared out the window and reflected on my life. By the time the sun had crept onto my pillow, I had a plan.

Phase one: ask Kendra to marry me and work my way out of the band, all while creating and completing a list of prerequisites to gain acceptance into a PA program. This phase began before the birth of the internet, so it took a lot of letter writing and making phone calls. Weeks passed until I had compiled a directory of PA programs from across the country.

With this list in hand, more questions arose: How will Kendra react to this? Where might she be willing to go, especially with Sadie? And although we began seriously discussing marriage, I sensed apprehension and doubt from her with each conversation.

At this time, I wasn't sure what her grand plans were. What would I do if she wasn't on board with any of this? Sadie's bond with me was not something Kendra would ever consider breaking... right?

Somehow, with my annual gross income of about $15k, I was approved to finance an engagement ring, and since our roommate, Roxanne, worked at a local jewelry store, I even finagled a small discount.

With the ring now in my possession, I began sincerely prying into Kendra's mind. I knew she had bigger aspirations, but was also struggling with how to accomplish them. As it turned out, she'd been looking at master's programs in psychology (she had already completed a double major bachelor's degree in Spanish and Journalism). The University of Kentucky was first on her short list. After discovering this juicy detail, I revisited my list of PA programs, and there it was: the University of Kentucky had a physician assistant program! This was meant to be, but was she genuinely feeling the same?

I planned on proposing to Kendra in the middle of one of our shows. It seemed fitting. It's kind of where it all began. Most of the people who had come to know us in the music scene would be there. After setting up my drum kit and finishing the sound check, I went into the bathroom, put on a collared shirt I had purchased at a thrift store, and a tie I found stuffed in the back of my sock drawer. When I emerged, the band knew something was up. I conspired with them to alter the ending of one of our songs, and they agreed.

The Portsmouth Brewery buzzed that night. It was standing room only. When the moment came, I called Kendra up on stage, pulled the ring out of my bass drum, and delivered the rather awkward proposal. Even more strained was her hesitant acceptance. The feeling I experienced didn't match what I had hoped, and my gut ended up being right.

Kendra and I were engaged for about four hours. After arriving back at our apartment late that night, the deconstruction of our relationship commenced while the construction of my life's next phase began. I think I was angry, but more so, disconcerted. We discussed how we were in different places. She thought we needed to enter into a period of discovery on our own, citing my intellectual immaturity as a driving factor, but also her profound fear of commitment. In the weeks and perhaps months to follow, I found myself craving redemption after being dismissed in that way. I needed to prove to her—to everyone— that I wasn't just a long-haired musician, house painter, and factory laborer from East Puckabush who was only destined for mediocrity. Do not misunderstand me—our dissolution was civil and friendly, but it still inflicted deep wounds.

Within days, my plan was coming together. I needed an associate degree in the health sciences, and I needed a 4.0 GPA. I needed to build the resume of a leader and to log at least 2,000 patient contact hours. Nothing else mattered. These were the priorities.

My bandmates—my brothers—held me together when they learned the news about Kendra's and my short-lived engagement. I couldn't have asked for more support than they gave. I'm forever grateful to my Pondering Judd brethren: Marty, Steve, Blaise, and Eric.

Over the next year, the band was able to breathe, coalesce, and reflect. Once we recognized that our days as a group were coming to an end, we began savoring Pondering Judd again, instead of treating it like a job that we dreaded. Approaching every show like it could be our last, each measure, verse, and chorus were performed with raw emotion and affection.

Since I was already enrolled in the University of New Hampshire's EMT-Basic course, one of my first inquiries was to their admissions department regarding their nursing major. As a New Hampshire resident, it made financial sense to choose a school with in-state tuition rates. This school was my top choice because it was only a twenty-minute drive from my apartment. I was still living with Kendra and Sadie. This was a convenient arrangement, which we'd hoped would cause the least disruption to my relationship with Sadie, but it was not sustainable.

I knew the deadline to apply for the fall semester was fast approaching, but it turned out to not matter. Admissions informed me of a two-year wait-list for the nursing program. Two years? And UNH's waitlist was not unique, at least for a BSN (Bachelor of Nursing). At 26, I felt old. The fire in my belly was stoking the retribution in my heart. Primed and ready, it was imperative that I start my mission immediately.

What about an associate degree in nursing? New Hampshire Community Technical College (NHCTC), also about twenty minutes from our apartment, had a two-year nursing degree, and for about half the tuition cost when compared to UNH. So, a few days after UNH temporarily crushed my dream, I met with the NHCTC nursing program director.

The news was only half as devastating. Their 1995 fall class was full, but I was told that 1996 could be an option if I applied right away. She could see the disappointment on my face. "Listen," I said. "Don't take this the wrong way, but I'm going to be a physician assistant one day and I need a steppingstone degree, plus at least two thousand hours of patient contact experience."

"Follow me," she said. "I think Dolores Stone is here. She runs the surgical technology program."

I didn't even know what a surgical technologist was, but I suspected I was about to have an impromptu interview.

"Dolores? This is Shawn. He aspires to be a physician assistant. He's about to complete the UNH EMT-Basic course and was in my office just now looking to apply to my nursing program, which, as you know, is full. Have you already filled your program?"

"I haven't. Have you applied to the college yet?" Dolores asked.

"No, but I can do that by morning."

"Okay. Terrific. Let's walk and talk as we make our way down to the admissions office."

By 4:00 pm the following day, my official NHCTC application and financial aid forms were in their hands.

A week later, Dolores called to tell me they had accepted me in to the New Hampshire Community Technical College's Surgical Technology Associate of Applied Science degree program.

A series of checkboxes in my life were marked off over the next few months, starting with that acceptance. I moved across town, got a roommate who was also in the surgical technology program, completed the EMT course, and passed the state certification exam.

That summer, I had two targets: saving money to avoid working during my first year of classes, and getting my head right. Nothing could derail me from graduating with a 4.0 GPA. It was time to start building my PA school application. Getting anything less than an A in each course would be considered a failure.

Word of my goals quickly spread and I was cautioned by several professors who were close to Dr. Larry Macklin, the anatomy and physiology professor. "I'm not saying that I don't think you're capable of getting an A in Larry's class, but you're gonna need to work your tail off to earn it."

Prior to every anatomy and physiology exam, I would create my own test as if I were the teacher. Mine were brutally long and extraordinarily difficult. A few students took my first test to gauge their own preparedness. With each successive exam, more and more students wanted a crack at it. At first there was a half dozen coming to my apartment, then ten, then twenty. By the midterm exam, I had to begin turning students away. I even made an enormous meal for everyone, typically multiple woks of stir-fry or a vat of soup. The group gatherings would last for several hours, and I couldn't help but notice a beautiful green-eyed brunette who always showed up. Her name was Karen. Let's just say that the more times she attended the group sessions, the more we got to know each other, and that led to some one-on-one "studying." With things getting serious, by the end of the first semester we had planned a road trip together.

On December 26, 1995, we left for North Carolina to visit my sister. Although we were only there a few days, one day was reserved for making the three-hour drive to Wake Forest, where there was a PA program at the Bowman Gray School of Medicine. I had already arranged to meet with their director and take a tour of the facilities.

I was feeling wildly inspired by our trip. Early in the second semester I found my groove, learned how to study, and my time management skills were becoming exceptional. However, I needed some leadership experience.

I took a job as a tutor at the community college, was nominated and inducted into the National Honor Society, became president, and co-founded a new chapter of Health Occupation Students of America (HOSA). I competed in HOSA's New Hampshire state competitive events, finishing first in the Surgical Technology and Extemporaneous Writing categories. This paved the way to the 1996 HOSA National Convention in Anaheim, California, where I won the bronze medal in Surgical Technology and was crowned the National Champion in Extemporaneous Writing.

In a short period of time, I had made my PA program application about as convincing as I could. The recommendation from most experts and guidance counselors was to submit eight applications, then pray to be granted at least two interviews. Nationwide, on average, programs were getting twenty-five to forty applications for each spot available. Most schools would interview only six to eight candidates per slot. I knew if I looked good enough on paper to get an interview that I'd have no problem convincing the interviewers why they should accept me.

My top choice was the University of New England (UNE) in Maine. It was expensive, but I'd have the option of commuting versus living on campus, which would certainly help my wallet. During my tour of the school, I was able to see the new state-of-the-art science facility that was being constructed on campus which would be the new home of their PA program core courses.

The application was rigorous, but the major deterrent was their "three + two" program. You take your prerequisites during your first three years at UNE. Then, and only then, are you able to apply to the actual PA program. Completing the first three years did not guarantee you a spot in the PA program. Although confident, that small risk, combined with it being a five-year master's program, was unappealing.

As luck (or fate) would have it, Karen and I, now living in her parents' basement during my second year of the surgical technology program and her in the second year of the biotechnology program, began wondering if we could find an institution that had programs for both of us. During her search, she stumbled upon Rocksville Technical College (RTC) in Rocksville, New York. They had a biotechnology program as well as a PA program, and both were bachelor's degrees.

Within minutes, I was on the phone and talking to Rocksville, requesting a PA program catalog and application. The decision had been made. This was where we would go.

If you recall the application and interview statistics I cited earlier, you should know that I pretty much ignored them. I was stupid. Don't be like Shawn. I was cocky enough to think that if any school granted me an interview, I'd blow them away and they'd have no choice but to accept me. RTC granted me an interview, so I needed a map of Rocksville, a suit, and the most brilliant answers to their interview questions.

I prepped like a madman and compiled a list of the top twenty questions asked at these interviews. I composed answers to them and committed them to memory, rehearsing them dozens of times in the weeks leading up to the big day. Each answer was one part "me" and one part "what are they looking for?"

The evening before the interview, I drove several hours to get to my hotel near the campus. I assured myself that I had done everything within my power to prepare over the past two years.

Not a wink of sleep was to be had. I lay in darkness. My heart rate never fell below one hundred. Dawn couldn't come soon enough. I showered, shaved, then applied eight coats of antiperspirant. At a local breakfast joint, I declined the coffee, but begged for extra napkins so

I could cover myself for protection, even though I had two more suits in the car as insurance.

I arrived on campus an hour early and made my way to the admissions department, so I could confirm where I needed to be. I then toured the campus independently to loosen up and air out before returning in time for my interview.

"Shawn Roussin? Come on back. The program leaders are looking forward to meeting with you."

I know the answers. Just be myself. Stay relaxed and poised.

The door closed, and I was given the seat of honor.

This is my MTV. It's time to be a rock star.

The show ended an hour later. I exited from the stage even more confident than when I entered. Reaching my gold 1990 Honda Accord, I collapsed into the driver's seat and looked around for witnesses. Confirming I was in the clear, I let out a monstrous scream, rested my forehead on the steering wheel, and started sobbing.

I recall nothing of the journey home, except the badgering voice in my head saying: *When will I know? How long until they reach a verdict? When will they call? They said it could be two weeks. What if they don't call? Do I call them? Did I do enough? Oh, my God! I need to apply to another school. Five more schools, at least. Is it too late? Dammit, I'm so stupid! Why didn't I apply to more schools? Idiot!*

Two days later, while at my clinical site for the surgical technology program, still sweating, sleepless, and becoming more and more convinced that I'd fucked up my entire plan, I scrubbed out of a surgical case in the operating room and started walking toward the employee lounge. My personal pager began vibrating and when I looked down I saw our home number. Karen's parents (Pete and Barb) refrained from paging me unless it was urgent. I altered course, thinking I'd need some privacy, and bolted to the locker room down the hall so I could make the call. After three attempts, my trembling fingers finally dialed the correct number. "Peter. It's Shawn. You paged? Is everything alright?"

"Well, I don't know. I just got home from some errands and checked the messages and someone from RTC admissions called. Said you can call them back. Do you have the number?"

Before Peter had time to enunciate his last syllable, he was hearing a dial tone. I knew RTC's telephone number like the back of my hand. I knew who had called, and before I could complete my next exhalation, I had flawlessly stabbed those eleven numbers into the keypad. First ring. "Good afternoon. Thank you for calling RTC admissions. This is David. How can I help you?"

"Hi David. This is Shawn Roussin, returning a call. I met with you and the physician assistant program directors for an interview two days ago."

"Yes, Shawn. I know who you are. I don't know if you want to be sitting or standing for this, but I'll let you decide. Are you by yourself?"

"Yes. I'm in the men's locker room at the hospital. My girlfriend's father just contacted me to let me know you called."

"Well, our PA program director, Helen, and clinical coordinator, Nadine, wanted me to let you know they would be thrilled if you would accept a spot in their physician assistant program for the class of 2001, and they wanted me to thank you for making it one of the easiest decisions they have ever had to make."

Slumping to the floor, the receiver still in my hand, for the first time in forever, I was speechless.

"Shawn...? Shawn?"

4

SKIPPING SCHOOL

I felt incredible relief in that locker room. The number of calls I made in the following twenty-four hours was just nuts. After all the conversations, fist bumps, hugs, and celebrations were behind me, I started thinking, *Okay, now the really tough work begins.* With everything that I had absorbed from books, shadowing, and questioning, I believed I had a clear understanding about the challenges I'd face over the next four years. Wow, was I ever wrong! And I still had to talk to my bandmates.

None of them seemed surprised. The writing had been on the wall in recent months. Treating the band as a job had led to less enjoyment in performing. We'd been having discussions about taking the next steps, as in, quitting our day jobs, getting an agent, buying a bus, and hitting the road. Since none of those things were in the cards, the band's exit strategy started taking shape. During the final performances, we'd celebrate the previous four years and honor all those who had supported us.

Within a few months, I communicated with RTC to plan my first semester, but my primary focus was on how the next one to two years would play out. As a four-year bachelor's degree program, they accepted high school seniors, which was not typical at the time. I was transferring numerous college credits, so I was hoping that maybe I could transfer into the current class of 2000. Between my inevitable associate degree, and the two years of credits from Berklee College of Music, a total of forty-four credits transferred to RTC, however, I lacked the prerequisite science courses required by the PA program. I needed a full year of biology and general and analytical chemistry. Organic chemistry and anatomy and physiology were also prerequisites, both considered sophomore level courses. RTC highly recommended that I enroll in their A&P course since they assumed it would be taught at a much higher level than the one I had already completed at my community college. Algebra II was expected, so I completed that during the summer before moving to Rocksville. My problem was that I was missing key building block courses which would pave my way for success. I needed a minimum of twelve credits per quarter to be considered full-time, but I would have to be creative to reach that. RTC's school year is based on four quarters, not three semesters. Ultimately, I'd have to start as a freshman and be the only transfer student in the class of 2001, but I thought my first two years should be a piece of cake.

Despite working as a surgical technologist for more than twenty-four hours per week and attending an Algebra II class at the community college, the summer of 1997 was about having a good time. Karen had been accepted into the RTC Biotechnology program, and would transfer in as a sophomore. We were methodically planning the next chapter of our lives together, surveying yard sales for items we'd need to furnish our one-bedroom on-campus apartment, spending time with friends and family, and engaging in conversations about the unknown journey ahead of us.

The band's final performance was on June 14, 1997, at The Stone Church Music Club in Newmarket, New Hampshire. The immense sadness of that night still haunts me more than two decades later. After the show, I took the head off my snare drum and wrote, "Thanks for the best four years of my life." The entire band signed it, and I had it enshrined in a shadow box.

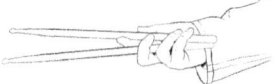

In preparation for the next four years in New York, Karen and I had a moving truck packing party the day before leaving. Knowing it would take approximately six hours to drive, while towing my Honda, and desiring to be at our apartment complex's check-in office when they opened at 8:00 in the morning, we made the bold move to leave New Hampshire at midnight.

Upon arriving at Livingston Manor, we found only a handful of students in front of us. Keys secured, we began the Herculean task of emptying the truck and hauling our belongings up to our third-floor apartment, all on empty stomachs and no sleep.

After finishing an exhausting day, Karen and I quickly learned that we were ancient college students (I was twenty-seven and she was twenty-five), and although we might have been there to further our education, it didn't seem like any other students at Livingston Manor were. I'd had no experience living on a college campus, but acquired it after that first night, the following night, and every Friday and Saturday night for the following two years.

It wasn't particularly enjoyable. It was horrific. I had Campus Safety on speed dial. Once our neighbors had figured out that I was the one repeatedly calling security, the regular harassment began. Their favorite tactic (when they weren't throwing empty beer cans at our windows) was knocking on our door and running away. At first, we ignored the door knocks, until one night, after realizing Campus Safety was useless, the situation with the "Community of A-holes" reached a boiling point.

That evening, the stars were all aligned (or maybe misaligned), and the posse of pricks from next door decided to push my limits. As many times before, they knocked on our door, swiftly dispersed, then gathered again when they judged it safe to repeat their pestering. Dressed and ready, looking out the peephole when the next knock sounded, I swung open the door and without making eye contact or saying a word, I closed it behind me. They were stunned. I made my way across the short landing, down three flights of stairs, and out to my car. I retrieved a twenty-eight-ounce, thirty-three-inch aluminum baseball bat from my trunk. I reversed course and made my way back up to the landing which had now been evacuated.

Using the bat's barrel, I love-tapped our neighbor's door. No answer. I tapped harder. No answer. I attempted to turn the doorknob, but it was locked. I was about to strike the door again when it opened cautiously. Three sets of teenaged eyes, on persons arranged from shortest to tallest, peered through the crack. Before anyone could say a word, I kicked open the door to reveal their quivering bodies. Each retreated deeper into the kitchen. I athletically positioned myself, left hand keeping the door fully opened, and right hand sealed around the handle of my bat, slung over my dominant shoulder. My eyes connected with their leader.

"We have tolerated your childish bullshit all year. The next time I catch either of you knocking on our doors or pounding on our walls, you're going to be in a wheelchair, shitting teeth and drinking from a straw, wondering why both of your legs are in casts! You think I'm kidding?"

"No, man."

Each of their Adams's apples seemed to rise and fall in unison.

"Great! Don't bother calling campus security. I've already notified them of our little discussion. I'm sure they'll be arriving any moment."

"Got it."

I worried that the "real" police might pay me a visit in the coming hours, or days, but it never happened. You know what else never happened? Unwanted door knocks.

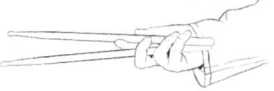

Karen and I left Rocksville to spend spring break back home. Avoiding arrest or expulsion from RTC was a tremendous relief. Upon returning to Livingston Manor before the new quarter commenced, it took me two weeks to realize the reduced traffic to our neighbor's apartment.

Wondering if anyone was even living over there, I inquired at the property manager's office, but they weren't willing to give out any information. With apprehension, I called Campus Security and was told, "You should just go talk to them."

The following day, I was sprinting up our stairs when the neighbor's door flung open. "Hey! You got a sec?"

I recognized him as one of the three. "Sure."

"My roommates are gone, like, not coming back. No one will bother you anymore. Sorry for any trouble we caused you and your girlfriend."

"Thanks. I appreciate your apology. But just to clarify, I want you to know that I still have my bat, and the wheelchair offer still stands."

I never found out where the other two students went or why. I wondered if the school got involved and informed their parents of the year-long torture. In the end, Karen and I decided we needed to get out of campus housing, but it would have to wait until we finished another entire year at Livingston Manor.

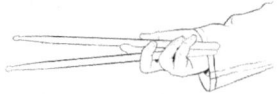

My freshman year in a word: comfortable. It included a full year of biology, general and analytical chemistry, more algebra, and a data analysis (statistics) course. It was just enough to retain my status as a full-time student.

Comfortable did not mean easy. As much as I was trying to keep my 4.0, I lost it during my second quarter. Frankly, I was relieved. The pressure I had previously placed on myself was entirely necessary, but now, at least retrospectively, I realized I'd been emphasizing the grade, not the knowledge.

Don't get me wrong: the grade was still king. It had to be. If at any point a student in the PA program earned a grade below a B in any core class, they were placed on academic probation. I joined that list, thanks to the data analysis course. Having to withdraw two weeks into my first attempt, I researched who the easiest professor was, and re-enrolled the following quarter. Even then, I barely managed to squeak through.

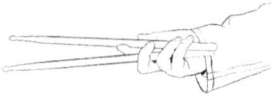

During my sophomore year, unlike landmines buried in the sand, the school planted obstacles in plain view. The beast to thin the herd came to us in the form of organic chemistry.

Here's my take. General and analytical chemistry is impractical advanced math based on structures that you can't see. Organic chemistry is the study of three-dimensional carbon-containing molecules, and for our purposes, how they act within plants and animals. Massive difference. I don't care for math, but as a visual person, organic chemistry just made sense to me. It's a good thing it did, because I had decided to attempt something unprecedented. At the time that I was at RTC, a full year of anatomy and physiology was required, but gross anatomy was not. I had been plotting a way to get into the prestigious gross anatomy course at RTC since the day I stepped foot on campus. Enrollment was limited to twelve students per year, making the positions highly competitive. One doesn't just register for the course; you must be approved.

Before I had completed my first assignment during week one of my freshman year, I had already figured out that Dr. Doolittle was the professor in the College of Science who taught gross anatomy, but he also taught the second quarter of biology. I ensured he was aware of my identity and ambitions. However, he wasn't the greatest obstacle. It wasn't Helen or Nadine (PA program faculty members) either. It was Dr. Lerner, the organic chemistry professor. There were weekly scheduling conflicts between the gross anatomy and organic chemistry lectures and labs. Despite gross anatomy being an optional course, physician assistant students had never dared to enroll in both classes. I was determined to break that tradition.

"Thanks for agreeing to meet with me, Dr. Lerner. Next year, having already received the blessing of Dr. Doolittle and the PA program faculty, I was hoping to take the gross anatomy course while simultaneously taking your organic chemistry class, but I'm under the impression that based on times that the gross anatomy lectures will be offered, I would need to miss nearly all of yours. A few of my fellow students have agreed to record those missed lectures and provide me with their notes throughout the year."

"I don't know if that would be wise," she countered. "If you were to just take those two courses alone, that would be an immense workload—and I'm sure you have others."

"Well, yes, but hear me out. I am the only transfer student in this program. I transferred forty-four credits. I only need twelve credits each quarter in order to remain a full-time student. With gross anatomy and organic chemistry each being four, I'd only need four more."

"So, you're thinking that you'll miss most of my lectures throughout the year and still pass?"

"Actually, I can't just pass. I need to pull a B, as required of the PA program. Otherwise, I'll get placed on academic probation, but you won't have to worry about that because I'll get an A in your class. Oh, and I'll get an A in gross anatomy too."

"Okay, Mr. Roussin. I admire your confidence and, quite frankly, I'm intrigued to see how this is all going to play out. I'll sign off on this, and I look forward to *not* seeing you in class," she said with a smirk.

And so, for one or two organic chemistry lectures per week for my entire sophomore year, I was somewhere else. I would hand my microcassette recorder to a fellow student before the class lecture, hoping they would remember to press record, notice when the tape got to its end, and then flip it without missing too much content. As soon as possible I'd have to arrange a time to retrieve it, collect the notes and handouts, listen to the lecture, transcribe it, and figure out what the hell was going on. Organic chemistry was the make-it-or-break-it class. It was designed to separate the dedicated PA hopefuls from the rest of the pack. And it did its job. We lost a few students from the program that year.

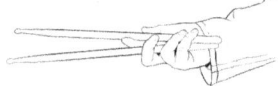

Dr. Doolittle prepared us for the first three-hour gross anatomy lab by delivering a thought-provoking, emotional, and poignant dissertation just prior to the class making our trek from the lecture hall to the lab. Like a scene out of the most epic of horror movies, he escorted us—the "chosen twelve"—in near-perfect silence to the western staircase of the College of Science building. I had never known this stairwell existed. It led us to a set of locked steel doors. Once ushered through, off to our right was a dark eighty-foot hallway that was unswept, musty, and riddled with cobwebs. The air was lifeless, and the echo was abrasive.

Professor Doolittle paused, and with his scarcely visible silhouette only a stride ahead of us, he reached up and tugged on a string dangling from the ceiling. A double fluorescent light, weak of wattage, came on and began flickering and humming. In the distance, where all our gazes took us, was a single black door. No one muttered a word. I could hear our collective heartbeats, and sense the unfounded fear of my comrades.

We paced behind our leader as he continued the march forward. He pulled another string, and another section of the tunnel became aglow. In perfect symphony, twelve frozen faces let out a gasp. The cold trepidation seeping from the walls had morphed into stunning anatomical images created from chalk powder and oil paints, applied by previous medical illustration students for whom gross anatomy was a requirement.

It was at this point that Dr. Doolittle broke the unbearable silence. "For years and years, since I began teaching this course to any RTC student who had earned the privilege, it's been my policy that if you successfully complete this course, you will be granted the honor of adding to the ever-evolving mural that grows down this corridor."

As we crept forward, we were awestruck by the artistic renditions of muscles, bones, and organ systems, as well as the poetic words of wisdom, inspirational quotes, and countless signatures of students who had endured their own rites of passage.

Arriving at the black door, Dr. Doo, as we affectionately called him, removed the padlock. Forcing the door ajar, it let out a dissonant squeal. He flicked on the overhead lights and we each entered the lab as he stood and watched us pass by, single file.

No one spoke. With our chins tucked into our chests, we hurried to our preassigned spots. I was first to enter and find my position, so I had the advantage of now observing my brothers and sisters as they experienced this moment. Each of us caught the powerful scent of formaldehyde in the still, cool air. A few were so bothered that they covered their noses and crinkled their faces. My partner to my right, a pale, red-headed medical illustration student from California, who was dressed as if she were heading to the Oscars, in red heels and wrapped in a pink boa, grabbed the material of her dress and stretched it over her face to filter out the odor, but it didn't seem to be working.

Three steel tables with boxy silver covers dominated the room, which didn't feel much larger than a kitchen pantry. Four students to a table. Synchronously, we each moved our attention to the door as it closed. We'd be trapped inside for the next three hours.

Dr. Doo declared, "No matter what your religion is, or lack thereof, three human beings lie before you. Each is a gift from them to you—to us. When we are in this room, your respect for them should never have to be questioned. Give them the dignity and thanks that they and their families deserve. Let's have a moment of silence."

The moment turned into two, then three. These moments became minutes. Once Dr. Doo noticed that all twelve sets of eyes were back on him, he reached above him and pulled down on a small rusty chain next to the door. A sudden pull of air rose from our feet as the hum of an exhaust fan launched the soundtrack of our year. "You may open your tables and begin."

5

IN A YEAR THAT WAS
SO IMPROBABLE...

One of the great foundations of a medical education is an understanding of human anatomy and physiology. Recognizing this, going into my sophomore year, I put everything that I had into my gross anatomy course. I would not forget the gift that Dr. Lerner had granted me, and the promise that I had made to her and myself. I was not present for over 60% of the organic chemistry lectures, but I *was* present for every gross anatomy lecture and lab. Furthermore, for the entire year, I devoted at least three extra hours every week in the gross anatomy lab.

I wore that formaldehyde cologne with pride, much to Karen's dismay (although her cats just loved it). I spent nine months dissecting a human body. The course was the ultimate test. It pushed individuals to their limits, leaving them with a sense of accomplishment and humility. I can't imagine a course anywhere requiring as much rigor and determination to complete than gross anatomy.

Still seeking a bit more experiential learning, Dr. Doolittle allowed me to do a one-credit independent-study project during the final quarter of my sophomore year. My project was to remove the entire central nervous system from our cadaver, dissect it, and write a paper about it. To conclude the year, I met with Dr. Doo in his office to do a final review of my work. I was surprisingly unemotional in his office, considering my tendencies.

Just when I thought I was ready to stand up, shake the hand, and thank the man who had given me a lifetime of knowledge in only a few months, he reached for a book from the corner of his desk. I immediately recognized it as an early edition hardcover of *Gray's Anatomy*. "This is for you," he said. "This was the anatomy book that I used in college many, many years ago. Throughout your career, I know this won't just sit on your shelf, but you'll open it from time to time, find what you need, and fondly reflect on your experience."

With a new unflappable stride, I stepped out of the College of Science building and felt the rare Rocksville sun on my face. Arriving at my car, I crumpled into the driver's seat. The only thing in my hand was *Gray's Anatomy*, so I opened it. The handwritten words, fittingly adjacent to a dermatome map of the nervous system, lifted off the page:

Shawn,

It was an honor to have you in the gross anatomy course. I look forward to the day I can call you a colleague and professional peer. You're a person of great knowledge and compassion; a rare combination.

Regards,
Dr. Doo

The next day, I joined 200 College of Science students in the organic chemistry lecture hall. After being absent for a year, I didn't recognize most of them. Nevertheless, it was time to take the last of my sophomore year's final exams. At promptly 10:00 am, the doors locked behind us and the gallery grew quiet. Dr. Lerner, standing at the podium, would normally start laying out the rules, but instead she said, "Nearly all of you were required to not only attend, but also pass this course. Some needed to carry better than a C average for the year as per the requirements of your major. Your fate may be determined by the outcome of this exam you are about to be handed. Many of you may have noticed as we progressed throughout our year together that there are more empty seats around you now than there were when we first convened many months ago. That is the nature of this course, I suppose. It's not every year that I get blown away by a student, and I mean completely blown away, but this year there are two such students who deserve to be recognized. The first student is in the pre-med program. There aren't many students we get to call perfect, but he is one of them. He attained a hundred and five average for the year. You know what that means, right? He got every question correct on every single quiz and test, including every bonus question. He simply made no errors. Joe Zalocha!" The lecture hall acknowledged Joe with applause as he waved from his seat at the end of the front row.

Joe stood across from me in gross anatomy lab (separated by only a cadaver's body) and was one of my closest lab partners (and also the dude who introduced me to whiskey at his Super Bowl party). I knew this guy was smart, but perfect?

"Shawn Roussin. Please stand. Most of you probably don't recognize Shawn because today is one of the few days all year that he has graced us with his presence. He's only ever set foot in this lecture hall for exams. With my permission, Shawn had a surrogate record the lectures on a cassette tape. He collected handouts from me in advance, and then worked with various note-takers each week so when he listened back to those recordings, he'd have a better understanding of the material. While you were listening to me lecture about your organic chemistry toolboxes, watching me draw molecules on my projector screen, and assembling ball-and-stick structures, Shawn was buried in a bunker somewhere on campus that I cannot disclose, dissecting a human body. Anyone care to guess his average, barring the outcome of today's final exam?"

Joe yelled, "A hundred and four!" The hall of sleep-deprived, heavily caffeinated, disheveled students let out a restless roar.

"He executed an A. Over a year ago, he sat in my office and told me he would, and he kept his promise. I don't know how he managed to pull it off. He's going to be a physician assistant one day, and it is that drive and dedication that will lead him to a very successful career. That is the type of person you want caring for you and your family."

After a critical review of my answers, I rose from my seat with confidence and made my way down the stairs to the podium. When I handed Dr. Lerner my exam, she leaned in and whispered, "Whatcha think?"

"I think I'm a much smarter person today. I will forever be grateful. Thank you for believing in me." We nodded and grinned, then wished each other a wonderful summer.

Karen had already begun packing up the apartment. As exhausted as I was when I strutted in, I couldn't wait to join in. The horrendous on-campus apartment where we'd lived for two years was going to be a thing of the past in a matter of days, and we could not have been happier. We had recently secured a one-bedroom place about two miles from campus. Even though we had to place all our belongings into a moving truck, drive back to New Hampshire, and unload it, only to repack it all into another truck ten weeks later and move it back to New York, we didn't care. We were elated to be leaving this hell behind.

We were going to attack this summer knowing that there would not be a "next summer," for when we returned to Rocksville at the end of August, a new sort of hell would await us. Well, maybe just me.

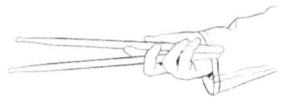

From this moment forward, you'll be reading edited text transcribed from my tape-recorded personal journal entries (not those of Dan,

Janelle, Alex, or Heather). Some are the words as they rolled off my tongue and onto the pages. Others are stories I crafted from actual events to the best of my memory. These are the chronicles of a physician assistant student.

PART II

LEARNING MEDICINE

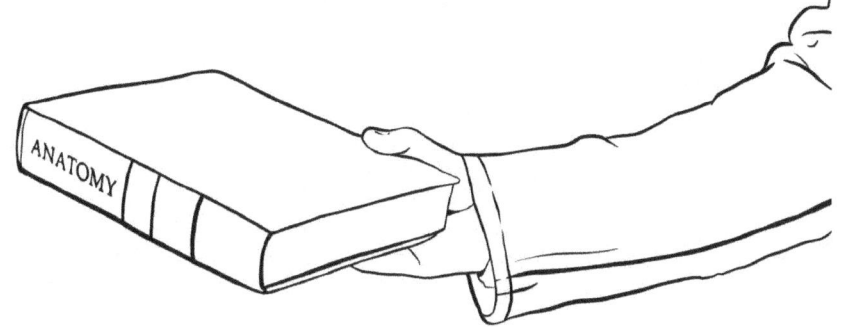

6

Just Press "Record"

August 31, 1999, Tuesday.

[The first journal recording]

I have been anticipating this moment for a few years, but I'm not engulfed in worry. I didn't feel much of anything for the entire summer, except relaxed. The PA program faculty warned us that this would be our last free summer, so we should make the most of it. Once we get back on campus, we're *theirs*.

I guess we were driving on the interstate and as we approached our off-ramp—that's when it hit me. I'm about to embark on the toughest year of my life.

Our program has orientation today from noon to 5:00 pm, then eight more hours of orientation tomorrow. Thirteen hours to prepare us for what the next nine months will look and feel like, and to set expectations.

Carrying a bag of microcassette recorders and blank tapes, I took one step onto campus and realized that I'm scared as hell about one thing: will I get enough material to write this book? I selected these fellow students based on several factors: dependability, trustworthiness, and individuality. Did I select the right ones? I don't want to harass them about recording content. We're going to be so busy and stretched so thin with the workload in front of us, I just hope they can find it in themselves to persevere and keep pressing "record."

Okay, day one of orientation is in the books. We met several transfer students and performed some team-building activities created by our academic coordinator, Taylor. The atmosphere was laid-back. There was one thing that genuinely disturbed me, though. Recalling the advice from previous PA classes, I proposed that we form small groups as a way to tackle the complex list of objectives associated with the daily three-hour clinical medicine lectures, but another student disagreed, "No, no, no. That's something we each do on our own." She was dismissive, and that ticked me off. So far, every ounce of advice we had been given by the students ahead of us had been spot on. Her intention was to gather her faction of friends and disregard the rest of us. What we don't need right now is the formation of competitive cliques. We need to all work together.

Seriously? Is this how we're starting the first day back? What will happen to the six new students who transferred in to replace the ones we lost? That's 25% of our program. We just met them. I can't imagine how they must be feeling. We should just put twenty-five numbers in a hat and have every student draw one. One through five form a study group, six through ten make up another. You get the picture: simple. Five groups of five. We could even decide to redraw numbers to form fresh groups at the end of each quarter. Everyone regarded the idea as excellent. Well, except the gaggle of girls who had already made plans to form theirs.

September 1, 1999, Wednesday.

[1 day since last entry]

Orientation, day two. Still feeling like I should be overwhelmed, yet I'm not. When will it happen? When does that shoe fall? I'm waiting.

Bailey, the newest PA program faculty member, will be the lead instructor for our history and physical exam course. I'm feeling confident that she will be great in this role. We already knew that Helen (PA program director) was outstanding. We are still unsure about Nadine (our clinical coordinator). I anticipate her being on par with the rest of the faculty. It's comforting to know we are in expert hands; there are some truly amazing and caring people here to educate us.

Viktor, a student who failed last year, but is being allowed a second chance by returning to be in our class, became the catalyst for our unity. With minimal resistance, he rallied the twenty-five of us into an agreement about the clinical medicine objectives and we formed several diverse groups. Despite his failure to succeed last year, he has experience and should serve as an unlimited resource for us. Or will he?

September 6, 1999, Monday. Labor Day.

[5 days since last entry]

We just wrapped up a meeting that included all the third- and fourth-year PA students. They scheduled it for when the fourth-year students who are doing their clinical rotations would be back on campus. As a transfer student and the former oldest in our class, I felt compelled to share some wise words. "I have waited five years of my life to get to this exact point. The information I sought is now in front of me and it's a damn good thing I don't have to wait another friggin' day to start learning it, so bring it on. I'm ready. We're ready. Let's do this together. I have one question for Taylor, though… How is it possible that I've attended only two days of classes, yet feel two weeks behind?"

September 7, 1999, Tuesday.

[1 day since last entry]

I got a letter in the mail about a month ago from Taylor. It announced that our class would be required to pass a medical terminology exam at the start of this year. We received an email reminder last night that it is happening this Friday, in three days. I'm not happy about this. They've already overloaded us with work.

Memorization alone is tedious, and I loathe that style of learning. I couldn't get Taylor to waive it for me, which rather surprised me. I have a surgical technology associate degree and passed a semester-long EMT course, so I think I can handle a medical terminology test. I'm looking for preferential treatment, I know. I've had a month to prepare, but neglected to do so.

I've seen a few classmates with flashcards. Dan said he had a foot-high stack of them. Maybe I can borrow them or suggest meeting him at the library soon. This exam is not a priority for me right now. Maybe I'm worrying about nothing. I have to study for it though, right? I can't assume that I can just breeze right through it with little to no studying. Imagine if I failed the very first exam. Oh, that'd be a good look.

September 13, 1999, Monday.

[6 days since last entry]

We interviewed our first patient today. Okay, not really. A classmate was the one playing the role. It proved to be a tougher assignment than expected. Our task was to document the patient's history. Maybe it was my lack of clinical medicine knowledge, or the fact other students were present… not sure. We took turns in small groups acting as either the patient or the PA.

Next week, we're required to submit a written HPI (history of present illness) for the encounter. A real patient in the hospital will be the next test. Damn! Less than three weeks into our didactic year (the year of learning medicine) and we are already seeing patients.

I'm getting very concerned about Karen. Every time I return to the apartment, she's curled up on the bed, watching TV. She's very distant. She laughs at nothing. I can be belly laughing over something and I'll look over at her. Flat. Blank. Stone-faced. She seems bothered by boredom and depressed about the job market.

Only needing two years of college credits, she graduated last spring. She's had a couple of interviews and offers. I think she's also realized that no one is going to pay her what she deserves. She received one offer for about 50% less than what she made during a summer internship back in Massachusetts. This isn't exactly a biotech hub out here. She has an interview at the University of Rocksville later this week. I guess they have a couple of open research assistant positions that she'd be qualified for.

It doesn't help that she has no friends out here. I'm in love with an introvert in a foreign land. I'm already so worried about her that I've contemplated sending her back home where I know she will be safe and probably happier. If she doesn't land a job that she's content with by next week, it'll be time to have that conversation. I need her happy, stable, and supportive. I know we've shared every step of this together for the last couple of years, but a change might be on the horizon.

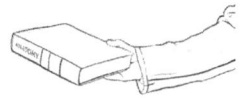

Our first clinical medicine exam for the OB/GYN unit is Thursday morning. I studied for more than sixteen hours this weekend for that exam. Actually, I can't call it studying. I just read 60% of the suggested material from our textbook and followed that up by reading over my group's answers to the clinical objectives. I wasn't ever "studying," per se.

The previous class recommended prioritizing the objectives, but this unit overwhelmed us with a staggering 120 of them. An example of some of the objectives:

1. Describe gynecologic malignancies, including risk factors, signs and symptoms, and initial evaluation.
2. Classify common breast conditions and outline the evaluation of breast complaints.
3. What is an APGAR score?

Despite those sixteen hours, I was only able to get through the first seventy objectives. The exam is in three days and this is just one course. One bleeping course! I found myself highlighting every single word of every paragraph of every objective. It's all important. All of it. But I've got to pare down these notes somehow. The volume of work is impossible. I'm incapable of narrowing it down to the most essential material. I need to think like a professor. If I were creating this exam, what would I ask? How would I word these questions? I wonder if other students are freaking out right now. Tomorrow morning, I need to connect with everyone in my study group and establish a plan. I'm thinking the next two nights we need to reserve one of the library's larger study rooms from 7:00 pm to midnight and get five to ten of us in there and just hash it out. Shit! And this is just one course. Have I mentioned that?

September 22, 1999, Wednesday.
[9 days since last entry]
Ugh! It's been nine days since I last recorded an entry. Where the hell did I leave off? I might have to listen to previous entries to ensure I don't leave loose ends.

Oh, right—the OB/GYN exam. It unfolded just as I had predicted. No surprises. I got an 85 on it. Despite not achieving a 100, an 85 is a commendable result, given the effort I invested. We went over the entire exam during class yesterday. My mistakes were dumb, but I only had a couple. I'll consider this a success.

Two days ago, while at the hospital, we interviewed actual admitted patients. The on-staff physician assistants led us in small groups of four or five. We went through the entire history-taking process with each student taking a section (such as the history of present illness, social history, or family history). Shockingly, it felt natural, which was odd because it shouldn't. The volunteer patients were great, and they seemed thrilled to help. It took my group about twenty minutes to collect their histories.

Karen still has her moments, although she seems better. Great days are rare. Most days are mundane. Yesterday, she reluctantly accepted a job at the University of Rocksville for $21k per year. She's disappointed with the salary because she knows someone from her graduating class who just took a job in biotechnology and will start at $35k with benefits, although not here in New York. Hopefully, this new endeavor will excite her a bit and get her out of her rut.

The plan over the next two years was for her to pay off her $30k in student loans, but now she's rightfully concerned about accomplishing that. That first payment is fast approaching. We even discussed the possibility of saving for a home once those loans were paid off. That's looking grim right now. One goal at a time.

At least she'll be out of the apartment and earning something. I shouldn't have to worry about this. These next twenty-one months will be a difficult time. I'll be under the burden of constant pressure to succeed, sleep deprived, and stressed to the max. My master plan of getting regular sleep, taking ten-minute study breaks every hour, varying my study habits, getting to the library, eating healthy, exercising, and not allowing myself to fall behind is already falling apart.

Speaking of that, I have the pathophysiology exam tomorrow and our endocrinology clinical medicine exam is on Monday. Looking at our syllabus, there will be times where we'll have three or four big exams in one week. These next five days will be an absolute grind.

September 27, 1999, Monday.
[5 days since last entry]
I'm fried. I'm so damned drained. I couldn't have prepared more for the endocrinology exam. It was three hours last night, five hours Wednesday, five hours Thursday, six hours Friday, ten hours over the weekend, and another three hours just prior to the exam this morning. After all that, I'm not even confident I passed. It felt like I hadn't studied at all. How the hell can that even happen? I thought I had made all the correct studying adjustments between the OB/GYN exam and this one, but now I'm not convinced.

These clinical medicine tests are mostly multiple choice, but each one has an essay question that is worth a certain percentage. We are at least warned beforehand. Taylor gives us three essay questions to prepare for, but only one of them appears on the exam. It's easy to crush the essay questions because we know what's coming, but the rest of it? Damn! I couldn't get on any sort of roll where I could assertively answer several questions in a row. I believed every question had two correct answers. I'll be thankful with a 70 (passing grade). Those who don't achieve at least a 70 must go through remediation and take a second exam. That's a list I suspect I'm about to land on.

Tonight, I'm kicking back with an adult beverage or three to reflect on a more cheerful milestone. We got our equipment (tuning forks, otoscope, blood pressure cuff, and stethoscope). Bailey rolled out this huge cart loaded with every student's equipment bags from the orders we had placed weeks ago, and when she called out the first round of names, a tremendous applause resonated through the classroom. It was awesome and uplifting, but also kind of funny. They knock you down with a grueling exam, then they reinspire you with dazzling medical swag.

7

WE ALL SCREAM
FOR ICE CREAM

October 8, 1999, Friday.

[11 days since last entry]

How do I cope with anxiety and depression? Eat ice cream! I'm not referring to a small quantity, and I'm not talking about having a bowl. I have a half gallon. And I don't mean plain. I top it with sauces, melted peanut butter, smashed up Girl Scout cookies, nuts, M&Ms, maraschino cherries... Last night was an ice cream night. How long did it take to arrive at one of these nights? Five weeks. Five total weeks. Five down, eighty-seven to go. It's too soon for this shit.

To make matters worse, I have to deal with my Red Sox. Arguably, I get more anxious watching a Red Sox playoff game than I do prepping for a clinical medicine exam. Those who know me well understand my passion for baseball, especially for the Sox. Two nights ago, they lost Pedro Martínez to an injury in the fourth inning of a game. They were ahead of the Indians 2–0, cruising right along, but ended up losing 3–2. I will try to keep my baseball emotions in check during these entries, but it will not be easy. Expect it to be a recurring theme. Listen, I had to watch the game. There are no two ways about it. The presence of a TV in the next room and the national broadcast of the Sox game made it impossible for me to focus on studying. Impossible.

So, yes, I watched the entire game, but as punishment, I studied from 11:00 pm until 3:30 in the morning. After a two-and-a-half-hour nap, I studied for a few more hours, then had my 9:00 exam. Oh, and I banged out an 85 on the most difficult exam (endocrinology) that I have ever taken. I am the model of consistency—and maybe a future model for diabetes, with all the ice cream that I'm probably going to consume over the next eighty-seven weeks.

Upon arriving home yesterday afternoon, the first thing I saw on TV was Cleveland's Harold Baines smashing a three-run homer in the fourth to make it a 6–1 Indians lead. Next inning, Jim Thome launches a grand slam to make it 11–1.

I walk to the freezer. Where's my ice cream? The entire time I'm prepping my vat of heaven, I'm dreading facing Liesl, one of my fellow PA students who is from Cleveland and is a huge Indians fan. Every time Cleveland defeats my Sox, she brings a sign to class that says, "Cleveland Rocks. Boston Sucks!"

With Cleveland up in the series 2–0, tomorrow afternoon the series resumes back at Fenway. I'll be watching, but I will make a run to Wegmans grocery store (Weggies—as we liked to call it) to collect some frozen antidepressants in case I need them.

October 11, 1999, Monday.

[3 days since last entry]

The Sox live to fight another day! I made sure I busted my butt studying before the game so I could enjoy it.

Karen and I joined Dan and his girlfriend, Bethany, for a night out on Friday. After dinner, we went to a concert on the RTC campus to see Guster, a trio that opened for my band Pondering Judd back in

New Hampshire about five years ago before they became a national act. They had just released their third CD and were doing a college tour to promote it. We had a blast. Not an ounce of studying was accomplished that night, but I made up for it on Saturday with eight hours, four on either side of the ballgame, then six more hours on Sunday so that I wouldn't feel the least bit guilty. But I did.

In three days, we have the clinical medicine HEENT (head, ears, eyes, nose, throat) exam. However, a problem lurks. Tonight is the series-deciding game five, starting at 8:00 pm. I need to allocate time for an hour or two before and after. I won't miss this game. My priorities are effed up right now. I am justifying it in my brain by recognizing that of all the clinical medicine exams this quarter, this one carries the least amount of weight towards our final grade (only 7 or 8%), whereby this Red Sox game is the most important of the year. I know... my logic is flawed.

Speaking of important, I guess Columbus Day is just so fucking important to these New Yorkers. Really? I'm driving around right now with about fifteen minutes to run some errands and everything is closed. I go to the post office. Closed. I had received a notice that a medical textbook I had ordered and paid extra to ship overnight, was ready for pickup, but nope. Can't get it today. Stupid. I drop by the Town Hall to get paperwork notarized on a scholarship application, which is due on October 31. Nope. Closed. Happy Fucking Columbus Day, New York!

October 12, 1999, Tuesday.
[1 day since last entry]
The Sox stormed back to win the series. Three in a row! Whoop-whoop! That's right. Now they're off to face the Yankees. This could get ugly. Our pitching is depleted. I'm in New York, albeit just outside of the big apple. The greatest rivalry in sports: the Sox and the Yanks. We never win. Since 1918, there's been this thing called the Curse of the Bambino. I will consume how much ice cream? How much will I neglect studying?

I got an 80 on the pathophysiology exam. That's about fifteen points higher than I expected. It was the first exam of the year whereby every student passed on the first attempt without needing remediation. But I feel a remediation day coming for me in the next two weeks, courtesy of the Red Sox and Yankees.

October 18, 1999, Monday.
[6 days since last entry]
I slept like crap. The Sox blew another one last night. I've never seen a Sox team play with as much heart as this one. I don't bitch about umpires, but we should bitch about umpires today, although it's not the reason why they lost. It's been fun, but I'm in New York and the Yankees will probably advance to the World Series. Suddenly, it's getting hard to walk around campus with my Sox cap. I conceded Game 1. Whoever wins Game 2 will win the series. If the Sox go down 2–0, they should take Game 3, but that'll be it.

I'm excessively preoccupied with these games. My grades are going to suffer. When a game is on, I can't focus. I just can't. Not for playoff games. I busted my ass all week, except those four hours that the game was on, but I can't be taking regular four-hour breaks during prime study time. And tomorrow is a massive pharmacology exam. It counts as 50% of my grade. On Thursday, I have a crucial exam that accounts for a third of my final grade. What the fuck am I doing allowing myself to be sucked into these games? I'm so ridiculous. I must study. It's why I'm here. But I absolutely have to watch the game. Damn, I'm so tired from treating myself inhumanely.

After a playoff loss to the Yankees, I can't sleep. My heart races, I can't quiet my mind, and I stare at the ceiling, feeling guilty about not studying.

During the last sleepless night, I dwelled on this book project. Now that I'm more than a month into doing my own journal entries, I can feel some direction taking shape. That still doesn't trump my inability to keep these playoff games from taking over my life. If I'm studying and the game is on, I'm thinking about the game. If I'm watching the game when I should definitely be studying, I'm overcome with guilt.

Can ice cream solve this dilemma?

Yes.

October 19, 1999, Tuesday.

[1 day since last entry]

I didn't think I would ever hear myself say it, but I'm relieved that the Red Sox season is over and I can get back to the task at hand.

I got a 74 on the HEENT exam. Considering the Indians and Sox played an intense five-game series leading up to that exam, I'm elated to have stayed off the remediation list.

October 21, 1999, Thursday.

[2 days since last entry]

I just finished an incredible week of studying for two exams. Pharmacology was Tuesday afternoon. That one counted for 50% of my grade. It was a total nightmare. The pathophysiology exam was six pages of either short-answer or essay questions, and I appreciated its brevity compared to the previous one, which spanned nine pages. I focused on the pharm exam because it carried more weight, but I think both went well.

Nadine returned to teach our history and physical examination (H&P) class for the first time since a brief leave of absence and it was absolutely amazing. She is such a phenomenal motivator, instructor, and lecturer. The grind of nonstop reading, studying, memorizing, and testing has bruised and bloodied the part of my brain holding the inspiration to become a PA. This H&P class, where we interact with patients, learn hands-on skills, and act as the medical detective, provides the motivation to keep me thrashing toward the finish line.

October 25, 1999, Monday.

[4 days since last entry]

Wow! I had one hell of a weekend. For the second time in my life, I got drunk and threw up. I don't know how people can do that repeatedly.

Classmates who live close to us had a Halloween bash. Karen and I went as Marge and Homer Simpson. We won Best Costume.

Then I won a trip to the bathroom floor, holding my trophy, the porcelain throne.

October 27, 1999, Wednesday.

[2 days since last entry]

My frustration level is through the roof. Our pathophysiology exam grades came in. I left the exam certain I got an A. My score on the first one was 102 (out of a possible 105 with the bonus questions). Despite using the same format and studying in the same manner, I barely passed it. Utterly inconsistent grading. It's bullshit. The entire class scored an average of twenty points lower. Un-fucking-believable.

We completed mid-quarter evaluation forms for all our professors and I expressed my dissatisfaction. This professor's grading is whacked. The way he tests us is idiotic. Eight pages of essays, which means regurgitating paragraphs from our textbook. He explicitly tells us which pages to read. It's asinine. My essays were killer.

The evaluations I submitted will surely come off sounding sarcastic and inappropriate. Though I was feeling guilty about it, I had the balls to slide it under Helen's door. Childish, I know. I fear getting dragged into someone's office and reprimanded, even though the evaluations are supposed to be anonymous.

When I'm pissed, I write, and when I write, I get too emotional. While I maintained professionalism and decency, it will unfortunately sound awful to the reader. It would have been wiser if I remained silent and kept my pen in my pocket. I'm not arguing against essay questions posed to evaluate a person's knowledge, but his essay questions seem illogical to me. They don't allow for your critical thinking to shine. It's all memorization and regurgitation in paragraph format.

His grading is entirely subjective. If all twenty-five students wrote identical essays to a question, there'd be twenty-five different grades. Most of our exams in other courses are multiple choice. At least on those, if the questions are well written, some deduction is required in order to get to a correct answer. We have been constantly reminded, "Choose the best right answer," because some questions may have a couple of suitable answers that could be correct, but only one of them is the best.

Those types of questions can drive me crazy, but they at least make you think. Plus, if you're wrong, you know exactly how many points will be marked off. One hundred questions? All weighted the same? Five wrong? Ninety-five. Done.

After our clinical medicine exams, Taylor would always dedicate time to review any questionable areas on them. If she saw that over half of the class got a question wrong, she would pick it apart with us as a class, and maybe even throw it out, thus raising our scores. That is the hallmark of an educator who cares. This other professor, Mr. Inertia, with his pages and pages of essay questions? It's so damn lazy. Takes no effort to write these, and his grading follows suit.

November 4, 1999, Thursday.
[8 days since last entry]
Either no one noticed or they're too polite to mention my four-day showering lapse. Or maybe other classmates emit a similar odor, which camouflages my stench. Welcome to finals week.

My H&P final is on Monday and it counts as 70% of my grade. Regrettably, I haven't been keeping up with the required reading in that course. I prioritize daily tasks, but H&P is consistently pushed to the bottom. That has to change. Devoting four consecutive days entirely to one subject or class is not something I typically do, but when a major exam is approaching, it becomes necessary. I need to be more consistent in doing something for each class every day. Perhaps that's where I screwed up this quarter. I am not confident about this H&P final next week. I'll be fine with the hands-on stuff. Chris (my skills partner) and I rehearse the practical stuff every week, sometimes twice, but when it comes down to the written material, that's where it's going to get dicey.

The next clin-med section is pulmonology. That test is in six days, on Wednesday. I completed the reading last night. It's weird how I have quickly gone from "Nothing short of an A is acceptable," to "Just pass, baby. Just pass." This pulmonology exam carries a weight of 14%, so you can see where I'm going with this... Studying for that exam will have to wait until after the H&P test.

Friday, eight days from now, is the pharmacology final. Since I pulled off an 87 on the midterm exam, I can drop that one down on the priority list as well. I won't attack that material until Wednesday night, after the pulmonology exam is done.

Lurking somewhere in this hellish stretch is the pathophysiology final. Fortunately, my average is pretty high (92 or 93) and this final counts as 23% of my grade, so I can sacrifice some time and effort there.

In summary, H&P gets top priority since the final counts as 70%. The pharmacology final is 50%, but I got an 87 on the midterm. Pathophysiology? I can slack off. Failing the final could still earn me a B. The clin-med pulmonology exam, which isn't a true final exam (it's just the next unit in the course), only counts as 14% of our grade this quarter, but I need at least a 70, otherwise I have to remediate. I don't want a remediation exam hanging over me during the quarter break.

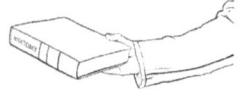

I haven't opened a single bill since we got back to Rocksville. We put everything in Karen's name, so I wouldn't have to worry about it; and I haven't. I'm assuming the rent is getting paid on time. The phone still works. Hitting the remote turns on the TV. Flipping the switch turns on the lights. That's a relief. This is a partnership. I can't do this without her.

I've been wanting to do something special for Karen. Over the last year, RTC has been putting a huge addition onto the College of

Science. The atrium is the highlight, but there will also be additional labs, classrooms, and faculty offices. There's a large open area that extends across several floors, but the bottom floor is the main feature. They intricately carved the marble with designs that represent science, math, physics, and medicine. The original artwork, named Principia, was created by Larry Kirkland. RTC created two-by-three-foot posters of that floor as gifts for the College of Science faculty. They aren't available to students, and you can't order or purchase them, so I had to figure out how to acquire one for Karen.

The dean's office advised me that the only way to obtain one would be to find a faculty member willing to relinquish theirs. Despite my efforts, I could find no one. Just a few days ago, I saw the poster in Taylor's office, mounted on a quarter-inch thick composite wood. It was spectacular.

Then I ran next door to Nadine's office. I asked her if she had her atrium floor poster, and she did. It was rolled up, slid into a clear sheath, and tucked away in the corner. I asked her what she planned on doing with it. I explained my difficulty in securing one, wanting to mount it like Taylor did, then surprise Karen with it for Christmas. She reached down, grabbed it, and said, "You can borrow it. I trust you. Do what you need to do with it. I don't care when I get it back."

I told her she had no idea the lengths I had gone through to get my hands on one of these. It's in my trunk right now. When I go to Kinko's tonight to do some photocopying of notes for my clin-med class, I'll have them make a high-quality copy of it. It's black and white, but huge, so I hope it's not too expensive.

The clin-med cardiology exam was this past Monday. I hadn't mentioned it because I have been relentlessly trying to track down this poster. Anyway, I think the exam went great. I enjoyed cardiology. While cooking, eating, walking between classes, and every spare moment that I could find, I studied. I can envision doing a cardiothoracic elective rotation next year. It sounds high-stress. Most PAs in that specialty perform vein-harvesting and function with remarkable autonomy. I suspect most of my patients would be over sixty-five, and I'm not sure I want to pigeonhole myself into any specialty so early in my career.

Looking ahead at the next ten-day stretch, the workload may break me, if my stench doesn't... When the strain of the workload approaches maximum velocity, as you know, I approach the freezer and grab a full bowl. It's time to stock up.

8

THE BEST-LAID PLANS

November 9, 1999, Tuesday.

[5 days since last entry]

The poster situation isn't going well. Kinko's made the copy, but it looked like shit. It was unusable. I visited the dean's office for the third time, hoping to get a list of faculty members who hadn't collected their posters. A secretary said, "Oh I can't give out that information."

"Why not? I don't understand."

"I just can't. May I suggest that you ask all your teachers?"

"I've already done that. When that failed, one of them suggested I come here for your help, so I'm just going in circles now."

Then a voice behind me spoke up. I spun around and this boy who looked like a student says, "Are you talking about those College of Science posters of the floor?"

"Yes! Can you help me?"

He introduced himself as Ben and said, "I've got several of those in my basement, or maybe in my dorm room somewhere. I was involved in the entire printing process. I took some of the first batches before they were discarded because some people didn't like the paper and printer quality. If you want, I'll bring one in for you, and if you like it, you can just have it."

Can you believe my luck? I am planning to meet him at the office on Thursday or Friday to see what he has for me.

I studied nonstop for four days to prep for the next H&P exam because I knew if I earned an 89, I'd maintain an A average; a 76 drops me to a B. I felt so confident leaving that room that I can't imagine I got less than a 90.

Cardiology? Frig. I got a 76. My second lowest exam grade in clin-med this year. What the hell is happening to me? I can't do any more than I'm already doing. I've already given up showering more than twice per week. What's next? The pulmonology exam leaves no room for error. A 70 (required minimum) lands me at 79.1 for the quarter. A 72 brings me up to a 79.8. That's the narrow margin between a C and a B: 2 points, the equivalent of one question. Below a 70 will result in remediation over break. No matter your performance on the remediation exam, the highest grade you can achieve is a 70. So, I need a 72, bottom line. Despite these numbers, I spent the entire time prepping for the H&P exam, which counts for 70% of my final grade. Priorities...

Speaking of more algebraic calculations, the pharm exam will require a 74 for me to finish with a B. That test is Friday. I reckon that's feasible, but I loathe pharmacology. I'm a hands-on guy. If I cannot see it, touch it, or work with it, I struggle. I didn't like my general and analytical chemistry or microbiology courses, and I don't like this pharmacology class. Securing a 93 on the pharm final would give me an A, but I'm giving up on that dream. Priorities...

I need an 85 on the pathophysiology final to keep my A. That is achievable. I only need a 41 to keep a B. That relieves some pressure.

Is it weird that I'd rather get straight Bs versus three As and a C? I reject settling for average, which is how I perceive a C. That's my new mindset. In my surgical tech program, anything below an A was unacceptable. Here, a C is unacceptable.

November 11, 1999, Thursday.
[2 days since last entry]
I'm an idiot. Crystal, Karen's 'little sister' from the Big Brothers Big Sisters program, called this morning. Initially, I was unsure if she was upset. She wanted to talk to Karen. Consumed by emotion, she wept as she revealed that her mother had just died. It caught me off guard. "Oh, well, Karen isn't here, but I can give you her work number." My response lacked sensitivity, and this was not the first instance.

About five or six weeks ago, while at the hospital conducting an interview, a patient told me that the man she had been with for several years had just passed away. I nodded, but was rendered speechless. A bunch of students were around me, watching and listening. Seconds passed before I gave a cold response. Awkwardly, I pressed forward into my history-taking. I felt awful at the time, and even worse now. Is this a trend? I'm not insensitive. That's not what I aspire to be as a clinician. Jesus, what is happening to me?

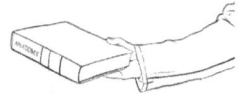

Last night, I slept for twelve hours. I guess that's what happens when you only slept forty-five minutes the night before. Karen had entered our makeshift study room at 6:15 am and glanced at me. "Please tell me you didn't stay up all night studying. Really, Shawn? Why did you do that?"

Losing one night of sleep is nothing more than losing one night of sleep. I can live with that if it means I will not have a C on my college record. By this afternoon, I might find out if it was worth it.

That said, I took last night off. Karen and I escaped for a drive and visited some stores. We were back by 9:00 pm. Lifeless, I lasted ten more minutes before crashing. I woke up at 8:00 am, so I must have slept for about eleven hours. I fueled up with breakfast and reviewed the pharm exam notes. A 74 earns me a B.

I learned that I secured an A with a 94 on the H&P final.

November 15, 1999, Monday.

[4 days since last entry]

I just walked away from my last final exam of the quarter. It was crazy! I feel a massive weight lifted from my shoulders after the immense demands of the last ten weeks. There's a new bounce in my step and a smirk on my face. It's so satisfying. I don't know what to do with myself right now. Nothing. How about that? Nothing at all.

I brought Nadine her poster back when the photocopy idea failed. But then Ben, the dude who was supposedly involved in the poster project, never emailed me or called me. So, I went back over to the dean's office, thinking that someone would know Ben and could help me contact him. I spoke to the dean's secretary, Cindy. She had never heard of Ben.

"You should try to connect with a faculty member who doesn't want theirs."

"I know. I've been through all that. I've spoken to every faculty member that I know. I was here a couple of weeks ago and someone at this desk declined providing me with the list of all faculty email addresses, so I could reach out to them."

"Really? I'll give you that list. Don't worry about it. Can I ask why you've been so determined to track down one of these posters?"

"Well, my girlfriend graduated from the RTC College of Science last spring, and she's been unsuccessful in tracking one down. She knows Dr. Fernandez, who was instrumental in this poster project. When he showed her one of the initial versions, she loved them, so I thought I would go on a quest to find her one, have it mounted, and surprise her at Christmas. I've been invested in this for most of the quarter and time is running out."

"Oh, my God. I just can't take it anymore," she said. "I'm giving you mine. What a wonderful story. I have no idea what I'd do with it anyway. I'd probably just give it to my son, and he'd either trash it, not appreciate it, or it would just sit in my basement collecting dust. You want it so much more than me, so it's yours."

She walked around the corner, returned moments later, and handed a poster to me.

"Cindy, you have no idea how much this means to me. I could just hug you right now."

I ran right over to the College of Science and told the PA faculty what had just happened. Everyone knew I had been trying to acquire one of these, especially Nadine, who said, "Just remember, Cindy really loves flowers."

Over break, I'm going to have flowers delivered to Cindy's office.

November 19, 1999, Friday.
[4 days since last entry]
I just drove away from the laundromat. I hate laundry. It was something I used to love doing during the school year. It offered a reprieve from studying. Now I can't stand it. In ten days, maybe I'll love it again.

We went out for Japanese food last night with Dan, Bethany, and Chris, my H&P skills partner who is one of the new transfer students. I'm becoming good friends with Chris and his wife, Carolyn. I had never tried sushi before. I loved it. Everyone at the table entered a pact whereby we all agreed to use chopsticks (something else I had never tried). Why do people use chopsticks? The fork is such a superior utensil. What could be easier? I can clean my plate with a fork. Chopsticks? Impossible, especially the rice. I don't have three hours to eat a meal. I'm a PA student. Mealtime is capped at three minutes.

November 29, 1999, Monday.

[10 days since last entry]

Welcome to the second quarter. I feel refreshed and ready. During the first week of break, I hung out in Rocksville and got together with Dan and Chris twice to practice physical exams.

Karen and I then spent a week back home in New Hampshire. What a hassle our travel arrangements ended up being, and Karen was none too happy about it. Because of her work schedule, I drove by myself a few days ahead of her, and she later flew out on a small prop plane. After landing in Boston, she took a bus up to Portsmouth. I think she wanted me to drive into Boston to go get her. On any other day of the year, I would have, but the night before Thanksgiving—one of the busiest travel holidays of the year? Hell, no! The bus was the way to go. She didn't appreciate that, nor did she seem to understand my point of view. And it showed the entire time we were home.

Then, on the trip back to Rocksville, we got into a tiff over whose money we would use to buy coffee at a rest stop. She rolled her eyes at me—the fourth time in three days—over something trivial. After that last time, I felt compelled to speak up. "Hey, how many more times are you going to roll your eyes at me?"

"I didn't."

"Yes, of course. I'm seeing things."

For the next three hours it was silent, which was not the right way to start a quarter.

Upon returning to our apartment, however, everything appeared back to normal. She was in a good mood.

Sometimes the silence allows your brain to settle down and refocus on what is important. This program is hard. I appreciate her being here, and I'm empathetic to the sacrifices she is making. I know she's not happy. I'm living with her, but seldom am I mentally present. She's lonely, I'm sure. It's difficult, if not impossible for me to mitigate those feelings.

It is now later in the evening and I'm on my way back from my H&P class over at the hospital. Nadine, who leads the course, is also my group's leader. I think we have five groups of five. She's harder on us than Bailey, who led the course until Nadine returned from her medical leave. We can all appreciate that. I learned a lot last quarter, but I'm not sure I felt pushed enough. Nadine is going to do that. I already know this will be my favorite three hours each week. We've got to come prepared, because Nadine grills us. But she makes it fun and she's a phenomenal teacher.

December 1, 1999, Wednesday.
[2 days since last entry]
We reviewed our pharm final in class. I scored a B. There were ninety questions. If I were to take this same exam today, I'd feel fortunate to answer 25% of the questions correctly. I just took it three weeks ago. None of this information is sticking. It gets smudged into short-term memory, regurgitated, then *poof!* Gone. They keep reassuring us, "Don't worry, you'll be able to recall a lot of this stuff when you least expect it. It's your first exposure to this material. You can't retain it all on your first pass, but it's in there, somewhere. We promise."

I'm not buying it.

December 8, 1999, Wednesday.
[7 days since last entry]
This morning, we were over at the hospital in the endoscopy suite and observed a gastroenterologist performing an upper endoscopy and colonoscopy. I've seen dozens of these, maybe hundreds. Some of my classmates, understandably so, were like, "Wow! That's so cool." The

"oohs" and "ahhs" echoed like a church choir. I'm sitting there, sort of zoning out, perhaps even yawning, hoping not to get caught. Then the doctor snared a polyp, zapped a tiny bleeder, and I thought a standing ovation was going to take place. It struck me that I could be the sole individual in my class with any medical experience. That is downright frightening to me. I think Chris was a licensed nursing assistant (LNA), but I don't remember if any of my other classmates had ever seen blood, stood at a surgical field, or held a stethoscope until a few weeks ago.

When I was contemplating becoming a PA, the typical applicant was a twenty-eight-year-old female with more than 2,000 hours of patient care experience and a health sciences degree. That was widely considered the minimum necessary, but the minimum would not guarantee you an interview. Yet, there I was two years ago, sitting in a class of twenty-four recent high school graduates. Now, in less than two years, those that have survived will be called physician assistants, and not a single one of them having ever received a paycheck in the medical field. Sorry, but that petrifies me. When I think about what I was doing between the ages of eighteen and twenty-two…

Later in our class, I took the role of the PA while Nadine acted as the mock patient with a breast lump. Since I had arrived late, I sat in the back but possessed a strong intuition that I would be chosen for something—and I was correct.

"We are going to have Shawn interview me in his office. I am here because I have found a breast lump. The information he gathers will be used to write a complete SOAP note." (Subjective, objective, assessment, and plan.)

I couldn't believe how difficult it was. Panic and stage fright immediately overwhelmed me. With no preparation or forewarning, there I was, a male PA interviewing my female instructor about a breast issue in front of all my classmates.

What happened? I don't know. I don't recall. Everything was a blur. I guess I did well. Afterwards a few classmates approached me to give me a pat on the back and words of encouragement. Ultimately, I appreciated being forced into a challenging clinical scenario, despite the uneasiness. I'd thought I was farther along in my interviewing skills. Any confidence I had been building feels like it took a hit today. Nadine's repeated interruptions made it exceptionally tricky for me to stay focused and maintain my train of thought, but experiencing that disruption was beneficial because it mirrors real-life patient scenarios.

After class, Nadine sought me out when no one was around and confessed that she chose me for this scenario because of my experience, candor, and maturity. She said that she was very satisfied with the job I had done. She confessed to being terrified by the younger "quiet ones" in this class, a fear that will plague her until their graduation, assuming they all reach that point. I knew who she was referring to. "You're right where you should be, Shawn. Keep working hard."

December 13, 1999, Monday.

[5 days since last entry]

I've got it! I've got it! It's awesome, and it's exactly what I wanted. Taylor had given me the name of the company that mounted her poster. The day after I finally got my hands on one, I drove over there and told them what I wanted. The woman at the counter laughed. "Yup. We've done a few of these in recent weeks. We know what to do. So, you're RTC faculty?"

"No, just a student."

"How'd you get one of these?"

I went through my entire saga from idea to acquisition. The woman loved my quest so much that she gave me the RTC faculty discount.

So now what? How do I get this thing back to New Hampshire without Karen seeing it when we travel back home for the Christmas break?

RTC has a major called Packaging Technologies, or something like that. I found their office on campus and spoke to an administrator who pulled a business card out of his desk drawer and said, "Call this place, drop my name, tell him who you are and what you need. The owner is an RTC graduate. He'll help you out."

This is crazy. I called, and now tomorrow I must carve out an hour to visit this custom packaging and shipping business on the northeast outskirts of Rocksville, meet with the owner, and see what he can do for me.

December 14, 1999, Tuesday.

[1 day since last entry]

I'm sitting in a parking lot in a suburb of Rocksville that I didn't know existed. The owner of the shipping company was so awesome. I went through the story with him, not leaving out any details, and when I pulled the mounted poster out of my backseat, his jaw dropped. "Holy shit! That's a marble floor over at RTC?"

"Yes, in the new College of Science addition."

"Damn! I've got to get over there to see it for myself. That's amazing!"

I told him I needed the poster packaged so there would be no chance in hell that any damage would occur to it, and then shipped to our home in New Hampshire, but that I needed it to arrive before Christmas.

"Don't worry," he said with confidence. "It'll be there."

Before I had even pulled out of the parking lot, I called Peter, Karen's father. After leaving two voicemails in a span of ten minutes, he called me right back. "Pete, there's going to be a package arriving at your house in the next few days. It's a Christmas gift for Karen. Be on the lookout for it. Hide it in a safe place."

"Is it that poster you've been talking about?"

"Yes. Wait till you see it. It's spectacular. Karen has no idea."

Sometimes you just have to scrap the best-laid plans, hoping a better one will come along.

9

LET THE TRUTH
SET YOU FREE

December 15, 1999, Wednesday.

[1 day since last entry]

Last Friday, I spent the entire evening attempting to complete the objectives for our next clin-med unit, general surgery, by using *The Essentials of General Surgery* textbook that we had been required to buy. I was eager to get this book, but became aggravated after reviewing the vascular surgery section, failing to see how this was supposed to teach us about actual "surgery."

Taylor informed us that at the beginning of each chapter there are a set of typical objectives, and she directed us to focus on those instead of relying on her to create a list, since she was happy about the ones in the textbook. I disagree. These objectives are vague and they pale in comparison to the precision of Taylor's objective lists (that we have become accustomed to). For three months, we acclimated to a particular set of expectations, and without warning, we get thrown a curveball.

Surgery is not a specialty of cutting. Surgeons deal with the same problems as family practice doctors, internists, and medical subspecialists do. After their own surgery rotations, last year's students had written these comments on their evaluations:

- "This section is not about surgery, but rather, it is about taking care of patients with medical and surgical problems."
- "This unit is about taking care of patients with a slight perspective towards the surgical patient."
- "Peter F. Lawrence, the author of the textbook, is one of the most famous surgeons out there. He does not see surgery as how or when to operate. Most surgeons spend a majority of their time evaluating and treating patients medically. They will, however, on occasion, use an operation as a method of treatment or for assisting in making a definitive diagnosis. I just wanted to make sure that you are aware of this, since I failed to do so last year."
- "You will get 'hands-on' experience next year on your rotations, and you'll read surgical atlases that study operative technique. Most of your time, however, will be spent taking care of postoperative patients and consulting on patients with problems that may need surgery."

Later this year, we'll have a unit called Surgery II, which is about caring for the surgical patient, suturing, trauma, shock, burns, and postoperative care. This section is presented now to coordinate with our H&P course and expand upon other subspecialties. Much of this content is review, designed this way to reinforce the material in other classes simultaneously.

Feeling irritated with the textbook, I had no choice but to call Taylor Friday night. I didn't see the relevance to surgery, and the objectives were unclear. Taylor confirmed she had omitted certain objectives because she wanted us to get a broad overview of a lot of topics that we had already covered. The unit emphasizes decision-making to prevent surgery, not the surgery itself.

At first, Taylor's response disappointed me. But I arranged a meeting with her so that I could better understand her philosophy on this. I felt much better after the meeting. In almost all cases, surgery should be a last option. A great surgeon avoids recommending surgery, except in specific circumstances. I believe this is what she wanted to instill in us.

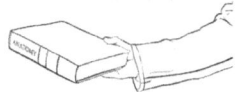

The College of Science Gala was this past Saturday. The event was quite formal. Prior to heading over, we attended a cocktail party at Chris and Carolyn's. I planned to have a few drinks for the first time since the school year began. We all let loose and worked up a sweat on the dance floor, but I soon began feeling guilty that I wasn't studying. Guilty that I was drinking alcohol. Guilty that I was having a good time. I had so much shit to get done on Sunday, and I didn't want to be hungover. I couldn't even give myself just a few hours of fun.

Why can't people get their clin-med objectives done on time? It's a simple ask. We all have specific clin-med objectives. We set deadlines, complete our work, and distribute copies on the due date. However, there always seems to be one person, occasionally two, that just can't pull their weight, and it pisses me off. These general surgery objectives were to be completed and distributed to everyone in our study group by 3:00 pm Saturday. That would give us Sunday through Thursday to study for Friday's exam.

Last night, while organizing objectives in my binder, I noticed I didn't have any objectives on the colorectal system. I figured out they were supposed to come from the same classmate who handled the spleen section, but I have those. Not messing around, I called her, and this is what I get: "Oh, um, yeah. I just didn't get to it, but hopefully you'll have it tomorrow."

Hopefully? Fuck you. That'll be Tuesday, three days after they were due, and only three days before the exam. I'm getting sick of relying on other people. I know that it's impossible to attack this clin-med material any other way than to divide and conquer, but it's still infuriating.

December 16, 1999, Thursday.

[1 day since last entry]

Received the half-assed colorectal section today from my classmate. Should've just done it myself. The quality was on par with a sixth grader. No offense to highly intelligent middle schoolers.

December 24, 1999, Friday. Christmas Eve.

[9 days since last entry]

It was time. I knew. Grabbing two shot glasses from the cupboard, I retrieved a bottle of Benedictine from the top shelf of the pantry. Karen's father, Peter, was in his basement workshop putting the final touches on the woodworking gift that he would custom-make for his wife every Christmas. When there was a break in the screeching of the spinning table saw, I yelled down to him. "Pete! Can you come up for a sec?"

"Okay. Be right there!"

When I heard his boots climbing the stairs, I ran over to the dining room table and pulled out a chair in front of one of the empty glasses that I had placed on the green tablecloth, patterned in animated candy canes, sugarplums and jolly white-bearded fellows. "Have a seat," I said as he came around the corner. He ripped off his Marine-themed cap and slapped his thigh with it to remove the sawdust.

"Oh, Jeez. What's this?"

"It's Christmas Eve. It's Benedictine; your favorite after-meal sipping drink." I filled both shots to their tipping points and took a seat across from him.

"Is this happening tomorrow?"

"What?"

"Are you proposing to my daughter?"

"Peter. C'mon. I would never do such a thing without your permission."

Raising his glass, he swigged enough to clear his throat and open his sinuses. "I'm listening. Make your pitch. It'd better be good."

Disregarding Peter's previous sound advice of savoring the Benedictine, I threw back the entire shot. If bad cough medicine came in a 750ml bottle at a liquor store, this would be it. Pete laughed as I finished hacking and wiping the tears from my eyes, however, that didn't prevent me from immediately topping off my glass again.

"She's the one. I don't know when I knew. It wasn't an epiphany; more like a body of work. I can't ignore it. She's always believed in me and supported me. When we met, I was a broke musician, eating one meal a day, and driving a 1986 Ford Aerostar cargo van, usually filled with drum gear. If that is all I was ever going to be, and all I was ever going to have, she would've been fine with it. And even though I had so little, I wanted to share it all with her. That feeling has only grown stronger. She inspires me to be a better man. I will honor her, protect her, and if we are ever blessed with children, I hope to God they look like her. And let's pray that the boys get your head of hair, not mine."

"You better not give Barb and I any bald granddaughters," he laughed. Raising the Benedictine to his lips, he withdrew the final sip. "Is your chest clear now?" After refilling our glasses again, Peter hoisted his as if to initiate a toast. "Cheers. I know I speak on behalf of Barb and I when I say that we look forward to the day we can call you our son-in-law, although we think of you in that way already."

And with that, I knew there was no way I was going to develop a cough for the remainder of the winter.

December 25, 1999, Saturday. Christmas.

[1 day since last entry]

Several days ago, Karen had headed out with her mother to do the last of their Christmas shopping, so I had plenty of time to wrap the box that the College of Science floor poster had arrived in the day before. Because it was packaged and sealed so well, I decided not to open it to verify it had survived the ground shipping from Rocksville.

The poster is black and white, so staying with the theme, I wrapped the box in a solid black paper. Karen's mother is a floral designer with a massive craft room. Raiding it for the perfect white, shimmery, four-inch-wide organza ribbon, I created the traditional crisscross pattern through the center, and finished it off with an extra-large pom-pom bow made from the same material.

Since there was no way to conceal this bad boy, I leaned it up against the faux stone fireplace next to the tree, pushed several other presents in front of it, then performed some reverse-Jenga maneuvers in hopes of deterring any would-be investigators.

When Karen arrived back to the house, she came into the living room where I was watching a Celtics game from the couch and she immediately alerted to the newly positioned gift. "That wasn't here when we left. Where did that come from?"

Playing dumb, I tried to downplay the holiday's newest arrival. "Oh, that? I don't know. Your dad summoned me downstairs about twenty minutes ago, asking me to help him carry it upstairs. Said it was something he made for your mom, but wouldn't tell me what it was."

Fortunately, she bought it and then dropped the subject.

Earlier this evening, we celebrated Christmas with Karen's side of the family. Her brother and sister-in-law were visiting from Kentucky. We hadn't seen them since Karen and I traveled down there four years ago, so it didn't take long to polish off a couple bottles of spirits amongst the six of us.

As midnight approached, debris from the dozens of unwrapped gifts lay scattered about the floor, but one remained unopened.

"Daddy? Do you want me to help you drag that one out so Mom can open it?" Karen asked.

"What? That's for me?" Barbara said. "You're kidding. Oh, my goodness!"

Karen and Peter lifted it and set it in front of her. Barbara removed an unmarked envelope from beneath the bow and handed it to Karen. Delivering her mother a puzzled look, Karen reluctantly grabbed it. "Ma, aren't you going to read the card first?"

"Why would I read your card?"

"No, Mom. It's your card. This is from Dad, to you."

"No, it's not. It's from Shawn, to you."

That's when she shot me the look. "Babe! What the hell? How did you...? But you and I were in New York, and..."

I will never doubt the RTC graduates who packed and shipped this thing. By the time she had all the protective layers removed, it seemed like a week had passed, and Dick Clark was beginning his final countdown to Y2K—the anticipated Armageddon. Still perplexed at what this could possibly be, she lifted the final veil of industrial packing paper and let out a gasp.

"Nooooooo! No way! Get outta here. Get the fuck outta here! Are you kidding me right now? Babe! How the hell did you...? It's even mounted. It's amazing."

No one around us knew why she was so excited. They couldn't comprehend the meaning it held and would hopefully always hold. As she wrapped her arms around my waist and buried her face in my neck, I whispered in her ear, "I needed to do something so special, so spectacular, and so crazy for you because of everything you have tolerated with me, and will undoubtedly have to in the next two to three years. This was the least I could do. One day, I will do more. I promise."

"But how did you get one? Only faculty received them. I tried for weeks and weeks."

"I know. I tried relentlessly for months. I'm just glad you never got your hands on one, or my surprise would have been ruined."

"Okay, but how did you get it to Portsmouth? That couldn't have fit in the trunk."

"It's a long story, but let's just say that I know people. Plus, I was a little lucky."

"No," Karen said, as she looked up at me. "I'm the lucky one."

"Well, I may need the collateral later in case I need to take a loan out on that luck between now and graduation."

"I think your credit score is safe for a while."

I hope so, because I'm about to submit an application.

January 2, 2000, Sunday.
[8 days since last entry]

Although we spent the better part of New Year's Day treating our hangovers with mimosas, leftover buffalo wings, and remnants from a charcuterie board, by this morning, Karen and I had recovered enough to head into downtown Portsmouth to hit the local shops.

The first window we arrived at was that of a custom jeweler. When I came to an abrupt halt, Karen was nothing short of surprised. "Check out these rings, babe," I said.

"Since when are you interested in sparkly things," as she tried to lead me away.

"No, look. These are pretty cool, simple, and no sparkles. Do they make them here? These look custom."

Now more curious, Karen cupped her hands over her eyes and leaned onto the glass, "I think so. Which ones do you like?"

"That one, for sure." I pointed to the ring on a stubby pedestal in the middle of the front row. "It's perfect. It's the most perfect wedding band I have ever seen."

"What? Wedding band? Are you still buzzin'? Let's go, Mr. Roussin. I want to get a coffee at Breaking New Grounds."

Sneaking up on midday, the cloudless sky allowed the New England temps to breach fifty, considered balmy for January. Peppermint shot for her, caramel for me, and always with extra cream, we used our large

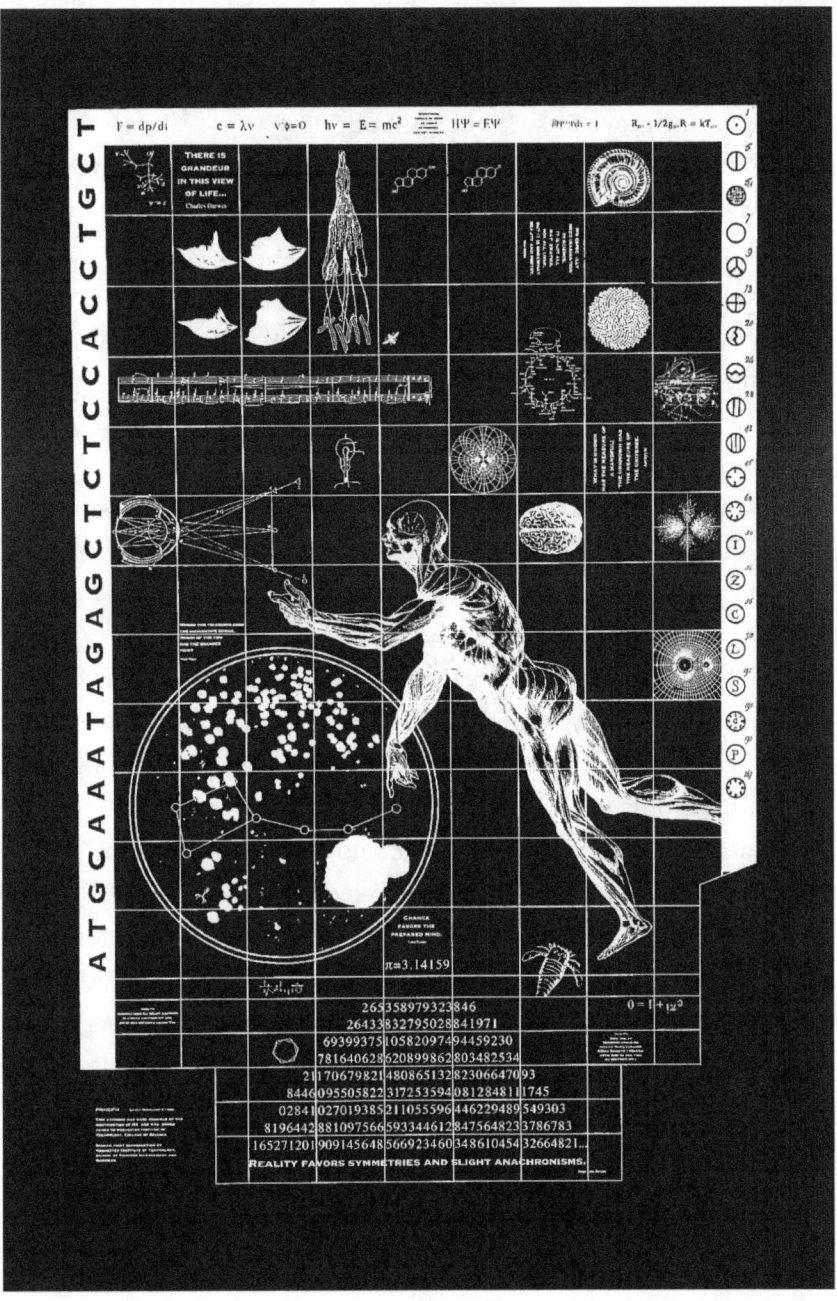

"Principia" by Larry Kirkland

steaming cups as handwarmers while we roamed Market Square in search of an open bench.

It didn't take long to locate an abandoned one, since folks were staying on the move to keep the chill off.

"C'mon, quick! Our bench opened up." I led her by the hand, narrowly beating out another young couple.

"Our bench?"

"Yes. The one we sat on during our first date. You don't remember?"

"Of course I do. I just didn't think that you would. But are we drinking the same exact coffees?"

Now she's pushing the limits of my memory, but I boldly confirmed, "We are."

"Dammit. You're right again. Not bad, my love. Not bad." She leaned into me and pecked my cheek.

"Do you recall some of the things we talked about?"

"Do you?" she countered.

"Hell no. Not a word. I was too frigging nervous. When I asked you out after one of my study groups, you told me you had a boyfriend. I had become enamored with you, so when you gave me that gut punch, I was crushed."

"But then what happened? There's no way you forgot that."

"You called me the next day and asked if my offer was still good."

"I dropped that other guy like a venomous spider. I was not going to let you get away."

Karen is deathly afraid of arachnids, venomous or not.

"And now look at us," I said. "A couple of years later, sitting on our bench, drinking the same coffees, still broke and living out of your parents' basement."

"Yeah babe, but look where we're going. Look what we're building."

Nodding as if she was gratified by the fulfilling of a prophecy, she looked across the Square to the Old North Church, closed her eyes, and extended her neck, allowing the warm rays to glow on her face.

I peeled back the covering of my fingerless gloves and reached into my black peacoat's front pocket. I slipped a ring onto the tip of my index finger, carefully withdrew my hand, and rested my palm onto her knee. She instinctively put her hand on top of mine.

"Speaking of offers..." I said.

Karen's eyes opened and she turned to meet mine. "Offer?"

"Yes. I was wondering if when we are done with all this education stuff, you might want to start planning our wedding. Because I'm not letting you get away either." I began lightly tapping my index finger on her knee.

The high-noon sun directed most of its light through the diamond, but some reflected up into her green eyes that could not have widened any further, or looked more beautiful as she looked down.

"You're serious? You're serious, aren't you? Yes, Shawn. Yes! Oh, my God! Yes!"

I slid the ring off my finger and transitioned it to hers. "I love you, Karen. You are my green-eyed sunshine."

"I love you, Shawn. And for the record, I would've said 'yes' the last time we sat on this bench."

January 3, 2000, Monday.

[1 day since last entry]

Despite the events of yesterday, the tension reappeared last night during our drive back to New York. I failed to complete nearly as much shit as I should have. I think I invested about eight hours, all dedicated to my medical lab testing exam that happens this Thursday. It's possible that I only absorbed eight minutes' worth of knowledge during my eight hours of studying. I'm lost in this course, and I don't think I'm the only one. Every classmate sounds defeated.

Our teacher might cancel tomorrow's class, and according to rumors, she may be absent for an extended period. With no estimated return date, many of us are on edge. Not a good way to reenter the earth's atmosphere after break. We've had four of the last seven weeks off, yet I don't feel rested or revitalized. The only person I can blame is myself. My plan to catch up on work in clin-med and get ahead to relieve early-return stress failed. Although I completed a few objectives for the next two units, I'm still way behind.

Thinking back, what I needed to do over break was absolutely nothing. I needed to sleep, be merry, and bored. I needed to empty my mind and decompress, but I didn't have the will, and now my seasonal affective disorder is coming full throttle. I didn't expect to feel worse after the break. It's like this one big, long "hurry and get me to graduation" feeling sitting on my chest.

Break wasn't a complete failure. Dan and Bethany came to New Hampshire the day after Christmas for my band's reunion show. We hadn't played together in a couple of years. During sound check, nothing was miked up, we had no sound guy, we whipped through a couple of songs, and I said to myself, "Fuck! Why am I doing this? We sound awful. This is going to be embarrassing."

But then, when we got onstage, everything came together and blew me away. It brought back fond memories and I needed that. I hadn't realized the significance of that time in my life, but I know I made the right decision. School is overrunning my existence. Yes, I try to find peace, but it's so hard. I'm going to make a more conscious effort to create diary entries not so wrought with cheerless thoughts. Playing with the guys last week, reminiscing, feeling that love for performing again, I think it had a profound effect on me. This time of year is always a psychological struggle. I'm sitting in the bullseye of the toughest year I've ever experienced, and I think it's about to get tougher.

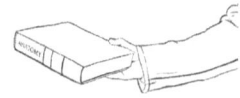

I get a big kick out of Heather. I chose her for this book because she's openly religious and always carries her Bible. I've seen her reading

Bible verses almost as often as a medical textbook. How the heck does she have time to do that?

Today, in clin-med class, we had an orthopedist talking about bone formation and remodeling. "Back when humans were evolving from the sea…" I look over at Heather and she's shaking her head, rolling her eyes, and smiling in complete disbelief. She looks like she's planning an exorcism on this doc. *God, I hope her entries are littered with disdain for evolution. Please, God, grant her the power to release those words into the recorder. That is precisely why I chose her. God, hear my prayers. Amen.*

January 4, 2000, Tuesday.
[1 day since last entry]

Yesterday, I think I spoke to ten classmates. We don't know what to do about the upcoming medical lab testing exam on anemias. I'm hoping that I didn't just make a horrible mistake, but I called our instructor, Dr. Jennings, and left her a voicemail.

"Dr. Jennings? It's Shawn Roussin. I'm one of the PA students in the medical lab testing course that you've been teaching at RTC. I'm calling on behalf of nearly all my classmates. Can you please create a condensed summary or chart of how you organize the different anemias before our 2:00 pm class tomorrow? No one, and I mean no one, has any clue what is going on, and it's only a couple of days before the exam. Thanks for your time."

That was stupid. That's going to backfire. I just know it. She is going to believe that we all think she's inept as a teacher. Maybe she is… We can't all be this friggin' lost… We can't. In my class, there are students much smarter than me, so if they're banging their heads against the wall, you know there's a major issue.

January 5, 2000, Wednesday.
[1 day since last entry]

After clin-med class this morning, I opened my email and found a message from Alex. He expressed the need to discuss some personal matters with me. My first thought was that he was dropping out of the PA program, but then I started freaking out that he was removing himself from this book project. Anyway, I met up with him later in the day.

I was right. Based on our conversations, he knew that truthfulness was paramount to me, regardless of the potential harm or interpretation. He told me he was struggling to remain honest when recording entries and he'd feel awful if he continued on—knowing he was holding back—and he didn't want to do an injustice to my project.

I'm thankful he came forward, but I wonder if Dan, Janelle, and Heather feel the same. Speaking for myself, I know that there have been a few times I've been apprehensive about the words spewing from my mouth when I press that record button. This is not about hurting people's feelings, though it's going to happen. It might be my classmates, friends, Karen, teachers, or faculty.

The content needs to be raw, expressive, emotional, and detailed, but most of all, truthful. Alex expressed to me he felt he shouldn't put down in words a lot of the thoughts he was having about people in his life. I need to honor and respect his decision. I'm having those internal battles myself. He also relayed to me that every one of his entries sounded monotonous and lacked any color, probably because he was restricting his sincerity. I confessed I was worried about the same with my own entries, so I'm sure others were enduring a similar struggle.

During sporting events, a color commentator is often present alongside the play-by-play analyst. The play-by-play analyst presents the events as they happen. It's bland and factual. The color commentator brings the event to life. They're the adjective junkies. The czars of verbiage. The drama queens. The spices in the carrot cake.

I must reach out to Dan, Janelle, and Heather to see how they're doing. This book may be doomed if they're feeling the same. The content might exclusively fall on me, and that would not be how this was all supposed to go down.

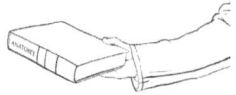

Despite my email plea, Dr. Jennings supplied us with no summary, chart, or explanation on how to best organize all the anemias into a memorable and meaningful way. At this point, without divine intervention, our exam results will be catastrophic.

January 11, 2000, Tuesday.
[6 days since last entry]
The entire tip of my right index finger is numb. I couldn't press the record button down. I have been doing so much writing that my fingertip is now devoid of sensation. It feels like frostbite. I needed to adjust the grip on my pens yesterday, and it's slowing me down. My penmanship resembles that of a third-grader. I might as well be trying to take notes in class using my nondominant hand. Try it. Tell me how that works out for you.

Temporary paresthesia aside, things have been awesome. There has been a lot of chatter about starting our internships and it's getting all of us excited. I haven't felt as impacted by my seasonal affective disorder symptoms as I usually am.

I've been a model of consistency, getting an 85 on my first three clin-med exams. At this point last quarter, I had started to fade a bit. I was unbalanced and burned myself out. Until recently, because I didn't make enough time to enjoy myself over the Christmas break, I could feel myself slipping into that dark place again. The chatter about hitting the halfway point of the year and Nadine beginning to set up our rotations has been reinvigorating. A renewed enthusiasm transports us back to our initial weeks two and a half years ago. This feeling is even stronger now than it was back in September.

Our H&P class took a bit of a turn. Dan lost his partner, Viktor, who I think was dismissed (again) from our program over break, so now I have two partners, Chris and Dan. These are the best friends one could ask for. We've each decided to step up our game. We're now practicing our physical exam skills a minimum of three and a half hours per week, on our own time; double what we have been doing.

Our competency exams are happening right after spring break, in six weeks. We acknowledge the vast amount of information we need to master, so we are prioritizing this course. Truth be told, performing the practical duties of medicine is what propels me toward rotations.

10

A Different
Kind of Stage

January 12th, 2000, Wednesday.

[1 day since last entry]

My belly still hurts. And so do my cheeks. I think I still have dried tears on my face. I have not laughed that hard in years, maybe ever, and the worst part was that I had to stifle it for an hour. The gentleman teaching our psychiatry clin-med class today brought in a bunch of videos. One of them chronicled the lives of several patients living with Tourette syndrome and obsessive-compulsive disorder (OCD). I'd never heard of Tourettes until today. This is a thing? Holy crap! Although one of the funniest things I'd ever seen, I also felt tremendous empathy for the patients and their families. Moisture was rolling down my ribs as I attempted to contain myself. There was just enough illumination in the room where I could tell that many others were reacting in the same insensitive way, so that made it even more difficult to suppress my response. I might like psychiatry, but I may not last long during my rotation before getting removed, possibly in restraints or handcuffs. Which, according to the other videos he showed us, happens to psych patients sometimes. I will need to figure out how to adapt to this uncharted world of peculiar mental and neurological disorders, and fast, or I may be starring in one of these videos in the future.

January 14, 2000, Friday.
[2 days since last entry]
I am done. I'm so sick of school. I can't endure this weight for another year and a half. It's absolute madness. Three days ago, I was talking about how great everything is, how inspired I'd been feeling, and how I've been able to stave off the burnout. That's gone. Gone, gone, gone, gone, gone. I'm tired of the torture. How do medical students and residents handle this type of immense pressure for one hundred hours per week throughout twelve consecutive years? Sincerely, that takes a very special person. That obviously ain't me, but I guess that's why I'm here, because I've already figured that out.

January 20, 2000, Thursday.
[6 days since last entry]
About that medical lab testing exam on anemias: I got a 59. One would interpret that as bad. Not me, folks. I may have failed, but I scored above the class average, and that, my friends, is something to be proud of. Will that get the attention of the powers that be? Do we have a teacher problem or a student problem? That's a rhetorical question. Let's summarize, shall we? Half the class is failing. We're halfway through the quarter. A grade of C is required to pass the course. Students who fail (after remediation) are not permitted on rotations. The program would never survive if they couldn't remediate half of the students about to enter their final year. Not a good look. So, are they going to listen to us now and fix this teacher problem?

January 24, 2000, Monday.

[4 days since last entry]

As I promised myself, I took the entire weekend off. I didn't think I could do it. Well, okay, I did thirty minutes of work last night at 9:00 pm, but that's it. Otherwise, I did nothing. I don't think I've done that this year, but I feel refreshed. I'm ready to attack the week. That feeling should last about twenty-four hours, then I'll be back to dropping F-bombs, worrying about everything, skipping showers, and getting three hours of sleep per night.

One of the biggest reasons I didn't open a book is because Dan and I spent over twelve hours in his parent's garage, installing my new car stereo, power amp, and rear speakers. The musician in me could not tolerate the factory system in my 1990 Honda for another day, so I used the Christmas money from my family and completed the long overdue upgrade.

To start the weekend, Karen and I dined at a small restaurant with Dan and Bethany. Dan was joining Bethany's dad onstage and playing some songs together on guitar. We needed a night out, but between that and the stereo install, the guilt began creeping in by breakfast on Sunday morning. I slept soundly all weekend too. Turns out you can reduce anxiety with high-quality sleep and avoidance of long nights studying, but one can only survive PA school for so long by making a habit of healthy behaviors.

January 28, 2000, Friday.

[4 days since last entry]

It's 6:15 am and I'm in the middle of mindless memorizing for the clin-med infectious disease exam. Every specialty has its common bugs and drugs, but this test isn't just for commoners. This is every drug and bug from all over the solar system—even the eradicated ones. I wish they'd concentrate more time and energy on pushing us to get proficient at the common stuff instead of exposing us to everything under the sun. Leave that for OJT (On-the-Job Training). Pounding us into submission with volumes of information is the unbearable part, not the complexity.

"Your patient has strep, so what do you want to prescribe to them? Oh, they have a penicillin allergy? That's fine. What's the best alternative?" Got it. But instead, "Your patient has an allergy to your first three options for antibiotic therapy, plus they have stage-four chronic kidney disease, ulcerative colitis, and are on twenty oral meds, so what would you like to prescribe, Mr. Roussin?"

What the hell?

Karen and I haven't kissed this week. I've been so busy that I haven't said two words to her. When she walked up to me this morning, I was already at my desk studying. The sun hadn't even begun to gleam through the window. She leaned over, kissed my temple, then turned toward the bathroom in silence. I don't think my eyes even left the page. I miss her. The day hasn't even begun and I'm already begging for it to end.

February 1, 2000, Tuesday.

[4 days since last entry]

Wildly successful Super Bowl party over at Chris's house two nights ago with all of our significant others.

As expected, Monday was a formidable battle against headaches and exhaustion. The fight continued relentlessly at the hospital.

Nadine gave us a real patient scenario and from it we had to perform the proper exams. A ten-minute stopwatch rested in her hand. Upon delivering the information, she started the timer. There was no opportunity for questions or clarification. After breaking into our groups, Nadine said, "Okay, who here is feeling confident now?" No one budged. Five sets of eyes, and not a single pair peered in her direction, but then I righted the ship and locked onto hers and she took note.

"Shawn, how about you? I'll even make it easy on you. Instead of a scenario, you can just pick any exam that you want: HEENT, neuro, abdominal, knee—whichever."

I fashioned a nervous response, "Um, well. Okay. I guess I'll choose an exam that I'm not confident in performing so I can get some constructive feedback."

"So what exam is that?"

And before I could spit it out, she interrupted me, "Wait, wait, wait. That was an admirable thing you just did. I'm letting you off the hook. Let's pick someone else."

Although initially disappointed, her pivoting away from me may have been a show of confidence. I don't think she's worried about me. She knows that Dan, Chris, and I have been dedicating extra time outside of class to practice, and maybe what she really wants is someone she can make an example of.

"Alex? You're up!"

Alex is exceptional. He's not the guy I would've picked if she was looking for someone to fumble through this exercise. Our entire group is strong.

Nadine's scenario would require Alex to perform vitals, as well as the cardiac and chest/lung exams. Being the only other male in our group, I was his patient. In practice, when performing exams, they instruct us to verbalize everything we are doing and why. The narration is reinforcement. Alex got off to a blazing start, but as each minute counted down, the pauses between exam maneuvers became longer, and his confidence appeared shaken. I'm not saying I would've done any better. The stage is an intimidating place. I've spent many nights on one. I'd like to think I would've just slain it, but who knows…

"You're done. Ten minutes," Nadine announced. "How do you think he did?" Silence. "Failed, but that's about where I expect most of you to be right now. You'll get there, but you have to keep working hard. The challenges will only become greater."

I took comfort in understanding where Nadine was coming from. We all need to work harder. Now is not the time to rest. She said we were right where we needed to be, but then Liz, one of the transfer students, stepped up to the plate. Nadine gave her a case whereby she had to do the complete HEENT (head, ears, eyes, nose, and throat) exam, and a full set of vital signs. Liz just knocked it out of the park. She is a star and everybody could see that from day one. She'll be extraordinarily successful no matter what she chooses to do. "Well, everyone take note. That's an A," Nadine proudly proclaimed.

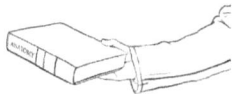

I stayed in Rocksville for our quarter break. I hoped Dan and Chris would be willing to practice these exams daily. Although Dan is slightly stronger than Chris right now, we should be fine as long as we don't become complacent. Today, Dan and I are practicing for a couple of hours. Tomorrow, the three of us are slated to meet. These competencies are huge. Passing these allows us to enter the final quarter.

I just learned that I got a 70 on my second medical lab testing exam, making my average... still failing. Getting a C in the course will require a miracle. My pharm grade was a 74. Not exactly where I wanted to be, but our instructor duped us. He's been clear about one thing: "You don't need to know drug names, just drug categories." Bullshit! Forty percent of the exam questions had actual drug names in them.

He also said, "And don't worry about drug interactions, because those are things that pharmacologists pick up on, or you can just look them up in the Physicians' Desk Reference." Bullshit again! So, I basically walked into that exam down forty points. Give me some points back on lucky guesses—and *boom*—there's my 74. It's so disheartening to put in the work and barely earn a passing grade because an instructor misled us.

February 5, 2000, Saturday.
[4 days since last entry]
I'm certifiably crazy. I need someone to assign me an actual diagnosis. Having been the only student in our class who had the honor of taking

gross anatomy, I had stellar notes, illustrations, and an understanding of neuroanatomy. So, I put together a full-color, forty-page review booklet. I dedicated twelve hours over the last week to finish it. Many students found out about it and wanted their own copy.

Getting it printed and assembled for everyone would cost more than $100. I could have made some sacrifices and gone with black-and-white, but I tried a sample run, and it just wasn't the same. I confided in Dan and, as usual, he came through in the clutch. "Hey, bring the booklet to my house. We'll scan all the pages, save the file, and then give it to Taylor so she can just upload the pages onto our class website." So that's precisely what we did. Taylor loved it. The class loved it. Every student was appreciative, which made the effort worth it.

But with all that effort, I had been neglecting my other priorities, and Karen was one of them. We used a gift certificate to go out to dinner last night. She was down and she was letting it out. No friends. An absent fiancé. She'd reluctantly go to work, come home to an empty apartment—or an apartment containing an emotionally unavailable man—then watch TV on the bed, fall asleep early, and suffer through the same sequence the following day. We have had conversations about her finding fulfillment outside of our relationship. I can't be the only thing she has, although right now I suspect she hates me. She's trudging along, isolated and depressed as we stride in opposite directions.

I revealed that I've been having unusual dreams about becoming a father for the past few weeks, and how much I'm looking forward to it. That time is coming, but not now. I'll be thirty in a couple of months. Karen wasted no time to stomp, "Shawn, do you know how much work kids are? What the hell are you talking about?" I misread her, thinking that might cheer her up. But cheerful, she was not.

I have this excitement building. Next quarter we have an awesome course called clinical skills where we'll learn to suture, perform joint injections, reduce dislocations, start IVs, and execute many other procedures. It's the hands-on stuff that I've been waiting for.

This six-year goal of mine is about to enter its final year. I can't pull back the reins right now, or let my guard down, but Karen is suffering and hurting, incapable of distancing herself from this evil that has been slowly creeping up on her. I don't know what to do, and I'm scared.

11

I HEAR THE TRAIN COMING

February 7, 2000, Monday.

[2 days since last entry]

In light of my most recent entry, I feel bad about what I am about to proclaim. I just left the hospital and I am on cloud nine. I am putting it all together. I've never felt more validated. Today, in our class over at the hospital, Nadine divided us into two groups. They assigned one group to write an admission note. When they were done, the other group had to construct a SOAP note based on the admission note. Then she pulled out a patient's chart and read us an emergency department note, handed us each a copy with personal information redacted, and let us get to work.

Despite the oddness of working in groups (too many cooks in the kitchen), we broke from our huddles after ninety minutes, proudly holding our first-ever composed medical documents. Throughout our program we complained to Nadine that we were forgetting important information. She kept reassuring us, "It's in there. It's a process. When you need to recall a piece of information that you had no idea you had stored, synapses in your brain will retrieve it for you."

Today solidified my calling. This was the first instance where I felt like I was truly practicing medicine, and I can't wait to do this every day.

February 9, 2000, Wednesday.

[2 days since last entry]

I'm leaving Dan's house right now. It's 1:45 am. We are now two days into the clin-med neurology unit and I see the struggle on the faces of many of my classmates. That's why I made that neuroanatomy review booklet that Taylor will now be able to upload to our class's website. Although it required a significant amount of time, I believe the effort will have been worth it. I needed to meticulously review that material anyway.

It ended up being a valuable experience for me, but I only averaged five hours of sleep per night over the last three nights as I was frantically trying to complete the pages. I wanted this to be an actual full-color reference document that each classmate could use throughout their careers, but it was cost-prohibitive for me.

Like me, Dan is a bit of a perfectionist. After seven hours of editing, scanning, and re-scanning, we had a ninety-five-page reference manual, complete with a table of contents. I have it stored on a CD and I'll be handing it off to Taylor later today.

Although the neurology exam isn't for another nine days, I feel several days behind. But I always feel that way. Yet, somehow, it all works out.

Okay, that's a first. Several times today, right in the middle of class, I just gave up the fight. I lowered my head onto the desk and closed my eyes. Others undoubtedly noticed it, maybe even the lecturers. That can't happen again. Every single moment of my life is a battle between studying and sleeping. Both have to somehow emerge victorious.

February 14, 2000, Monday.

[5 days since last entry]

I'm sure this is not how Karen and I envisioned our Valentine's Day. It all started when I got back to our apartment on Friday. I headed directly to my makeshift desk and dove in like any other day. Karen's arrival disrupted the harmony. She had a plan. For how long? I don't know, but tonight was the night she had a colossal task to complete. Viewing it as petty was my first mistake. Complete with graph paper denoting our two-room floor plan, and miniature cutouts of every piece of furniture, Karen seemed poised to embark on a renovation.

Our living room is set up as a bedroom, which is open to a small kitchen, and our bedroom is a quiet space where my desk (an eight-by-four-foot folding table with stacks of milk crates holding textbooks) is located, and not much else. This setup has been working brilliantly since August—or so I thought. She can enter and exit the apartment, watch TV, use the kitchen, use the bathroom, and sleep, all without ever entering the "bedroom."

She announces, "I'm going to figure out how to switch these rooms."

"Um, now? Like right now?" I'm in the middle of creating a study plan for finals which start in two weeks. "Why are you going to do that now?"

"I'm sick and tired of it. I hate being in an apartment set up like this."

I couldn't tell if the fluttering in her voice was sheer anger, a manic break, or her depression's shattering point. Witnessing her cry for the first time left me completely bewildered. Where is this coming from? Why is this so bothersome to her? No one ever comes to our apartment. We don't host cocktail parties. Our extended families aren't coming for dinner. Fuck! It's mid-February. I don't even think we'll be living here in three months.

"Well, if it's possible, I'm doing it, 'cause I hate it," she screamed.

"Fine. It's your damn apartment anyway. Who the fuck am I? Do whatever you want. How much time do you need?" I stormed into the study room and began ripping textbooks from the shelves. I yelled through the wall, "I'll pack up my shit and go to the library until they close, and when I get back after midnight, at least you'll be happy."

"Happy? Really? You think that is what'll make me happy? Nothing makes me happy around here. Not this apartment, this city, my fucking job. Nothing!"

Nothing? I guess that included me.

It became quiet. I stared at my suitcase, packed full of books. For minutes, all I could hear was my breath through the dead air. Was she waiting for me to leave? Was she mounting another offense?

I grabbed the armrests and pushed myself up. The hydraulics under the chair released a soft, breathy tone. Removing my jacket from the hook behind the door, I begrudgingly slung it on, zipped it up, then pulled my Red Sox winter beanie over my ears and eyebrows. I slid the telescoping handle out of my case and began towing it. At the end of the hall, I pivoted into the living room and there she was, her back leaning against the door, looking my way. Our eyes locked.

"Don't go," she said.

Karen abandoned her post, walked past me into the kitchen, and disappeared. The makeover had been cancelled, or at least postponed, so I retreated back to my desk.

That was two nights ago. I couldn't focus on anything the entire weekend after that. Until 1:30 pm yesterday, we hadn't spoken a word to each other, or even made eye contact. So, I broke the silence. "Hey, we've got to talk about this. This is stupid. You're obviously not going to find a shred of happiness here in Rocksville. It's better for you to go back home. This isn't working for either of us."

Karen misses her family. I love that family is so important to her. She hates her job, especially the compensation. She could triple her income back home. I don't think she feels valued here. She's bored. I'm here, but not *here*. I can't be, and she knows that. We've talked about what these years were going to be like, but now that she's living it, she's finally breaking.

"Go home, Karen. We'll get by. I'm sorry. Just go home." She extended her arms to me and we embraced. "Listen. This exam on Monday counts for seventy percent of my grade. It's the only chance I have for an A in any course that I'm taking this quarter, but I will not open another book between now and that exam if it means you and I have to work through this all weekend. That's what matters right now."

With the tension resolved, but not the plan, we looked at each other with wide smiles, and in synchrony said, "Let's go."

We kept our reservations for dinner and then went to a rock concert to see the band, Live.

I resent having to return home every night and dedicate five or six hours to studying after enduring seven or eight hours of classes, and then spending the entire weekend compensating for areas where I lagged behind in preparing for the week ahead… Unfortunately, that is the current reality. Nevertheless, there is another aspect to consider, which is the decaying relationship. I've been doing a lot of reflecting this weekend, and when it comes right down to it, I must sacrifice my education a bit. What if I just let everything slide by a full letter grade? If that means a B instead of an A, or a C versus a B, can I accept that? I might not be able to. Is that worth the relationship repair? That would force me to enter a mindset that I have never permitted before.

I'm sitting in the parking garage after finishing a near-perfect exam (so it feels). Walking away with the knowledge of your triumph is an incredible sensation. I rarely experience that feeling anymore. Nadine's exams are the perfect balance of verifying what you should know, without getting lost in details of minutiae. I wish all our instructors were like that. The world needs more Nadines.

February 15, 2000, Tuesday.

[1 day since last entry]

Well, that was a kick in the nuts… I'm up. I'm down. I'm confident, then unassured. Ecstatic, then depressed. I had strutted out of the medical lab testing exam, knowing I aced it. Nope: 78.

I'm still fighting to pass this course. Shit, most of us are. That raised my average to 72. If my math is correct, to pass I'll need a 67 on the final. Some of my classmates will need better than that, since the entire class failed the first exam. Our administrators and instructors have articulated to us that there will be no curve. Well, I just don't believe that. What is Helen going to do if 75% of her students fail this course? We know what the policy says, but they intended that policy to be for the one or two students per quarter who may need some remediation in a single course, not for twenty of us all at once.

Sulking over my likely fate, a cup of coffee in hand, I shuffled over to Nadine's office for some help with my mental health.

"What happens if I don't pass a course?"

"Remediation," she said. "It's like a make-up test. If you get a seventy on the remediation test, you pass. And if you don't get a seventy, a formal meeting with our faculty will occur, whereby you'll have to make a case as to why we should allow you to remain in the program. Look, I know your situation, Shawn, just like I know the situation with every one of your classmates. Since you've been at RTC, you've earned a 3.8 GPA. If you get a sixty-eight in one of your courses this quarter, for example, knowing you've never earned anything lower than a B, especially knowing that you came to us with an associate degree for which you earned a perfect four point zero… If you should have to sit in front of us because you could not pass a remediation test, that is the case I would make for yourself if I were you. That's all I'm saying. You hear me? Conversely, if you've snuck by at RTC with a 2.8 GPA, and you've been on academic probation for multiple quarters, good luck at your trial, right?"

Well, this is where I am. And I didn't even mention my 70 average in pharmacology. Plus, I've just come to terms with sacrificing a full letter grade in all of my classes to help save our relationship?

February 22, 2000, Tuesday.
[7 days since last entry]
In a few moments, I will be walking into the pharm final. I have studied more for this exam than the previous three combined. If I don't score at least a 70, I'll have to undergo remediation. That's why I studied ten hours on Sunday, ten hours on Monday, and awoke at 6:00 am this morning to consume another six hours of "drugs." (Ha! See what I did there?)

So, if twenty-six hours in three days isn't enough, something is wrong. I am feeling confident though, more so than before any other pharm exam this year. Most of the exam is on antibiotics, so you can imagine where the focus should be: interactions, side effects, and how they kill their intended target.

No surprises. *Phew!* That was everything that I expected, and nothing that I didn't. I'd be shocked if I didn't pull a 70 on it.

Okay, on to medical lab testing. That'll be the most intimidating exam of my RTC career. Well, maybe not quite reaching the level of my gross anatomy exams.

February 24, 2000, Thursday.
[2 days since last entry]
The quarter is over. I think I did enough to be allowed into spring quarter without remediation. I am the happiest man on the face of the earth, but that could change with one ring of my phone over break.

Will that call come in, advising me of my failure? Or will I be ensured of another ten weeks?

February 25, 2000, Friday.
[1 day since last entry]
When I got home yesterday, I took a four-hour nap in the middle of the day because I only had thirteen hours of sleep over the previous four nights, combined. After that medical lab testing exam, I didn't have that usual feeling of jubilation.

I'm teetering on the edge of not only failing one course, but two. This is uncharted territory for me, and so unexplainable. Nevertheless, I find a peculiar and unsympathetic comfort knowing that I am not alone. For some of us, this may be where the train stops and lets you off. What if it's me? What would I tell my parents? The dream would be over. What would be next? I'd be an embarrassment to my family—a failure. How could I possibly face any of them ever again? Everyone would have proof that I wasn't smart enough and that I was incapable of doing anything important with my life. Maybe they were right. Perhaps I just needed more time to go through the motions until I ultimately failed. I guess no one around me had the heart to tell me that this dream was a terrible idea. I wish someone would have.

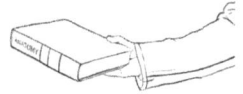

After crawling into bed, I hit the mute button on the television, rolled over, and watched Karen sleep for a while. I hadn't done that in ages. Even during rest, I could see the depression etched into her face. It's been so hard for her this year, but especially this quarter. When it comes right down to it, she's always been there for me, but the resentment is building. Can we make it another quarter? Will we even need to, or is this where the train lets me off?

12

THE COIN FLIP

March 3, 2000, Friday.

[7 days since last entry]

It's shallow, I know. A couple of nights ago, Dan, Chris, and I went to a massive auto show at the convention center in downtown Rocksville. It's shallow because it was rather inspirational. Oh, my, that sounds awful! I'm driving a reliable Honda Accord that hasn't given me a single issue since I bought it four years ago. Despite having over 150,000 miles, I know it has a lot of life left, but I'm looking forward to a major upgrade not long after I graduate. To what, I have no idea, but it was fun to walk around the auto show and dream.

Yes, I checked my grades, and yes, I made it. No remediation needed. I will have a final quarter, but I earned my first C in college. A pair of them. Am I disappointed? Yes, but I accept that I couldn't have done any better or worked any harder, so I'll move on. There's nothing I can do about it now. It's time to rest, reboot, and begin that last push toward my internship.

March 7, 2000, Tuesday.

[4 days since last entry]

The quarter break (called spring break everywhere else) ended two days ago. During it, Liam (a good friend in our program), Chris, Dan, and I practiced our physical exams three hours per day, and it didn't feel like schoolwork. We enjoyed ourselves and maintained a lighthearted yet focused approach. I believe that will be evident the next time Nadine requests one of us to perform on stage.

Karen and I went out Friday night. We tried an elegant European restaurant. And I decided to try Brussels sprouts for the first time. I like cabbage. They look like a baby cabbage, so why not? I plopped one into my mouth, bit down, and immediately began searching for a place to release it back into the wild. I mean, this wasn't a black-tie event, but we were dressed formally.

Without causing a scene, I had to spit out this sprout at once. I thought the best option would be the linen napkin in my lap, but there were couples, families, and waitstaff surrounding us. I'd be caught in the act. The bitterness triggered my gag reflex as I scanned the room, searching for the perfect moment to unleash this mini-cabbage-from-hell into the napkin above my cupped hands. And *now!*

"Why didn't you warn me, babe? That was the worst thing I have ever tasted, aside from beets. People eat these and enjoy them? Maybe if wrapped in bacon and smothered in native New Hampshire maple syrup."

As if I didn't have enough to worry about, they denied my credit card. Apparently my student loan checks haven't been deposited yet.

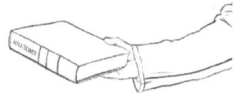

We took our H&P competency exams last night at the hospital. Liam was my partner. The structure of the exams has been consistent, which helped mitigate some concerns. We know precisely what to expect.

One of us, who will be the acting PA, picks an envelope. The other sits on the exam table as the patient, knowing they'll receive the remaining envelope. After the scenario has been read aloud to us, the timer is started and the ten-minute countdown begins. Liam did awesome; he was much better than I was. I felt satisfied with my performance, though. I was calm and confident, but malodorous. I need to remember to slap on some deodorant in my car prior to walking into the next practical exam.

For fun, this weekend, Karen and I test-drove some cars. We got into a Camry and an Avalon, for comparison's sake, then we ran some numbers over lunch. Her Corolla is dying. In the beginning, death was a gradual process, but now the firing squad is arming themselves.

Could she finance $30k right now? Not unless she wants to abort her plan of paying off $1,000 a month in student loan debt. Our goal is to leave her parents' basement within two years after I graduate. I will be thirty-three and she will be thirty-one by then. However, she will need a newer, reliable vehicle if she works in Boston this summer and has a long daily commute.

March 10, 2000, Friday.
[3 days since last entry]
After my near disaster last quarter, I decided I would attack this quarter's coursework alternatively by studying at least some material from three courses each night, even if it's just a quick review. In previous quarters, I would go all-in on a single course for multiple days in a row right before an exam, only to regret not spending time on others. I'm hoping this minimizes stress while it maximizes learning. We'll see how long it takes me to fall back into old habits.

March 11, 2000, Saturday.

[1 day since last entry]

I've been provided false information. I'm one week into the final quarter—a quarter that those with experience have touted to be the easiest of the year—and I can assure you right now that they are all effing liars.

I just came from the library where our group discussed several issues regarding our essay questions for the clin-med objectives. We're planning to address these issues with Taylor, the academic coordinator. The issues revolve around both courses that she teaches. We vehemently think the essay questions she gave us in advance are unreasonable. She's adamant that they are legitimate. "You need to do a good job based on what I think is a good job. Even if you do great work, if it's not the work that I was looking for specifically, you'll get a seventy, and that's it. That's the highest. You better not snow me by trying to cut around the answers and do them half-assed." We were none too pleased with her.

You could write pages upon pages upon pages trying to answer her ridiculous essay questions. They are all lists, charts, and algorithms. She warned us last quarter that things would be different this time around because she believed we were all just memorizing and regurgitating, versus genuinely learning the material. She expressed her dissatisfaction and was actively seeking change. Well, she's on an island by herself. I thought the way she presented the essay questions in last quarter's course was optimal and practical. They included real clinical scenarios, requiring us to discuss patient presentations and employ critical thinking to solve the problems. But these new ones? Just regurgitate your notes from memory and you're golden. It doesn't stop there. Some influential students complained to her about the extensive detail required for the previous essays, so now she's giving us five when previously there were only two (although only a couple of those will make it onto the exam).

It's just way too much. Those responsible for influencing her must now think this whole thing has backfired. The class agreed that I would email Taylor to let her know that our cohort wanted to have a closed-door meeting with her after our hematology lecture on Tuesday.

We also wanted to discuss the Special Topics course she's teaching. That class meets every Friday for two hours and combines the knowledge from our freshman year Computers and Medicine course with internet technologies. We each have to give a fifteen-minute presentation on one of the five key topics covered. One of them is telemedicine, another is handheld devices.

Frankly, I think the actual course material will be invaluable. Our gripe: because we have so many speakers and guest lecturers booked, all with worthy presentations (Surviving the Surgical Rotation, CPR Certification, Intro to Public Speaking: Presenting at Rounds), the exams will be scheduled outside of normal class times. What? We are already swamped. That's unreasonable and absurd. And who was nominated to compose and send the email again? Yours truly. I didn't want to be the bad guy here, but Taylor has already come out on record stating that PA students are the biggest whiners, although she claims she said it jokingly.

In the very first week of this quarter, Taylor has given us enough to complain about for an entire year. You know, that "easiest quarter of the year." And it's only with *her* two courses. The expectations are too high. It's like she has forgotten where she came from. Why is she angry with us? This isn't the Taylor we know.

But she holds all the cards and can make our lives miserable if she so chooses. We're powerless. How do I play this?

The essay question is only worth ten points. I could just leave it blank. I can still pass her exams. If we all did this, that strategy might backfire as she could then just assign a higher value to the essay questions on subsequent exams. But, of course, it's a moot point because seventy-five percent of the class are timid twenty-year-olds who'd never agree to a revolt anyway.

All I can do is approach Taylor with professionalism. Then we'll see which direction the group discussion goes after class, and hopefully cooler heads will prevail.

March 13, 2000, Monday.

[2 days since last entry]

Disaster averted. I was getting into my car last night and right after I opened my door, both of my feet went right out from under me and I fell hard. Aside from the embarrassment, I didn't feel injured. When I got home, I opened my books and began the evening's work.

After about two hours, I began composing that email to Taylor. After I clicked the send button, I began pacing neurotically, contemplating if I had done the right thing, when suddenly my back went into spasms.

While not as severe as I have experienced in the past, it significantly disturbed my sleep. I log-rolled out of bed at 1:30 am, still struggling, and found some leftover expired oxycodone. I cut one in half and took it. By 4:00 am, I had nodded off on a bag of ice.

Five hours later, my eyes begrudgingly opened as I thought I had pissed the bed (ice bag had sprung a leak). It was 9:00 am, and I was supposed to be sitting in my clin-med class. Shit!

I hobbled back into my study and sent an email to the entire PA program faculty explaining what had happened. Nadine called me and told me she'd relay my message to Taylor ASAP, not to worry, but wondered about the second half of our H&P competency exams that were scheduled tonight over at the hospital.

"I'll be there, Nadine. One way or the other, no matter how my back is feeling, I'll be there."

Besides the planned absences from my organic chemistry lectures last year, this was the first class I've missed in four years. Unlike high school, though, they don't give awards for perfect attendance.

March 14, 2000, Tuesday.

[1 day since last entry]

I made it to competencies yesterday. My back cooperated. Had I not gone, I think some of my classmates would've been a little suspicious.

Yesterday was the first collegiate class I had missed due to unforeseen circumstances, so it's hard to question my reliability.

Speaking of that, Taylor said nothing to me either. For some reason, she didn't receive my email two nights ago. I had the chance to talk with more classmates, and we're in agreement about the workload. It's pathetic. It's smothering our entire world right now. I just can't fathom it getting any worse, but I suspect that it's going to. Taylor seems different this quarter and hasn't been as helpful when we've had questions. Initially, I believed it was solely my perception, so I observed and stayed silent. When I ultimately decided to disclose my concerns to trusted classmates, we agreed, she isn't right. Now I'm feeling uncertain about my next steps.

Do I have a plan B? Sort of.

I spent the entire weekend composing and memorizing my answer to only one of the two hematology essay questions that were provided to us. Holy crap! It's way too long. It covers too much. When I began structuring my answer for the other essay, I soon discovered it was simply reiterating the entire unit. It was an impossible task, so I threw my hands up into the air and said, "Fuck it." I'm going to sit down to take that test knowing that it'll be a coin flip whether I'll be completely fine, or I'll be handing in the exam with the essay question left blank. The extraordinary amount of work necessary to have a chance on that second essay question is not worth the ten points. You can keep 'em. If Taylor has anything to say about it, there might be two dozen PA students heading to the dean's office.

I'm back in my car. The exam is over. I should go to Vegas. Deep down, I knew there was no chance Taylor would include that impossible essay on the exam. So, I rolled the dice, chose correctly, and dodged a bullet. Or maybe it was Taylor who did the dodging. When the exams were distributed, all of us turned them over in unison, shuffled to the back page, read the essay question, and a massive cheer burst out. It appeared as if Taylor had been expecting it. She snickered then chimed in with her defense.

"Someone in the class emailed me at the end of last quarter, requesting a change to the essay portion of these exams. They convinced me it would be better to have fewer essays with more complexity versus several essays with more focus."

Here's my problem. One student emailed you? One? Really? There are twenty-six of us now. Does one student's suggestion have the power to change how the exams have been structured since we stepped onto campus this year? That's bogus. I'm so glad it's over, but I still think we need to have a discussion with her. We'll wait until everyone is in a better state of mind to address this.

March 18, 2000, Saturday.
[4 days since last entry]
Welp. Shit is getting real. Yesterday was a very odd day in the Special Topics class that Taylor teaches. It's safe to say that she read all our evaluations and she wasn't happy. I'm still angry. I can hardly remember anything from that infuriating display she put on in front of our class. I haven't stopped shaking and I couldn't sleep last night.

This is so out of character for her. The entire class is just taken aback. I'm not sure what anyone's next move is going to be. I think we should just sit back and await her counterattack, but if she pulls this crap again, to the dean's office we go. Does the rest of the PA faculty know what's going on? They must. Do we go to Helen first? We should. That's a horrible look if we go above her. This is her program. Helen, Nadine, and Bailey have been nothing short of amazing. Hell, until recently, we all thought highly of Taylor as well. Something isn't right with her. Something is going on here. Marriage? Health issue? I don't know. I need to sleep on this. Pffft. Sleep? Yea, right.

March 20, 2000, Monday.

[2 days since last entry]

As we took our seats in clin-med class this morning, Taylor addressed the class, asking us if we wanted any essay questions on the exam for our next unit, oncology. Wait, what? We never asked for the essay questions to be eliminated. We valued questions that were reasonable, practical, and better focused. She doesn't seem to respect any of our suggestions or concerns, which I honestly believe have been delivered constructively. She concluded by telling the class that she would make a decision later this week, after she had time to consider several factors leading up to today.

Frankly, I'm petrified that if they eliminate the essay questions, the multiple-choice questions would now reach a new level of epic. If I have gauged her agenda astutely, her goal would be to make us come crawling back to her, begging for a return of the essay questions. This is what she wants. She can't admit to being wrong. She believes we're all conspiring against her, but she's flat-out wrong. That's not the case. No one wants this fight. Our aim is to have our voices heard. She's always given us that until now.

The seniors warned us that we would learn to dislike Taylor this year. We all thought they were crazy. She's a great teacher and leader. She's dedicated, hardworking, inspirational, and a lot of fun, but she's become this abrasive toddler we've come to despise. It's sad. I hate feeling this way, but the seniors appear to have been right.

13

CALL ME

March 22, 2000, Wednesday.

[2 days since last entry]

Big news. I think Karen and I are moving back to New Hampshire for my final year. That was definitely not the original plan. We hashed it out on Saturday night. Nadine and Bailey, our clinical coordinators, are responsible for setting up the rotations. Eight of the ten are required, and two are electives that we can choose. I'm wondering how many of the ten I could arrange closer to home. I sat down with them, and they believed arranging half of my rotations back home was possible, with the remaining ones all in the Rocksville region, but no promises were made. They advised me it's a distinct possibility that I may end up with only two back home, but they vowed to work with me.

This could save us thousands in rent and other living expenses because we'd move back in with Karen's parents. I'd have to work out my living situation whenever assigned to a rotation in this area. I have plenty of contacts and friends here, so it shouldn't be a problem. Although Karen could at least double her income back home, my primary concern was her happiness. Her parents were supportive, but wanted us to have complete ownership of the final decision.

Yesterday afternoon I spent a considerable amount of time on the phone reaching out to a plethora of healthcare contacts from home. Four of my six leads that I tracked down are very strong, and each one of them would be less than an hour drive from Karen's parents. Nadine hasn't even looked at her complete list of potential clinical sites for Maine, Massachusetts, or New Hampshire yet.

We need to decide soon. The property managers need adequate notice, and we'll need to reserve a moving truck during the busy rental season.

Some downsides exist. I need to be on campus for testing, meetings, and presentations at the end of each rotation. They call those Recall Days. It is also the time when you might have to move after securing a place to live for the following five weeks. Chris and his wife, Carolyn, own a home right here in Rocksville and may let me use their spare bedroom a couple of times throughout the year if I need it. They said they'd discuss it tonight.

Not big news, but I've got to tell you, this alternative approach I am taking is absolutely working. I'm completely revolutionizing how I'm organizing and attacking my study time. I'm just trying to review a bit of everything nightly, emphasizing more recreation time, and hitting the pillow at a much more reasonable hour. My stress levels seem to be reduced, I'm keeping up, and dare I say that I may be retaining more information. Who knew?

March 28, 2000, Tuesday.
[6 days since last entry]
Taylor had emailed me over the weekend requesting a private meeting, which I just walked out of. I set aside about twenty minutes, but I needed ninety. Although she had some sensible insights, it felt like she was winging it for the most part. She had answers for everything, like she wants me (us) to believe she has this big master plan. Maybe

she does, but I am skeptical. The meeting unfolded as anticipated. No matter what I said, she manipulated the conversation so she would appear calculated and crafty. Did she listen to me at all? I believe so. Do I think she heard me? Yes. I don't doubt that she has our best interests at heart. I wonder if she has simply lost touch with the realities of being a student. She claims that the program's faculty are purposefully trying to create stressful situations for students to navigate in order to better prepare us for our clinical rotations, which she affirms will be far more taxing than anything we've experienced up to this point in our college careers, maybe ever. I can appreciate and accept that. A specific type of stress arises in clinical scenarios where one must quickly make life-saving decisions, as opposed to the intimidation of memorizing thousands of facts for impractical exam formats, and that immense amount of work makes it difficult to remember crucial information that'll need to be recalled during rotations. Both sides are walking a fine line, neither of whom are clear on how to wave the white flag and surrender.

I need to step back. I can't keep getting worked up over every little thing. My fresh approach this quarter has been effective. I'm not feeling as overwhelmed, and I need to keep that momentum going.

March 30, 2000, Thursday.
[2 days since last entry]
This past Monday, I had an assignment due. I finished it last Thursday, and I carried it with me in a black folder every single day. The black folder holds 100% of my completed assignments until the day I need them. Today, we were instructed to bring only minimal belongings to the hospital as we would be walking the floors, so storage space would be limited. I heeded the warning and arrived with only the essentials, but of course that didn't include my black folder. I had entered the hospital thirty-five minutes early when the realization—and panic— hit me.

Class started at 4:00 pm. If I raced back to the apartment to fetch the folder, I would have been late and lost upon my return, not knowing where all of my classmates were dispersed, but at least I'd have my assignment in hand. I made the executive decision to stay put and try to negotiate through this. Trina, the lead PA for our group, was having no part of it. She deferred to Nadine, even though I had offered to go get it, miss class, and bring it to any location that she desired. Trina made it clear to me that it would not look good if I dismissed myself from class. I knew Taylor was leaving for an educational program tonight, not that I wanted to approach her with any issues right now.

The next morning, my first stop was Nadine's office. I handed her my assignment and attempted to explain.

She was empathetic, but said, "Well, you do understand that by rights I can't accept this. It's a zero."

"Actually, I don't."

"Well, it's in the syllabus."

"I don't recall reading anything to that effect… And if I had known that, I would've taken a chance and attempted to retrieve my assignment before class."

"You should have. You probably would've made it."

"Yes, but if I hadn't I would've likely been late, not been able to find my group within the hospital, and missed class altogether. I was convinced it would've been the greater of two evils."

"I suppose you're right, so in that light, I agree that you had to make a tough decision, and you made the correct one."

"Nadine, I swear to you I had that assignment done four days before it was even due. I even carry it in this black folder everywhere that I go. In compliance with instructions, I brought minimal belongings to the hospital—just one folder too few."

"Well, there was one other student who didn't turn it in last night. I suppose I could give you both warnings and reiterate to the entire class that handing in assignments late is unacceptable and will result in zeros for the remainder of the year, but I have to consult with Bailey, since she takes equal ownership over this course."

Well, that was two days ago, and today the hammer came down. It's a zero. I'm mad, of course, but the old me from last quarter would have entered a fit of rage. The new me is just gonna let it roll off my shoulders. The mistake is mine, and I accept responsibility. It would be foolish to make a scene over a single assignment when the locations of my rotations are at stake.

April 10, 2000, Monday.
[11 days since last entry]
You can only feel so many fake breasts, slide your finger into so many rubber buttholes, and fondle so many pairs of silicone balls before you long for actual flesh. Today we finally performed our inaugural procedure on a living person by starting IVs on each other and drawing blood. It signaled further confirmation that we are inching closer to the big dance. Procedures are something I love doing. I'm a visual learner. I believe I have good manual dexterity (except with chopsticks). Show me, teach me, and then let me do it.

April 14, 2000, Friday.
[4 days since last entry]
Hell week is over. Four exams in eight days. Two clin-med, a pharm, and a diagnostic medical imaging test. This weekend can kiss my ass. I'm doing nothing. It will be the epitome of complete nothingness. Normally, I'm looking at ten or fifteen hours of work just to catch up from the previous week's massacre. The only massacre that will be happening this weekend will include Karen and me engaging in some bourbon sipping and batting cage shenanigans on Saturday; then Dan, Chris, and I are playing a round of golf on Sunday.

We are five weeks from our first rotation. The seniors forewarned us that once you enter the last month of didactic learning, you're sick and tired of everything and just want to get out there and do it.

They're right. I *am* sick of sitting on my ass for eight hours per day in a classroom listening to lecturers, studying for eight hours per day in my apartment, practicing physical exam techniques on the same two classmates repeatedly, surviving on a few hours—some nights only minutes—of sleep, and cramming for exams, all weighted in such a way that it can make you or break you.

I will not be broken. I did not come this far to only come this far.

April 19, 2000, Wednesday.
[5 days since last entry]

I have never been book-smart. Reaching the same level of achievement as others requires intense work on my part. Until five years ago, I had also never applied myself. Learning from words on a page has always been a struggle. Throw me into an experience, give me hands-on instruction, and I will thrive.

Soon we'll all be able to take everything that we have learned and apply it to real medical patients. The pressure will be different, but it's a stress I expect to shine in versus suffocate. There will still be reading and testing, but it will feel more purposeful, and I expect the learning curve to be astronomical.

This year has flown by. I anticipated it being the most challenging year of my life. That prediction was not an overestimation. Sometimes I wanted to throw in the towel, but that's not how I feel right now, so I'm glad that I didn't just pack up and drive away. Some students did, but others weren't given a choice. Some couldn't handle the intensity and were let go from the program. With five weeks remaining, I think the writing is on the wall for two more of my classmates. As much as it came together for me, it didn't for everyone.

Faculty routinely reminds us, "Don't worry. By the time you get to rotations, you're ready." I hope they're right. I have found my strengths and weaknesses, but that makes me no different from anyone else in my class.

April 20, 2000, Thursday.

[1 day since last entry]

Well, if it wasn't already cemented, I'm sure that it is now. Karen is applying for a loan to purchase a new car. She's going home for my final year. The Corolla that she's had for years is approaching 200,000 miles, and she'll need an upgrade if she's going to be commuting to Boston five days per week. Both of our cars are about ten years old and have fairly high mileage. Since she'll be able to significantly increase her income and won't have many expenses aside from fuel and auto insurance, we can justify it.

April 26, 2000, Wednesday.

[5 days since last entry]

Yesterday, Nadine and Bailey were off campus together in a bunker somewhere, quarantined as they began pairing up rotation sites with students. I just had to drop in on Bailey today to inquire how it went. She had no new information to provide me. I wanted an update on the leads I shared with her. "Well, you know, we're doing the best that we can. There are only so many times you can call and email these people, and if they don't respond, well, you eventually have to assume that they are just not interested."

Dammit! As of right now I only have two rotations back in New Hampshire. I gave Nadine and Bailey several strong leads, or so I thought. Is this Bailey's way of telling me she is giving up on them? I can't tell Karen about this. Can you imagine if I'm only home for 20% of my rotations when I was banking on 50%? This is just not fucking happening right now. I should've been more proactive and made more calls myself, but I was complacent. This is devastating.

April 28, 2000, Friday.

[2 days since last entry]

I've made all the calls I could, dedicating every spare moment I could find. I reached out to some surgical technologists I've worked with, asking them to help me find new opportunities. I tried calling several hospitals to gather the office numbers of providers who had previously hosted students. I even called a few of my old surgical technology classmates. One of them, Vicki, made several calls on my behalf and even reported back to me rather quickly, 99% confident that a general surgeon she has worked with would take me on. She's trying to get me a definitive answer by Monday. She also had a solid lead on an orthopedic practice in New Hampshire that she has connections with.

Over the phone, Vicki and I composed a letter that she was going to print and give to a colleague so they could hand-deliver it to the board of the orthopedic practice which meets next week. Vicki said, "Shawn, I don't see a problem. It's a formality. They love having students."

One urologist I scrubbed a lot of cases with, Dr. Shepard, returned my call. He gave me a couple of leads, but he didn't seem confident that anything would come of them. I've got nearly two dozen leads now, but I'm running out of time to do the legwork.

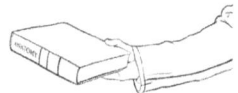

Yesterday, we did a suturing lab on pigs' feet. I've done several similar labs. I was the first to complete the in-class assignments, and Nadine allowed me to move on to next week's lesson independently. After swiftly completing those assignments, I began walking around the lab and assisting any other classmates appearing to need help. Nadine granted me permission to leave early, but I preferred to be the last student to leave the classroom. I used that time to pry Nadine for an update about rotations. I was wondering if she had the same take as Bailey, and sadly, she did. She obviously wants to make everyone happy, but she has a duty to find the best fit for the student, their preceptor, and the site. Our education is their top priority. I discussed my new leads with her and emphasized my need for a few more days.

She reiterated to me that the information I am attempting to track down was needed last week. Affiliation agreements and other necessary documents need to be agreed upon and signed. In thirty-one days, our first clinical rotation begins.

I haven't been in the best of moods in recent days. While speaking with Vicki on the phone, Karen figured out what was going on. "I love you," she said, "and if this is the way it has to be, then this is the way it has to be. It's only a year. I'll find a way to keep myself busy. It's not the end of the world. It won't be easy, but we'll get through it."

That was the comforting message I needed to hear.

14

A CASE OF PRE-
SENIORITIS

May 3, 2000, Wednesday.

[5 days since last entry]

I don't feel like moving. I don't feel like doing anything. This is senioritis, except I'm no senior. I need this year to be done. I need a break from everything, but especially from the classroom. You can't teach me anything more in the next ten days. Okay, that's not entirely true, but you understand what I mean. I need to escape and enjoy myself for two straight weeks.

With Vicki's relentless footwork and phone calls, I turned in five lead sheets today at the last possible moment. In four weeks, we start our first clinical rotation. In two weeks, we'll know that location. Some of us will have a few blanks to fill in along the way. Last-minute changes do happen. Those students that are assigned a distant location have two weeks to set up housing and move. Then, at the end of every fifth week, we pack up and transfer to the next site.

May 4, 2000, Thursday.

[1 day since last entry]

I went to see Nadine this afternoon and asked her if she had contacted anyone from my lead sheets. I'm sure she wanted to punch me for repeatedly nagging her about this. She confirmed that she had reached out to each of the contacts. However, she was only able to leave voicemails. Why do people do that? These were fantastic leads. Providers initially appeared eager to share their contact information and accept a student, but then they end up in the witness protection program. No one returns calls. It's infuriating.

I know Nadine and Bailey won't give up, but there are only a few grains of sand left in the hourglass.

May 5, 2000, Friday.

[1 day since last entry]

Nadine informed me she hadn't received the signed affiliation agreement for my emergency medicine rotation, which I thought was already guaranteed. Jesus! Are you kidding me?

Karen and I continue to justify our decision despite a mounting concern that we may only have a few opportunities to see each other in the next year.

May 10, 2000, Wednesday.

[5 days since last entry]

In our last H&P class, prior to our speaker presenting on communication skills for providers, Nadine asked us to stick around because she and Bailey would announce which students would be going out of town for their first rotation. This means that some students' rotations would be located forty-five minutes or more from campus—and possibly requiring them to secure alternate housing, so they wanted to give them forewarning.

The entire mood of the room changed. Before the guest lecturer even released his first bit of advice, I could tell that not a single word of it was going to be heard. For an hour we sat, grinning from ear to ear, writhing in our molded plastic chairs, watching the clock behind the presenter's head. We appeared attentive, but we were staring right through him, fixated on the countdown. It felt like the longest hour of our collegiate careers (even longer than a three-hour pharmacology lecture).

When the sixtieth minute struck, there was an outpouring of applause. Like a father and bride making their way to the altar, Nadine and Bailey marched to the podium, arms swinging in synchronicity, Nadine gripping a solitary piece of paper as if it possessed the nuclear codes. We all rose when they made their way down the center aisle, our bodies rotating as they passed. Bailey arrived first, then paused while Nadine proceeded to the whiteboard. With each name she wrote, a gasp poured out of our lungs, and all heads turned to briefly focus on that student. Nobody looked my way, as my name was not written. Perfect. This is just how I wanted it. I know I'll be here in Rocksville for my first rotation. I have no idea what I'll be doing, but now I know that Karen and I can go back to New Hampshire and enjoy a week off together before I return here alone.

When I arrive back, I don't know where I'll live for the following five weeks, but I have some options. Because of my extensive surgical experience, I wholeheartedly believe I'll start in general surgery. I'm not saying it will be easy, but it'll at least be familiar.

Nadine and Bailey can put me there and not have to worry about me. We've all heard the horror stories about certain surgeons who ruthlessly abuse their students. I'm the only student in this room with experience dealing with hazing, so they know I'll be safe in such a den of wolves.

In the middle of recording this entry, I called Karen and left her a voicemail. When she called back, she asked, "What's the deal? Is it too late to back out?"

"No. There's nothing to back out of. This is how it's going to happen. This is what I wanted. I've got this." I informed her that my first rotation would be in Rocksville, but that was all I knew at the moment. I shared my suspicions about it possibly being my surgical rotation with the particular surgeon who everyone notoriously fears.

I mentioned I would be working fifteen-hour days, studying for three to four hours each night, most likely doing rounds on weekends, and enduring some mental abuse over five grueling weeks.

Over the next forty-eight hours, I still have three final exams and a major project to complete. It's time to get jacked on caffeine, seclude myself from the world, ward off any temptation to sleep, and make this last push.

May 19, 2000, Friday.
[9 days since last entry]
I commend the PA program faculty for their astonishing work in organizing and executing their first annual white coat ceremony. The new atrium in the College of Science served as the backdrop. Two sets of twenty-five chairs were arranged in a five-by-five formation, separated by a center aisle, where we, the honored guests, were to sit.

On either side of the podium was a large table; on it lay fifty white coats—pressed for success: twenty-five short and twenty-five long. The short ones denote the student, while the long ones befit the graduate. The atrium was jam-packed with family, friends, and other students. It was standing room only. Each of the PA faculty gave inspiring words of confidence as they stood at the mic. Then, one by one, we were called to approach. When they announced my name, Lloyd, a senior and my big brother in the program, held out my coat for me, sliding it up over my shoulders. I hugged and thanked him. Then I hugged and thanked Taylor, Bailey, Nadine, and Helen.

My coat fit perfectly. A bit short, but it represented having fulfilled the next step in this journey, and for that, I felt invigorated and ready, yet not quite satisfied. There remains another leg to travel.

May 28, 2000, Sunday.
[9 days since last entry]
It's been a while since I recorded an entry. I needed time away. Let me fill you in on everything.

Our finals were surprisingly laid-back. They were the easiest of the year. Our faculty made sure that we felt the heat, but these exams were like a congratulatory parting gift. Even as someone who has been obsessed with grades since I was just a budding flower five years ago, I couldn't tell you what any of my final exam grades were. Either you have just completed the second hardest year of your life (the worst is about to come), and they hand you your first five-week assignment, or they show you the door and ask you to pack your bags.

The moment finals were over, Karen and I went on a mission to pack up our apartment and race home to New Hampshire. While doing so, we were handed some rather shitty news. We had planned to sublet our apartment to Karen's coworker, but his application was rejected because he didn't earn enough money. He earns the same as Karen, while I earn nothing. How is that logical? The manager of our apartment complex suggested that he get a cosigner, then they'd review his application again. With his boss as a cosigner, he received approval. Unfortunately, the complex informed us they would only allow him to finish the remaining four months of our lease. Once the four months were up, they would terminate his sublet agreement. Who the fuck would want to move twice in four months? I don't blame the guy for withdrawing his application after that. When that happened, we knew we'd have to take a hit.

Since we had signed a one-year lease, and we were about to break it, the building manager would fine us twice our monthly rent, plus we would forfeit our security deposit. We knew they were determined to fine us, keep our security deposit and rent out our place as soon as we left, providing them a double profit for four months. Makes all the sense in the world. To ensure that didn't happen, and since the financial difference was nominal, we decided to just move out, but pay the rent for the remainder of our lease.

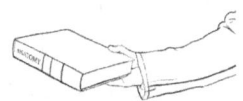

What a great vacation! We got to see everybody. Karen and I checked out different wedding venues and settled on The Governor's Inn in Rochester, New Hampshire. It meets all our criteria. We want an outdoor venue that can transition to indoors if the weather doesn't cooperate, but also has grounds that are perfect for photos. They'll take care of the decorating and food too. The expense exceeded Karen's parents' budget by a small margin, but they eagerly agreed to it with little convincing.

No vacation is ever complete without going to the batting cages to tear the cover off several hundred balls, rip open some calluses, and throw your back out. We even made it to Fenway Park, overpaid for scalped tickets, and were ecstatic to watch Pedro Martínez pitch from the best seats I have ever had.

While I was home, about 20 of us celebrated my thirtieth birthday by going to the greatest pizza place on the planet: Roger's Pizza in Dover. I've been going there since I was in diapers. My mother and stepfather surprised me with an awesome laptop. Karen and I were just discussing the potential difficulties of traveling over the next year with an outdated, bulky desktop and printer.

I have to tell you about a call that I received last night while we were at my brother-in-law's. It was Karen's mother, Barbara, which I found rather odd. "Hey, I got this envelope here from RTC and didn't know if it was something important."

I demanded she open it.

It was my grade report for spring quarter. Four As and two Bs. What a huge turnaround from my winter quarter! I attribute that to having found my balance; less time buried in books, and more time with Karen and friends.

Now, on to my rotation assignments. I'm happy with them at the moment, but they are subject to change. Our program includes eight required rotations: outpatient medicine, inpatient medicine, emergency medicine, obstetrics and gynecology, psychiatry, orthopedics, pediatrics, and general surgery, as well as two elective rotations. Since I am certain that I'll start my career in surgery after I graduate, I wanted to do one of my electives in an ICU (intensive care unit), and the other in neurosurgery. I was granted both.

To my surprise, I'm not doing general surgery first, as I think the world expected, but instead, I'm off to the ICU. I was able to connect with a senior, Brian, who just completed his last rotation precisely where I've been assigned to do my first; he put me at ease. Apparently, my preceptor is great, but I'm jumping from the frying pan into the fire. As a first rotation, taking care of the critically ill will be intimidating.

A couple of days ago, as instructed, I called the contact number that I had been provided for my ICU rotation, and almost immediately went into a panic. The number was not in service. I reached out to Nadine and Bailey and they instructed me to call Glenwood Hospital's main number, ask to be forwarded to the ICU, and see if that got me anywhere. I requested to speak with Dr. Orlando, who was the preceptor listed on the contact sheet, but was laughed at. "Um, yeah, you won't ever see him." Eventually, I was able to speak with a physician assistant on the team with whom I'll be spending my time. He instructed me where and when to meet on Tuesday.

"Tuesday?" a bit confused. "I'm supposed to start Monday."

"It's Memorial Day. Enjoy your three-day weekend and we'll see you Tuesday, but I won't be there until Thursday."

Great. I know how this will play out. I'll show up on Tuesday, find the ICU, stand around like an abandoned puppy, and no one is going to have any clue who I am or what they're supposed to do with me for the following two days. Despite the holiday, I'm making a call on Monday afternoon to plant a reminder.

At the moment, I have three rotations closer to home. I wanted half of them there, and it may still happen, but for now I know that I'll be doing neurosurgery and emergency medicine in New Hampshire, and pediatrics in Falmouth, Maine. Each location will be about half an hour or more away from Karen's parents—our home base.

Unfortunately, I won't be home at all during the summer months, as my first four rotations are in New York.

One of the hardest things that I have ever had to do in my life was move to Rocksville, New York. That meant leaving behind the band, my friends, my family, and the life I knew, and embarking on this dream of mine that, five years ago, seemed impossible. But a few minutes ago, I left Karen to begin the drive out of New Hampshire, and that just became the new hardest thing. It will be five months before I return home. I have not been separated from her for more than a week since we met. This may be our biggest test yet.

PART III

APPLYING MEDICINE

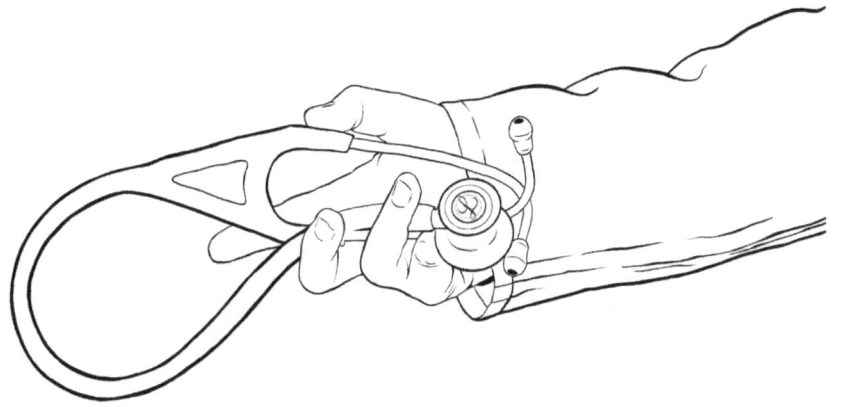

15

ROTATION #1—
INTENSIVE CARE
UNIT (ELECTIVE)

May 30, 2000, Tuesday.
[2 days since last entry]

It's 6:30 am and I'm heading to my first day in the ICU. The move into Barb's place was simple. Barb is a fellow PA student in my class who is living in the same off-campus apartment complex that Karen and I just moved out of a week ago. Barb's roommate is away for the summer and she had an available room, so it worked out perfectly.

I purposefully went to bed very late two nights ago, then awoke extremely early so I'd be tired by 7:00 pm last night. That way, I'd fall asleep easily and get a good night's sleep. That backfired, so I'm going to be a zombie all day.

As intended, I called the ICU yesterday afternoon and pleaded with them to remind any physician assistants that were scheduled to work today that I'd be arriving at 7:30 am. The woman on the call seemed uninterested, so I have no idea who I'm meeting or what they will expect from me when I show up.

It was inappropriate to be whipping out my recorder in the middle of the ICU, and I don't know how often I'll have the chance to record entries on site, but here's my day one summary:

My first shift was eleven hours. The first six, I felt out of place and wanted to leave. I was overwhelmed; I felt I didn't belong there. I was approached by several staffers who asked, "Is this your first day? And you're in an ICU for your first rotation?"

Here's something we weren't taught: how to gather a history from intubated patients. Or how to perform a physical exam on a patient in a drug-induced coma! None of this is what we've been practicing for the last year. I was about to call Nadine in utter frustration when I was instructed to go to the noon conference (a daily educational event where lunch is served and any hospital employee or student may attend). I ran into several recent RTC graduates that I knew, and they set me at ease. "You're in a tough spot, Shawn. Observe everything and be assertive. Introduce yourself to everyone. Tell them you'll help them with whatever they need. Follow anyone around who will let you. Ask a ton of questions."

It instantly reminded me of the three books I had read by Dr. Robert Marion. I'm the lowly intern who needs to prove myself by offering to do all the scut work—never-ending remedial tasks that must be completed but are usually delegated to those at the bottom of the hierarchy—for anyone who will give me the honor. This is how the system works, and I need to learn how to leverage it.

During the noon conference luncheon, Jade, an RTC graduate from two years prior, took me under her wing. She was heading to radiology rounds and said, "If you're not busy right now, come with me."

Of course I wasn't, so I followed. Dr. Hargraves, the instructor who taught our radiology unit earlier this year, was leading the rounds. Combine that with seeing Jade, a familiar face providing me with some direction on my first day, and I started to lighten up.

After radiology rounds, I ascended to the ICU and discovered only two doctors on duty for twelve admitted patients; one bed was vacant. That made me somewhat invisible, but it only lasted about fifteen minutes. Belinda, one of the ICU nurse practitioners, ran into me and introduced herself. "Oh, hey! Follow me. We need to take out this guy's femoral line and you're gonna help. Actually, you're doing it." (A femoral line is a large IV that has been inserted into the femoral vein to provide a rapid and reliable route for administration of medications.)

I felt my mood change over the course of a single heartbeat.

No sooner had I removed the femoral line when Belinda's pager went off.

"Go find the patient's chart while I answer this page. In the progress note section, write a procedure note and sign your name," she instructed.

I knew the components of a procedure note, but had never written one for when it was me who had removed something. Consent wasn't necessary, but an intubated patient wouldn't be able to sign one anyway. It went something like this:

May 30, 2000. 1335 hrs. / Shawn A. Roussin, PAS, Procedure Note

Removed dressing overlying right femoral line insertion site. No evidence of infection noted. Pulled line out in its entirety. Applied immediate direct manual pressure to the site for approximately ten minutes. No bleeding observed once pressure released. New sterile dressing applied. Patient appeared to tolerate it well. Distal pulse 2+.

Belinda cosigned.

"Let's go. That was the ER paging. We've got a stroke victim to assess."

I followed her with great enthusiasm. It was my first opportunity to find the ER in this place. She runs over to the attending physician (the doctor in charge), gets the scoop, and points to a glassed-in trauma bay. "His name is Ralph. Go find out what's going on and report back to me with your findings."

Ralph couldn't respond to any commands. He was shouting obscenities, not making any sense, and was very combative. The stroke team ignored me while getting him in restraints. Meanwhile, this idiot (me) is trying to conduct a neurologic exam. Not happening. Whatever portion of it I managed to fumble through was the stuff of amateurs. Humiliated, I wanted to go home again. Not looking forward to my first official beat-down, I left the room and found Belinda. It only took a few seconds to give my full report.

"See, that was an easy one, right?" she laughed. "When they're disoriented, not alert, or combative to a point that you can't conduct a meaningful physical exam, the subjective and objective portions of your note are done. You just document that the patient is confused and uncooperative."

Well heck, she's right.

"Let's go find his wife. After we gather some details from her, we need to order some testing, so think about it."

There I was, practicing medicine.

May 31, 2000, Wednesday.
[1 day since last entry]

My roommate and classmate, Barb, is also doing an ICU rotation, but at a different hospital here in the city. Compared to my first day, hers sounded superior. It's a personality thing. I was clearly displaying a pensive and fearful demeanor. Shyly sitting on my hands all day, lips sealed, and keeping to the perimeter of the action will not work. I need to stick my nose out, ask questions, and volunteer. Barb went for it and it appears to have paid off for her. That was the right move. Today is a new day. It'll be important for me to strike a balance between using charisma and assertiveness.

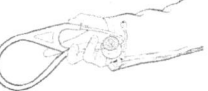

Boom! That's how I imagined my day to go when I walked through the doors of the hospital this morning. It took everything I had to hold back tears of excitement. My attitude and approach did a complete one-eighty, and one day later, everything changed. I'm flying high again.

I performed more procedures, including an ECG (electrocardiogram) and an ABG (arterial blood gas), I communicated with patients' families, and even called a spouse at home to provide them an update.

Yesterday, I had feelings of quitting. Today reaffirmed why I began this voyage.

Upon walking out of the ICU, the wife of our admitted stroke patient was entering. She remembered my name and thanked me for everything that I had done for Ralph.

"But I'm only a student."

And before I could get another word out, she kindly interrupted, "Yes, but you took the time and let me know everything that was happening in such a warm and compassionate way. That meant the world to me."

June 4, 2000, Sunday.
[4 days since last entry]
Only one week has passed since I left Karen in New Hampshire, and it serves as a harsh reminder of how difficult it is without her presence. Colleen, our PA classmate, joined me, Barb, and her date for a fun night of drinks, darts, and dancing at a bar. It was a much-needed escape. A couple of girls were trying to grind on me while we were

all tearing it up on the dance floor. It was reaffirming to know that I still got it, but my heart rejected it. I miss Karen so much already, but I won't have to miss her much longer because I just found out that there was a change to my schedule and I'm going home for my second rotation!

This weekend I studied renal issues and electrolyte imbalances. I swear, every ICU patient has kidney issues.

It's gorgeous out, so Dan, Chris, and I are going to go play nine holes of golf this afternoon. After I return to the apartment, I intend to prepare a healthy dinner, spend an hour or two reading, and retire early to ensure I am well-rested for the beginning of my second week.

June 5, 2000, Monday.

[1 day since last entry]

Every time I look up from what I am doing, I get asked, "Are you following this patient?" "Hey, you following bed nine?" "Excuse me, you're following that lady in six, right?" "You got those morning lab results on that diabetic guy?"

Just because I hang out in the ICU, pop in and out of rooms to examine patients because I've heard that they have some sort of obscure physical exam finding, doesn't mean that I'm "following the patient," or does it? This ICU has thirteen beds: ten have patients in them right now, but only two that I would say I am "following."

When I saw my preceptors, Belinda and Shane (an ICU physician assistant), I asked them, "Am I doing what I'm supposed to be doing? I feel like I haven't progressed as much as I should have."

Shane chimed in. "Shawn, only one week has gone by. You're putting way too much pressure on yourself. Stop worrying. You're doing your procedures wonderfully."

Belinda was quick to add, "You're helping every chance you get. The ICU is the hardest rotation, and you were the student that RTC trusted to put here on the first day of your internship. Don't worry too much about learning the medicine. Seize the opportunity to do as much as you can with your time. This is where you can learn ABGs, insert central lines, place nasogastric tubes, and maybe even insert chest tubes. The actual medicine will come over the next year, but here in the ICU, get your hands dirty. Do stuff. Other than the ER, this is the only place that such opportunities will present themselves. In the operating room, you'll have to hold retractors for three hours while the residents and attendings try to embarrass you with impossible board questions. Does that make sense?"

I inquired about trying a fresh approach this week, wondering if it would be okay to shadow them throughout a patient's entire ICU stay. I wanted to watch Belinda and Shane at rounds in the morning and afternoon, observe their exams, read their notes, listen when they communicate with families, and understand the rationale behind the daily tests they order. They were completely on board with that, but advised I still try to see as many patients as I can, especially the ones that ICUs are most likely to see, such as patients with COPD, pneumonia, congestive heart failure, post-surgical sepsis, and drug overdoses.

I felt better as the day progressed. The voices from our PA faculty kept repeating in my head, "Whatever you see during the day, read about at night."

Before leaving the hospital today, I had a strong desire to visit a patient whom we had admitted early last week and who had been transferred out of the ICU on Friday. This gentleman won an NBA championship in the 1950s. He'll probably be the tallest patient I will ever see in my career. Unfortunately, he has liver metastasis, likely from his prostate, but had also presented with renal failure and hyperkalemia (high potassium); his was 8.7, which is critically high.

When I arrived at his room, he wasn't there, and there was a sudden settling of dread in my chest. I was relieved to learn from a nurse that he was downstairs getting dialysis. There was a moment when I thought I had lost my first patient. I scooted down to dialysis and found him. He immediately recognized me and smiled. He told me a few of his favorite basketball stories, but I could see his energy was fading, as was his life. His liver was twice the size of a normal one, and his kidneys were essentially dead. Despite his age and grim prognosis, he told me he wanted everything done to keep him alive.

Chemo is off the table, and his cancer is inoperable. I don't know squat, but I don't think he'll be going home from here. He will probably die here. I vowed to visit him each day, but his remaining days are limited. He seems to understand his condition. "I've lived a good life, a great life," he confessed.

I held the hand of an NBA champion and I will never forget him.

June 7, 2000, Wednesday.
[2 days since last entry]
Best day yet. I must have done four or five unsupervised ABGs, but also did my first central line into a subclavian vein (large vein beneath the collar bone). That was a sweaty one, and a supervised one, and one that I needed a lot of help with, but I did a central line!

I wrote SOAP notes on two patients that I've been following this week. While it thrilled Shane, I could sense his impatience as I took a long time to finish them. There is a vast amount of information to analyze and contemplate, but as I become more familiar with the system, I'll improve my efficiency.

I can recognize when someone requires a chest X-ray. I'm aware of the proper method for delivering an ABG to the lab. Whenever I need supplies, I can find them. They're letting the leash out on me a bit and I'm taking that gift of autonomy and running with it.

I didn't stop moving today. Ten hours of exhilaration!

June 9, 2000, Friday.
[2 days since last entry]
I scored two last-minute tickets to an outdoor concert in downtown Rocksville last night. Barb ended up coming with me. Melissa Etheridge, the headliner, opened the show unexpectedly and performed a short set.

I wanted the tickets because my band Pondering Judd had frequently performed in New England with Guster, who were part of the lineup. Edwin McCain was also playing, and I wanted to see him too.

At 9:45 pm, Guster took the stage, and when they did, I called Karen on my cell so she could listen. It brought me such happiness to hear her voice, although the show was so loud that it was impossible to comprehend much of what she was saying. She seemed annoyed by the call. When I got home, I wondered if she was thinking, *Seriously, Shawn? A Thursday night, and you're at a concert having a great time? I thought you went out there to learn medicine...*

Dammit. Now I feel guilty.

The pimping has begun. In the medical profession, "pimping" is when students are asked preposterous questions, given one second to respond, and then mocked after attempting to provide a reasonable answer. This week I became the target, and I think I know why.

A few days ago, I examined a patient after rounds and detected a lower abdominal mass. By my estimate, the mass was about 8 cm x 12 cm. I wrote this in my SOAP note, but also recorded that the patient had not moved his bowels in seven days. About a half hour later, Shane was reviewing my notes and said, "You felt an abdominal mass?"

"Yes, the size of my fist, right below the umbilicus. It was a bit tender to palpation."

He jumped up, kicked back his rolling chair, which nearly took out the printer stand behind him, and he ran into the patient's room. "Show me."

I repeated my exam, but it was gone. *How? What the hell?* "Sir, did you move your bowels after I saw you?"

"No," he said. But he was now sitting up in a bedside chair. He had been lying almost flat in bed when I examined him earlier.

Shane began feeling around the patient's abdomen. "Nothing."

"Shane. I'm telling you right now that I felt a mass. I would not have written that in the chart if I hadn't. I figured it was stool. It didn't pulsate like an aneurysm so I assumed it was feces since he hadn't produced a bowel movement in a week. Should I have told you as soon as I found it?"

"No, no, no. It's fine. I was caught off-guard when reading your note. Since I have to sign off on it, I have to go see for myself."

The rest of the week was strange. Shane's demeanor had changed. I felt a lack of trust. He and the team were dropping facetious jokes about it, so it seemed less of a big deal, but that's when the pimping began.

The beatdown commenced during rounds with the ICU attending physician, Dr. Cho, medical staff, and other students. Dr. Cho is an obese Japanese fellow who always wore a clip-on bow tie, had pants six inches too short, as if he was preparing to wade through a puddle, and never matched his socks. He grabbed a chart while we were all gathered in a room, then he turned to me (not calling me by name, of course), and motioned with his open hand to alert the team that this next question is for me and me only. "This patient is anemic. His hematocrit is twenty-four. I wonder what this could be… What is the primary test for determining hemolysis?"

"Ummm, a low hematocrit…" My voice trailed off as the wheels in my head were churning. I swear to you, less than one second had passed when he let out a sarcastic chuckle and rolled his eyes. The answer was to analyze a blood sample with a microscope. I'm standing in an ICU, so I'm trying to think practically. Initially, I wondered if the answer was to use a microscope to examine the red blood cells, but I was assuming Dr. Cho was seeking a specific lab test or bedside assessment that could provide a quicker result. Unfortunately, my lack of confidence made me the laughingstock of the department. And this comedy show repeated itself multiple times each day, all week.

At the educational luncheon today, I was able to speak with two medical students I've seen in the ICU. They both laughed and said the same thing, "Isn't it great? Don't worry, next week they'll move onto someone else. It happens to all of us. It's part of the process. It's a test to see how tough you are... Can you handle it? How badly do you want this?"

June 13, 2000, Tuesday.

[4 days since last entry]

I haven't had my psych rotation yet, but this has got to be what being bipolar feels like. I'm up. I'm down. Some days I feel like I'm just killing it and learning a lot. The next day, I'm the village idiot on Team ICU. And really, am I doing enough procedures? I've got the ABGs down. No one needs to look over my shoulder anymore. I still haven't started an IV yet. How is that even possible? I've done more central lines than IVs. I still want someone nearby while doing those lines, but that's only in case I puncture a lung or hit the carotid. I'd especially want Dr. Asad in the room. In Pakistan, he worked as a surgeon, but here in the US, he's a critical care fellow transitioning into nephrology (a branch of medicine that deals with diseases of the kidney). You can always find him in the ICU with us. Everyone here knows him as the Line King.

While Dr. Asad has been an outstanding mentor, he has no patience whatsoever. That's because it only takes him seconds to get a line in, never failing on his first attempt. It's unbelievable. Today, he was supervising me while I was doing a subclavian line. I had the patient prepped as swiftly as he would. I grabbed the needle, found my landmarks, and went for it. I hadn't quite introduced the tip deep enough when I felt the resistance of the clavicle, so I decided to withdraw a few millimeters and readjust my angle. As I did, the Line King let out a quick, frustrating groan and said, "Step aside. We don't have time for this."

Was he serious? What was I supposed to do, hip-check him into the patient's recliner? I just needed another second, but I guess he couldn't spare one. I was pissed.

It's only my third week in the ICU, but I am feeling as if I should be further ahead than I am. It's self-inflicted and overwhelming.

Sometimes I wonder if I should've become a nurse because I truly enjoy the more frequent personal interactions with patients. I have an impeccable capacity to learn and perform procedures, but maybe I'm not cut out for the actual "medicine" part of medicine. That's where I struggle the most. That may be my downfall. Or maybe I should shut up and be patient.

June 19, 2000, Monday.
[6 days since last entry]
Late last week, Bailey called me at the hospital to discuss my site visit project. Each PA student is required to do a presentation during our internship. These lectures take place on Recall Day, typically by two or three students, but first needs to be discussed with a member of the PA program, which usually occurs mid-rotation. I told her I had decided to do my paper and presentation on "hepato-renal syndrome secondary to cirrhosis." After ending the call, I had the impression that she was worried about my topic, although found my direction intriguing. I wondered if she doubted my ability to present such a complex topic effectively. So, on Friday, after getting my ass handed to me again at morning rounds, I cornered Dr. Asad and asked him if he would take some time to talk to me about HRS (hepato-renal syndrome).

He guided me back to one of the conference rooms and spent over an hour with me. He presented it like a thesis. It was magnificent. He covered the pathophysiology, management, and treatment of HRS, cirrhosis, and ascites so I could understand. Frequently, as he articulated his mastery of the subject, I gushed out laughing because it made so much sense to me. It felt good to grasp such a complex topic. "I can see that you are comprehending this," he said, "and I will tell you right now that you know more about HRS than any of the residents in this hospital."

As soon as I got home Friday night, I threw out the entire paper I had written and started over from scratch. I worked on it for five hours that night and the majority of Saturday. On Sunday morning, I reviewed it, made some adjustments, and felt excited about the progress I had made, prompting me to spend several additional hours crafting the oral presentation. It was going so exceptionally well that I kept my afternoon golf date with Dan, his father, and Chris. After getting home last night, I tackled the oral portion again until satisfied.

This morning, at 7:00 am, Bailey met me on site so I could give my presentation. It blew her away. "Wow Shawn. You just taught me a thing or two. You demonstrated a strong understanding of this rare syndrome through a very confident presentation. You were able to explain things in such a way that any medical professional would be able to understand."

Bailey and I had a wonderful conversation afterwards. She posed many questions, attempting to poke holes in my work, but I mounted a strong defense. I didn't want to miss anything and I welcomed the constructive feedback. It will only make me a better clinician. Regardless of what happens next, that moment made this rotation all worth it.

Pathophysiology is so important. That we only get one dedicated course in it during a single quarter of our didactic year is mind-blowing to me. I didn't have this perspective during the course, but I do now. In retrospect, this should have been a year-long area of study. If you can understand disease processes, everything else is more comprehensible.

As Bailey and I ended our meeting, I told her I wanted Shane, Belinda, and the other preceptors to pimp me more. I can handle it. Sometimes I feel like certain preceptors are not comfortable putting students on the spot, but that I welcomed it and wanted more. She was only concerned about my reading log. We are required to track the title of the book, journal, website, or article that we read, the topics they included, and the number of pages read. That list is submitted to the PA program clinical coordinators at the end of each week. I have been averaging only twelve pages per day, and she said that twelve isn't horrible, but it's not enough.

I'm reading as much as I can manage. I have a perpetual weakness in reading comprehension. I read slowly—and it almost always puts me to sleep.

After leaving the hospital, I refuse to consume caffeine and I won't compromise the successful life balance that I discovered last quarter. The apartment I'm staying in doesn't have a desk or study area. I'm on the couch in the living room or in my bed. These are ideal places to quickly succumb to shut-eye when there's a book in front of me.

But I know that Bailey is right. I need to read much more. She reminded me of the day when seniors emphasized the importance of fully immersing oneself in patient experiences at the clinical site and then reflecting on them at home every night. It's an invaluable connection that we must make in order to succeed. Not making this investment every twenty-four hours would set one up for failure. The perfect opportunity to study for boards happens with nightly reading.

Helen has beaten this into our heads, too: "Read, read, read. It's a dirty, four-letter word, but it has to be done every day."

How I made it this far is something that I will never understand. I must find a way. If I can add two to four hours more on weekends, I think I can bump up my daily average to twenty pages. They won't ever view that as enough, but they'll acknowledge it as an improvement.

Anyway, Bailey must have said something to my preceptors right away because twenty minutes later at the 9:00 am rounds, we entered the second patient's room and Dr. Cho, who was reviewing the morning lab results in the chart, says, "Look at these eosinophils, they're up to seven percent. I think that is high." (Eosinophils are a type of white blood cell)

Shane, who rarely pressures me, wasted no time directing a question my way. "Shawn. Why would someone have eosinophilia?" Well, I asked for it.

"Allergies, like hay fever, or perhaps a drug reaction."

"Right! If seen on a complete blood count with differential, suspect drug allergy," Dr. Cho concurred.

Feeling redeemed, perhaps I earned some respect today.

June 20, 2000, Tuesday.

[1 day since last entry]

It's 9:00 pm and I'm just leaving the hospital. It's not because there was so much to do or that it was exciting beyond belief, but rather, there was nothing to do. Last night, I devised a plan to take care of a couple of needs. I decided that to complete more procedures and increase my reading, I would bring all my reading materials with me to the hospital. While studying in the ICU, I'd be readily available to anyone and everyone who may need my assistance. By dedicating an additional four hours from 5:00 pm to 9:00 pm, I could crush these goals.

That said, the first evening was a total failure. I completed all my reading, but otherwise I just sat on my ass and listened to the chorus of telemetry machines and bed alarms going off. Was tonight an outlier? Should I continue lurking until 9:00 pm each night just to do another ABG? I envy Barb, who is performing triple the number of procedures. It's so frustrating. At least the uncomfortable chairs in the ICU prevented me from nodding off while reading, so that was a win.

June 21, 2000, Wednesday.

[1 day since last entry]

Busy. That describes today, and that is just the way I like it. I did my first central line independently, and it went masterfully. It was the first of many procedures that kept coming my way.

Most of my day was with Belinda. Between patient care responsibilities, we were able to chat multiple times, dissecting several different topics. I love the one-on-one preceptor-student interactions, as opposed to being pimped in front of peers.

But that wasn't the highlight. Yesterday, I wrote the admission note for a lady who had a heart attack. Throughout the day, multiple medical professionals tried to convince her to have an angiogram in the catheterization lab, but they all failed. And that's where I came in.

I saw her this morning, wrote my SOAP note, and looked at her ECG again. She clearly had anterior wall ischemia with inverted

T-waves throughout her precordial leads (this is ECG speak for "bad"). When compared to her previous ones, there was definitely a concerning change. I was perplexed by her refusal to rectify it with a stent in the cath lab. Since I was the one who had seen her in the ER, spent the most time with her, and written her admission note, she likely had a bit of trust in me, so I sat down with her to try my luck. We talked about her family, her children and grandchildren, upcoming life events, and holiday gatherings. Widowed a year prior, she had lost some will, and her sense of value was vanishing.

After almost an hour at her bedside and missing part of morning rounds, I was finally able to get her to agree, but she was outwardly scared, tearful, and requiring reassurance. I told her I had no idea if they could do the procedure today, but I would come by every hour to see how she was doing. And if I could get the interventional cardiologists to allow it, I would be in the room with her during the entire thing. "That's the only way I will agree to this," she said.

Under the cover of fluorescent lights, I couldn't sneak back into rounds undetected. "Oh, look, he *didn't* quit. I can't wait to hear the excuse as to why our student started his day with us at this hour," mused our facetious attending. I was sure I'd be in trouble for this.

When rounds were mercifully over, Gavin, the PA I had been with this week, escorted me to a secluded area. "This better be good, although it's still going to be unacceptable."

I pleaded, "Listen, Gavin, the lady who has refused the cath lab? I spent an hour with her and she finally agreed, but there's a catch—"

Cutting me off, he said, "Wait. What? We were going to just discharge her later today, against medical advice. How the hell did you do that?"

"I don't know. I just acted like her grandson, I guess. I held her hand, we talked about her family, what her late husband would've wanted, and she agreed."

"Okay…" Gavin suspiciously waited for the punchline. "You said that there was a catch."

"I have to be in the cath lab with her."

Gavin looked over my shoulder, deep in thought. He put his hand behind my neck, turned my body, and forced me forward. He was charging towards the shelf of charts, me as his shield. After finding hers, he removed it, and thrust it into my chest, "You're up. Call the operator. Ask them to connect you to the cardiologist on call. Tell them exactly what you told me. Get them up here and get her to the cath lab. When it happens, don't miss it. When you're done, find me. I have an assignment."

The cardiologist agreed to visit her, and told me I was welcome to be at the patient's side throughout the procedure.

Moments later, I found Gavin. He had an ambiguous grin as he hung up a phone. "Here's the deal," he said. "I've got this great patient. Read his entire chart, go see him, do your exam, and write your SOAP note, but I want you to concentrate your assessment and plan on his cardiopulmonary and infectious disease status. When done, report back to me on how you plan on caring for him today, and we'll sit down to review it."

He gave me a summary before sliding the chart across the counter. The synopsis made me realize I was in over my head. I'm not ready for this. This case is too complicated. That's when I stepped in it. "Gavin, I think this is too complex for me. And you're probably unaware, but earlier in the week, Shane and I agreed that I would begin arriving at the hospital later in the morning so I could stay later in the evening to handle necessary procedures and dedicate more time to reading. But today I did start very early and had planned on leaving at five."

His eyebrows shot to the ceiling, stunned. "Um, alright. I wasn't aware of this. I didn't know that you were just here to do procedures and read by yourself." Perplexed, palms in the air, he walked away. Although I stayed until 9:00 pm, thus making it a fourteen-hour day, Gavin didn't say another word to me, or even look in my direction.

Honestly, I couldn't blame him. I had let my fear and apprehension get in the way of an educational opportunity. When the clock struck 9:00, I closed my book, having not put a single word to memory, and shuffled to the exit.

June 22, 2000, Thursday.

[1 day since last entry]

I'm on edge. I just fucked up my rotation and I've got to fix it, but I'm running out of time. I went about my normal morning routine, arriving before 7:00 am, attending rounds, and accepting my lashings.

When Gavin came in at 1:00 pm, he didn't acknowledge me. Iris, one of the ICU fellows, approached me to tell me about the newest patient that had been admitted overnight with pancreatitis and was going through DTs (delirium tremens = body tremors) from sudden alcohol withdrawal. Although we rounded on him this morning with the team, I was too preoccupied with my situation with Gavin to remember much. "Well, pick him up today and start following him. This is a classic ICU patient that you'll see many times in your career," Iris said.

"Yes, of course," I agreed. Knowing this, when Gavin came in after the luncheon, I found him standing on the other side of the ICU and I decided to put on my big boy pants and confront this head-on. "Hey, Gavin? This new patient; can I follow him with you?"

Without looking up from the note that he was writing, "It's DTs, pancreatitis. That's it. Easy enough for you?"

Yup. There's my answer. I'm hosed. I earned this. Dammit! I'm such a tool. I just walked away. He's pissed. In his head he is thinking I don't have what it takes. I'm here fourteen to fifteen hours per day, and I will now forever be known by this one passive mistake.

For the rest of the day, I was sad, lost, and hopeless, but then Belinda ran over to me and said, "Don't forget about your date with the cath lab tomorrow. Hey, are you okay?"

I ran through what had happened with Gavin yesterday. "Don't worry about Gavin. He's fine. He gets easily frustrated, and when that happens, he withdraws. There's no reason to get worked up about it. Shane and I think you've done great here. This place is not an easy lake to get your feet wet. You put too much pressure on yourself. Don't take it to heart. Everything is going as planned. Keep doing what you're doing."

June 30, 2000, Friday.

[8 days since last entry]

I'm heading back to New Hampshire after having just completed our first Recall Day back on campus. Here's my summation and commentary about the past week. I needed a few days for reflection. It is true what our faculty have said, "The moment that you start to feel complacent, it's time to move on to the next rotation."

Five weeks at one location and then you pack up your things, move out, return to campus, take an exam, give a presentation, fill your fuel tank, and go set up camp at your next destination. During the initial week, you experience a sense of displacement. I know I was hesitant to ask foolish questions, yet felt bombarded with unanswerable ones, just hoping to appear somewhat intelligent.

First week goal: avoid looking incompetent and soiling your khakis. The easy part should be finding the elevators, cafeteria, stairwells, your preceptor, and the bathroom. But it's a hospital, so none of those things are easy. Hopefully, by the third week, everyone has accepted you into their tribe, and conversely, you've figured them out and accepted them (not that you had a choice). If that occurs, you can start learning some medicine.

By week four, you're comfortable, but barely. Your H&Ps sound more like conversations, your hands tremble less when starting an IV, your deodorant lasts past 10:00 am, you've smartly traded in those khakis for black slacks, and the attendings—if you've proven yourself—may accidentally call you by your name.

But then you enter week five, a shortened week, and the goodbyes and thank-yous enter every conversation. You exit stage left, only to let out an enormous sigh of relief, knowing this same cycle will now repeat many more times until the tenth rotation has been completed.

Recall Day was great, but weird, at least for me. We did some housekeeping, then each of us had ten minutes to share our thoughts and stories about the first rotation. I expressed my story about missing rounds to convince the lady who had the heart attack to go to the cath lab. I wanted to communicate to my classmates the value of human connection, patient relationships, and its potential to make a difference. This woman had been a volunteer at that hospital for more than twenty years, so I told her, "Look, I know you are scared. You have selflessly given everything to this hospital. Now it's our turn to give back to you. Please have this done for you, for me, and for your family."

I followed through on my part of the bargain by holding her hand and maintaining conversation throughout the entire procedure. As I recounted the story, a lump swelled in my throat, realizing the immense impact I made on this person and her family. As tears began streaming down my face, the class grew silent. I needed several deep breaths to compose myself.

"For six years, this is what I had waited for, and it was at that precise moment that I realized I was going to make it. I was going to be a physician assistant. It's the best decision I had ever made."

When we had each taken receipt of our ten minutes of fame, we took a break for lunch and many classmates sought me out to give me hugs and thank me for having the courage to tell that story.

After lunch I gave my presentation, Hepato-renal Syndrome Secondary to Cirrhosis. I was the first classmate on our first Recall Day to present.

There are only two or three presentations per Recall Day, so everyone does one during the year. I estimated mine would be about forty-five minutes, but it ended up an hour and a half. It went well, despite the faculty's repeated challenges, but I didn't mind.

That presentation, and of course all the preparation, provided me with some confidence that I may even want to teach one day, or at least be a preceptor myself.

I had called Karen when I left Rocksville. I'm forty miles from home now, and I can't wait to roll up that driveway, jump out of the car, and leap into her arms. Although the absence hurts, this distance will be a beneficial experience for us. It's time to crank the windows down, and the tunes up. I'm coming home, baby. I'm coming home.

One down, nine to go—but the next one is in New Hampshire, at the hospital where I was born.

16

ROTATION #2—
EMERGENCY MEDICINE

July 3, 2000, Monday.

[3 days since last entry]

I'm just now pulling out of the parking lot after day one of my second rotation, and what a difference. No nervousness. Everything was much easier. I am going to get along great with my preceptor, Jack. Our personalities and sense of humor mix like a good PB&J, but not that mint flavored jelly that tastes like toothpaste.

The emergency room brings variety, and I like that. The possibility exists to observe, learn and perform many different types of procedures, just like in the ICU. It is fast-paced for a community hospital, although Jack tells me it is not uncommon on a weekday to have three-hour breaks between seeing patients. I think I'd prefer a more challenging and intimidating tempo, so long as there is still ample quality time for learning.

They will have me doing four ten-hour shifts each week, from 9:00 am to 7:00 pm, but my preceptor won't always be Jack. They have a fast-track, or what they call an "express care" side of the ER, and I will divide my time between there and the main emergency department.

At the end of this mandatory rotation, I must prepare for an exam on Recall Day, so my efforts to read more need to be better than last rotation. As expected, that was a theme on our last Recall Day. *"No one is reading enough."*

July 8, 2000, Saturday.

[5 days since last entry]

This week I did two ten-hour days, an eight-hour night shift, and a ten-hour night shift. I was with Jack in the express care for most of it. On the second day, we saw a ten-year-old boy who had just fallen off his bike and was having hand pain. Jack purposefully didn't let me examine the kid. Instead, he called me over to look at the X-rays. "Alright, what do you see?"

Looking at the two X-rays hanging on the light box, "Yup. Fractured the base of his fifth metacarpal," I proclaimed.

Jack looked surprised and shifted his eyes to the X-ray in front of me. "Mm-hm, yes. You got it. Well, I can see that I won't have to worry about your ability to read X-rays. Most students, especially six weeks into their training, would have alerted me to this kid's normal growth plate (often mistaken for a fracture line) and totally missed the subtle fracture."

We read every film together during our shift. The day passed without any mistakes. I guess my X-ray interpretation is better than expected at this point.

During the two night shifts, I was with the docs in the main ER and it was there that I met my twin, Dr. Ed. I'm taller, and he's much more athletic in appearance, but otherwise we're both thirty-year-old bald dudes with dark-rimmed glasses and brown goatees. Whenever we entered a room together, people thought they were seeing double and although double vision could be a sign of head trauma, we assured them that they hadn't recently suffered a brain injury. I played his shadow for the first few patients, but an hour into the shift, he grabbed a chart, flipped through the pages, and handed it to me. "Here. Go see this one. Don't take all night; then come find me and tell me what you wanna do."

This patient was a thirty-eight-year-old guy with chest pain. After gathering a history and performing an exam, I found Dr. Ed in the provider's office with his feet on the desk, eating an ice cream, and presented my findings.

"Okay, student, but what do you want to do? You have to figure out why he's here, make him better, and send him home. Or you must come to the realization that he is too sick to be sitting here in your emergency department and send him off to a place where someone else can fix him, preferably before he dies. Be proactive in plotting your patient's exit strategy to prevent ER overload. Is that clear?"

Frankly it wasn't, but I suspected that at some point it would be. "I want to initiate a line, perform an ECG, and order a troponin, but I don't suspect his chest pain is cardiac. Oh, and maybe a chest X-ray."

"If you think it, get it," he instructed.

Dr. Ed was a superior pimper when compared to my first couple of days with Jack, but Jack is a PA and probably just taking it easy on me. I hope Dr. Ed puts more pressure on me as we go. When he would hammer me with questions, if my answers weren't adequate, he'd immediately send me away to go read about it. When I was done, he'd welcome me back to ride shotgun.

By 3:00 am on my first overnight, and after sitting around doing nothing for two hours, Dr. Ed turned to me in the office and announced, "Hey, I'm going to go to the call room to take a nap. Why don't you go home? We might go another two hours without a patient."

I was unsure how to react to this. Was this a test? Was I supposed to decline his offer to abandon a completely empty ER? What's the right response here? I didn't want to repeat my misstep with Gavin from the ICU.

"Um, okay. Well, thank you. No really, thank you for having me tonight, and especially for pimping me. It gets me thinking and endorses what I know and what I don't. I appreciate that."

"Great. I'll do more. Now go! Get the hell out of here. I'm going to bed," he said, bounding down the hall past multiple empty gurneys, ECG machines, and a cluster of IV poles. He vanished, and so did I.

Not that I want to make it a habit of comparing my preceptors to myself or famous people, but during the second overnight in the ER, I was with the medical director, Dr. Otis, who looks like Patrick Stewart playing Jean-Luc Picard on *Star Trek: The Next Generation*. Dr. Otis has an unmistakable French-Canadian accent. Rather than allowing me to see any patients without him, he instructed me to just follow him everywhere and pay close attention. We'd swoop into an exam room, collect information, escape back to his office, and sit. Then he'd ramble off what he thought, why he thought it, what he expected, and then asked me if I had any questions. If I had none, he'd stand up and dart to the next patient's room. This routine lasted all of an hour, then the pimping started.

His questions were from left field and I had no chance. When I answered incompetently, I lost confidence. Then when he asked a straightforward question, to which I should've known the answer, my brain seemed to automatically assume it was a trick question. It was bizarre and relentless.

"What antibiotic do you want to use? Why? What if they're allergic? Any jugular vein distention? No? Good, because there wasn't any. Did you hear that murmur? No? Well, I heard an S-three. What does that mean? You're taking too long. Why don't you go read about heart sounds and murmurs? Once you are sure you have the correct answer, report back to me. You have to envision the cardiac cycle in your head. Imagine what is going on physiologically. When you can give me the answer that I am looking for, you can join me in seeing patients again."

Overwhelmed, I marched off to his office and began digging. I had been in there for almost an hour when he entered and took a seat. "So, what did you find out?" he asked.

"I'm sorry, but I am having a difficult time visualizing the cardiac cycle and how it relates to an ECG tracing, but I promise that before the next time I work with you, I will. I need to illustrate it because I'm a visual learner. Words in a book or on a screen don't cut it for me."

Dr. Otis was sympathetic. "It's okay. There are plenty of resources out there."

I'll be working with him again in two days, so I need to be prepared. He'll remember. I know he will. If I'm not able to rattle off an award-winning speech on the cardiac cycle, this rotation is going to tank before it even starts.

Later on in the shift, a drug-seeker showed up. She saw Dr. Otis the night before and received twenty hydrocodone tablets for a dental abscess. She hoped a different provider would be at the ER because she wanted more narcotics. Dr. Otis slid open the curtain and you could tell he was not too impressed. He looked in her mouth, pushed on her pretend abscess, knowing it would illicit the dramatic yelp for help and crocodile tears. "Sit tight. We'll be back soon."

The entire encounter was under fifteen seconds.

"What do you know about dental fractures?"

I said, "Well, we didn't have a dental unit during our training, so I couldn't tell you anything."

"Go look up the Ellis classification for tooth fractures and report back to me," he said as we returned to his office. "That book right there in front of you," he pointed.

On a shelf that was bowing from the weight, sat the condensed version (800 pages!) of an emergency medicine study-guide. "I memorized that book word-for-word before I took my boards. I can tell you everything about the Ellis classification. Actually, I can tell you anything you'd need to know about emergency medicine."

Without taking a breath, he launches into a lengthy monologue about dental fractures. Holy crap! He's an emergency medicine physician, and he knows everything there is to know about dental fractures. I may have an advantage over the competition now. Who else will have heard what I just heard? And he did this to me the entire night, despite how busy it became.

In the blink of an eye, this night received a shot of steroids. Outside of the automatic glass doors leading to the ambulance bay, a frantic pounding overtook any chaos that was occurring within the department. A woman was seen on the security monitor, kicking at the doors. She was holding the body of a violently convulsing child. The charge nurse surged across the floor towards the bay while a staffer closest to the button that would open the doors, slammed it like a contestant on *Family Feud*.

I had been off in the corner writing a note and immediately became panic-stricken. "Where's Dr. Otis?" At this moment, I was the closest thing to a clinician within earshot. As the woman was handing off the child to a nurse, I ran towards her, screaming, "Find Otis!" Before I could take my next breath, he calmly appeared out of thin air, passed me with purpose, and ducked into the trauma bay. "Shawn! Get in here!" he demanded.

I followed his orders, and the woman followed me. At the top of her lungs, distraught, she cried, "This is my son, Mikey. Oh, my God! Help him! He's thirteen months. I just went to check on him before going to bed and he was shaking all over. I grabbed him and got here as soon as I could."

With eight staffers in the room, Dr. Otis instructed, "Shawn, hold his head still so I can examine him." I went to the head of the bed, leaned over this little boy's face, and secured him. Others grabbed his limbs. Two IVs were plunged into him. Stripped of his jammies, diaper removed, a full assessment of any obvious injuries concluded. There were none. Realizing the IVs were in place, Dr. Otis ordered diazepam (an antiseizure medication).

Observing Dr. Otis was like watching a master conductor and his symphony. I quickly drew my attention back down to the boy's face as vomit exploded from his small mouth. "On his side! Now! I need suction!"

No one seemed fazed when I barked out these orders. A suction was thrust into my hand and a non-rebreather mask was slung over my shoulder. I cleared the boy's airway and placed the mask over his nose and mouth. "It's at ten liters," a team member announced.

Dr. Otis left his maestro's podium, demeanor still unwavering, and came to my side. He put his hand between my shoulder blades and leaned over. "Shawn, you're in charge of this airway until I say otherwise. Got it? Do not, and I repeat, do not let him aspirate."

For the next two and a half hours, the seizing and vomiting continued. As Mikey's upper airway filled each time, I'd slide the mask to the side, clear his mouth and nostrils, then return the mask to his face. Repeated doses of diazepam didn't work for long, so we switched to phenytoin and the seizures finally ended.

It was past 2:00 am, and I had been hunched over the head of this gurney, my elbows straddling this boy's head, for hours. I don't recall muttering a single word after demanding the suction. Without moving, I watched in awe and made sure his airway was clear. I was exhausted and my back would not allow me to stand up straight.

Stabilized, breathing on his own, and resting, his mother clung to his side. Finally, I left Mikey's room and began a lonely stroll down the hall towards the breakroom, clutching my lower back. Coming towards me was Dr. Otis. He cut me off and thanked me. "Great job. You helped save that boy's life. Welcome to the Emergency Department."

I could see myself working as an emergency medicine PA. I went home at 5:00 am and I can't wait to come back.

July 12, 2000, Wednesday.

[4 days since last entry]

I opened my financial aid package on Monday night and could have cried. The bad news outweighs the good. The bad news is that I've borrowed as much as is allowable from the federal government prior to completing a bachelor's degree. They gave me about $6,000 less than what I had received in past years. The good news is that RTC provided me with $10,000 in scholarships, but I'm still going to be about $9,000 short of what I'll need to cover my projected expenses over the next ten months.

The main issue is my inability to earn money this summer because of rotations. I'm being charged full tuition for the summer quarter, which seems unfair since I will only be on campus for two days.

Yesterday, I called the financial aid office and kind of went off on them. I just don't understand where they get their formulas. They're giving me $250 more in aid this year than last, but charging me for an extra quarter of tuition. They accounted for only $7 per month for rent, food, and living expenses. Where did these fucking geniuses earn their economics degrees from?

Fortunately, I have a master's degree in foreshadowing and saw this as a potential stick in my spokes three years ago. A few weeks prior to moving to New York, on separate nights, I sat down with both sets of parents and created a backup plan. I asked if they would each attempt to save $5,000 in case I needed it for expenses during my final twelve months. Ironically, I called them two months ago, after Karen and I had decided to move out of our Rocksville apartment and for her to go back home to New Hampshire. When we made that decision, we thought we wouldn't require that money from my parents anymore, as our expenses would significantly decrease and Karen would start working. That was before they delivered this embarrassing financial aid package.

My parents are so much wiser than I. When I discussed finances with them two months ago, they each told me, "Well, you never know what is going to happen. We have the money if you need it. Until you graduate, it'll be here."

After I made that call to the financial aid office, I had lunch with my mother and stepfather. I showed them my financial aid letter and ran the numbers. "Whatever you need, just let us know, and we will get it into your account," my mother said. I immediately felt at ease, but if it's not $5,000, it won't be enough.

Then last night, I went to my father and stepmother's house for dinner, letter in hand. I had drawn up a spreadsheet displaying my expected shortfalls. "Whatever you can do to help," I said. "I'm going to have quite the need between now and next summer."

My mouth fell agape when my dad said, "Well, I don't have any cash in my pocket, but we'll write you a check for $5,000 right now if that'll work."

"Holy crap! Are you kidding me?" I couldn't contain myself. I buried my face in my hands, planted my elbows onto the table, and bawled with such inconceivable relief.

Additional loans won't be necessary, nor will I need to earn an income. I'll be able to concentrate on learning, reading, and studying for my board exams. The clouds have parted, and the sun is shining. This is actually happening. I'm going to get through this.

July 13, 2000, Thursday.

[1 day since last entry]

I'm leaving the hospital after another eleven hours. I'm convinced I will work in emergency medicine one day. Could that change in the next ten months? Of course, but this rotation is so exciting.

Today, I worked in the main ER with Dr. Ray. I just grabbed a chart out of the rack and said, "Hey, do you mind if I go see this patient?"

"Heck no," he said. "Just report back to me before you write any orders. And whenever you want to snag a chart and get started, you're welcome to."

I'm in my second week and being allowed the liberty of taking the lead. I would see a patient, present the case to the attending, and we would agree on the orders. Then, I would write the orders in the chart, get them cosigned, and communicate the plan with the patient's nurse. When done, I'd move on to the next patient.

As results began pouring in, I'd review them on my own, find the attending, confer with them, and plan the course of action. This could involve sending a patient home, calling a hospitalist (a medical provider that admits and cares for patients during their stay), consulting a surgeon, or performing a procedure like reducing a shoulder (popping a dislocation back into socket), draining an infection, or stitching up a wound.

That terrified look plastered on my face during my ICU rotation is slowly melting away.

July 14, 2000, Friday.
[1 day since last entry]

I was taken for my first ride today. I attended to a fifty-five-year-old man, who was experiencing lower back pain. He happened to be a colleague of my father at the Portsmouth Naval Shipyard. I spent over twenty minutes with him, and because he knew my dad, we traded a couple of memorable stories. I didn't think much about it, but he was in a room separated from another patient by only a curtain.

The next chart I grabbed from the rack was for a twenty-year-old woman, also with lower back pain. She had been placed in the trauma room next to my dad's coworker. I walked in and was immediately accosted. "Well, it's about fucking time you got here! I've been sitting here in fucking agony, while you were having your little story hour next door to me. You know what? Fuck you! Forget it. I'm outta here. I don't want you fucking guys laying your hands on me now. No one gives a shit around here. I can hear you all laughing out there by the desks. I'm getting dressed. Everyone can go fuck themselves. And you'll be hearing from my lawyer too."

I've been on the wrong side of the operating room several times when surgeons have unleashed a few choice offerings to the swear-lords, but this caught me by complete surprise. I tried to smooth things over. "My apologies. Thank you for your patience. Please understand, this is an emergency room and we must address the most urgent or emergent patients first. It doesn't mean that anyone is ignoring you. In the last hour, we've had two ambulances arrive with critical victims that had to take priority. We are prepared to treat you, so now that I'm here, how can I help you?" The multiple ambulance thing was a lie. I also falsely claimed that many of the staff were busy attempting to resuscitate a gentleman who had experienced cardiac arrest and this did give her pause. With guilt flushing her face, I continued, "If you leave and go to another hospital, I can guarantee you they are having a similar night, and your wait may be even longer. Tell me what's going on?"

Tossing her dirty, worn-out Converse All Stars on the chair across the room, she started whimpering. Open in the front like a bathrobe, she clenched her gown to cover her chest. I lost count of the number of piercings she had, and that was only from the ones I could see above her neckline. Colorless tattoos decorated each arm, and the black lacquer on her fingernails were perfect as if she had just driven here from the salon. She claimed she had been painting at a friend's house, picked up a full five-gallon bucket of paint, and experienced a sudden sharp pain that shot down both legs, leaving her with a burning sensation in her ankles, but there wasn't a speck of paint on her.

I helped her into a position of comfort, but during this maneuvering, she bellowed so loudly that the cafeteria employees had to have heard her on the other side of the hospital. "How much longer until you can give me something strong for the pain?"

"I'm a student, so I can't do that, but I'm going to go track down Dr. Ray who is here tonight, and I'll have him come see you." I flew through the curtains and observed several smirking faces glancing in my general direction. Across the ER, I spotted Dr. Ray writing in a chart.

"Dr. Ray, I know you're busy right now, but can I pull you into the office right away so I can present a patient to you?"

After I closed the door behind us, he started laughing. "I couldn't help but overhear the belligerent one. What's up with her?"

I gave him the very brief history and asked if we could give her something for pain right away.

"Before we do anything, let's go see her," he asserted.

As we made our way to her bay, I caught the eyes of a few more staffers; they all seemed amused. I didn't know what to make of it. Without a doubt, they had to have heard her drop a full barrel of F-bombs on me.

I thought I had taken command of the situation, calming the patient down, and convincing her to stay so we could help.

The moment Dr. Ray pulled the curtain aside, the moaning and writhing began, and she laid right into him. "Are you the doctor? I need fucking pain meds. I've been here for hours."

Dr. Ray gathered the same history that I had and seemed to compile similar physical exam findings. We walked out of her room together. "I think her pain is real," I told him. "I don't think she's faking it."

As he leaned over to the secretary, she questioned. "You thinking what I'm thinking? I think she's a frequent flyer and we're this week's location of choice."

Dr. Ray penned some orders in her chart then motioned for me to follow him into his office. Sitting at the desk, he called two area hospitals to ask if the patient had visited them in the last few weeks and why. While he was on hold, I excused myself and ran out back to the express care wing where I knew Jack was working. "Jack, I think I just got burned."

"Yup! You did. We've already heard the story down here. She took you for a ride. It's something that happens to all of us, even now, but you'll become more adept at recognizing it. The fun part is when you catch them, confront them, and get to witness the looks on their faces—watch how fast they run out of the ER. It's precious. That usually deters them from coming back anytime soon."

Walking away, I realized I have a lot to learn, and it seems to have nothing to do with actual medicine. Apparently, you need intense intuition and investigatory skills. For the rest of this rotation, I might as well be walking around with a sign on my back that says "Kick me" or have "Dr. Gullible" written across my forehead in a black marker.

What I want to do, but never would, is walk right into that patient's exam room and say, "You deceitful son of a bitch. Get the hell out of this ER." Can't do that, though. Apparently, it's considered unprofessional, especially as a student. I wonder if doctors ever just lose it on a patient... I'd pay to see that.

After I returned to the main ER, I was curious what Dr. Ray was giving her through the IV. He told me he had recently gone to some educational conferences on treating pain and he has a new concoction, which doesn't include any narcotics, yet does the trick. As it turns out, this patient didn't get opioids, so she didn't get the fix that she was seeking. This will do one of two things in the future: it will keep her from coming to this ER and seeking the "good stuff" or she'll come back with a different fabricated complaint in hopes that she'll pull the wool over the eyes of the next provider she encounters.

I went back to Dr. Ray's office. "I just got off the phone with Lilac City Hospital a couple of towns over. She's been up there several times with back pain over the last few months. I'm not convinced that she's legit, but that's okay, we're treating her pain."

Twenty minutes after she received her meds, I returned to check on her. "How are you doing? Is your pain getting any better?" No response, because she was *snoring*! I have to make a note of Dr. Ray's magic potion. When she could eventually mumble some coherent words through her drool, we had her call a friend to come pick her up without further confrontation.

The next couple of hours were slow as hell, so Dr. Ray, Jack, and every staffer in the ER were just hanging out, shooting the breeze, and joking around. One nurse turned to Dr. Ray and said, "Man, we've got to hire this guy. He fits right in."

"I was thinking the same thing," Dr. Ray said. "If we've got an opening, he's welcome to apply. I'm sure we'd take him."

Later on, as I was leaving the hospital, I thought, *I'm on a five-week job interview.*

July 19, 2000, Wednesday.
[5 days since last entry]
I went in at 7:00 am. A half hour later, an ambulance brought in a seventy-seven-year-old lady who appeared to be having a severe COPD exacerbation. We learned she had a DNR (Do Not Resuscitate)

order on file. The EMS crew told us they had given her a continuous nebulizer treatment on the way over.

Through her nebulizer mask, we could hear her demanding, "Help me. Help me. Help me." We kept trying to tell her we were doing everything that we could. She received morphine and a sedative to calm her so she'd get her breathing under control. Moments after she was wheeled to her room, the family started arriving. Her husband showed up first, then her daughter, then two sons. I was a passive observer. I was available, but never received directives. Astonishingly, their family doctor showed up. He moved to the front of the group and began rattling off pertinent history details, along with the family's wishes. Although I had stepped out for about ten minutes to go see another patient, when I had made my way back, the room was somber. I think in those ten minutes, someone communicated some harsh decisions, and they grasped the reality that she would not make it.

The patient's breathing was shallow, but no longer labored. She was becoming less and less responsive. Her three children, all in their fifties, further crowded the bed. A horrible feeling crept up into my throat and my eyes welled up. I paced a bit, hands and fingers intertwined and clasped at my waist. Her daughter looked up, frantic, and began shouting, "Oh, my God! Where's Daddy? Where's Daddy? Just hang on for Daddy, Mom. Hang on!"

I watched her heartrate on the monitor: 51, 47, 43, 40, 37.

Now all three of her children were pleading chaotically. "Where is he? We need Dad."

A nurse, hearing the tension from outside of the room, poked her head in and asked for a description of him. One of her sons responded. "I think he went to the cafeteria to get a bite to eat. Navy blue shorts, hiking boots, white short-sleeved shirt with a Bruins logo." The nurse sprinted away. We all knew where she was headed.

Spotting a tissue box on the crash cart in the corner, I ambled over to retrieve it. After offering one to everybody in the room, I secretively removed two for myself and slid them into my coat pocket.

"Mom! Please hang on. They're getting Daddy. Hang on until he gets back." Their heads turned towards the curtain, then back towards their mother, then towards the curtain again. My eyes zeroed in on the daughter who was clinging and pleading with urgency.

For a second, I mentally traded places with her: I was suddenly clutching my own mother's hand, looking at my mother's last breaths, hearing my voice letting out pleas, and allowing my tears to fall from my cheeks and onto her chest.

Interrupting that moment, the patient's husband parted the curtains and rushed to his wife's side. As Dr. Otis reached up to turn off the alarms on the monitor, the room finally became still and peaceful. Beats per minute: 28, 27, 26, 25, 24. Dr. Otis made eye contact with every employee in the room, and we all knew to silently follow him into the hallway. I glanced back one last time. A hand settled onto my shoulder and my gaze turned toward it. I followed the black sleeve from the cuff link to the forearm, then to the shoulder, the neck, and finally met the eyes of a priest. I nodded, reached into my pocket for a tissue, stepped aside, and drew the curtains to a close behind him. Just outside in the hall, I listened as the last rites were read.

I left the emergency department, made it outside, and just started walking. I had no destination or deadline. It was time to wander and regroup. No one would be searching for me. I had no desire to see any more patients, but my shift was due to last another ten hours. I knew I couldn't hide for that long. By the time my second tissue began disintegrating and had lost all absorbency, I looked up and could no longer see the hospital.

I turned around on the sidewalk and strode back into a headwind. The air was still thick from an early shower, and the freshly cut lawns were damp and glistening. Through some trees, I could see the outline of the hospital again. I took a deep, cleansing breath as the clouds parted. Although I was now facing the sun, I could make out the big red letters: E-M-E-R-G-E-N-C-Y.

In the distance, cast over the tree line, faded the last remnants of a rainbow.

Re-entering the ER with bloodshot eyes, I somberly removed the next chart from the top of the rack. I didn't look at the name, age, or chief complaint. I found the room number and went in. My eyes met theirs and I froze. For a brief moment, I saw the face of my mother, but then it vanished.

"Hi. I'm Shawn, a physician assistant student. How can I help you today?"

July 22, 2000, Saturday.
[3 days since last entry]

Jack was working today, and even though I hadn't been doing many weekend hours, he invited me to his eight-hour express care shift. It's the summer and express care routinely had patients with rolled ankles, poison ivy, and what I like to call the "fall down, go boom" crowd (skinned elbows, dirty lacerated knees, and other aches and pains from hitting the ground from whatever height and from whatever speed). These days allow you to get good at the common things. It's also a break from the high-intensity pace of the main ER.

Today was just that; if I wasn't picking dirt out of an abrasion, I was reading X-rays; and if I wasn't applying a cast to a teen's wrist, I was throwing stitches into yet another body part when Dermabond (skin glue) just wouldn't cut it. Sometimes a laceration comes along and its location is bewildering. Its size may lack impressiveness, but its degree of difficulty reaches a nearly insurmountable level. And well, only a student would be crazy enough to give it a go.

I had just finished lunch and was doing some charting when I heard our triage nurse announce as she passed by, "We got a live one, Shawn. I think this one is for you."

I swung around in my chair and saw my sister, Crystele. "Hey," she sang sarcastically. In tow was her boyfriend, John, hobbling a bit.

As he passed, John said to me, "Despite the blood you're about to see, Crystele would not bring me to the closest hospital. Oh, hell no!

We drove right on past that one. So, thanks. Because you're here today, my suffering had to last an extra seven miles."

Laughter filled the hall as his chart was slid across the counter to me. Jack held his hands up and took a step back. "She's right. You take this one."

When I entered the exam room, I was met with objections about removing his boot, and thus removing the direct pressure that John proclaimed was the only thing keeping him from bleeding out.

John explained to me that just after sunrise, he made a pot of coffee for himself and his parents, with whom he lived. After his first cup, right on cue, duty called, so he shuttled towards the bathroom. The doorframe to the bathroom, which had been in the same location since the home was built, grabbed John's pinky toe. As if an exorcism was occurring, he let out a blood-chilling scream, followed by a litany of choice four-letter words. The narrow bathroom walls provided all the balance points he would need to find his way to the seat that he needed most—the toilet. Whether it was his high-pitched screams, or the cacophony of barking dogs in the neighborhood, John's mother woke up and rushed to the crime scene and flung open the bathroom door. Shirtless, and with shorts around his ankles, "Ma!" he yelled. "Close the door!"

Traumatized, she fled. John had looked down to see his baby toe not facing the same direction as the day he was born, and a pool of blood had collected on the floor. Lacking any medic skills, he found a roll of double-ply toilet paper and began mopping up the puddle, like a biscuit sponging up the gravy from a Thanksgiving platter.

When John realized he couldn't keep up with the river, he began wedging paper between his toes. Eight feet worth of toilet paper later, and upon finishing his duties on the throne, he limped back to his bedroom. After getting dressed, he put on two pairs of socks, cinched up the boot laces like a tourniquet, finished his coffee, and downed a small handful of ibuprofen.

Later on, he set out to complete the monumental task of an overdue, inaugural mowing of his parents' lawn. Pushing the grass cutter in near-perfect squares, the single-acre lot took two hours to complete. After shoving the mower back into the shed, he looked down at his boots. Both were covered in grass stains and crud, but one felt like it was in four inches of water, yet that boot appeared bone dry.

By late afternoon, worry was beginning to set in, so he called Crystele. "Hey, I think I need to go to the ER. I hurt my little toe."

"You need to go to the ER for your little toe? Seriously? Your baby toe?"

"Yes, Crystele. Can you come get me and bring me?"

She reluctantly obliged, and they ended up here, at the Daniel Webster Hospital express care.

The outer layer of his compression dressing was a snugly wound Timberland boot. Unlaced, it effortlessly slipped off. "Christ, John. This sock is filthy," I joked.

John got a glimpse of his sock. "A tad bloody, too, wouldn't ya say?"

"Oh, my God, John! Is that toilet paper?" Crystele provided her two cents. "That happened, like, seven hours ago? What the hell?"

"Shut up!," John said. "It was all I had. I was on the shitter."

With both socks now shimmied off, it was time to pick away at the eight feet of blood-soaked toilet paper dressing.

The last layer removed, we were relieved to see no active bleeding, and his little toe, although looking more like his big toe, seemed to be properly aligned. "I thought you said the toe was pointing the wrong direction…"

"It was, at least before I put it into my boot."

"You probably either dislocated it, or maybe fractured it," I said, "but cramming it into your boot popped it back into place and realigned it. With safety goggles on to protect me from any arterial gushers, I slowly separated his toes. "Wow. How the frig are we going to close that gash?"

Jack, peeking over my shoulder, let out a laugh. "Ha! You're not."

Dropping into my best *The Thinker* pose, I paused. "Well, let's get him down for an X-ray while I think about this. If there is a fracture, he'll need IV antibiotics and I'll need to get ortho down here to take a look. If nothing is busted, I can close that wound. It won't be easy, but I can do it."

Jack and I left the exam room and proceeded down the hall. "What are you thinking?" I asked.

"I'm thinking I wanna watch you try to stitch that up, but I can't let you do it because if you fail, I can't come bail you out on this one. That's an impossible location. I've never seen a laceration between the toes like that. Hopefully he broke it, thus it becomes an open wound so ortho will have to come down and deal with it."

"I can close it. What's the worst that can happen? I try, fail, and then we go to plan B?"

He asked me what I thought Plan B was. I thought I needed to tell him right up front, believing that would convince him to let me attempt Plan A. "Well, the wound is already very clean, but we will clean it exceptionally well, give him a shot of antibiotics, leave the wound open, get a nice dressing on it, make him non-weight-bearing, send him home on oral antibiotics, and make sure he gets close follow-up for dressing changes over the next few days, unless my sister can do them."

Jack's eyebrows went up as the corners of his lips angled down. "Okay. You're on, but only if the X-rays are normal." And off he went to grab the next chart.

The X-rays were normal. No fractures. No dislocations. As I'm delivering the news to John and Crystele, a nurse set up a suturing kit on the Mayo stand. "On your belly, buddy. Get comfy. This could take a minute," I warned.

Technically, the time I had to close this wound had run out. Depending on several factors, lacerations should be closed within so many hours, otherwise, they should be left to heal on their own. Since John's had happened in a clean environment, he had protected it from the elements, and he had bled enough to effectively wash it out, we figured that afforded us additional time.

I don't know how many times I stopped to adjust the bed, had John log-roll left, log-roll right, or had the nurse maneuver my light source, requested more sterile gauze, and asked someone to wipe my brow so the beads of sweat wouldn't splash into this work of art, but after fifty minutes and fifty demands of, "Okay, John. Don't you move," I had successfully completed the mother of all repairs.

While creating this eighth wonder of the world, news had spread throughout the ER, "You've got to go see what Shawn is doing back there."

Jack was the final spectator to arrive back on scene, and as he was looking over my shoulder, I trimmed the tags off the final knot. "Well, I'll be a son-of-a-bitch," he whispered. Raising his volume, he sarcastically announced, "I quit. I can see that I'm no longer needed here anymore. You're hired. I'm going home now."

And after that repair, so did I.

August 2, 2000, Wednesday.

[11 days since last entry]

That final week in the ER wiped me out, plain and simple. I don't think I did any reading—even during the three days I was laid up with back spasms, which hit me the day after the epic toe closure of my sister's boyfriend. If I wasn't at the ER, I was trying to sleep.

Mentally, I was exhausted. I'm thirty years old, so physically I'm capable of almost anything, but the pace, variety, and unpredictability of the ER was mind-blowing. ER personnel experience burnout at an astronomical rate, and I can now appreciate why.

On one of my final few days in the ER, I met a woman in her late sixties who was there with her two children: a son and a daughter, each in their thirties. She had come in with chest pain. Several times during their stay with us, I had given them updates on results which almost always turned into a somewhat lengthy Q&A session. As a student, I took it as a challenge, wanting to not only treat and comfort my patients, but also to educate.

I detected new abnormalities in this patient's ECG, as well as a cardiac murmur on exam, which surprised her. I tore out a blank progress note page from her chart and flipped it over. After removing the printed ECG from her chart, I explained the findings that might be a cause for concern. Using drawings, I showed her how murmurs occur and discussed why they may or may not be worrisome.

"Now I understand what you mean. That makes sense. I can see it and hear it now," she said, as her two kids nodded in agreement. "I really love PAs. They spend more time with you and they never appear rushed or have God complexes. You were really great. How long have you worked here?"

"Oh, I don't work here. Maybe one day, but I'm just a PA student now. This is only my second rotation, so I've got a ways to go."

"You're kidding. That can't be true."

"Yup, about nine more months."

When Dr. Ray and I had finally determined that she could be discharged, we walked back into her room together. "Shawn and I have decided that it is safe to let you go home, but you need to have a few outpatient tests that can be ordered by your primary care physician. Although not urgent, try to get them completed within the next few weeks. Your PCP will get a copy of our notes so they'll know the direction to take this once you follow-up with them. Before we get the IV out and get you all disconnected from these wires, do you have any questions?"

"No, Shawn answered them all. Thank you. Hold on to this one," she said as she pointed in my direction.

"Yes, he's great, huh?" Dr. Ray said. "Thanks for coming in. Glad we could take care of you."

In front of Dr. Ray, a patient endorsed my capabilities, and with everything I had just encountered over my entire rotation, that may have been the highlight. Small, but meaningful and validating.

The thrill and elation that I experienced while in the ER would be hard to match, and it had me thinking about a special Emergency Medicine two-year residency program for physician assistants offered by Alderson Broaddus University. I had heard about it from several people, including two of my preceptors, so I spent some time investigating it further. If accepted, during the first month on campus, you have to complete several courses such as ACLS (advanced cardiac life support), ATLS (advanced trauma life support), and PALS (pediatric advanced life support), but also complete the instructor certifications for each.

You are provided a small stipend to work in a hospital ER for two years, Friday through Sunday, while taking courses back on campus, Monday through Thursday. I'm intrigued, although it flies in the face of my master plan with Karen. It's two more years of training and minimal income. I'd be thirty-four before starting my career.

Then there's that wedding and honeymoon thing that might be impossible to work around at this point. That's a lot to think about. My wheels are turning. Jack and two of the ER docs said I should get the ball rolling on the application, which I've already started, and they would write me letters of recommendation. I'm not obligated to dive in immediately. I could take a year, get a job in an ER after graduating, pay off some loans, then do the residency program. That might work. This possibility hasn't yet reached the level of requiring a discussion with Karen, and until it does, I think I need to secretly keep it in my back pocket.

August 6, 2000, Sunday.
[4 days since last entry]
On Friday, I sat for the ER exam on Recall Day. I feared I might fail, as I had only managed to read 500 pages of the recommended 750-page

textbook. Every single time I opened it, I fell asleep. I never felt like I retained anything, but you never know when, at some random point out of the blue, you're going to pull a factoid out of your ass when you least expect it.

Except for ten hours on Thursday, the day before the exam, I hadn't actually studied, only read. My focus was on completing hundreds of practice National Board exam questions. Nonetheless, I scored a 90 on the ER exam, so it paid off. Jack gave me an A for my final rotation grade, and since I had also received an A on my ICU evaluation (there wasn't a test, as it was an elective), that gave me a 4.0 for the quarter.

17

ROTATION #3— OUTPATIENT, FAMILY MEDICINE

August 7, 2000, Monday.

[5 days since last entry]

Grab a seat, folks. This entry will be a doozy. I need to catch you up on a few things. It's about 10:30 am and I start my third rotation in about ninety minutes. After a few practice runs this weekend, I found the most efficient way to get to my site in just over half an hour. It's an office-based private practice that sees patients from infancy to the elderly.

The excitement factor will be absent over the next five weeks, so I'm concerned that my recordings will be as boring as white rice and skinless chicken breasts. That may be some people's cup of tea, but not mine. I don't ever see myself working outside of a hospital setting. I know I have a lot to learn about managing chronic conditions. In the

ER, you manage patients for a brief time. I often heard the saying, "Treat 'em and street 'em." In the ICU, you manage patients that often can't speak or move. But now, I have to learn to provide care for patients who take actual medicines at home, only after I have been given twenty minutes to diagnose and/or manage their ailments. Three rotations, and three completely different ways medicine is applied to provide healthcare.

Meeting and meshing with your preceptor, as I have learned, is a major key to success. During the last Recall Day, Bailey and I had a conversation about Dean, my family medicine preceptor. Dean had been Bailey's preceptor when she was going through the program several years ago. She said he was a very soft-spoken, even-keeled gentleman with a tremendous gift for teaching.

The school instructs us to call our next preceptor several days before our rotation starts, but I hadn't actually spoken to any of them until Dean. I'd usually end up leaving a pre-scripted voicemail and never receiving a return call. So, when Dean picked up the phone, it was a pleasant surprise. Evidently, he was aware of my time spent at home in New Hampshire during my previous rotation and inquired about whether I had attended any Red Sox games on a student's income. The conversation, albeit brief, relieved some anxieties.

While home, I prioritized spending time with Karen. And it was all going amazingly well... until recently.

Karen had started her new job last Monday. By lunch break on her first day, she was ready to quit. She hated it. The fault was with the company, not the people. You'd hope one could figure that out during the interviewing process, but I guess she didn't. The place was in complete disarray. She now regrets not taking a higher paying job in Boston, but the horrific commute is what deterred her.

After the first day, her recruiter called to check in. The first words out of Karen's mouth: "I'm not staying here."

It's understandable why she felt discouraged and was so disengaged during my last few days at home with her. I felt helpless. She has a new car coming in six weeks. We have no money. We're planning a wedding, but we haven't made any progress. Opting for her grandmother's self-made dress, she acknowledged it will need some restoration and minor alterations. We received no response from any photographers we contacted. The Governor's Inn, our ceremony and reception location, could not arrange a time to have us up there for dinner and formal consultation. I didn't reach out to a single DJ on our list. When I asked Karen if she had picked a honeymoon spot or spoken to any travel agents, she just let out a frustrated sigh.

She's the one who has been unemployed for over a month. She's had ample time to get things done. I keep getting on her ass about it, but all she does is procrastinate.

I arranged my room and hung up new pictures of Karen, including Post-it notes she had randomly placed for me to find during our time together. Leaving her this time was harder. I won't be returning to New Hampshire for ten weeks. I may not see her until mid-October. We talked about her coming out for a long weekend, but it's a several-hour drive and flying is cost-prohibitive. This will be a true test for us.

Last weekend, I met with my dad and stepmom. As previously mentioned, they had saved $5,000 in case I needed it during my internship year. It was time to collect the first installment. As a thirty-year-old, I felt shame in even asking my parents for this money, let alone accepting it.

They signed the check and slid it across the table, making it officially ready for deposit. Never at a loss for words, I moved my eyes from the signature line to their faces. That lump developed in my throat again, and my breathing needed to be reeled in carefully, like a six-pound trout on a two-pound test line. As I reached the eye-welling crossroads, I extended my neck and fixated on the ceiling fan above me. My cracking voice broke. "I'm grateful for everything that you have given to me in my life."

"We know, Shawn," my stepmom said, as Dad nodded.

"I'm probably not going to need all of it."

"Shawn, it's fine. That's what it's here for. It's yours."

"It's not mine. This is a loan, remember? And you will be the very first that I pay back."

"We know you will," Dad said.

"And when my next need arises, I will go to my mother and Norm."

"That's fine. Whatever you need. We don't doubt you. You've come this far and we know it hasn't been easy. Now go finish what you started."

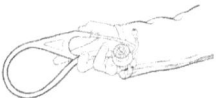

Speaking of challenges, last weekend reminded me of the immense difficulty I had faced transitioning my life from music to medicine, trading my drumsticks for a stethoscope. Karen and I went out to a local music club, Biddy Mulligan's, to watch my old band, Pondering Judd, do a headlining show with their new lineup. Unbeknownst to me, Steve, our former bassist, was visiting from Sacramento and also dropped in on the show. I hadn't seen him in more than two years. "It's hard to watch the band play," I told him. "I wanna be up there so badly. I really miss it."

"I don't know, man. It's their time now. We had ours, and it was great, but that is in the past."

I understood, though I was a bit surprised by his differing stance.

People filled the venue, standing shoulder to shoulder on the dance floor, around every table, and at the bar. The crowd appeared baffled when the band finished their encore twenty minutes before last call.

"We have a couple of special guests in the house!" Marty, the lead singer, announced. The place started going crazy. Everyone there knew who we were, and although I made a beeline for the drum kit as soon as they invited me, it took some coaxing (and synchronized chanting from the fans) to get Steve to join us.

We played a handful of our most popular tunes. I'm not sure how many beers were in his belly, but John, my sister's boyfriend, with still-fresh stitches between his toes, was dancing on the bar, scattering half-empty glasses, cardboard coasters, and bowls of salted peanuts.

When the dust settled, I didn't want to leave the stage. It felt like old times and reminded me of an era without responsibilities. For this one night, I didn't give a shit. It imposed the briefest of peace upon me, and I realized it would probably be the last time I would ever play with this extraordinary group of musicians and friends. I wondered if anything would ever bring back the lost balance in my life.

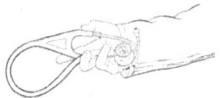

My first day is over. I'm just sitting in the office parking lot. If you could hear my voice, it would convey immense relief and happiness. Dean met me at the door when I arrived. I was expecting a short, fifty-something year-old gruff dude, but he was almost my height, six foot two, slender, balding, wearing silver-rimmed glasses and a long, pressed, white lab coat over a lavender dress shirt and pink paisley necktie. Bailey was spot on. He did have a gentle, calming demeanor.

Throughout the day, I had to keep laughing at myself. All my perceptions of what my third rotation was going to be like had been shattered. As usual, instead of allowing the experience to come to me, I lost sleep, predicting all the worst-case scenarios before even setting foot in the front door.

Anticipating the pimping in a style consistent with my ICU experience, I instead found Dean's questions practical and scripted in a way that I could actually provide an intelligent answer. Or maybe, just maybe, I had retained enough material over the last two years to appear competent—at least for a day.

I had been Dean's younger, chubbier shadow during the first two patient encounters, but by the third, he was willing to let me fly solo. Handing me the chart, he said, "Here, you go see this one, write a SOAP note when you're done, come find me. We'll review it, then I'll go see the patient, write a SOAP note, and we'll do a comparison."

It couldn't have been more perfect. For the rest of the day, this was our approach. Since each appointment took me about forty minutes, I only saw seven of the twenty-one patients that were scheduled. Dean wouldn't sit with me to review until we had each completed a patient's SOAP note. He was conscientious about not falling behind. You could tell this wasn't his first rodeo. His knack to balance the care of his patients while carrying a new student on his back was astounding.

By mid-afternoon, I already knew the questions he was going to ask me: "Why do you want to do that? Why did you choose that medicine for this patient? Can you inform the patient about the potential side effects? How urgent is it to complete this test? What labs do we need to order? Does this patient need a referral? When should we see this patient back for follow-up?"

Dean never asked an irrelevant question. He had no intention of embarrassing me in the presence of others.

Of the handful of patients I saw today, all but one had simple complaints (earache, cough, rash, etc.). She was a two-year-old whose mother had concerns for developmental delay. Her only word was "Ma." If the child wasn't being held by her mother, she'd lash out, cry, and throw a tantrum. She'd start smashing up anything in her way if the attention was ever taken off her.

Examining her was out of the question. She'd pull her own hair, slap her mother's face, and let out unprovoked screams. I didn't want to get beaten to a bloody pulp by a child on my first day. She didn't have any of the classic features of Down syndrome, but my mind kept going there. I didn't hesitate to explain to the mother that I was in over my head. "I'm unsure what to do, or if tests need to be ordered, but I suspect when Dean comes in, he'll want to send her to a behavioral specialist for children. She looks normal, but I do question if her hearing is intact. She doesn't seem to respond to voice commands at all."

Dean shared my concerns and referred them to a pediatric psychiatrist. And although her records indicated that she was not up to date on her immunizations, that would be a fight for another day. "Besides, I'm not getting near that kid with a sharp object," he said with a chuckle.

August 10, 2000, Thursday.

[3 days since last entry]

Nothing can replace experience. Dean has more than twenty years, and it shows. He's brilliant, confident, efficient, and collected, but perhaps more importantly, he takes no crap. Today I watched him do a complete head-to-toe annual physical on one of his fifty-year-old male patients, and the entire time he is chatting away like it's dinner conversation, collecting the ROS (review of systems = a list of closed ended questions intended to uncover any symptoms that have not already been alluded to), and getting an updated family history, all while the patient is chatting about his oldest son who is heading off to college in two weeks.

Mid-physical, Dean discusses how it's time for this patient's first colonoscopy, without missing a beat. The rectal and genitalia exams were conducted so casually that they might as well have occurred during happy hour at the local pub. From start to finish: eight minutes.

When we arrive back at Dean's office, he asks, "So, any questions?"

Stunned at the absolute perfection I had witnessed. "Um. No. I'm blown away by how seamless you just made that look."

"Experience. That's all," he says. "You'll get there. I've been doing this a very long time."

"You make it look like art. So smooth. It was fun to watch you." I grabbed the next chart and proceeded down the hall, jaw still dragging on the carpet.

My complete physicals are horrible. Remembering only half of my training seems impossible. Nasal exam? I don't test the sense of smell or look at their mucosa. Neck exam? I never get behind the patient to palpate the thyroid gland as they swallow. Lungs? I don't perform egophony or percussion. Cardiac? I don't have them squat to assess how their murmur changes. And the list goes on.

If I hadn't just witnessed Dean do the most comprehensive physical that I have ever seen (in under ten minutes!), I would not have thought it possible. But since I did, I know it is.

Because of my struggle, I thought it would be helpful to do my weekly write-up on a typical adult complete physical. RTC requires that each student submit a complete note to our preceptor for review by the end of each week. It can be on any patient that we've encountered. When I handed it to him, along with the evaluation forms, he looked annoyed. "Evaluation? RTC does everything crazy. Everything is crazy there. The way they grade you is crazy. It's all backwards. There is the yellow sheet and the orange sheet, and assigning numerical grades, and providing signatures. It's so foolish. I take students from six other PA programs and no one else does it like this. It's ridiculous. It should be pass/fail, or satisfactory/deficient, or honors, and that should be the end of it. No grades. No testing. No write-ups. This is a professional program. It's just absurd."

I don't know who to believe, RTC or Dean, but I know I'm not qualified to render an opinion. It sure sounds nice to just show up to rotations, see patients, and read about their conditions and diseases, but how can you argue with RTC's reputation and track record of producing competent entry level physician assistants?

August 14, 2000, Monday.
[4 days since last entry]
During our first Recall Day well over a month ago, our class learned that Liam, an amazing friend of ours who had been with us since the start of freshman year, was dismissed from the program. I believe he had been on academic probation multiple times. We were aware of his struggles, but receiving that news was still saddening.

The day after it was announced to us, I called Liam. He was not in a good place, and not forthcoming about what he had been going through, but I was reluctant to ignore it. I told him just because he won't be a PA next year, doesn't mean he'll never become one. It's just not his time right now. I knew he could recover from this setback, but should refrain from making any life-altering decisions in the near future. I reminded Liam that he isn't defined by a degree or letters after his name. There's a reason why everything happens. I've attempted to reach out several times since, but have failed to reconnect.

Two days ago, I finally spoke to his father. His parents may have been more surprised than the rest of us. Apparently, Liam had become withdrawn from them during the final quarter. I now suspect Liam knew he was trapped in a hole he couldn't escape from, silently harboring his expected fate, likely feeling some shame. His parents have had three face-to-face meetings with the program leaders during the subsequent weeks after his dismissal, pleading with them to allow their son to continue, but RTC would not budge. I was angry, so I instructed Liam's parents to schedule another meeting and come prepared with the following details: Viktor, the transfer student in his fifties (also released in May), had been expelled from this program twice before. The program allowed Viktor to have another chance by giving him a spot in the following year's class after he failed to make it through his didactic year two other times. Why? I suspect because his wife, an MD, serves as a clinical preceptor for the RTC PA program. Makes sense, right? It's all in who you know and the power you may hold. Having said that, RTC has a maximum number of PA students they can graduate each year. What I didn't know was whether there were any open spots in the class behind us. If there weren't, then I suppose Helen's hands were tied. However, I floated that to Liam's dad, so perhaps he could use that to his advantage. Speaking as if Liam's life was at risk, he was grateful to me for reaching out.

Since I had scored some free tickets for a hypnotist/comedy show, I invited Liam. I wouldn't take "no" for an answer. Although we talked about my rotations, I tried to redirect the conversation away from that as quickly as I could. He pushed, and was genuine in his interest, but it became awkward.

Ultimately, Liam seemed back to his usual self, showing no signs of depression. I'm sure I'd be despondent if I had been dismissed entering the final year of my goal.

August 17, 2000, Thursday.

[3 days since last entry]

I received bad news via email from Karen last night. She can't fly out between the end of this rotation and the start of my next, so we'll have to endure ten weeks of separation.

Aside from that crushing communication, today was a tale of two different patient encounters that had me on the highest of highs one minute, and the next, feeling like an incompetent fool.

I saw a forty-two-year-old man who had been feeling agitated and jittery for a few days. He also had blurry vision, tremors, and diarrhea. The patient firmly believed it was his thyroid. I looked through his chart and discovered that two years ago he was having similar symptoms, although not as intense. His TSH (Thyroid-Stimulating Hormone) came back on the very low end of normal. He'd been sent for an ultrasound that showed a dominant nodule, which was eventually biopsied, but the pathology was inconclusive.

Despite being advised to schedule a close interval follow-up ultrasound in 3-6 months, he hadn't returned to the office for any reason until today. While examining his neck, I let out an intriguing gasp. "My apologies. I've never felt an abnormal thyroid before, so this is pretty cool for me." After I completed my exam, I left to locate Dean.

"This next guy has thyroiditis," I told him point blank.

"Really? He's hyperthyroid? Why do you think that?"

I went through his list of complaints and history: "Well, two years ago, his TSH was barely normal, but his physical exam was not, plus he had some mild symptoms. He had an inconclusive biopsy, but we haven't seen him since. The endocrinologist suggested repeating the ultrasound in three to six months. I bet his TSH is undetectable now. Besides that, his thyroid gland is grossly enlarged. Wait until you see it."

Dean and I returned to the patient's room, and after just a few moments, he agreed. He ordered a full thyroid panel, called an endocrinologist, and scheduled a biopsy for as soon as possible. The patient was scared, but grateful. "Looks like you have a budding star here, Dean."

"Well, I taught him everything I know," Dean said with a smile.

And so, the confidence was high, but as a student that can turn on a dime—and often does. Just hours later, Dean was occupied in a room with a complex patient while I was writing some notes, so when I was done, not wanting Dean to get too far behind I glided down the hall to the next exam room to find two charts outside on the door. Perusing them quickly, it was a mother and son "two-fer." Is that allowed? Two patients in a room? Together? This means twice the work in the same amount of time, right?

After knocking, I pushed open the door and was immediately struck in the nuts by a flying reflex hammer. If I'd been wearing a long white coat, it may have better protected me, but I'm still in the short one. The four-year-old, built more like a Division 1 linebacker, was yanked by his arm back into a chair by his mother. I estimated his length of time in the chair at three-tenths of a second before he escaped, dove on to the exam table, and began rolling his body up into the razor thin paper that is supposed to act as a barrier to the faux leather.

Once cloaked in multiple layers, he let out a roar, tore through his new paper garment, and announced, "Hulk don't like *him*!" With his arms free again, he crammed a few cotton balls into his cheeks, turned on the water to the sink, wet his hair, then began whipping it around like he was filming a commercial for a male showering product.

In the midst of the pandemonium, I gathered a history and avoided further injury. The Hulkster provided me no safe moment to write anything down because I was either warding off an attack or attempting to retrieve my pen from him since he kept swiping it to practice writing his alphabet on the exam room walls. With enough data to present to Dean, I escaped. It felt like I had been in the room for an hour, but it may have only been five minutes. Dean hadn't yet emerged, so I went back to the office and began writing my notes. No sooner did I get the subjective component completed when Dean walked in. My forehead crashed to the desk.

"Shawn! Are you okay? What's the matter?" He ran to me.

"I am such a moron!"

"What do you mean? What's going on?"

I told him I had gone to see the next patient to keep the line moving, but it ended up being two patients, a mother and son (who thinks he's the Hulk). I ran down their reasons for coming in and then returned to the office to start my notes. That's when it hit me. I hadn't examined either of them. How could I leave the room without conducting an exam? Is this amateur hour?

"Well," he said calmly. "That's why we don't send students into rooms when a 'two-fer' is waiting, especially if one of them thinks they're a superhero on steroids."

August 18, 2000, Friday.

[1 day since last entry]

Because Dean had today off, I accompanied one of the docs whom I had seen at the office but never interacted with. I made a conscious effort to remain alert and communicate effectively with him throughout the day. I thought we got off on the right foot and had a great day, but at closing time, the shit hit the fan.

The first patient was a six-year-old who came in for a school physical. The doc let me go in ahead of him. Within twenty minutes, I exited the room with his school's medical clearance forms completed. I gave the forms to the doctor and briefed him at the nurses' desk. I asked if he wanted me to write a note in the chart.

"No. Let's just go see him."

I actually didn't write a single note the entire day. I would occasionally catch him dictating notes in his office between patients, so I thought he was just keeping up on his notes like any other provider would.

Today was a day of school physicals. I think there were at least six on the schedule for us. I asked the doctor I was shadowing if I could perform all of them, since repetition is how I learn most effectively. He agreed, so off I went.

Despite not having completed my pediatric rotation, I expect it will resemble today's experience of conducting multiple well-child care visits (WCC) and school physicals. One room I entered was a brother-and-sister combo (another "two-fer"), ages six and eight, both there for school physicals. I've already determined that with kids, the younger they are, the more difficult the interaction can be. Below four and it gets challenging. Can't talk? More challenging. Infants? Ugh! Between four and fourteen? Great ages. You can have an immense impact on their mental and physical health. They are generally receptive to education, but you must speak with them on their level.

I feel like I'm developing my schtick for working with kids. For instance, these physicals require a test for color blindness. The Snellen chart for vision features prominent red and green circles. When presented, I ask patients if they can tell me which one is blue and which is yellow. By simply gauging their puzzled reaction, I can tell whether they are color-blind. It works every time and is an icebreaker since I perform the test very early during a complete physical.

On the same duo, I stumbled on to a good stale-air buster when I examined the belly of the six-year-old boy. After auscultating (listening with a stethoscope) and palpating (feeling with hands), I did a little percussion. "What are you doing that for?" his older sister asked inquisitively.

"I'm trying to figure out where his air is. Can you hear the difference?" I tapped on his belly, then his chest, then his thigh, then went back to his belly.

"Yup! It sounds different, but why do you have to do that?" she asked.

"I do this to determine if I should issue a warning to you."

"Warn me?"

"Yes. Warn you. I can tell by the sound that your belly makes if you are going to have to fart soon. I can say without a doubt that your brother is going to be tooting up a storm this afternoon, so I'd stay far away from him if I were you."

Infectious giggling ensued. When the sister got up on the table, I made the uncontrollable laughing worse. As I was tapping, I said, "Oh, boy. This is not good." I paused and gave everyone in the room a deathly concerned look. Her brother was still hysterical in his chair. "I've got some really bad news. Her farts are going to be ten times worse than yours. You're going to have a fart fight later!"

When we were done, the young mother said, "You're a student?"

"Yes, and for another nine months."

"Are you going to come back to this office when you're done? I mean, work here?"

"Very unlikely. I'm from New Hampshire and I plan to go back there."

"That's too bad. If you were working around here, I'd ask you to be their doctor. You are so great with kids. I've never seen them have so much fun at an appointment before. And thanks for staying with them when they got their immunizations. That helped, and I know you didn't need to do that."

If only all kids were perfectly healthy and between the ages of four and fourteen…

The rest of the day went on without a hitch. The last two appointments were, you guessed it, school physicals. It was approximately 4:30 pm when I wrapped up the last one and proceeded to the office to seek out my preceptor. He looked up from his chart. "So, where do you stand with all of your note writing?"

"What?"

"Your charting. Completing notes in the chart. Writing notes," he tried to clarify. "You've been writing notes on all the patients you saw today, right?" he asked, seeing the stunned look on my face.

"Ummm, no?"

"Well, why not? It's what we do, right? We see a patient, we write a note, we see a patient… This isn't a new concept for you, is it?"

He was steaming. These patients, charts, and notes are technically his. He realizes it's 4:30 on a Friday and his student has seen half of his patients today without documenting anything, so he might have to stay for an additional hour to complete his work.

"What should we do?" I asked. My voice was barely audible through the whistling noise coming from his ears.

"We? We?! No, *you* are going to pull the charts on each patient you saw today and write notes on them."

Shit! That's eight charts. Eight notes. And I didn't write a single detail down all day. I was irate. Prior to entering the first patient's room, based on what the presiding doctor said to me, I was under the impression I wasn't to write any notes. I thought he was doing them. After all, he saw every patient after I did, and I heard him dictating notes in his office several times throughout the day, including during lunch. I presumed he was doing them. Nope. I spun around and stormed out. I wanted to keep walking right out the front door, get into my car, and drive into the Ashokan Reservoir.

"Hey!" he yelled. "Bring the stack of charts to me and we'll divide them up so we can get out of here."

That was kind of him, but I wouldn't take him up on his offer. The whole thing had been my doing, and I would not compound my failure by making more work for my preceptor.

The staff nurse saw me pulling charts. "Hey, Shawn. What's up?"

"Well, I was just informed that I was supposed to be writing notes on all the patients that I saw today, but I thought he was, and of course, he wasn't. So, I guess I'll be here a few more hours. Can you just show me how to turn the lights off and lock up?"

She helped me track down all the charts that I needed. I took the stack and headed back to an office on the other side of the building, as far away from the doc as I could get. Thirty minutes and three completed charts later, he came to find me. "Hey, give me half of those remaining charts. I'll dictate them. It'll be so much quicker. Pick the ones you want. Actually, take the easy ones. I know the physicals are the easiest notes to write, but they tend to be long, so do the rash kid and the guy with gout. You saw them, right?"

I really didn't want to acknowledge him. I was still fuming, but his tone had completely changed, so I felt obliged. "That's very kind of you, but I'll finish them. I'm sorry for the miscommunication. It won't happen again. I'll get them done tonight and lock up. Can I just put them on your desk for you to cosign and maybe we can review them together quickly at some point next week?"

I think he knew he wasn't going to win this one. I was going to fight him tooth and nail.

He nodded. "Okay, we'll figure it out next week. Thank you. I've already heard from multiple patients today that you were great, and I agree."

Suddenly, spending two hours on a Friday night in August, all alone in a medical office, handwriting notes, wasn't stinging so much.

August 22, 2000, Tuesday.

[4 days since last entry]

Today, at the end of lunch, that doc pulled me away from Dean to review the Friday night charts. "Shawn, you're writing way too much. I mean, way, way, way too much. You don't have to write every single thing. Just get the general stuff in there. They're school physicals. And your exam notes are too detailed."

Dean had mentioned the same thing after my first few days here. "I understand. I've been told that before, but I enjoy writing everything I do because it provides reinforcement and helps me to learn. When I find my rhythm and develop a routine, the repetitive process of doing and recording becomes incredibly valuable. If I write it down, I have better recall later."

"Well, you write too much. My history notes on a single acute complaint are rarely ever over three lines. You had at least six or seven sentences for a patient with sinus congestion. You can't do that. It's completely unnecessary."

Here I am, thinking that I'm going to be criticized for notes that don't contain enough detail, but instead, I'm being reprimanded for notes that are too thorough. I can't win. I strongly suspect it's a style issue, a student issue, or an experience issue, but most likely all of the above. Whatever... I'll do whatever it takes to maximize my experiences. That is nonnegotiable.

August 24, 2000, Thursday.
[2 days since last entry]
Nadine called me on Monday. We talked about my upcoming site visit, but I also had to present the topic and draft of my paper for this rotation.

This weekend, I wrote the entire paper, so I didn't do any of the suggested reading from the rotation's syllabus. Ten days ago, I emailed her my topic, outline, and bullet points. Since I received no response, I assumed I was good to go. Unbeknownst to me, Nadine was on vacation last week, so when she called, I was informed that my topic was too broad and that it needed to be narrowed down and redone. "It needs a lot more work," she said. Nadine considered my cited articles to be unacceptable because they were more than two years old.

I'd sunk twelve hours into writing my paper this weekend. I reached out more than a week in advance of Nadine's site visit, received no response, and now I'm told to toss it onto the scrap heap? Ridiculous! But I can't say anything, right? Of course not. I'm the student. Keep your trap shut, Roussin. This is not the moment to start digging your own grave. Just skip another weekend of reading, redo the entire paper, make it the best it can be, present it with conviction, and move on.

August 30, 2000, Wednesday.
[6 days since last entry]
I am figuring out my style as a provider, and it's happening quickly.

I entered a room this morning for a well-child visit, where a nine-year-old boy and his father were waiting. After introducing myself as a PA student, I joked with them that they'd get two physicals today, but only get charged for one, because when I was done, Dean would come in and do a physical too.

The dad was not amused by my attempt at comedy. Actually, this guy wouldn't be amused by anything. He seemed irritated and impatient throughout my entire visit with them. Maybe he was just having a bad day, but his son and I had a great time. The schtick works. I thanked them for their contribution to my educational experience and went to get Dean. When he concluded the visit, I headed to my preassigned area in the hall to write my note.

An unexpected tap on the shoulder, "Hey, Shawn. Thank you. I really appreciated how awesome you were with my son. You have a great future ahead of you. Don't ever lose your sense of humor. Good luck to you."

Holy shit! Where did that come from? In a surprising turn of events, this father, who avoided eye contact with me and acted annoyed the entire visit, made an effort to find me to give me a compliment.

He shook my hand, I gave his son a high-five, and they went to collect their discharge instructions at checkout.

Jenna, a staff secretary, looked up at me. "Shawn, you're so good with kids."

"What? How would you know that?"

"We hear things out here. Our patients talk to us, you know. They've all said wonderful things about you. Do you have kids of your own?"

"Not yet, but it probably won't be long. I'm engaged and not getting any younger. I'll be thirty-one next May when I graduate."

"Thirty? You're still a baby. You're going to be an awesome dad. I can tell."

"Thanks, Jenna. I have a long way to go. Some days are tough, but hearing your confidence in me reassures me that becoming a PA was the right choice. You would be surprised to learn about the bizarre path I took to get here. I could write a book about it one day."

September 4, 2000, Monday. Labor Day.

[5 days since last entry]

I'm sitting on the side of the road in Cooperstown, New York, about three hours from home, and three hours from my temporary apartment. Despite the lingering sunlight, a sense of darkness envelops me as Karen drives away in the opposite direction, her taillights fading from sight.

Since we couldn't justify her flying out to see me for a mere forty-eight-hour visit, Karen proposed we meet at the Baseball Hall of Fame. I had always wanted to go. It made perfect sense as the halfway point between us. However, I needed Nadine's blessing. Lucky for me, she is also a huge baseball fan. Karen and I booked the trip prior to me requesting permission. The cost of a seedy hotel room at $35 per night, along with a single day-pass to the museum made it affordable.

"Nadine, I'm thinking about meeting Karen in Cooperstown for the long Labor Day weekend. I haven't seen her in a month and may not see her again for over another month, but I must confess that if I go, this would make two weekends in a row that I haven't done a single page of reading—"

"Just go," she interrupted, not an ounce of hesitation in her voice.

"But I'm so far behind. I had to redo my paper, and then—" she cut me off again.

"Shawn, just go. Don't worry about the exam."

What on God's green earth is happening here? Did she just say not to worry about the exam? I made her repeat herself at least three more times. "Okay, I'll go. Thank you, but I think I'm going to need you to put that in writing. Do you have an attorney that can draw something up for us to sign?"

I mustered up the courage to ask Dean if I could leave my rotation early on Friday to meet Karen at the motel and he didn't balk either. "Absolutely! Enjoy."

The moment I saw her, I began dreading the departure. Exhausted from the drive, and after getting settled into the motel, we took off for Main Street, Cooperstown, to find a place to eat.

The village was quiet so we easily found a small tavern and sat at the bar, mostly away from other patrons so we could snuggle up to each other. Escaping from the deeply grained wood that surrounded us, the slight scent of tobacco was diluted by the welcoming late summer breeze that offered itself through the screened door. After catching our reflection in the mirror behind the bottles of liquor, the bartender grabbed the remote that lay in front of us and asked, "What you drinking tonight folks?"

Giving a verifying nod to Karen, "Two seven and sevens, with lime, please. Tall."

"Coming up. I'm about to put on the Yankees-Royals game. Hope you like baseball."

"Sort of, I guess. Why? Is this a baseball town?" I asked.

"Ha! What gave it away? If you're interested, there is this museum down the street with a bunch of baseball stuff in it that you may want to check out if you have time."

As our drinks were placed in front of us, I said, "Babe? Did we make the right decision?" Looking at me somewhat stumped, I continued, "You're home. We're apart. I'm lonely and sad, but I know you're safe and with your family, so that is reassuring."

"We did," she replied. "I hate it too, but this needed to happen. Next week, you'll already be a third of the way done. I know it's hard, but it's kind of flying by, right?"

She was right. Next Friday, I'll take a test after completing my third rotation out of ten. It's crazy, but deserving of a celebratory toast.

After the clink of our glasses dissipated, we heard a deep, raspy voice from several seats away. "Pardon me. You, in the Red Sox cap. What are you celebrating, if you don't mind me asking?"

Over Karen's frosted glass, directly in my sight line from the darkest section of the tavern, a figure rose from his seat. Stepping into the next dome of light from overhead, the blur of his body came into focus and the clatter of metal cleats strode across the fissured and coarse wooden floor. My glass hit the bar with such precision as to cause a plume of whiskey to rise like a mushroom cloud. I swiveled my stool towards this majestic giant. A chorus of brass and tympani drums flooded my ears as the anthem to *The Natural* filled the room. A tattered, short-brimmed Yankees cap, high onto his forehead, abutted this man's thick brow. The emblem, tanned with a season's worth of clay, was still recognizable. From neck to knees, baggy white pants with navy-blue vertical pinstripes fought to thin this man, but were failing. Using the back of my chair for leverage, he climbed upon the barstool next to me. "I couldn't help but notice your Boston Red Sox cap. The Sox should have never sold me to the Yankees in the winter of 1920. Because of that, I had no choice but to curse your team, and the curse endures."

Am I looking at a ghost? I turned to Karen on my right, wondering if she could see him too. I glanced at the figure, then back at her. I panned the pub. Surely, someone else had noticed him. Removing a nearly translucent white linen cloth that was slung over his shoulder, the bartender began drying a glass. I caught his eye as he pitched me a curious smirk. *Yes, he can see him. Good, I'm not losing my mind.*

"Buster," he introduced himself as he extended his palm.

Grasping it, I immediately knew what a thirty-six-inch hickory bat felt like. "Shawn. And this is my fiancée, Karen."

"Nice to meet you. You're here for the Hall of Fame?" he asked.

"Yes. Well, Karen and I are sort of having a bit of a temporary long-distance relationship right now, and until an hour ago, we hadn't seen each other in about a month. I love baseball—have never been here, if you can believe it—and so Karen, who at least pretends to like baseball, suggested that we meet here. And, holy shit, the resemblance to Babe Ruth is stunning. Obviously, you know that. Do you work for the Hall?"

He allowed me to catch my breath and said, "No. I'm a diesel mechanic from Ohio. About ten years ago, my daughter saw a picture of the Bambino in a *TV Guide* and thought the likeness was uncanny. Before long, I became associated with a management group, and here I am."

"So, this is what you do?"

"This is for fun. I still work. Been married to Cecile for over forty years. The kids don't understand, but men like you who cherish history and collect memories, well, that's who this is for."

"And to be clear, I don't hold you personally responsible for the Curse." Since the Red Sox have not won a World Series since 1918 (before they inexplicably sold Babe Ruth to the Yankees) they are said to have been cursed.

Chuckling, he said, "What will it take to break that, not that I will let it?"

"Your Yankees have the second-best record in the American League right now. My Sox are a couple of games out of a Wild Card spot, so it ain't happening this year," I said, rolling my eyes. "Listen, it's a sluggers' game now, right? McGuire? Sosa? What they did a couple of years ago… that's where the game is now and where it is going to stay for the foreseeable future, so the Sox need a couple of big bats. I'm talking Hall of Fame hitters, back-to-back, three/four in their line-up, but it has to happen while Pedro is here. If they do that, your Curse will get reversed. Mark my words, Buster."

He reached into his back pocket and pulled out a baseball card. It was him, dressed just as he is beside me. "That will never happen. Not on my watch, but I do wish you luck." Collecting a pen from the bar, he signed the card "Buster the Babe." As he lumbered off towards the exit, we could hear several patrons calling out, "Night, Buster!" The now-familiar march of his cleats on the hardwood dissipated into the street. His silhouette visible through the windows, the great Bambino's pinstripes faded around the corner.

The following morning, after grabbing a bite at the Doubleday Cafe, we all but jogged to the Hall of Fame as it prepared to open. "Karen, we talked about this. We do not stop and look at anything, nothing, no matter what, until we get to Carlton Fisk's plaque, remember?"

Grabbing her hand and weaving my way through the crowds, I pulled until her feet were dragging, like a child searching for Santa at the mall. "There he is. Hon, that's my boyhood idol's Hall of Fame plaque. We're here. He's here."

It took Karen several attempts to break my stare until she could convince me to take some pics. Once I filled over half the memory card on the digital camera, I said, "Okay, as far as I'm concerned, we can leave now. My trip is complete." I was being facetious, of course, although I don't think I entirely convinced Karen of that.

After finishing up at the museum, we walked to Doubleday Field— the place where legend has it, the first baseball game was played. It was named after the inventor of baseball, Abner Doubleday, a Civil War hero who was credited with creating and developing the game in 1839. That's largely inaccurate, as baseball's origins predate that by many years. It is thought to be derived from two English games from the late 18th century: rounders and cricket.

On Sunday, we hit all the memorabilia shops downtown. As we entered the first one, a gray-bearded gentleman in an old pair of denim overalls almost long enough to reach his Birkenstocks, politely greeted us. I returned the greeting, reflexively waved, caught a glimpse of his coffee-stained teeth, then froze. He acknowledged I was peering over his head and turned to look up onto the peg-boarded wall behind him. "He was just inducted, you know?" The man announced.

Karen, having arrived back at my side, said, "Oh, shit."

"But I guess you knew that, since you have that Sox jersey on. Number five? That's Nomar, right?" he offered.

I didn't move. I wasn't trying to be impolite. He looked back behind him, then back at me and Karen.

Fixated on this framed two-foot by three-foot photo, he provided the historic details. "That is Fisk's walk-off home run from game six of the '75 World Series, but you probably knew that too."

I had no saliva in my mouth, but I attempted to swallow.

"Oh, shit," Karen muttered again.

"Excuse me? But um, is that signature real?" I asked.

"Yes. It is number 53 out of 1,975 that he signed when he was here during his Hall of Fame induction ceremony back in July."

"Okay. Hey, Karen?"

"Oh, shit," making it a trifecta.

Whispering her direction, "I don't care how broke we are, or how much that costs, I am going home with it."

And with one credit card signature later, I did.

And so, like hitting the game-winning home run in game six of the World Series to losing game seven the following night (speaking of the '75 Sox), I had just gone from complete euphoria to having to leave Karen.

"Don't make me go back. I'm not ready yet."

"Shawn, I didn't realize how hard this was going to be for you."

"I didn't either, but now that I know what it's like to not see you for an entire month, I don't know if I can bear doing that again."

"Hey. Your third rotation ends this week. You're almost there. *We're* almost there. You got this."

September 7, 2000, Thursday.

[3 days since last entry]

I snuck out during lunch break to sit in my car where I had left my recorder because I wanted to tell you about a patient encounter.

A man in his forties came in for a blood pressure check. When I walked into his room, he looked at me rather befuddled. "I know, I know," I said. "People aren't expecting to see me. I'm Shawn, a PA-Student. Is it okay if I get started with you?"

"But I was supposed to see Dean. He's been managing my blood pressure for ten years."

"Dean will still see you. He's down the hall finishing up with his previous patient and asked me to come and see how you were doing. Is that okay?"

"You're a student?"

"Yes. A physician assistant student."

"So, you're not a doctor?"

"No, but neither is Dean."

"I think he is," the patient said, now perhaps confused.

"He's a PA, and that's what he's training me to be."

With some reluctance he agreed, but only if I promised him that he would see Dean too.

After the pinkie-swear ceremony was over, we chatted about his blood pressure and medications. I completed a brief exam, and the only abnormal finding was that his entire right lung exhibited wheezes. The old stench of a Winston throughout the room and the pack rolled up in his sleeve were dead giveaways that he was a smoker. "How long have you smoked?"

"Well, I didn't start until after high school, so, I don't know, twentyish years?"

"On average, how many per day during those twenty?"

"Pack and a half, I'd say."

The math was easy. Medical math is not always as simple as calculating pack-years (average packs per day multiplied by years smoked), but this is one math problem that even a third-grader could do. "So that's over thirty pack-years. I ask because you didn't come to us today with any sort of complaint indicating you were sick, but I hear wheezes from your right lung. Your left lung is completely clear, and that is a bit concerning to me."

He admitted to me he had been congested with a productive cough, but denied hemoptysis (blood-tinged mucus produced during coughing). He wasn't short of breath and had no history of asthma or regular inhaler usage. There were no classic symptoms of infection such as fevers or chills.

"I feel fine. I've been coming here a long time, and no one has ever told me I wheeze. Can you go get Dean, please?"

Right on cue, Dean knocked and came in. In front of the patient, he asked me to give him my full assessment.

After I presented my findings, Dean rechecked the patient's blood pressure and gave a listen to his chest. "I agree with Shawn. If you had bronchitis, both lungs would typically be affected. With pneumonia, we'd usually find a fever, or you might have some shortness of breath. Shawn suggests you get a chest X-ray because of your smoking history, and I agree.

"Well, okay," he timidly approved. "I guess you're training this guy pretty good, huh?"

"Yeah, Shawn knows his stuff. When he gives me a report, I listen, and I always follow-up on everything. He's doing a fantastic job here and today is his last day with us."

And with that, I'll never know what that patient's X-ray showed or what happened next.

I'm pulling out of the parking lot. That's a wrap on rotation number three. Learning under Dean was a tremendous honor. Every person who encounters him, whether as a patient or colleague, has nothing but praise for him—and rightly so. Unless something changes, I will probably take him up on his offer to write me a recommendation when I apply for jobs.

This morning, he had asked me to arrive early so we could review my evaluation without disrupting patient appointments. One form had fifteen questions. The preceptor must choose between five ratings: unsatisfactory, below average, average, above average, or outstanding. My eval was about half "above average" and half "outstanding." His final grade for me was a 90. Now that I'm contemplating a master's in emergency medicine, I am back to emphasizing grades, so I'm a little disappointed about the 90. It's stupid, and I'm disgusted with myself for falling back into this mindset, but here I am. It's ridiculous. Sitting in my car, I'm crunching the numbers with a scientific calculator to determine the mark I need on the Recall Day exam to achieve an A. I can't go back to doing that. I missed eleven days of reading during this rotation and have only three days to catch up.

Time to lace up the gloves and start this fight again.

18

ROTATION #4—
INPATIENT MEDICINE

September 11, 2000, Monday.

[4 days since last entry]

I studied for the Outpatient Medicine exam during the final three days of my last rotation, reading for seven hours each night and doing one hour of board review practice questions. Those eight hours wouldn't start until I arrived back at my apartment each of those nights. Despite the investment, I only scored an 80 on the exam. I got what I deserved. I'd love to tell you I'm over it, but I'm not. I don't know if I'll ever be able to break free from this obsession with grades. Despite a temporary reprieve, the earning of a master's degree has reignited my previous state of insanity.

Friday afternoon, as is customary, I placed a call to my next preceptor. Sounds like a very nice gentleman. Can't pronounce his real name (Srikarthikeyan), so I hope he has a nickname.

The usual butterflies fluttered around in my stomach all weekend, despite Taylor emphasizing that my new preceptor is a great guy. She told me he is known as the Golden Child (can't derive a nickname out of that) because he is so bright. Fantastic. I'll grab my hunter-orange dunce cap and jump to the front row during rounds. That way, there will be no question who should receive the bulk of the pimping questions.

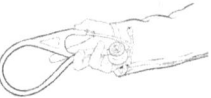

I was worried for no reason. Smoothest first day ever. The Golden Child is golden (and goes by his first name, Amrit), but it helped that I ended up tagging along with Marianne and Jeanie, two PAs that graduated from RTC a few months ago. They're on the hospitalist team and swooped in to take me under their wings. Their capabilities astonished me, especially considering they have only been employed as PAs for a few weeks. Marianne and others told me my preceptor is a tremendous teacher and to always do the reading he recommends. I was assured that if I stay the course, do those readings, and trust the process, I will end up where I should be.

That said, Jeanie warned me, "When you least expect it, he *will* ask you what you learned from the readings. This could happen during rounds, at the nurses' station, a luncheon, or in an elevator. He will dedicate time several days per week to meet with you privately for discussions.

So, this guy enjoys teaching and doesn't seek to intimidate or humiliate? We'll see about that.

September 13, 2000, Wednesday.
[2 days since last entry]
Three days have passed and I am hating this inpatient rotation. The complexity is terrifying, and I detest the lack of predictability. It's not for me. I will gain valuable knowledge, but the menial scut-work tasks are miserable. It's horrible sifting through paper charts (when you can

finally get your hands on them); attempting to translate the chicken scratches of hundreds of different medical personnel is impossible.

Hospitals are nothing more than three-dimensional escape rooms. Every corridor looks the same. Doors lock behind you. Not all elevators lead to the floor you want. Furthermore, jockeying with other students and residents for the experience to perform procedures is as unappealing as a three-day-old potato salad left on a picnic table in Georgia during August. No thanks. I'll pass.

Before I left today, I was talking to Dr. Amrit in a hallway when a resident approached and asked, "Hey, either of you two good at hearts?"

Dr. Amrit didn't seem to recognize this physician. "What do you need?"

The young doctor insists, "You must come hear this for yourself," gesturing only to me.

Dr. Amrit and I followed him into the room of a recently admitted patient in his sixties. The only information he provided was that he came to the hospital with a fever. The resident closed the door behind us. "Take a listen."

I opened my mouth wider so the ear buds of my stethoscope would sink deeper into my canals. Squinting, which always makes people hear better, I looked to the ceiling and crinkled my nose. My face said, "*Holy shit!*" My brain brought up the image of a chart I had once made of all the abnormal heart sounds. It was buried in a small black leather-wrapped binder in my coat pocket. I understood it would take years of regularly referencing that chart before I might put it to memory. I wondered if I could access it without being detected while it was Dr. Amrit's turn to listen.

Switching positions with Dr. Amrit, I reached into my pocket and allowed my hand to rest on that pint-sized binder, waiting for the perfect opening to extract it, or hoping the data on the page would magically transfer to the decoding centers of my brain.

"He's also got CLL," the resident added, as if the patient's form of leukemia was a piece of the puzzle that was going to help us solve the mystery of the unusual heart sound.

When everyone had completed their turn at the man's chest, I was the one being stared down. *Oh, right, I'm the student here.* Cutting off the comedic pause of the doctors waiting for me to say something impressive, I gave it my best shot. "That might be the first time I've heard an S-three gallop." (That's a sound linked to high atrial pressures, often found in heart failure and dilated cardiomyopathy.) "But there is also a constant high-pitched scratchy noise in the background. I don't know of a murmur that sounds like that." That's all I offered. Would it be enough to impress them? Are they looking for a diagnosis, something more specific, a plan?

Nodding, Dr. Amrit confirmed. "That's an S-three. Good job. That scratchiness is a pericardial friction rub. Unless you work in an ICU or cardiology practice, you may never hear one of those again."

"A friction rub? Man, I hadn't thought of that. Okay, but what do we do? Do you think it's related to his CLL, or his fever?" I asked.

Now verified to be an intern, the doc who recruited us into this patient's room announced, "We're getting an echocardiogram and cardiology said they'd be up in about an hour."

Dr. Amrit instructed me to review the patient's chart, do some reading, follow-up on the echo results, and try to be nearby when cardiology arrives. The resident grabbed the chart from this patient's breakfast tray and handed it to me.

I scurried to an empty nurses' station and began my review. According to the notes, it appeared as though others had also noted an S3, but described it as an "odd murmur." Oh, good, I'm not the only one who didn't identify the friction rub.

September 14, 2000, Thursday.

[1 day since last entry]

It took getting into my first week of my fourth rotation to have my first run-in with a nurse. I was only expecting it because of the series of Dr. Robert Marion books that I had read years ago. Different era and circumstances, I suppose, but my senses had been on high alert anticipating a confrontation. Having at least some experience in healthcare, let me preface this by saying that I have the utmost respect and admiration for all nurses, especially the floor nurses who are in the trenches working long hours, often without a break and in understaffed hospitals. Society undervalues and underestimates their worth. This anecdotal scene I'm about to set isn't terrible. But when you're exhausted, in a new environment, and stressed as a student, even a mosquito bite can make you lose your cool.

I grabbed the chart of a new patient I was going to begin following and headed for a designated area where clinicians gather to write notes and orders, only to find that every seat was occupied. I noticed an old-fashioned metal swivel stool being neglected off in the corner beside a document shredder. Since it was curiously vacant and I could use the shredder as a desk, I plopped down and began my work. After finishing a SOAP note, I flipped through the chart to find the order's tab. I'd just taken a sip of my coffee when, above my left ear with the strength of two megaphones, I heard, "It's over here! This guy has it!"

Startled, I inhaled reflexively, aspirating my coffee into my lungs. I coughed and gagged for several minutes while surrounded by unsympathetic staffers in scrubs and white coats. Not a single one of them looked up from their charts to assess me. Lacking any empathy, like the rest of the crowd, this nurse, who direly needed the chart I possessed, continued to tower over me, arms crossed, now impatiently tapping her clog on the tiled floor.

Judging by her expression, you would've thought she'd been searching all of greater Rocksville for this chart since before smoking tobacco was considered a healthy habit.

Once able to breathe again, I said, "Sorry. Do you need this chart?"

"Who? Me? No. I'm good. Take your time."

I recognized the sarcasm. She continued to hover, tap, and stare, so I finished out my orders. "Do you know where Dr. Burke is? I need his signature on these." She didn't move or acknowledge me, so I tucked the chart under my arm and left. *Wanna be that way? Okay. I'll play.*

Excusing myself from the makeshift workstation I had set up, I ran into Dr. Burke down the hall as he was leaving a patient's room.

After attaining the co-signatures, I roamed the floor for a bit longer, frequently passing by the nurses' station. With each lap, I made sure to display the chart that she needed, one time, even carrying it like a waiter holding a tray of drinks above their shoulder. After my fourth orbit and many frigid stares, I decided to end the torture.

Hoping for a cooler head, I snuck up to where she was sitting. "Are you Shauna?" I had learned that Shauna was my patient's nurse, and sure enough, "Shauna" was on her ID badge. No response. "Well, your badge says you are. I'm sorry that your hearing aid batteries have died. I'm Shawn Roussin, a PA student. I've been following Mr. Johnson and have a stat CBC order that Dr. Burke just cosigned. We need it drawn right away."

Not looking up, "Oh, my God. You're so smart. You know that stat means right away. Thank you for clarifying."

"His crit came back at twenty-four. It was thirty-one when he got admitted two days ago. If it drops again this afternoon, we're transfusing. Oh, and to clarify, you know that twenty-four is less than thirty-one, yes?"

"Got it. Twenty-four is bad." Still refusing eye contact, she held out her hand expecting the chart. I set it down beside her and began walking away. Not exactly from under her breath, I heard her say, "You can't just take charts and leave. There is an area for charting. Use it like everyone else does."

"Sorry. I assumed it would be sexual harassment if I sat on someone's lap without their permission. Besides, I was in plain view. The location of my charting harmed no one."

"Don't do it again."

Bitch.

September 18, 2000, Monday.

[4 days since last entry]

Dr. Amrit asked me to see a patient this morning who had been admitted last night. He is a seventy-one-year-old male who had gone to his PCP (primary care provider) on Friday with several complaints:

lack of coordination, loss of peripheral vision, worsening golf game (was slicing every shot), left leg and arm weakness; he had also lost confidence in his ability to safely drive a car.

His PCP was able to get a head CT completed by the end of the day and it showed a 6 cm mass with 2 cm of surrounding edema in his brain. Since he was to undergo a more extensive work-up early in the morning, they were able to get him a private room in the hospital last night.

The case seemed overwhelming. The simple task of writing a daily progress note, which I had been doing for months, was unnerving. I was certain it would be the most challenging case of my early training.

I slipped into the patient's room to find that his bed was empty. The aroma of fresh hospital coffee wafted over my face. Natural light was pouring in through the window, settling on a fully opened newspaper being held by a gentleman sitting in a recliner. "Excuse me? I'm looking for James?"

"You found me."

This guy didn't appear sick. I was expecting a frail, gaunt, jaundiced man lying in bed next to the Grim Reaper. Minus a stethoscope draped around his neck and a lab coat, he could've passed for an attending physician walking the very halls of this hospital.

"I'm Shawn, a PA student, and I guess I'm on the team that's going to be following you while you're here."

"With Dr. Amrit? He just left."

"Yes. He asked me to review your chart, introduce myself, and complete a progress note on you each day."

"Glad to have you aboard, Shawn!"

After a pleasant interview, I picked up on several neurological exam findings that had been mentioned in his PCP's office note and subsequent hospital admission note. Knowing where his mass was, coupled with his exam findings, it began making sense. He inquired why I seemed anxious and hesitant. As best as I could, I explained my fear of coming to talk to him, apprehensive by how I might handle such a complex clinical scenario.

"Maybe I don't truly understand the severity of what's going on, but I think I do," he reflected. "I only get upset when I see people around me getting upset. I don't want or need anyone's pity."

"Sir, you have every right to feel whatever you want, or nothing at all. I will not pretend to have any idea what it must be like to be in your shoes." I explained to him what I knew, what the plan for the day was, and encouraged him to remain positive, taking one moment at a time.

I could see his eyes welling up. His lips began trembling, and he moved his gaze back out towards the rising sun. "I'm not worried about myself. I am worried about my wife and children."

He began fidgeting with the buttons on his shirt, wiping invisible crumbs from his lap, and adjusting his socks unnecessarily. I found a ceiling tile to fixate on and began blinking rapidly, forcing back my heartache for this man and his family. After allowing ourselves to form this bond, I took a few slow, deep breaths.

"One moment at a time," he whispered. "One moment at a time."

September 19, 2000, Tuesday.

[1 day since last entry]

James had his MRI yesterday. We expected the results to roll in rather early today. In the morning, he was my first stop. Although he kept asking me if I knew anything, I didn't, and that was the truth. I needed to locate Dr. Amrit. He had to have known something by now, and I needed to be with him when the news was delivered. I paced the floor, passing the nurses' station about every thirty seconds. Where is he? Am I supposed to be somewhere? Is there a meeting or educational conference that I'm supposed to be fighting to stay awake in right now?

I couldn't take it anymore, so I bolted for the elevator. I'll locate radiology myself and find someone who can review the MRI with me. This family's life is being held hostage, and I'm not making them wait another minute.

Students don't know where anything is. They often appear lost because they are. I had become professional at disguising it. Because I wore the short white coat, I was generally treated as a legitimate target for pranking, so I played it cool and refused to ever ask for directions.

After several minutes of roaming the halls, I began observing personnel wearing scrub tops with the word "Radiology" embroidered across their chest. I knew that I had struck gold.

"Hey, Shawn! In here," a familiar voice beckoned. It was Dr. Amrit. "We just pulled up James's MRI. Take a look. You don't receive training in reading anything but plain films, right?"

"Correct," I nodded. "But give me a shot at it." The radiologist started hanging the sheets on a lightbox in sequential order. The lights were already at their lowest setting, though not approaching that of a photographer's darkroom. I know that the most sinister of brain masses is the glioblastoma, but I didn't know which features to look for on an MRI that would suggest the diagnosis. Since the MRI included contrast dye, the doctor could examine vascular structures and blood flow, but I also had no idea what AVM's (arteriovenous malformations) would look like.

My eyes scanned back and forth, up and down, sheet to sheet. "Here. The mass is obvious." I raised my pen to an image, the first one that appeared to show anything abnormal. With confidence, I scrolled, frame by frame, until the mass disappeared. "It's solid," I said sadly. "It's not vascular, right?"

"Correct," the radiologist agreed. "It's probably a glio. And I'm no surgeon, but I suspect that it's inoperable. It's too deep and too close to major blood vessels and other critical structures."

The radiologist began removing the images from the artificial light and voiced no further interpretation. Nothing needed to be said. My eyes met Dr. Amrit's, and he fled to the elevator. I followed, knowing he had one goal: find James.

Sequestered in a six-by-six rising room for what seemed like a lifetime, I knew my place in the hierarchy. We did not speak in the elevator until the bell chimed for our floor.

"You good?" he asked.

"I'm good."

Upon exiting the elevator, I had the privilege to walk beside my superior for the first time, but as we approached James's door, I let my stride lag and Dr. Amrit took the lead.

Needing the support, James had seemingly recruited everyone in his bloodline who was still living to be witness to his fate. His wife sat within an intimate distance, grasping his hands. As we entered, his children rose and went to their father's bedside. Two brothers were also present, his neighbors of over thirty years, four teachers he retired with, eleven athletes he had coached, five grandchildren, one of which was asleep on his chest, and his pastor.

Dr. Amrit took a spot at the foot of the bed and remained standing. Content to hang back as a passive observer, I fell at ease on his flank.

A hush came over the crowd and Dr. Amrit, unwavering, began. "We've just returned from reviewing your MRI images with the radiologist. The radiologist, Shawn and I agree that this appears to be a glioblastoma, as we had feared. It is surely the basis of all your symptoms. I have many calls to make. So long as you agree, things will begin happening fast, meaning someone from radiation oncology, neurosurgery, and oncology will get involved in the next twenty-four hours. With your permission, we will present your case to our weekly multidisciplinary team to decide on the next best course of action to aid in diagnosis and treatment."

The floor quickly became slippery with tears, none of which came from James. After answering a battery of questions, Dr. Amrit and I stepped back and began somberly weaving our way to the door.

As James's loved ones surrounded him, his body became obscured from my view, but the solar rays imposed their will onto his face from the only lonely window in the room.

September 25, 2000, Monday.

[6 days since last entry]

By the end of the week, I hope to be adopted by a team of about a half dozen physician assistants, and I don't mind at all. This will be a good thing. I've seen Dr. Amrit in passing, but that's it. He is spread way too thin. When he was present and engaged, he was fantastic, but lately he hasn't been fulfilling his commitment to me and RTC. I also wonder if someone had planned this, and if so, was Nadine involved? Did I do something or am I just paranoid?

I am failing to follow patients adequately here, and I'm unsure how to address this issue. On my own, I called several residents, attendings, and hospitalists, offering to help manage patients on their service. "I'm looking to work. I'll do whatever you need. Here's my number."

The hours ticked away. Nothing. By 6:00 pm, I hadn't seen a patient, done any exams, reviewed any test results, written a single note, ordered any labs, or fetched a single cup of coffee for anyone.

My ears were the only thing that served a purpose today, gathering intel. I listened to every conversation around me, whether it was a dietician calling in orders for TPN (total parenteral nutrition = when all calories are provided intravenously), two interns standing in a hall arguing over the initial work-up for their new DKA (diabetic ketoacidosis) patient, or a third-year resident pleading his case to the gastroenterology attending on the urgency of an upper endoscopy. I just listened. There was nothing else to do. I was on my own.

Another day of this would require me to reach out to Nadine. However, before leaving for the day, I spoke to a PA on the hospitalist service and she put me in touch with Colette, the chief of physician assistants, who agreed to meet with me after rounds tomorrow.

September 26, 2000, Tuesday.
[1 day since last entry]
My meeting with Colette was brief, but productive. She had spoken with Dr. Amrit, who was very understanding and apologetic. He agreed to take on a more active role, but ultimately, I would be handed off to Colette and her team of hospitalist PAs. They typically only take a PA student every other rotation, and as luck would have it they were without one right now.

Colette told me she'd review the patients on their service and get back to me with a plan by morning. Until then, I tagged along with anyone who whisked me away somewhere. My first whisking was to the library with Jody, a PA on Colette's team. Her routine involves going there often, finding a secluded corner, and engaging in reading and research. She always carries blank progress note pages with her, the ones that go in the charts, and she'll write her notes in the library to escape the chaos of the floors.

After she presented her three patients to me today, we had a Q&A session. She asked me if I would've done anything differently and why. Some things she referenced were familiar to me, but accessing many of the details in my brain was challenging. When we were done, we headed upstairs, found each of her patients' charts, and inserted her completed notes.

I need more of this and I'll soon have it. Colette caught up with me before I left. I learned that I'm going to have three patients starting tomorrow. She gave me a synopsis of each so I could focus my reading tonight.

September 28, 2000, Thursday.

[2 days since last entry]

Today was the second day rounding on my three patients. The first day was uneventful. I had worked myself up for no reason, or maybe I was overly prepared. The team took it easy on me while we were feeling each other out. Knowing one of my patients was going to be discharged, they asked me to see a different patient around 2:00 pm. She was in her nineties with severe dementia. She was asleep when I arrived, and I tried like hell to wake her up to see how she was doing, but she wouldn't budge. Through the curtain, a voice yelled out, "She doesn't talk!"

Well, she needs to. I have a note to write. Shaking her a bit and getting right up next to her ear, I said, "Good morning!" Silence. "Good morning!" Still nothing. Now loud enough to drown out an oncoming marching band, I tried one last time. "Good morning!"

"I told you, she doesn't talk!"

"Okay. Yes, I heard you." *Shit, is she still alive? Her color is good. Her chest is rising and falling. She's so thin and frail that I could see* her carotids trying to bust through the skin on her neck. These signs are compatible with life. Last resort was a sternal rub. Still no response. What the hell is going on? I ran out to the nurses' station and found Colette writing a note at the counter.

"I need help. My patient won't move or wake up. I yelled at her and did a sternal rub, but she didn't flinch. Neighbor says she doesn't talk. She looks fine. Has a pulse. Breathing. Can you come check her?"

Colette dropped her pen and headed down the hall, in no rush. "You just need to agitate her; piss her off. Keep pushing and prodding and they'll wake up. They always do. That's end-stage dementia for ya."

Disrespectful of her near-vegetative state, Colette hoisted her off the bed and transitioned her to the recliner. The patient's lids lifted and her eyes widened. Colette said, "Good morning!" and the patient lit right up. "Sometimes words don't work and you just need to force the issue. Don't give them any options."

Colette removed the lunch tray lid to find that nothing had been touched. She settled beside her, grabbed the Jell-O, unwrapped the white plastic spoon, placed a napkin on the patient's chest, and began feeding her. She reached for a mug on the tray and handed it to me. "Go to the break room and put this in the microwave for a minute."

When I returned, Colette took the mug back and removed the cover. The slightest hint of steam escaped. Colette brought the mug to her lips and let the broth make contact, as a young mother would do when checking the temperature of her child's baby food before starting the engine to the make-believe airplane. "Perfect." She put the lid back on and slid a straw into the center. For the next fifteen minutes, Colette sat with this woman and fed her while I admired this simple act of kindness.

September 29, 2000, Friday.
[1 day since last entry]
I was cruising through my eleven-hour workday until about 2:30 pm when I was instructed to go to the ER and admit a twenty-eight-year-old female with recurrent pancreatitis. It should've been

straightforward, but she was born with a congenital defect of her pancreas called pancreatic divisum that hadn't been discovered until recently. Over the years, she experienced pancreatitis flare-ups that were alleviated with standard treatments.

In January, she had her first of three pancreatic ductal stents placed, but each one fell out. She had a "super-stent" inserted a month ago, but now it appears as though this has also failed. The story gets better. In the last three months, she has passed multiple kidney stones. The work-up revealed persistent hypercalcemia (high calcium), and shortly thereafter the doctors diagnosed her with hyperparathyroidism, so surgeons removed three of her four parathyroid glands.

Through all of this, the patient developed a dependence on morphine and hydromorphone, two powerful narcotics usually administered by injection or intravenously. Someone dropped the ball in managing these medications. The prescriptions were halted, and the patient went into withdrawal. That was around the time she began seeing a psychiatrist and received a diagnosis of bipolar disorder, so she was now on paroxetine (antidepressant) and gabapentin (a neurologic agent used for a variety of conditions). To treat her recurrent pancreatitis, the doctors have been administering TPN through a PICC line (an IV that can be left in for several weeks).

She was in the ER yesterday with a fever. Suspecting an infected PICC line that had reached its usual lifespan of six weeks, the ER removed it and sent it for culture. They gave her a shot of ceftriaxone (an antibiotic) and sent her home.

Today, when she arrived at the outpatient procedures department to get a new PICC line inserted, the doctors found she still had a fever, but now also had abdominal pain, vomiting, and diarrhea. So, they wheeled her to the ER for evaluation. By the time I arrived, most of her labs had come back. Her lipase (a pancreatic enzyme) was over 600. Normal is around 300 or less. Despite what she had been through, she was in good spirits and grateful, but understandably frustrated.

Although it took me nearly two hours from the time I arrived in the ER until I had finished my interview, exam, admission H&P, and orders, I had at least completed all of the work myself. I located one of the staff physician assistants to review everything. Having been at the hospital for ten hours, it was now 5:00 pm, and I realized I hadn't eaten or drunk anything all day, so I went to find some water, hoping it might subdue my massive headache.

Returning with a drink, thinking I'd be going home in about ten minutes, that staff PA pulled me off to the side and said, "You're not going to like this, but I need you to redo your entire admission note."

If my cup was made of glass, it would have shattered and left me bleeding. Without saying a word, I went and grabbed a blank progress note from a nearby stack.

"I'm sorry, Shawn."

"It's fine. This has to be done right. I'm the one who is sorry." As pissed as I was, that was the truth.

"Okay, come here. This is what I would do and here's why."

By methodically cross-examining that admission note, she made me realize it appeared as if a fifth-grader had written it. It was choppy, disorganized, and lacked crucial material. Although it wasn't my best work, it was exclusively mine. The tired, undernourished mistakes in that note made me think about the Bell Commission (a committee that evaluated the training and supervision of doctors, and developed a series of recommendations that addressed several patient-care and safety issues, even putting restrictions of the number of hours a physician can work in a day and a week), which New York had first adopted in the mid-1990s. It was a prominent feature in the Robert Marion book *Rotations*, although writing a poor note paled in comparison to the experiences of those interns in his book.

I took a moment to gather myself and then began. Half an hour later, I surfaced with a final product that I hoped would be worthy of a supervisory signature and insertion into the chart.

"Excellent, Shawn. That's what I'm talking about. Great job. I've got it from here. You go home now."

It was a relief to be set free. I needed a double-decker Advil sandwich right now, especially since I had weekend duties with Dr. Amrit to look forward to in the morning. I only need to round on his patients with him and write notes on the three patients that I'm following, one of them being Miss Pancreatitis. Once I'm done, I can leave, hopefully by noon.

One thing is for sure: I'm not accomplishing any reading tonight, but I am calling Karen to see if she got the card I mailed to her a couple of days ago. It features a bride and groom holding hands while wearing handcuffs. I thought it would be fitting since we're getting married one year from today: September 29, 2001.

October 3, 2000, Tuesday.

[4 days since last entry]

I'm getting tired of working with some of these residents who have chips on their shoulders, especially the interns—the first-year residents. They repeatedly go behind my back and change my orders. I'd appreciate a heads-up or sidebar conversation before they did that. When a resident spots the "S" after the PA student's name, they instantly label us "Captain Incompetent." They're not entirely incorrect in their assumption. At the end of my notes, I leave my contact info. If someone with more experience doesn't agree with what I've written, or God forbid, if they may want to collaborate, they could easily reach out to me for a professional conversation.

On Sunday, I went to Stalwart Memorial Hospital in Rocksville to visit my patient from a week ago, the one with the brain tumor. They had transferred him there to undergo surgery. The fact that it was operable is generally an encouraging sign when it comes to cancer. That hospital, with its associated University of Rocksville Medical School, covers 5.4 million square feet and has about 900 beds.

I'm trying to find a single patient. My investigation confirmed that he had his surgery on Friday, so I expected he'd be in an ICU. Most ICUs are like gated communities. Knowing this, and the fact that I did not have a Stalwart ID badge, I wore my short white coat and packed all my pockets with gear. On my chest was my shiny gold RTC name tag. I thought the uniform might serve as a secret password during my visit.

Arriving near the ICU entrance, I pretended to be looking up some medications on one of my pocket reference guides. Seconds later, two surgical residents, still wearing blood-stained booties, gained access. I snuck through the doors behind them. Acting like I had been there before, I strutted up to the counter. "Hello. I'm Shawn Roussin, PA student. I'm looking for James. My team took care of him across town before he was transferred here for surgery. I'm dropping by to visit. What room is he in?"

She turned to a woman at the desk. "The post-surgical guy in room twenty-one? He left this morning, right?"

"Left? No, he was transferred to the regular floor," the woman replied.

"Oh, okay." Turning to me, "Let me locate his new room number for you."

Amazing! This guy must be doing extremely well. Armed with a new destination, I set back out on foot. Lost in a hospital so enormous that it has its own zip code, the commute to his floor took about fifteen minutes. I found the closest nurse and inquired as to the room number for James.

"James? He's not on the floor right now."

"Is he having a test?"

"No. His family arrived a short while ago and since it was so beautiful out, they brought him outside."

"Any idea where? This campus is massive."

She pulled a map off the counter. "Here's where most patients and their families go," she said, circling a couple of nearby locations.

The first exit I escaped through led to a sunny courtyard. A paved path led to an interstate of walkways. Fall was consuming New York, so every leaf was taking on the colors of fire, and the breeze made them flicker. I looked for a wheelchair holding a man donning a white gauze turban.

Not thirty yards away, there he was. I approached from behind, came around the back of his chair, and stopped in front of him.

"Oh, my God! Shawn. Look, honey. It's Shawn."

I shook his hand, then squatted at the tips of his feet. His grip was unexpectedly strong.

"Thank you so much for coming by."

"I told you I would, but I've got to say, I thought I'd find you in the ICU. Instead, you're outside working on your tan. I guess things went pretty darn well."

"You're a man of your word. You are the spirit that kept me going throughout this entire ordeal. Oh, bless you."

His son chimed in, "Yes, so far, so good. We won't know too much for another day or two. He hasn't yet stood up, but Dad's mind seems to be intact, so we're probably most grateful for that right now."

I visited for a while longer with hearty conversations and funny stories. I felt so connected to him. James's appreciation was genuine. It's moments like this when I realize I am doing what I am supposed to be doing, even though I have a lot to learn.

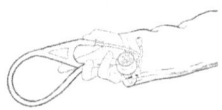

I had been waiting for Karen to call ever since our last conversation about a week and a half ago. The last time we talked was a catastrophe. I was not about to reach out to her first. She had felt angry because I had been hounding her about getting her ass moving on the wedding plans, and she didn't appreciate it. I didn't appreciate being unappreciated for attempting to help while doing my internship hundreds of miles away. It became a big mess, and I was in no mood to talk to her. I was hopeful the card I sent her last week would be an icebreaker. It worked.

We had perhaps the most exceptional conversation ever. That was a weight lifted off my shoulders. Neither one of us needed that hanging over our heads, especially since I'll be returning home in ten days to do my pediatrics rotation.

I called my next preceptor, Sharon, and from what I could gather, my daily commute from Portsmouth, New Hampshire, to Falmouth, Maine, will be just under an hour. Not great, but at least I'll be home.

Still no word back on the Master's in Emergency Medicine residency. If I don't hear from them by early next week, I'm going to reach out to them. Ever since I began getting serious about it, my excitement has skyrocketed. The ER is for me. I will never be employed by a hospitalist service. Never.

October 5, 2000, Thursday.

[2 days since last entry]

They call it constructive criticism. I call it a good old-fashioned ass-reaming. At 10:30 this morning, I got hauled into a room with Chief Colette and Alan, a PA I had spent the day with yesterday. After morning rounds, Alan sent me to the ER so I could admit a patient. Looking to avenge my previous admission note failures, I was going to pay a little extra attention to detail and knock this one out of the park.

When I hadn't contacted Alan by noon so he could review my work, he arrived in the ER, found me, and was noticeably perturbed. For whatever reason, he thought I was some sort of fantasy novel wizard who had been admitting patients and whipping up potions and spells for centuries. It was a very complex patient, and only my second attempt at an admission note while flying solo, but Alan was not cutting me any slack.

Colette explained. "Shawn, since you've come to our service, I've spoken to several of the providers that have had direct contact with you. They have assessed your work, and we all agree that it is of very poor quality. Yesterday, your admission note took you at least three hours. Other PA students that we have had during their fourth rotation, we expect full notes and orders to be completed in half that time, and with better organization."

For ten minutes, I wasn't allowed to talk while the assault continued. Alan began submitting his analysis. "Every minute of every day should be for learning. Whenever I see you, your nose should be in a book. There is no idling. You should be either writing, reading, tracking down labs, or looking at films."

Then, as I expected, he goes off on the HOPE trial. HOPE stands for Heart Outcomes Prevention Evaluation. It's a study that correlates reduced blood pressures with improved cardiovascular outcomes by using ACEIs (angiotensin converting enzyme inhibitors, a specific class of blood pressure–lowering medications). At one point last week, while rounding on our patients, a brief discussion about hypertension occurred. Alan brought up the HOPE trial and suggested that I read it.

Immediately, I removed the 5 x 7 mini-binder from my coat pocket, flipped to a page of notes that I had been keeping during this rotation, and wrote "HOPE trial—hypertension." I should've known that I was being set up for a pimp session. I should've gotten the hint when the following day as rounds began, Alan handed me a seven-page journal article titled: The HOPE Study.

In passing, Alan said, "If you get a chance, you should read this. It's no big deal if you don't get to it right away, but you need to know this." Like I said, it made my to-do list, but it didn't make my "must memorize before breakfast" list. Every damned time I ran into him over the next few days, he'd ask, *"Did you read HOPE? Reviewed that study I gave you yet? Don't forget to read that paper."*

With my tail between my knees, I seized the soonest opportunity to inject a rebuttal to Colette and Alan. "I have not read the entire trial front to back. I perused a few parts and read the conclusions, but that's all. It's on my list of readings to complete before my Recall Day test, but admittedly, because of the nonchalant way that Alan had presented it to us, I hadn't put it at the top of my list, and for that, I apologize. Had Alan been clear and said, 'Shawn, go home and read this tonight because you and I are going to discuss it tomorrow,' I would have."

I think Colette and Alan heard what I was saying, but I felt the need to continue my defense. "Guys, I read about my patients' conditions every night. I'm the first one here each morning so I don't have to fight for possession of the charts with thirty other people, risking not being prepared for rounds. I also have rotation-specific objectives that I'm studying, as well as trying to complete a few practice board questions each night. I know you remember what it's like to be a student. Neither of you is that far removed from your training. I am sorry that I am failing you. What can I do better?"

I'm not sure if I was patching up cracks or unleashing a flood, but I think it was the latter. I don't mess around. I arrive early, take quick lunches (if at all), and leave late. My first two weeks were all messed up because my preceptor was a ghost. Despite advocating for myself and talking to Colette and Nadine, I haven't been able to find my groove here. I feel like an outcast, a burden, a footnote.

Just when I thought the meeting was concluding, Colette kept browbeating. "And we noticed you skipped grand rounds last week. That is not allowed, and we have never received an explanation." Grand rounds are meetings of hospital personnel to share clinical expertise, experiences, and discuss topics of interest to help improve patient outcomes. As a student, missing them is a sin, punishable by public hanging.

"I slept in because I had a fever, headache, sore throat, muscle aches, and lesions all over my gums. I hadn't slept for two days and almost didn't come in at all. I loaded up on ibuprofen and Tylenol, and got some throat spray. Since we had agreed to keep Dr. Amrit as my primary contact, I called him that morning and left him a voicemail."

Alan says, "Well, it's not a good look. Dr. Amrit was the main presenter at grand rounds and his student skips it…"

Oh, shit! I didn't know he was presenting a topic. We weren't handed a schedule. We just know where and when it occurs each week, and that there's a free lunch spread. "Well, Dr. Amrit didn't mention anything to me about it when we bumped into each other down in radiology. He said he got my message and asked me how I was feeling."

"That's fine," Colette agreed. "But he is increasingly concerned about your effort."

Now I'm getting fired up. *How the hell would he be able to evaluate anything that I have done in the last week or two? I don't see him cosigning my notes. We don't have educational meetings anymore. His absence and subsequent removal as my preceptor due to lack of time speaks volumes. You want me to believe that he's voiced concern over my effort? Prove it.*

The pressure is going to be on me from here to the finish line. I will get here earlier. I will skip eating. I will only drink if someone makes me. I will stay later than the custodians. I will find a urinary catheter, insert it each morning, and attach a bag to my leg. I'll wear an adult diaper and apply cologne to mask the smell of shit in my wake. Game on! I got the shaft here and they know it. Lack of effort? Bullshit!

With sincerity, I tried to resolve matters. "I do honestly appreciate you sitting down with me today. And I am grateful all of you stepped up when called upon. I know they put you in a difficult position, but also please understand my side. This rotation has been abominable, disorganized, and has lacked any semblance of consistency. It's been the complete opposite of my previous three rotations. It's important we all learn from this. So, where do I stand?"

"Stand? What do you mean?" Colette said.

"Like, if you're assigning me a grade right now…" They are going to fail me, probably out of spite, but I wanted to afford them the freedom to say it to my face and not cop out by simply writing it on an evaluation form that would get mailed to RTC after the rotation ends.

"Average. You have a chance to be average," she said, and Alan gave an agreeable nod.

Colette began collecting some things from her desk. Alan placed his pen into his coat pocket, they both backed up their chairs, and rose. I shook their hands and thanked them again.

I haven't done anything average since I started this quest six years ago. That's not how I roll. Was this a motivational speech? Do they really think that? Did Nadine put them up to this? I can't imagine that. No way. Average? A *chance* to be? I guess that's a C.

Look at me. What a surprise, worrying about grades again. The grade they assign counts for two-thirds of my rotation grade. If they give me a C, I'll need a 100 on that Recall Day exam to get a B for my final grade, which is not good enough, but a C? Unacceptable.

Like John McClane in *Die Hard*, for the rest of the day, I was walking on shattered glass. It was difficult looking people in the eye. I figured the rest of the team all had at least secondhand knowledge of "the meeting." I was off my game, not that my game had been worthy. Colette and I had no communication for the rest of the day, making me question if I would even be returning tomorrow.

Later in the afternoon, Colette can usually be found in her office, either making follow-up calls or completing charts, so I sought her out just after 5:00. "Colette? Are we good?"

"Yeah, we're good."

"I took an ass-reaming this morning and I honestly feel that it all stems from a single incident that happened on a day that you weren't even here. Alan blows everything out of proportion. And I don't appreciate him accusing me of screwing around all day when he couldn't possibly understand what I do because I am hardly ever around him. He exaggerates everything. Do you really think that it took me seven hours to do a single admission note? Let's be serious here."

"Okay, tell me your side, because I agree: something doesn't sound right."

"It was 8:20 am and rounds had just finished when he sent me to the ER. I was writing my notes and orders by about 9:00. I was almost done when we had to attend the 11:30 meeting that lasted until 1:00 pm. At 1:30, Alan showed up in the ER and asked me what I'd been doing all morning. I told him I was doing what he told me to do, plus I had already seen my other two patients and written progress notes and orders on them. That wasn't good enough for him, I guess. He was pissed, and made sure everyone around us knew it. He had no interest in what I had to say. He just said, 'Alright, that's it. I don't want to talk to you anymore,' and he stormed off. He didn't review my work or cosign anything. Nothing."

She sat back in her chair. "Okay. Good to know. Let's just start fresh tomorrow."

They warned us. Everyone is going to have a bad rotation, maybe a couple. We're going to have great ones too. Well, I hate this one, and I'm not overreacting, which I often do. It's been fucked up from the start. I can't wait to leave this city.

October 9, 2000, Monday.
[4 days since last entry]
This morning, I got "the call" from Nadine. Guess what? We're having a meeting. Colette had contacted her about my "slowness." So, the next time Colette, or anyone says, "We're good," I'm going to assume they're lying.

Apparently, not only am I slow, but I'm also not very "kind." Not sure what that's about. Now I'm trying to plan a strategy. How do I act? Do I just keep my trap shut, let them slap me around? That would seem rather phony of me, but may end up being in my best interest. I only have two days left here.

Oh, frig, I just saw Bailey walking by in my rearview mirror. Is she joining us as well? I'm in for a real massacre, yet I still can't recall any "unkind" acts. Slow? Maybe. But unkind? I'm at a loss here. I don't know what's going on, but I smell a rat. Let's get this over with.

After I left my car, I went to the main lobby of the hospital and waited. In the middle of my fight-or-flight response, Nadine and Bailey walked in, waved and smiled, and I could do nothing but look away.

Ten minutes later, they came to escort me to the pressure cooker. I got off to a good start, explaining my perception of how this entire rotation played itself out, taking ownership of my lack of efficiency in completing notes.

They threw each accusation at me in the form of a question. It implied they wanted an answer, so I gave them one. Bailey interjected, "Now, I know you will not like what I'm about to say, but I want you to accept this as constructive criticism. I've noticed a theme with you, Shawn. Since I've known you, whenever someone presents allegations against you, you become very defensive. It comes across as arrogant and unprofessional; something you should work on."

I cemented my blank facial expression and created a perfectly placed pause. I thought, *That's fine, but I will always defend myself against allegations, and when I'm wrong, I'll take ownership of my actions. In this field, I am going to have to find better ways of concealing my stress reactions, but that is a process.* I couldn't find the courage to say it out loud. At this point, anything I muttered would be deemed arrogant and defensive, so why bother? Since speaking would gain nothing, I needed to just be agreeable to everything for the next forty-eight hours.

Then they brought up an "incident" from three weeks ago. In jest, I had casually made a statement that I never thought would be interpreted in the way that it was. Only Nadine and Bailey know that I'm potentially writing this book, and although they did not allude to that in the meeting, Nadine leaned into me and softly said, "I don't think this issue needs to be discussed ever again." I knew exactly what she meant, so I will honor that. They wanted me to know that they thought this was out of character for me, and they expected it to be an isolated incident. Although they believed it was misinterpreted, they acknowledged that it should have never been said. Not that what I said was right, but it pales in comparison to what you hear hourly from other students, docs, PAs, nurses, etc. But I can't say anything because I will appear defensive.

Even though it didn't feel like it, I figured we were done. Sure enough, Colette wasn't finished. "Another disrespectful act that we witnessed from Shawn occurred when he put a foot up on a desk during a presentation by one of our nephrologists."

Again, I chose silence over defensiveness. I thought, *Good grief. Seriously? Those are incredibly informal meetings attended by about a dozen people, usually in any open space we can locate. Some people are eating, chewing gum, and sitting on the floor. By having my foot on a desk, I was merely blending in.* But my grave had already been dug. I wasn't about to nose-dive into it. "Agree. My apologies. That won't happen again."

It was silly for me to believe that the meeting would adjourn then. Colette went to her next line item. "And another thing that won't happen again is missing grand rounds, especially when your preceptor is presenting. Right, Shawn?"

For fuck's sake! This woman wants me maimed, disfigured, or dead. When I told them my side of the story, Nadine and Bailey were mercifully more compassionate than Chief Colette, but still upset that I didn't inform them when I was sick. Or maybe they really wanted this meeting to end too.

To lighten the mood, while escaping to the door, Nadine sarcastically muttered, "And when someone asks you to read the HOPE study, just do it. Meaning, like, that day."

I directed an apology to each of them for conducting myself in a way that ultimately led to such a meeting. It truly was a valuable experience. Prior to departing, I felt it was important to tell them one last thing. "I sought out Dr. Amrit two days later to apologize for missing his presentation. He apologized for not informing me about his lecture and for passing me off to others after committing to mentor me. By the way, I'm a bit surprised he was not at this meeting. I assume he was invited, but I'm sure he was busy with other more important responsibilities. Prior to completing my final evaluation, I hope you seek input from him."

I didn't tell them what else he said to me. "Don't take this the wrong way, Shawn, but I hadn't even realized that you weren't at my lecture. Had Colette not informed me, I would have never known. Truly, I'm not bothered by this. I have had many RTC students. You are not even halfway through your training, yet you are doing exceptionally well. I've expressed this to Nadine and Colette, and I'll tell them again before we complete your final evaluation. Your assessments are well thought out and thorough. So, again, my apologies."

October 11, 2000, Wednesday.

[2 days since last entry]

My final eval went down today. Colette told me I had done excellent work and that I was a model student. She was happy with how my assessments and plans progressed, and how the "incident" proved to be isolated. Who is this person? Is this the same one I just sat in a meeting with two days ago?

She listed my confidence as a weakness. "It's good to be confident, but sometimes it comes across too strong, cocky. To others, it communicates arrogance." I never want to be off-putting like that. I honestly believe that I communicate with patients and families extremely well, but during this rotation I didn't always communicate with my team or faculty on the level that I should have or show them the respect that they deserve.

Choose your words wisely, or zip it. I don't care what grade they give me. It may not be as bad as I expect, but... It's over. I'm going home.

19

ROTATION #5—
PEDIATRICS

October 30, 2000, Monday.

[19 days since last entry]

I'll double-check, but this is likely my longest journaling hiatus. I have been home for more than two weeks, about to start my third week in pediatrics. I needed time for reflection. Let's face it, things were said during my last rotation that triggered my defense mechanisms. The reactions I had to criticisms of my performance required some serious scrutiny. It was humbling, and perhaps the most valuable experience of my training thus far.

I promised to never listen to any of my entries until I was actually ready to sit down and begin transcribing, but I couldn't hold myself to that over the last two weeks. Instead, I rewound all the tapes from my previous rotation and during my one-hour commute between Portsmouth, New Hampshire, and Falmouth, Maine, I simply pushed play.

I had entered some dark, angry places. My tone was often harsh and combative. When I wasn't muttering obscenities, some barely audible to the microphone, I was lashing out at everyone except the one person I should've been targeting: the man in the mirror. I was definitely coming across as arrogant, often defending myself when I was to blame. I dug myself into a deeper hole with every conversation. People were justified in throwing dirt on me. Slinging it back at them was unbecoming.

I don't know how to implement a fresh approach, but I must change. I am the student. People are sacrificing their time and energy for me and not receiving a dime in compensation. I admire them, but I need to respect them more. When asked to jump, I will jump. No need to wait to be told how high. I'll just make it as high as possible—and on the first try. And if criticized, I'll accept it and be grateful.

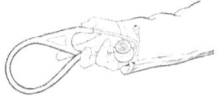

In pediatrics, when you're not seeing a patient with an earache, you're seeing one for a cough. When you're not seeing one for a cough, it's a sore throat. When it's not a sore throat, it's conjunctivitis. When it's not one of those, it's a mysterious viral exanthem (rash). Every fourth patient is a well-child check (WCC), whereby a detailed list of developmental milestones needs to be checked off for the patient to receive a clean bill of health. Failure to connect on a milestone could lead to blood draws on veins the size of dental floss, ordering imaging studies that will likely be difficult to interpret due to motion artifacts, or require a referral to a specialist in a distant metropolis, carrying with it a four-to-six-month wait. How my preceptor, Sharon, and all pediatric providers can remember every milestone for every single WCC visit is astonishing.

Pediatricians are typically present at the hospital for deliveries. They'll see a newborn in the office when less than a week old, then have a WCC at one month, two months, and four, six, and nine months.

Then again at twelve, fifteen, and eighteen months. When a child is two years old, they finally start coming in annually, although some might slip in a thirty-month visit. During each WCC, the healthcare provider tracks growth and development, discusses nutrition and safety concerns, advises and administers immunizations according to the recommended schedule, and performs a head-to-toe exam. At around age twenty-one, pediatricians often transition patients to adult practitioners.

So far, this rotation is amazing. I don't think my new attitude and approach is contributing to that. Providers here love having students, and parents are generous and usually accepting.

Coming from my last rotation, this is the perfect environment for me right now. It's laid-back, but admittedly a bit boring.

That's awful to say. I'm equally not excited about my upcoming site visit, which, because I'm hundreds of miles from RTC, will take place during a phone call tomorrow with Nadine.

Seven of my ten rotations are in New York, so you'd think that the team would just schedule my three site visits during three of those seven, but oddly, they didn't.

This morning, I sent her my presentation, but it's going to feel weird delivering it over the phone.

October 31, 2000, Tuesday.
[1 day since last entry]
My presentation wasn't as clumsy as I had imagined it might be. It went great. Before I even started, Nadine delivered some good news, as she called it.

"Well, Shawn, last night I opened your final evaluation from your inpatient rotation and I'd like to go over it with you now, unless you want to do your presentation first?"

"Hell no! Let's hear it."

"They gave you an eighty-five, and I know you won't be happy about that, but allow me to read you all the comments they provided before you fixate on the number, okay?"

An 85? Disappointed? Damn, I'm floored; stunned. I was expecting the equivalent of a D or worse.

Nadine rattled off remarks made about my performance: *"Shawn's knowledge base is appropriate. He has demonstrated a great rapport with his patients. He conducts himself in a highly professional manner. He handles constructive criticism well. He has regularly shown the ability to adjust to stressful situations. Throughout Shawn's rotation with us, he progressed wonderfully, was a pleasure to be around, and will make a fine physician assistant one day."*

I'm being pranked, right?

"Are you sure my name is at the top of that eval?"

"If you're Shawn Roussin, then yes."

"Nadine, I'm dumbfounded. I was quite literally expecting that I would somehow have to repeat that rotation after graduation. I can't believe they passed me."

"Sometimes your perceptions don't match reality, especially when attempting to function in high-pressure situations."

Okay, I know this will sound far-fetched, but now I'm wondering if this was all a set-up. Are other students having similar encounters with preceptors and meetings with faculty? Is this part of the curriculum? Is confronting and cornering us into stressful situations to gauge our responses, another type of learning experience they've incorporated? Would they really go that far? Are they that good? Maybe, just maybe.

November 3, 2000, Friday.

[3 days since last entry]

Sharon gave me a glowing mid-rotation review today. Everyone here is great, though I wish the patient encounters were more interesting. Maybe this is completely by design, but I'm only seeing simple acute visits and well-child checks. They seem to shield me from all other visit types.

Most kids don't need chronic diseases managed, and they aren't usually on two dozen meds, or have to submit to various screenings and interventions, but there has to be more to pediatrics than this.

The assigned readings I complete nightly convey a different tune. My exposure here is limited, and it's making me nervous about the boards, for which I have stepped up my game. I'm spending more time doing practice questions. They're heavy in those milestones, as well as acute illnesses, so the focus of the rotation seems to fit. I will trust that I am getting what I need here.

November 4, 2000, Saturday.
[1 day since last entry]
Karen and I did something fun today. Well, at least fun for me. On a whim, since it was about sixty degrees and sunny, I talked her into visiting different auto dealerships to test-drive cars. Although we had no intentions of making a purchase, we dressed up and concocted an embellished story about ourselves so they'd take us seriously. It worked like a charm. We started with a VW Passat. In deference to my practical side, we also drove a new Toyota Avalon, but it wasn't sporty enough for me. Then we hit a used car place where I took out a two-year-old Audi A4, then an A6. Oh, my! That A6 was money!

I want a nicer car so badly. If you could see some of the beaters I've tooled around town in over the years, you'd understand. My '90 Accord is sneaking up on 175,000 miles, and although it has been so damn good to me, one of the first things that I will do when I become a PA is reward myself with an upgrade.

I already have that first paycheck spent, although there is that wedding thing…

November 5, 2000, Sunday.
[1 day since last entry]
How do I say this? There is no place for smut in this book. Sorry to disappoint, although by now you should have figured that out. This is not going to be a young adult romance novel, but I will admit that this is the horniest I have been since I was a twenty-year-old musician living in Boston. This is absurdly different. This is a deep, driving,

paternal instinct. It's an incredible urge that I've never had before. The moment I hop into my Honda and head home each afternoon, I immediately start thinking about becoming a father. Okay, that's not exactly what I'm thinking about. I'm thinking about how quickly I can get Karen naked. I could certainly blame the absence of opportunity over the last ten weeks, but this happened in October last year, too, and perhaps the year before that.

What's different now is that if it were to *accidentally* happen, at least by the time a little Shawn or Karen were to arrive, we'd both be done with school and gainfully employed, so although it's not the right time, at least it's no longer the worst time.

November 8, 2000, Wednesday.
[3 days since last entry]

My preceptor, Sharon, wasn't in, but I volunteered to come in to the office to help the staff with whatever they needed, whether it was pulling charts or giving immunizations. Dr. Jordan was there and invited me to see patients with her. She gave me permission to join her in the exam room next door once I was done giving my current patient their vaccine.

After a light double-tap on the door, Dr. Jordan said, "Come on in." She introduced me to a man who appeared to be in his mid-forties. At the base of his feet was a car seat, and still strapped into the five-point harness was an infant, only a few months old. Lying on the exam table was a female teen, maybe one-hundred pounds with long, straight black hair. Her black trench coat didn't cover the dozens of holes in her jeans that were ragged at the heel.

Dr. Jordan asked the family, "Is it okay if he stays?"

I reached out to shake the man's hand. Unamused, he didn't reciprocate, but rather, glared at Dr. Jordan and said, "Um, no, that would definitely be a distraction."

This was my first experience with any patient not agreeing to have me present during an encounter, so I needed a moment to process it.

At the very most, three seconds clicked off the clock, then he brought his stare over to me. "I said, no. He'll be a distraction. Leave."

Well, alrighty then. I wanted to slap him silly and tell him to go to hell, but there is apparently a code of conduct agreement that I signed which forbids this, so rather than ending my career before it started, I abandoned the room.

Several staffers, who had just witnessed my entrance into the room were surprised to see me exit so quickly. One asked me what was going on.

"They kicked me out," I told them.

A nurse said, "We think there are three generations in that room. You saw the baby, right? Well, we're not sure if the baby is his daughter or granddaughter."

"Wait, what? That guy is like in his forties?"

"That teenager is his daughter. She and her mother, that guy's wife, were both pregnant at the same time and delivered their babies within a week of each other. I don't know which baby is with them. The funny part, or sad part, is his granddaughter is technically older than his daughter."

As you may recall, it took me two attempts to pass my data analysis course at RTC, so I was struggling with the fuzzy math. I started mapping out a family tree in my head but succumbed to confusion after the first branch.

I grew up in Maine. I love Maine. I would never disparage Mainers, but many people hearing this story would laugh and say, "Well, it's Maine. What did ya expect?"

Dr. Jordan was in there nearly an hour. When she finally exited, I slipped into her office so I'd be spared any eye contact with the gentleman. Dr. Jordan apologized for the guy, but did not provide any further details about their visit. It ticked me off at first, but I know I shouldn't take it personally.

Thirty minutes later, the next attempt at banishment occurred when I entered a room to see two sisters, Casey and Courtney, aged two and four. With the memory of my previous encounter still fresh,

I should have recognized the patronizing glare of the middle-aged mother. "I'm sorry, no. We need to see LeeAnn," she said, as if she had been forewarned of a student's presence. The office was a few people short, and every kid needed at least one vaccine today, so LeeAnn, one of the nurse practitioners, found herself well behind schedule soon after a shortened lunch consisting of two grapes and a wedge of cheddar cheese.

Trying to rationalize with the mom, I said, "Oh, you'll see LeeAnn. She's right next door finishing up and she didn't want you waiting any longer than you already have, so she asked me to come in and at least get started."

"Okay then," she yielded.

She informed me about the older one's recurrent left ear pain. The history was brief. Courtney had ear tubes placed a month prior, and the mother thought one had come loose. My exam revealed a normal right ear with a blue ear tube in its proper location, but excessive cerumen (wax) in her left ear. Specific for ear wax removal, I grabbed a small plastic curette from a clear jar next to the sink. "I'll need to remove some wax to get a better look because I can't see her eardrum. This may feel weird, or even tickle, but it won't hurt. I'll just need you to hold her still."

"No, no, no, no, no. That's not going to happen. If that needs to be done, LeeAnn will do it. No student is sticking anything in my daughter's ear."

Setting the curette down on the counter, I reluctantly conceded. "That's fine. I understand. Why don't we switch gears to Casey?" The younger child was also there with a complaint of ear pain.

My history questions were identical, and the mom was getting short with me. "I really don't know how much you're going to be able to help us here today. They've both had ear issues since birth. I don't want to go through their entire history with someone new. LeeAnn knows us. The last time we were here, we saw someone new who spent one second with her, looked in her ears and said that those were the worst ears she had ever seen, then put her on an antibiotic because it "tastes good." I'm not going through that again. I know you're a student, and I'm sorry. Please don't be offended, but I would really appreciate it if you could just leave and go get LeeAnn. I mean, you can come back in, but only with LeeAnn. Thank you."

I would not win this, not today, and not with this mother. I just nodded and reached for the door, wanting her to witness my disappointment.

"I'm so sorry, Shawn. Please don't take it personally."

"Not a big deal at all. Your time is valuable. I'll go wait for LeeAnn and bring her in when she is available so we can get you out of here."

I caught LeeAnn in the hall and gave her the rundown. She said, "Don't worry about it. I'm not surprised. I know exactly who that mother is. If she has to wait more than five minutes, she threatens not to pay or leave the practice, but she never does."

I decided to sit this one out so LeeAnn could try to catch up and get back on schedule. Meanwhile, I saw that everyone else in the office was becoming frustrated. Four clinicians were here today and three of them were a couple of patients behind as darkness was approaching. I resumed doing menial tasks, while staying alert for an opportunity to assist.

At one point, within earshot of everyone around the main work area, Nurse Debra asked, "When is your last day? Is it Friday?"

"No, it's next Wednesday, a week from today."

"It has been a pleasure having you here. We want to keep you. You're not allowed to go back to New York. You're staying."

"Well, thank you, Deb, but I'm the one who is grateful. Everyone here has been so welcoming and helpful."

"We talked at lunch yesterday. We're writing a letter. People only tend to write letters when they are angry or have negative things to say, so we need to send one that is nothing but positive. We appreciate when someone, especially a student, goes above and beyond, and their teachers should know that. This will be totally separate from whatever evaluation that Sharon has to do."

November 13, 2000, Monday.

[5 days since last entry]

As soon as I arrived at the office today to start my final three days, one by one, I tracked down every employee and asked them if they'd help me with a little prank. It was not a secret that I had baby fever during my entire rotation. Everyone played into it, and they knew how much it annoyed Karen. If a newborn was in the office, I was first to be notified.

I told everyone that I had swiped Karen's camera. She'll never know it's missing. The goal was to get as many pics as possible of me holding babies (with permission of the parents, of course), and then sneak her camera back into the case before I returned to New York. At some point—a week from now, a month from now, after graduation—Karen would discover the pics and be like, "What the heck are these?"

The office was more than willing to take part. We only had two newborns coming today, but the team was combing the provider schedules and creating a plan for tomorrow and Wednesday. My mischief has become the staff's top priority.

November 15, 2000, Wednesday.

[2 days since last entry]

I'm driving out of Falmouth for the last time. The photo ops were a success. Parents were enthusiastic about participating in the prank. Pediatrics was fun, and I really liked it. I'm not going to say that I loved it, but close.

Baby fever may have clouded my judgment. I've got a feeling my next rotation—number six: obstetrics and gynecology—will cure that. If it only makes it worse, I'll be back home again for rotation seven when I'm slated to do neurosurgery. Karen will again have to contend with my nightly advances.

Despite my long drive tomorrow, I'm hoping for a sleepless night, if you get my drift.

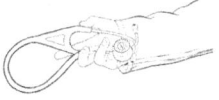

At the end of our freshman year, the RTC program faculty connected each of us with a sophomore mentor. That sophomore had a junior mentor, and so on. It's like a big brother, big sister relationship.

Lloyd, my mentor, gave me some extremely sound advice about a week before my first rotation, yet it wasn't until completing pediatrics that I could finally grasp what he meant. He said, "Be sure you can instantly recognize normal because you're going to see a lot of it. That way, when something abnormal appears, you won't miss it. You may not nail down a diagnosis on day one, but you'll know something isn't right, all because you became an expert in normal."

Thank you, Lloyd. I get it now.

20

ROTATION #6—
OBSTETRICS AND
GYNECOLOGY

November 20, 2000, Monday.

[5 days since last entry]

My last experiences in Rocksville were far from pleasant. I felt ill just reentering the city limits. Whatever I can fit in my Honda travels with me. I live out of suitcases and laundry baskets, and drag 100 pounds of books wherever I go. The weekend was dedicated to setting up my room and working out the nausea.

Today marks the halfway point of rotations. Number six will start this morning. I feel awful about how few journal entries I made during pediatrics, but it was rather uneventful when compared to the previous ones. Now entering OB/GYN, I have some thoughts linking the two.

During the pediatric rotation, there were four female patients with medical issues concerning their breasts or genitalia, but these patients (and their parents) refused to have any males present during the examinations. As a result, four unique learning opportunities passed me by. The first was a fourteen-year-old girl who discovered a breast lump. Like other visits, Sharon sent me in ahead of her. I was immediately met with "the look" from Mom, followed by the teen and the mom's eyes anxiously connecting. Apologetically, I was discharged from the room. I was discriminated against for being male—not because I was a student—which is completely understandable.

The second time, a thirteen-year-old girl had found lumps in her armpit and groin. This patient was with her dad. Multiply that "look" times a hundred, and you understand my challenge. "Hi. I'm Shawn, a PA student working with Sharon. She sent me in to get started, but she'll be joining us in a few minutes."

With a worrisome frown, the young patient's father says, "So, you'll be examining her?"

"Yes, but if any private areas are involved, I'll get a female in the room. We'll slide that curtain over and you can stand behind it, so long as your daughter is okay with that."

"I don't think that is going to happen."

Trying to put him at ease and convince him to let me proceed, I said, "I understand your concern. This is my sixth and final year of schooling—"

"I don't care," he interrupted. "No kid is going to be looking at my daughter's personal areas. Am I clear?"

And with that, I was ejected from an examination room again.

This scenario played out two more times. Here is something for all of you non-medical professionals to consider, and I mean this with the utmost respect: if students cannot get the training and experience that they need during these rotations, when thrust out into the real world, patients (and parents) should not act surprised when we aren't able to effectively assess patient complaints.

I suspect that over the next five weeks, I will do multiple pelvic and breast exams per day, but until this point, I've only observed three pelvic exams and performed zero.

Dan was at this site a few months ago and completed the same rotation. He relayed to me that he had a good experience, but warned about certain players to be cautious around. Tips like that are key to survival.

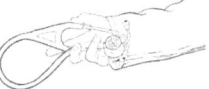

I didn't last two days back in Rocksville without needing to talk to Karen, so I called her last night. We talked for over an hour and I confided in her about some battles I had been waging. On Saturday night, my old band Pondering Judd had a CD release party—their first since getting back together with almost all new bandmates. Karen, my dad, my sister, Crystele, and new brother-in-law, John, went to the show. If I had gone, I'm unsure of how I would have handled it.

Music had always been my outlet. I can't say it was ripped out of my hands. I simply set it down and walked away, not because I wanted to, but because I had to. It still hurts. I dream of being back on stage, especially with P-Judd, and I hope one day that'll be possible.

The freshman fifteen is really a thing. Apparently, it's also a sophomore thing and a junior thing. I've put on forty-five pounds since starting at RTC. Nothing fits anymore. Buttons are flying off my pants. Belts are my saving grace. I don't dare bend over or squat. I'm one pound away from disaster. Tucking in shirts is hell. I'm envious of every person I see wearing scrubs.

We just relinquished our daylight savings, so my seasonal affective disorder will soon arrive, right on cue. After six years of full-time school and busting my ass every summer so I wouldn't have to work during the school year, I'm fucking fried. I need to be done. I want to be home. I can't live like this any longer. Yet now I need to step up my game and buckle down to prepare for the national board exam in April. Passing the boards early, before graduation, will give me an advantage in the job market.

There's no way I'll ever work in OB/GYN. That took one day to realize. I've never felt so uptight in my life. Urban areas provide regular occasions to interact with diverse nationalities and races, enhancing the learning experience. Of the ten women I saw today, seven were Latino, one was black, and two were white. Fifty percent of them were completely covered in hickeys, and yes, in places where clothes would normally provide cover. Despite their average age of twenty-one, not a single one of those ten were experiencing their first pregnancy. The twenty-nine-year-old was on her eighth, and with a fourth different father. Under social history, it listed "never been married." Only a couple of the patients I saw spoke English.

My preceptor for the day, Ellie, was amazingly fluent in Spanish. It must have been a job requirement. She was not timid either, throwing me right into the fire. She handed me the first chart. "Go see why she is here, but if you feel that she needs a pelvic exam, come and get me. You'll need a chaperone."

I quickly realized that I needed to ask all closed-ended questions. Any question requiring more than a single word answer would be met with a grunt, shrug, and shake of the head. The patient never answered "yes" or "no" with any conviction. My interrogation was over in less than two minutes.

Ellie was just standing in the hall. "That was quick. You nailed that one down already?"

"The only thing I'm sure of is that she didn't understand a single word I said."

After a quick laugh, I followed her in. She carried on in Spanish for a few minutes, then turned to me and said, "She's agreed to let you do the pelvic exam."

I went into panic mode. *Shit, shit, shit, shit, shit. I'm not ready for this. I don't wanna do this. Can I go home now? Is it possible for me to watch a few hundred of these first?* In my best professional colleague's voice, I mustered up a single syllable of my own. "Why?" It was a brilliant question; one she was probably hoping I'd ask.

Ellie explained. "She took a pregnancy test two weeks ago, and it was positive. We confirmed it with a blood test a few days later. She began spotting last night, so we're worried that she is having another miscarriage. You need to look to see if you can see any products of conception in the vaginal area and evaluate her cervical os (opening to the cervix) to verify that it is still closed."

And so, thirty minutes into my OB/GYN rotation, I had reluctantly completed my first pelvic exam. It turned out that neither of us saw any blood, so we set her up for an ultrasound and a quantitative hCG test to measure the level of a hormone that should be present during pregnancy. If the hCG is still rising (it usually doubles every forty-eight hours in viable pregnancies), then that would be good evidence the pregnancy is okay.

Repeat this similar scenario another nine times, and that sums up my day. Before leaving, Ellie asked, "Enjoy your first day?"

"Well, yeah. I thought it was great. You made me feel relaxed when I clearly wasn't, and you wasted no time in tossing me out of the frying pan. I needed that push."

"You know Dan, right? Did he give you a heads-up on anything? Good? Bad?"

I wasn't sure how to tackle this one. "Even if he did, it would not be my place to say anything. As a student, I try hard to not begin any rotation with presumptions. He told me he learned a lot and I would like it here."

"Really? I'm surprised he didn't say anything about how a couple of people treated him—pretty unfairly and unjustly, I might add."

"No. Not a word."

That was a lie.

November 21, 2000, Tuesday.

[1 day since last entry]

What a difference a day makes. My anxiety did not follow me to work today. Once I got the first pelvic exam out of the way, then nine more, I was freed.

I also met Jim, my assigned preceptor. He handed me a thick folder overflowing with papers. "Here. Read and study all this material. On your last day here, I'll give you a seventy-question exam. It'll count toward the final grade I give you for this rotation. It will be much harder than the RTC exam."

Dan had warned me about this and verified that his exam was much more difficult than RTC's. "And from now on," Jim continued, "you won't come in on Mondays unless I can find someone to take you, but I'll let you know the week before. I'm off on Mondays. What is your surgical experience?"

"I have a surgical technology degree and I've scrubbed cases in every specialty aside from open-heart."

"Sweet! On Fridays, we're usually in the operating room all day, but also cover the ER for any emergencies. Whenever we do a case together, I'll tell everyone involved about your background. They're more likely to let you get your hands dirty that way, instead of only holding retractors. Surgeons will ask you questions. I'll pay attention to your answers. They like right answers, if you know what I mean."

November 22, 2000, Wednesday.

[1 day since last entry]

Still no cure for my baby fever. Today may have made it worse. I examined a woman forty weeks pregnant. I could hear the baby's heartbeat using a Doppler and could feel that the baby's head was right where it needed to be: not breech. He was highly active and his kicks were visible from across the room.

Karen won't want to hear this report. I think she hopes this rotation will remedy the fever. It still might. After all, I haven't seen a delivery yet, nor have I witnessed any of those nightmarish situations that I recall watching on *ER* every week.

November 24, 2000, Friday.

[2 days since last entry]

First day with Jim, first case in the OR. It was an exploratory laparoscopy with an excisional biopsy for suspected endometriosis. A laparoscopy is when a couple of very small incisions are created, one for a camera and usually two others for long thin instruments. Endometriosis is a cyclically painful condition that occurs when the uterine lining grows on other structures outside of the uterus. I don't know if Jim had dropped any hints about my experience, but immediately I felt respected. The room had a reassuring vibe. Astonishingly, I received no pimping questions. It seemed apparent that the surgical technologist was fairly green, maybe even a student himself. It gave me perspective on how I might have looked a few years ago.

The day was about to get better, so I thought, but between cases someone from the department of surgery approached Jim and told him that the provider running the pre-op clinic (where they clear patients for upcoming surgery) needed to leave unexpectedly for personal reasons.

"Jim? Hey, sorry to have to ask, but we need you down in the clinic to provide clearance for two patients that are on the schedule this afternoon. Can you head down?"

"Ah, dammit, Jess. The next case is an abdominal hysterectomy and I never get to assist in those anymore. I was really looking forward to it. And I still have to go write post-op orders for the previous patient."

"Well, I don't know if I can find anyone else, and if I can't those cases will get canceled."

"Wait. I can send Shawn down." Then he introduced me, "He is an RTC PA student and a former surgical technologist. He's halfway through his training."

Turning to me, Jim said, "Would that be okay?"

As if I had a choice… "Jim, of course. Whatever you need me to do."

"Are you sure, man?"

"Just same-day, outpatient cases, right? I can figure it out. When does the first case start?"

Jess jumped right in. "An hour. Maybe sooner."

"Well, we better get moving then. Show me the way."

As Jess led, Jim yelled, "Just a brief note. Nothing fancy or extensive! You find anything questionable, you come find me in the OR and I will get down there as fast as I can!"

It only took a minute to weave our way over to the pre-op staging area. In my head, I let out a collection of curse words. *I've never done a pre-op physical or cleared anyone for surgery. What the hell did I just agree to?*

Jess opened both charts and removed a two-page form from each. These forms listed the clearance requirements, a standard practice for all surgical patients. Then she pointed to the rooms where the two patients were and fled the scene.

After looking at the basic blank forms, I thought I'd start by reviewing the charts and learning why these patients were even here. I hit the jackpot! Staring me in the face was a previous office visit note from their PCP, including a full social history, past medical history, family history, allergy list, and current medication list. This was basically going to be a cut-and-paste endeavor.

Pulling the curtain aside, "Hi, Clarissa. I'm Shawn, an RTC PA student. If you hadn't heard, the provider who usually interviews and examines you before they wheel you in, had to leave to tend to a personal emergency, so I volunteered to come down and get started. My preceptor, Jim, will come down, probably ask a few questions, and do an abbreviated exam as well. Is that okay?"

During my interview and exam, I could sense my awkwardness, so I reverted back to my pediatric rotation one-liners and jokes and it totally worked. The patient and I were laughing so hard that the tension in the room fizzled out.

After the exam, I stepped away and began completing the form. On the second page I saw the words "Breast exam." *No!* I didn't do one. I couldn't go back in there. Why was this a requirement? Is that really necessary? No way. She's only twenty-four. I'm not going back. I can't. Is Jim going to call me out on this if I leave it blank? Would he notice? Would he let it slide? I had to be honest on the medical form, so I went back in.

"Sorry, Clarissa. I need to apologize. I had no idea that a breast exam was necessary for pre-ops. I showed her the spot on the form as proof that I needed her to remove her bra and open her gown.

"Really? You're kidding, right? Fine, I guess. My bra is off. My gynecologist just did one last month. I need another one?"

She doesn't need a breast exam. "I'm sorry." *Could this get any worse?*

Yes, because guess what I didn't do… I failed to get a chaperone.

Nerves affect clarity of thought, and your reactions to them can be uncharacteristic. They have a place in medicine, but they must be expertly controlled. My nerves were on full tilt. I could feel her staring right at my face the entire time, like she was trying to catch me doing something inappropriate. I'm supposed to look for asymmetry, dimpling skin changes, and nipple inversion, but I just focused on the floor between my feet, wondering if that drop of sweat on my nose was going to make a sound when it hit the tile.

I never imagined a breast exam being clumsier than a vaginal exam, but this one was. If I never have to do another breast exam again, I'll be happy, but there was another one to do in fifteen minutes, so I needed to get over this fear—and fast.

The next examination was uneventful. It was probably the fact that the patient was about fifty, had delivered four kids, and didn't give a shit who saw what, who touched what, or who went where. Plus, I remembered to call in a chaperone.

Jim was impressed by my thoroughness, and grateful that I stepped up without hesitation. Throughout the afternoon, I gave him reasonably intelligent answers to his questions, and I felt as relaxed as I had ever been with any previous preceptor.

Still, I couldn't help but recall Dan's notable warning, similar to Ellie's, so I wondered what was lurking around the next corner.

November 28, 2000, Tuesday.

[4 days since last entry]

These three-day weekends are the bomb. I completed a ton of board review questions and nearly finished all my Christmas shopping. Next weekend will compensate for that. I am required to do a twenty-four-hour shift on the labor and delivery unit. I show up at 7:00 am on Saturday, and leave at 7:00 am on Sunday, so having Mondays off will be a saving grace. Morbidly, I'm kind of looking forward to that experience.

But right now, it is 4:00 am, and it is crystal clear why I don't ever want to go into any sort of specialty that requires rounding on admitted patients in a hospital: because it's 4:00 am!

I was asked to see two patients, examine them, write SOAP notes, and present them to Jim when he arrived. Additionally, he asked me to be prepared to give him a five-minute oral presentation on ectopic pregnancies (when the fetus develops outside of the uterus). I did the reading that he asked of me, extracted the highlights, organized them into a brief speech, then memorized it.

Unable to find either of those two patients, a wonderful nurse took pity on me. After the fourteenth time she saw me pass her in the hall, she gave me the correct GPS coordinates. According to her, one of the patients had been discharged the evening before. Concerned that this was some sort of trap, I verified this with at least three others on the floor.

This is awesome. I have at least an hour to see my one and only patient. No sooner had I walked into her room, and Jim shows up. We chatted with her and both examined her, then he told me to write a note and be ready to present her at rounds.

"Sure, no problem," I said. I was feeling good about this one. I even had time to go down to radiology and look at her X-rays from the previous morning since I couldn't locate the report in her chart.

Organizing in one of the smaller conference rooms for morning rounds, I nervously held my handwritten notes on an index card, and unbeknownst to me, the chief OB/GYN attending was sitting five feet in front of me. When my patient's name and room number were announced, I deferred introducing myself and started right in. Moments later, the attending slammed his fist down on the desk beside him. "Vait, vait, vait!" (German accent? Maybe Russian?) "Vat you doing? Not how you present case. You not organized. You skipping 'round. I do not know vat going on. You skip and skip. Is this how we do things here? Huh?"

To say it became dead quiet for a second would be an understatement, but that didn't last long. This guy loved to put on a show, and since he enjoyed the sound of his own voice, he berated me some more. My face may have been blank, my heart rate may have been nearing two hundred, and perspiration may have instantly penetrated my collar, but I would not disengage his stare. I don't think he liked that, so his other palm hit the desk. "Vell?!" he screamed impatiently.

Not missing a beat, I said, "As I was saying, there was no official report on the chest X-ray, so I went down to view it myself, and it was normal."

Looking for any reason to butt in, the attending doctor said, "Oh, really? It normal? Is dat vat you think? You radiologist now? Who else following dis patient? Anyone?"

Jim piped in. "I am. I was extremely busy this morning, so I couldn't get down to radiology to review all the films, but it's the first thing we'll do once we complete rounds."

The attending, still steaming and apparently tormented by my presence, "You don't know vat go on with patient? Patient get sick and die. Dis bullshit! Okay. Next patient. Who has next patient? I hope you more organized."

For the remainder of rounds, I stared at my shoes, compulsively counting the tiny air vent holes, unable to look up.

When rounds were over and the entire team (residents, PAs, and students) was dismissed, I stood up last, allowing the others to turn their backs on me as they left the room. I waited for Jim. Kindly, he also waited for everyone else to leave. When the final white coat had departed, he said, "Shawn, I'm sorry things went down that way. Don't take it personally. It's no big deal. He blows up like that all the time. It's because he doesn't know you. He'll do the same thing to the next new student."

"Jim, I'm fine. I can take it."

"I know you can. We should go see those films and update him, as I promised."

Thirty minutes later, we found the attending back in his office, watching TV, feet up on the desk, and eating a donut. Jim pulled up a chair beside his desk as I stood behind him. He acknowledged Jim, but not me. I was far from offended. Jim gave the rundown on his patients and this jackass barely nodded, like he couldn't care less.

Jim and I left and got ready for the next case—a quick laparoscopy. In the OR, the surgeon handed me the camera and said, "Can you run this?"

"Yes, I can." I grabbed it from him and smoothly slid it into the cannula (a hollow cylinder placed through the skin to introduce surgical instruments into the abdominal cavity).

Using two other ports (cannula sites), one with a retractor, and one with forceps, the surgeon began moving things around and calling out orders. "Find the liver. Look at the gallbladder. Zoom in. Closer. Swing to the stomach. Good. Nice. Over the omentum. Great. Done here. Let's head to the pelvis. Left ovary. Perfect. Right one now. Where'd you get this guy, Jim?"

"Who? Shawn? I thought you brought him…"

"Well, I know you didn't train him on the camera. He's too damn good." The entire operating room laughed.

Sarcastically, Jim countered, "Well, fuck. I'll scrub out and go eat lunch then."

"I'm good with that. We're done here, anyway. I don't see any pathology. Everything is normal. Let's all scrub out and go get lunch. I'll finish up with Shawn. Can you close these incision sites with me?" Since Jim had already torn off his gown, I assumed he was talking to me.

"Yes, sir. I can."

"Great. Jim, go write the post-op orders and I'll meet you in the cafeteria in thirty."

And with that, I began closing my first surgical wounds. The surgical technician handed me the needle driver with a perfectly loaded suture. That had never happened before. For years, I delivered instruments to others. Now, I was the receiver.

With calm direction, the surgeon guided me through the closure. After cutting the final tags above the knot, he stepped back and de-gowned. "I trust you can dress those wounds, Shawn?"

"Yes, sir. I'll meet you in recovery."

Down in the cafeteria, while I was gathering lunch items, Jim saw Captain Jackass eating by himself, so I was pissed when Jim made his way over to his table and sat across from him. I plopped down next to Jim and, in an effort to avoid speaking, I made sure that I was constantly chewing. I knew the attending wouldn't have the patience to ask me questions if he had to wait for answers because I had a mouthful of food. As it turned out, he just kept treating me like I didn't exist, which was fine with me. At the conclusion of the insufferable banter between he and Jim, the Captain gave a tension-driven directive, "He need be more organized. Teach to present better." Grabbing what was probably his fifth coffee of the day, he walked away.

When the tail of the jackass disappeared around the corner, one of the third-year residents, Mike, asked to sit down with us. "Shawn, don't worry about what happened this morning. It's no big deal. He is very regimented, anal, and not very malleable. And he does that to everyone. Present quickly, provide only essential details, and conclude with your plan for the day. Do that and you'll be fine."

"Thanks, Mike. When rounds were over, I couldn't stop shaking. I just wanted to run and hide somewhere."

"Well, you obviously shook it off pretty quickly. Word is already out on your brilliant camera work during that last case." Mike stood and patted me on the shoulder. "You're okay, man."

Because of my experience during my inpatient medicine rotation, I feel like I'm under a microscope, so I'm consciously trying to put forth greater effort to succeed. I can't have another rotation where I get pulled into detention.

I impressed Jim with the ectopic pregnancy spiel today. Later, when he cosigned my SOAP notes in the patients' charts, he didn't add a single word or addenda, so I'm assuming they were thorough.

I'll arrive at the hospital tomorrow morning at about 4:30, get my rounding done, prep my notes for rounds, and pray Captain Jackass doesn't ream me another one.

December 4, 2000, Monday.

[6 days since last entry]

Thank God I have Mondays off. I completed my twenty-seven-hour shift this weekend, so today is for recovery. I woke up at 4:30 am on Saturday to visit my assigned patients. At 8:00 am, I uneventfully presented them at rounds and then the team began answering one pager-call after another. I don't have a pager; I'm just attached to the hip of whoever will allow me to ride along with them.

The team included a third-year resident, a second-year resident, an intern, and me. Technically, the attending is on the team, too, but we only communicate with that person if the third-year gets in a pickle and needs help—something they try desperately to avoid.

We have to cover calls from the ER, continue to manage the OB/ GYN patients on the floors, including those in pre-term labor, those in labor or false labor, and anyone with vaginal bleeding (possibly miscarrying), all while taking on emergency C-sections. This shift was my introduction to the labor-and-delivery floor. Until this weekend, I had only witnessed one cesarean five years ago while working as a surgical technician.

At 2:30 am, that changed. The night was very routine or so I was later told. All women in labor on the floor are constantly receiving internal exams to check how many centimeters their cervix is dilated. Once you hit the magic ten centimeters, you're ready to push. Each exam usually accompanies a review of the fetal heart tracings, which look for fetal distress and potential umbilical cord compression.

I was gloved, wrist-deep, and reporting, "Five centimeters here," when I heard the resident's pager go off. We were summoned down the hall to another patient's birthing room, and upon arriving, the intern told us that this patient was a twenty-year-old non-English-speaking, one-hundred-pound woman at forty-one weeks gestation (currently, thirty-seven is considered full-term), with a fetal weight thought to be greater than nine pounds. She had begun pushing about thirty minutes before we were paged but then gave up, refusing to put forth any more effort due to severe pain, despite having had an epidural.

The fetal heart rate began dropping rapidly and was not returning to baseline. I took one look at how petite she was and, knowing she was nulliparous (having never birthed a child vaginally), I assumed this could get ugly. I don't know much about giving birth, but I knew there was no way that baby was coming out of her vagina without a fight. The resident immediately called for the suction device. The patient's husband, gripping the hand of his wife at her bedside, now had concern flashing across his face. These devices are just what you'd imagine. It looks like a mini toilet plunger attached to a hose that provides suction. It's applied to the baby's head, and voilà, you can now pull the baby while the mother pushes, doubling your chances of a successful vaginal delivery. These are somewhat controversial. Why? I have no idea. If you have to save the life of the baby by getting them out immediately, I don't see the argument. It's like advising against chest compressions for fear of a broken rib.

Within seconds, the device was on. I was astonished at just how hard those things are pulled. A few times it disengaged, and the resident nearly fell to the floor. But she just threw it back on, increased the suction and, with both hands, started pulling even harder. Angle up, angle down, move left, move right, rotate clockwise, then counter, all while pulling. "No chance!" The resident called for the episiotomy tray.

After a quick injection of anesthetic, she made a cut with scissors and continued cutting until the baby's head started to advance, but it never felt sufficient. She grabbed the scissors again. Another centimeter. Nope, so she cuts again. Now down to the edge of the anus. With one last snip and pull, Mom let out a bone-chilling scream. Her vagina exploded as if a grenade had detonated, and the head finally delivered.

The growing episiotomy wasn't enough as she ripped apart in two other places. The suction was removed and tossed aside and they handed the resident a bulb syringe to aspirate the nose and mouth. The head was shaped like a butternut squash. After a few recovery breaths for Mom, who was still crying out, the next push created a volcanic eruption of amniotic fluid that covered the delivering resident. Fortunately, she was wearing a gown, gloves, mask, and face shield because she would need every bit of that personal protection equipment to keep from drowning. Despite being agile enough to sidestep and dodge most of the overspray, I still got hit by some smaller shrapnel. The episiotomy allowed the body to be delivered with the next tug. Since the dad had long since excused himself to go vomit in the bathroom, they tasked me with cutting my first umbilical cord.

Blood-covered, the baby let out its first cry while being wiped down. Two residents, looking at each other in disbelief, recognized the responsibility of repairing the wounds of war. One said, "We need to call." That meant waking the sleeping attending at 3:00 am, dragging them out of whatever sweet dream they might have been enjoying, and into this nightmare of a bloodbath. The delivery room resembled an emergency trauma bay after treating multiple gunshot victims. How does one sew together a pile of ground hamburger? I'll tell you. It takes three doctors, fifty milliliters of anesthetic, seventy sutures, eighty sponges, and more than ninety minutes.

And about my baby fever? Cured!

After the final stitch, the team retreated to the on-call room and collapsed onto three sets of bunk beds. All was quiet for almost two hours. When the resident's pager alarmed at 6:45 am, it was because the next team was letting us know they were ready to receive their report on all the patients that we'd be signing over to them.

On our way down to the nurses' station, one of the residents apologized. "I'm so sorry that you didn't get to see a normal delivery. All of us were hopeful we'd be able to get you in position to guide a baby out, catch them, wipe them down, cut the cord, and hand them off. Instead, you had to witness one of the worst deliveries that any of us will ever see throughout our careers. That's not how they typically go."

"There will be other opportunities," I told them. "The last week of my rotation, I'll be on the Labor and Delivery floor, so I'm sure it'll happen then."

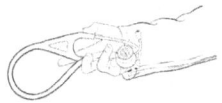

I want to address some uneasiness I encountered with a patient during this rotation. I needed time to mull over how I would tell the story. Now that I've had closure on it, it's time to share.

During my first week in the office, I performed a pre-op H&P on Alyssa, a twenty-five-year-old single mother of a one-year-old. Alyssa had horrible endometriosis and recurrent hemorrhagic ovarian cysts. I had learned she was an aspiring physician assistant, yet hadn't reached the point of completing school applications.

Since her surgical clearance was a breeze, we spent most of the encounter just talking about becoming a PA. Although she fired off question after question, what she was most interested in knowing was what it was like going through my PA program. She was clearly struck by the bizarre path I had taken to arrive at where I am today. "Wait. You played in bands? Your hair was longer than mine? You wore spandex pants, leg warmers, and makeup? No way. I need to see pictures."

In no stage of denial, I kept nodding and smiling. She kept disbelieving and laughing.

"How the hell did you get your start in the medical field?"

I rattled off a few of the major highlights, and right on cue, she said, "Shawn, you *have* to write a book about that."

"I know, right? What would the title be?"

She paused and looked around the room, then she grabbed my hand and yelled, "I've got it! I've got it! How about *From Hair Band to Healthcare: Becoming a PA?*"

I had to admit that it was clever. That'll get filed away for sure. As she let go of my hand, I reached into my coat pocket and pulled out my microcassette recorder. "What if I told you I started writing that book sixteen months ago?" I held the recorder up to my mouth and began talking into it (without pressing the record button). "Alyssa is a pleasant, and obviously brilliant, twenty-five-year-old mother of one who presents with ongoing cyclical pelvic pain…"

She burst out laughing even harder and I thought she was going to roll out of her chair. "You get the hell outta here right now! No way! Are you serious? You are, aren't you? Am I going to be in your book?"

Of all the patients I had come into contact with through my first six rotations, Alyssa was the one I felt the greatest connection—and in the shortest amount of time. Essentially, I was going to be writing this book for her and thousands of others like her.

We chatted for another thirty minutes without a single break in the conversation. I felt so bad for her, having to put her career on hold after unintentionally getting pregnant at twenty-three, just a year away from completing her BSN (Bachelor of Science in Nursing).

She's obviously bright, but I told her that it will take more than brains to complete a PA program. To quote a medical student from the PBS NOVA documentary *The Making of a Doctor*, "To become a doctor, you don't have to be smart; you just can't be stupid."

A week later, Alyssa returned for her surgery and I went to see her. Both of her parents were huddled in the corner of the pre-op room. Her mother was holding her granddaughter as a nurse was starting Alyssa's IV. Sitting in a chair at the head of the bed was a beefy, rugged, heavily tatted, clean-shaven male wearing a flat-billed Yankees ball cap slightly to the side and a waist-level black leather jacket.

"Shawn! Oh, my God! Thank you for coming to see me. Mom and Dad, this is Shawn, the PA I've been telling you about all week. He's writing a book." She whispered to them, "I might be in it."

At no point was I introduced to this man caressing Alyssa's hair. He paid no attention to me; he kept his eyes only on her. He grew creepier with each passing moment. I also couldn't help but notice a subtle aversion she had towards him. Aside from her annoyance at his touch, she acted as if he didn't exist. He never contributed to the conversation. His actions were limited to stroking and staring at her.

After signing the consent forms, the nurse administered a sedative. I tied on my mask and we wheeled her into the operating room. The surgery, which took place last Friday, went flawlessly and we hoped she would only need to be admitted for a couple of nights.

Since I was off on Monday, I was worried when I arrived on Tuesday that she'd be gone, so I made it a point to go to the hospital over the weekend, just to check in on her.

Happily shocked, she asked, "What are you doing here? It's the weekend."

"The hospital doors were unlocked, so I thought I'd drop in and see if anyone needed help. You know this place doesn't close over the weekend, right?"

"Shouldn't you be home writing a book or spending time with your fiancée?"

I didn't recall mentioning my relationship status, but maybe I did. We had talked extensively, but that was over a week ago. Was this a feeler question? "Oh, Karen? She's back in New Hampshire."

"So, you're just out here by yourself?"

"Well, no. I'm renting a room in a house a few miles from here." I tried to redirect the conversation. "Are you in any pain? Have you been able to eat anything yet?"

"I'm fine. Just tired. I hate the hospital. My entire life, I've never had a positive experience in them. Well, until this time."

"What do you mean? You've only been here overnight."

"I met you. That's what I mean." She didn't really look at me when she said it, but she blushed from ear to ear.

"I think your anesthesia hasn't worn off yet, or your blood sugar might be too low. I should call a nurse."

"I'm sorry," she said, sensing she'd made me uncomfortable.

"For?" I stood up.

"I don't know. I'm alone. I'm depressed. I'm stuck. I live with my parents." Her lip began trembling and her voice cracked, so I did the only thing that a compassionate human would do, I sat down on the bed and handed her a tissue. Practically swatting it away, she lunged forward and put her arms around my neck. The floodgates opened, and she sobbed on my shoulder for the next few minutes.

Still secured in an embrace, I asked, "Alone? What do you mean? Who was that guy with you yesterday?" He surely wasn't acting like a brother.

"That's Nate." Finally, she pulled away and fell back to her pillows, wiping tears away with the sleeve of her hospital gown.

"He seems very supportive and attentive."

"That's one way to describe him. Too controlling is more like it. He's alright, I guess. We were supposed to have gotten married two months ago, but I called it off. He's not the one for me. And he's not supportive at all. Don't let him fool you with that act. He does what he wants, when he wants, and only cares about himself."

"Then I think you know what you have to do, especially if you want to take the next steps towards becoming a PA, right? Listen, my high school sweetheart, Wendy… Shortly after we graduated high school, gave me a mug with a saying on it that has always stuck with me: Success Is Loving What You Do. I like to think about success as five percent ability, and ninety-five percent motivation. You have the ability, Alyssa, but if you want to be a PA, you'll need to find that other ninety-five percent. I believe that you can and you will, but now *you* have to believe that."

She kept nodding as her tears dried up. Because her emotions were so real, and she was so genuine in her interest, I felt like I needed to extend a hand to her. My cell number was off limits, and since I live hundreds of miles from her, I figured providing my physical mailing address to her was safe, so I wrote it down on the back of her menu.

Reciprocating, she said, "You can have my address too. Can you just get it from my chart, or should I write it down for you?"

"I have no idea if that's ethical or not, so just write it down for me. But listen, down the road, if you have questions about this whole PA path, drop me a line. I'll probably set up a new email account after I graduate. When I do, we can begin communicating that way."

I told her I'd drop by the next day, but she had been discharged by the time I made it back to the hospital. I began wondering if I'd ever see her again, let alone hear from her, so after a couple of days I picked up a get-well card. In it, I wrote:

Alyssa,

As promised, I came by to see you on Tuesday, but you must have been doing exceptionally well because they informed me you had been sent home earlier in the day. I know how much you hated being in the hospital. I hope this recent surgery provides you with many pain-free years to come. Its people like you that make being a PA worth all the time, effort, and commitment it takes to become one. I never required a thank you, yet you were always so gracious to provide one. Since you have said the things that you have said to me, I have walked with a bounce in my step, a deeper pride, and a new air of confidence. I hope you will keep in touch. If there is anything that you need during your quest in becoming a PA, please contact me. We need more people like you in our profession. I believe in you. Get well soon.

Your friend and future colleague,
Shawn

December 14, 2000, Thursday.

[10 days since last entry]

Just before lunch, Jim and I scrubbed in on a laparoscopic ablation procedure for endometriosis. I stood there while the surgeon treated Jim like crap. The guy was a pompous ass. I know surgeons. I've been around enough of them to know the good ones from the bad ones. Many are asses; however, you don't hire a surgeon for their bedside manner—you hire them for their ability to make impeccable decisions and for the skill of their hands. This one was a dick *and* lacked good hands.

Several hours later, right before I was supposed to sign my patients over to the evening crew, I ran up to the floor to check on a patient. That same surgeon was standing at the counter chatting to a nurse. I watched him for a few moments. The conversation seemed flirtatious and not exactly work-related. I could see the chart I needed, resting under his hand. I was running out of time. I needed to interrupt him, but I knew exactly what would happen if I did.

"Pardon me. Sorry to bother you, but could I just look at that chart for a moment since you're not using it?" I asked. "I won't even move it from in front of you."

"No. Just go see her," he said, leaning firmly onto the chart with his forearm.

Okay. I'll play. I went into the patient's room, asked her a few questions, and examined her. She was feeling well and wanted to eat. I scampered back to his side, still with his paws on the chart. This guy is fucking with me. It's like he knows I have to present this patient to Captain Jackass and his indentured servants in seven minutes. I stood closer so my sleeve would graze the pages of the chart and used my tuna-fish sandwich breath as a weapon. Disgusted, he took his glasses off. "What can I do for you again?"

"I just need to know if she still has a fever."

"Did she say she did, or did you not go see her after I told you to do so?"

"Subjectively? Nope, but I want to see the number."

"So, go look at her chart."

"I am looking at her chart. The one you're not using. It's under your arm." I tapped it three times and threw him a sarcastic smirk.

"They keep vitals in the room." He said. "There's a sheet on a clipboard that's hung at the foot of the bed. She doesn't have a fever."

"My apologies. Normally that is correct, but this patient's vitals sheet is clipped to the inside cover of her chart, the one you're leaning on, the one you're not using. I just want to see the number. One second and I'm gone."

He keeps his eyes on me as he returns his glasses to the tip of his nose, then flips to the front cover. Glancing down at the vitals sheet, "Well, look at that, yes, she *does* have a fever. So what? Some people have fevers after an operation." With a thud, he closed the chart, tucked it into his armpit, and began walking away. "I hope you don't have any more questions because your one second is up."

"I do. What's the number?" To be flippant, "I mean, is it like really high, like 109? Or is it a low-grade fever, like 80-ish?"

Without breaking stride or turning around, "Who cares?" He yelled.

I sprinted to the stairwell, galloped down a flight, and whipped into the afternoon sign-out room just in time. "Yes, room 311 is an extremely healthy thirty-year-old female on no medications from home, who had an endometrial ablation procedure this morning. I just came from her room. She has exceptional pain control, will be ordering dinner, has voided on her own, and has already been out of bed to the chair twice. She has a low-grade fever according to the surgeon who I just spoke with moments ago. They are going to watch her overnight, and so long as nothing comes of it, we should discharge her in the morning."

I'm sure that exchange with Dr. Pompous is going to get me in trouble. He won't report me, but any one of the dozen bystanders might. When will I learn?

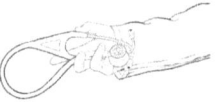

I delivered my first two babies a couple of days ago (the way it's supposed to go). Somehow, I ended up in a patient's room with Malcolm, a medical student, and one of the other residents. The resident's pager starts beeping. He looks down, then says, "My patient is going." (meaning ready to deliver, or start pushing.) "Who wants to come?"

"I want to!" I blurted out. "I haven't delivered a baby and only have a week remaining."

Malcolm was too slow, but he agreed to sit this one out to grant me the opportunity. The resident jogged out, and I jumped into his draft.

"Okay, now who are you?"

"Shawn. PA student from RTC."

"You haven't caught a baby yet? What the hell have you been doing?"

"This is my first week on the OB floor. I've only seen two vacuum deliveries. Oh, and a vagina versus grenade."

"I heard about that one. Damn. You were there? You better not be some sort of bad omen or something." He cut in front of me and charged into the room. "Okay. Act like you've been here before. Mom will freak out 'cause it's her first too. Be cool and confident. I'll talk you through it."

This intern put gloves on and completed a quick check of the baby's head. "Get Shawn some gloves. Come over here. Sit. Okay, there's the head. She's ready to push. The baby will be out soon."

A nurse popped her head into the room. "Hey, you're on your own with this one. The attending is in an emergency C-section."

Technically, perhaps hospital policy, I thought an attending was required to be present for each birth? Instead, they got me. I looked over at the intern and he said, "You're up, Shawn. Here we go." I placed my hand over the baby's crown and provided a slight pressure. Mom had one heel dug into my hip on the bed. She reared back, sucked in a breath, crunched forward, and everyone in the room began counting down from ten as she bellowed. Out of nowhere, an unfamiliar voice behind us called out, "I'm here." A midwife threw on a gown and gloves and settled in beside me, hand on my shoulder, peering in.

I'm the lowest guy on the totem pole, but currently sitting in the highest position. This is the intern's duty, and they are supposed to deliver under the direct supervision of someone above them. He was kind enough to bring me with him, but seconds before the big event, I was getting ousted by the midwife.

"And you are?" she asked, with urgency.

"Shawn. PA student. I'm assuming you need me to move?"

"Umm. No. Do you want to move?" she laughed.

"Actually, I don't."

"Good. I mean, you're already in position, and that baby is coming any minute now. You guide the head out with the next push, and I'll hand you the bulb syringe to suction the mouth and nose. When the rest of the baby's body delivers, you better catch him. They're slippery little buggers."

We perfectly executed the play. I clamped the cord and handed Dad the scissors and instructed him on what to do.

Life…

December 15, 2000, Friday.

[1 day since last entry]

Somehow, I averted disaster today. I was certain Jim told me he wouldn't be in on Friday and that I should spend the day on the labor-and-delivery floor, hanging out with the team of med students and residents. Before we left yesterday, he didn't advise me to round on anyone. So, I walked into rounds at 6:50 this morning and I saw no one from the team there. I leaned over and asked one of the senior residents, "Hey, Jim is off and I'm in OB today. I wasn't supposed to round on any patients, was I?"

"Here is how you can tell. Look at that board on the wall. If you see a tiny red "PA" beneath a patient's name, then it's assigned to the PA for that day."

"Oh, shit. That is going to be a problem." There was a red "PA" under one name near the bottom of the board.

The senior resident echoed, "Yup, that's definitely going to be a problem."

"I'll be right back." Like Fred Flintstone starting his car, my feet ripped up the tile beneath me and I was gone. I gathered just enough info on the patient to finagle my way through rounds, knowing I'd go back up later to write my note and orders.

At 7:07 am, I attempted to sneak back into the rounding room. I tiptoed to my seat, looked up, and there was Jim, giving me a "*Where the fuck have you been?*" death stare. What is he doing here? He's irritated. He's steaming. He's tapping his foot so fast that it looks blurry. His face is beet-red, and I'm pretty sure I saw blood coming from one of his eyes.

The attending turned to Jim and said, "Bisson?"

"Yes. Umm, Shawn, would you mind presenting Bisson this morning for the team?" Jim's got that "gotcha" look. I know he thinks I showed up late to rounds and didn't round on the only patient that was assigned to us.

"Sure, Jim, be happy to." Oh, the look on his face. He was not expecting that at all. He thought I was about to jump from a plane without a parachute. Instead, I landed that plane blindfolded in a blizzard, and the passengers were cheering.

Immediately following rounds, I was puzzled when Jim sent me to scrub in on a scheduled C-section that he excused himself from assisting.

After the case, I left the PACU (post-anesthesia care unit), changed, and headed up to the floor to write my note and orders on Bisson. I opened the progress note section and began flipping pages until I saw an entry with today's date, and there was Jim's handwriting and signature. *Fuck!* I'm screwed. I slammed the chart shut and began frantically looking for Jim, building my defense as I scurried around the floors of the hospital. I asked every person that I recognized, "Have you seen Jim?"

Finally, a senior resident told me she'd just seen him walk towards the elevator. I high-stepped it and just caught the doors closing. I threw my hand in the crevice and the doors reopened. "Jim, can I chat with you for a second?"

"Sure. What's going on?"

"About this morning. I'm sorry. I was certain you had the day off and I was supposed to be on the OB floor all day, so I didn't think I had any rounding obligations. Just before rounds, a resident informed me on how that big dry-erase board works, so I ran out to go see the only patient assigned to the PA, which is why I was late to rounds. That's why there wasn't a note written. I didn't have time. My intent was to write it after the C-section, and, of course, I just saw yours, leading me to have an "Oh, shit!" moment. I hope you understand."

"It's okay. I should have been clearer about today's expectations and plan. Frankly, I'm impressed with how you handled it. That was kind of funny. It wasn't funny at the time. I was pissed. I thought I had you dead to center, so when you presented Bisson perfectly, I was like, what the fuck just happened? It's no big deal."

"Well, Jim, it's a big deal to me. I messed up and I feel bad about it. I just needed to man up."

"Shawn. It's alright. Thanks for finding me. We're good, okay?"

As the day progressed, I reflected on my entire experience here and began to question if I would be detained by the RTC faculty again. Less important, but still a consideration, was my grade. I'm presenting another oral topic, abortions, to Jim on Tuesday. He had given me about a dozen articles to read to help prepare for it, so I read them all again as soon as I got home last night and began creating my concise sidebar speech for whenever he asks me. I have through Monday to perfect it.

In five days, I'll have to take his seventy-question exam. Then the following day, Recall Day, is the PA program's OB/GYN exam. That week will be hell, but I've survived worse.

December 18, 2000, Monday.

[3 days since last entry]

Much like I don't announce to anyone that I'm carrying an audio recorder around with plans to write a book about this experience, I don't feel like it's important to hand out copies of my resume every time I enter a room.

I'm most comfortable in surgical situations. By now, we all know that, but when I enter an operating room, it is assumed, and rightfully so, that it's my first time. I'm the new guy—the student, the one who everyone needs to pay the most attention to (but often gets completely ignored, or worse yet, hazed and pimped).

After leaving the scrub sink, I raised my arms away from my body, letting the water drip from my elbows, backed through the swinging door, and entered the OR. The team was still draping the patient, but surely the scrub tech felt my presence. I sidestepped to the left, getting into her peripheral vision. The back table, where all the secondary surgical instruments were arranged, had a folded gown with a hand towel on top, neatly laid out near the edge closest to me. I knew it was mine, and the best thing to do is to have the towel handed to me, rather than reach for it, risking contamination of the sterile field, so I remained patient and waited.

With draping complete, the tech maneuvered her Mayo stand over the patient's legs, transferred the first batch of tools onto it, and set up an electrocautery pen. By this point, I have air dried and I do not need that towel, but it was covering my gown. She had time to hand me the towel, but was avoiding it. I needed to make my move before my arms started tingling. With her back turned to me while she performed the sponge counts, I removed the towel and properly did a quick pat down, dropped it into the linen basket, and retrieved the gown. As the gown unfolded to my knees and I inserted my arms, the tech whipped around and said, "Hey, hey, hey! What are you doing?"

"What do you mean?" Introducing some lighthearted humor, I said, "I'm going to need a gown for this part, right?"

"You don't touch things back here. Ever. Now my table is contaminated." She unfolded some sterile towels to cover the former location of the gown and surrounding area.

"I did *not* contaminate your table." By now, the room has fallen silent.

"You touched my table; therefore, it's contaminated." She's feeding the flames.

"Ma'am, my apologies if you think that, but your back was turned when I properly retrieved my towel and gown. Nothing is contaminated. Can we please get off on the right foot today? The patient is under anesthesia and the surgeons are waiting. My name is Shawn. I'm a PA student, but I have been a surgical technologist for three years and I have scrubbed about a thousand cases."

Not sure how to respond, the scrub tech began fiddling with whatever was in front of her, and under her breath she said, "Well, you can't just grab things."

"Can I grab my gloves?" They, too, were awaiting me on the back table. Defeated, the tech turned, grabbed my gloves, and held them out for me to slide into. I asked for a spin (the final move required to tie up a surgical gown) and I stepped to the patient's side.

Less defensive now, she said, "I'm sorry, but you know how we get." We entered a truce. We understood each other. It's a surgical technician's job to create and maintain a sterile field. We have to be prepared to meet the surgeon's needs promptly, in all situations. The table and instrument set-up are meticulously created and maintained with an obsessive attention to detail.

By now, word is out that I'm okay to be here. The attending and chief resident became reassured with my presence. They used my name (which never happens), let me get my gloves bloodied, and gave me things to do (like running the suction and cutting sutures). They never stopped teaching. Halfway into the case, the tech leaned towards the attending and said, "He's rather relaxed for someone who just got yelled at by the scrub nurse." I tried to stifle a smile under my mask, but my crow's feet gave it away.

In recovery, I was helping the resident with the post-op orders (actually, he was helping me), and the tech came over and offered me one of her freshly baked chocolate chip cookies. "Good job in there. You can scrub with me any day."

December 19, 2000, Tuesday.
[1 day since last entry]
Sometimes I feel so dumb. I wish I could learn to get over my fear of answering on-the-spot questions because sometimes I may actually be correct and appear intelligent.

One of the attendings, Dr. Newsom, with whom I had worked several times before, and who had always been so nice to me, was doing a scheduled C-section with her chief resident. While scrubbing at the sinks together, Dr. Newsom asked, "Shawn, what are we worried about here?"

I'm thinking, *For fuck's sake, could you ask a more generalized question than that? But, this is part of the game.* "What do you mean?"

"You know she has diabetes, right?"

"Actually no. Until five minutes ago, I had no idea I'd be doing this case."

"Well, she is a diabetic and you should've known that."

What? Where the hell do some of these docs come from? I should've known that a person I didn't know existed until two seconds ago, has diabetes?

"Regardless, she has diabetes, so, what are we worried about?"

Yeah, I heard the question the first time. The second time is only slightly less general than the first.

"Postoperatively," she added, in an attempt to clarify.

The longer I'm silent, the more clues she offers. If I don't say another word, she'll eventually be able to answer her own question. "With diabetes? I don't know. Fetal size? Polyhydramnios?"

"No, Shawn. Postoperatively."

I always feel like these answers should be more complicated, so I don't spout out the first thing that comes to mind.

"How about infection? Does that sound like something we should worry about in a diabetic patient, Shawn?"

Dammit. "Yes. Where sugar resides, bacteria thrives."

"Mm-hmm," she said as she disappeared into the OR. I followed, ready to accept my fate of standing around holding retractors and being ignored. And that is just what happened. She was short and impatient with me. I was annoyed, but understood her reasoning. I'd failed to earn her respect.

I took my lumps and just kept quiet, doing what I could to help. During this case, I learned by listening and observing. When it was almost over, and there was no trouble on the horizon, Dr. Newsom asked the chief resident, "You got this from here?" The chief affirmed and Dr. Newsom left.

Once in the clear, the chief said, "Shawn, come over here. Can you help me close?"

"Yes, I can first-assist while you suture."

"No. You're closing and I'll assist *you.* You right-handed? Let's switch places." As I left my position and walked to hers, she rotated to the spot where I had just been standing. The chief called for two retractors and told the scrub tech, "Hand this man a suture."

This is the part where I act like I know what the fuck I'm doing, even though I don't. *Stay calm. You've seen this done hundreds of times. Handle the instruments with confidence and don't let them see you shake.*

"The peritoneum, Shawn. I'll present it to you. Work from me to you, a running stitch," the chief resident instructed.

"Can you tie the initial knot? My one-handed knot-tying is weak." I told her. I ran the suture down the length of the incision as she followed me (keeping the last stitch out of the way, yet snug). She tied off the final knot and I asked for the suture scissors. Holding out my hand, I felt and heard the beautiful slap of them hitting my glove. This repeated itself for the muscle fascia and subcutaneous layer. The chief resident called for two forceps. "Give Shawn the stapler. He's got this." I grinned so hard that the tape holding my mask in place over the bridge of my nose lifted clear off my skin.

Once the final staple was in, she said, "Hey now. Not bad at all."

"For my first time," I added.

"Oh, shush! First time? First time, my ass…"

"No really. I've never closed a surgical site before. When you offered, there was no way I was going to pass up the opportunity, so thank you. I really appreciate it. That meant a lot to me."

"You're welcome. So, have you landed a surgical job yet, or are you just fielding offers right now?" she laughed. "You're going into surgery, no doubt. That's where you should be."

Ever since that moment, that's all I can think about. Someone saw something in me, enough to comment in front of others. I feel at ease in the operating room, but I know that it's best for a new graduate to start their career in primary care so they can lay down a solid base of practicing medicine and managing chronic diseases for a few years. But it's *that* path that's intimidating to me, not surgery.

Since this may be my last entry before Recall Day, I have to say, Captain Jackass has lost his title. Now I feel awful about having graced him with it, although he clearly earned it. He never yelled at me again. He allowed me into his surgical cases and included me in his conversations with Jim and the residents. I gained an understanding of the incredible pressure he is under to oversee an entire OB/GYN department. As with most doctors, until you walk a day in their shoes, you never truly know what it's like to be them.

21

ROTATION #7—
NEUROSURGERY
(ELECTIVE)

January 2, 2020, Tuesday.

[14 days since last entry]

I'm back in New Hampshire, staying with my brother- and sister-in-law. Their place is forty-five minutes closer to the hospitals where I expect to spend most of my days during this rotation. The neurosurgery practice has multiple offices across a few cities. I could end up in any one of them on any given day.

The disappointing factor in all this is that I could only get scrubbing privileges (written permission to participate in surgeries) at one of the three hospitals, and it's the hospital that I worked at as a surgical technician. Why RTC still sent me on this rotation is baffling. I think there will be days when I'll be standing in the corner of an operating room doing nothing, not able to see inside of the surgical wound or hear the conversations of those performing the surgery.

We're going to need to get creative to make this a valuable experience. I'm supposed to be excited about an elective rotation (my other was the ICU), but I'm not feeling it right now. While all of this was coming to light, I finally connected with Brad, the physician assistant who will be my preceptor, around 8:00 pm last night. My first actual day was today. Of my previous six preceptors, not a single one of them ever asked me, "Shawn, what do you want to get out of this rotation?"

So when Brad asked, my answer was swift and matter-of-fact. "I want to learn how to manage patients postoperatively and be able to conduct a complete neurosurgical exam with confidence and efficiency, but also understand what my exam findings mean."

"Wow, you've given this some thought. I like it. Then that's what we'll try to do."

I don't know how often he takes students, if ever, but he seemed impressed by my answer, perhaps befuddled that I even had one. I didn't admit to him my intentions of going into emergency medicine. During rotations, I always tried to give the impression that whatever specialty I was doing at the time was where my passion lay. Doing so probably encourages the preceptor to invest more effort into a student's experience.

I also voiced that I was about to embark on a three-month plan to prep for my boards and, thus, I was hoping for a rotation that was less demanding than my previous ones. He was very understanding. This felt like a good time to let him know that later during the rotation I would need to get out a few hours early because I had received an unimaginable Christmas gift from Karen: tickets to the annual Granite State Baseball Dinner, where my boyhood idol, Carlton Fisk, would be a guest of honor.

"Of course, Shawn. No big deal," he said. "That sounds awesome. No worries. You seem excited about this rotation, and so are we. We'll make this relaxed, stress-free, and keep the demands to whatever level you need."

But I'm not excited at all.

January 8, 2001, Monday.

[6 days since last entry]

It never gets old being right. I'm bored out of my mind because I'm not scrubbing any cases at all. I commute to a hospital, do nothing, drive to a second hospital, do nothing, then commute back home. I wanted time to study for boards, but the boredom is becoming intolerable.

On Friday, I spent almost three hours observing a surgery behind the wall of drapes that separate the surgical field from the anesthesiologist. I couldn't see or hear anything. Darren, one of their newer PAs, was trying to teach during the case, but it was pointless. At least when I'm in the office seeing patients, every patient has imaging studies—either CT scans or MRIs—so I'm getting some excellent guidance on reading those. Our radiology course last year focused on plain films. Learning to read advanced imaging studies is reserved for on-the-job training, and that appears to be the standard across PA programs.

I feel like I've lost all ambition, though. I don't know what's wrong with me. No reading in five days, but I completed an eighty-question board review practice test. Any second now, my phone is going to ring and either Nadine or Bailey will be on the other end reading me the riot act. I need to get my shit together. I'm exhausted from doing nothing. There have been some late nights and my commutes are terrible. Sixteen hours per day, I'm either standing in a circle the size of a dinner plate, or I'm sitting in a car driving to the next place where I will stand in another circle.

Though I go back to New York for my final three rotations once this one is over, I'm not enjoying being home.

This morning, I'll be at one of the offices with Darren. It's my first clinic with him. During the first week, I didn't see any patients solo; I only shadowed the provider I was with, so I hope Darren pushes me a bit. If he doesn't, I may need to be more assertive.

I don't know if the two PAs in this practice are talking about me, but I assume they are. There are three surgeons in the practice—Dr.

McJamison, Dr. Jackson, and Dr. Farley—each with his own level of experience, demeanor, style, and tolerance for students.

Dr. McJ never says a single word during cases, and when he does, it's under his breath, behind a mask, and with a thick Irish accent. Dr. Jackson is boisterous, always cracking jokes, and is hard to read. I can never tell if he's being serious or sarcastic. I swear he spends his nights trying to come up with ways to test how gullible I am. The third, Dr. Farley, is as formal as they come. He's classically trained (old-school), and probably months away from retirement. He's the guy who asked Brad why I was standing with the anesthesiologist last week. "If Shawn can't be standing where you're standing, he can't receive the proper training. If the hospital cannot grant surgical privileges to a student, they should not be allowing students at all." He told Brad not to take on any more students unless that issue is resolved.

Once the clinic was over, Darren looked at the afternoon's surgical schedule. "Hey, since you can only scrub at Hillsborough Hospital, Dr. Farley has a one-thirty laminectomy over there. You should get in on that one. Go grab some lunch, find either him or Brad at the scrub sink, and ask if it's okay. I'm sure they'll be fine with it."

Rather than waiting at the scrub sink, I went to the pre-op area, found our patient, and read the chart. My experience in the last rotation taught me a lesson; if I get in on a case and the questions start flying, I need to be ready by having some knowledge about the patient.

As I closed the lid on the chart, Brad walked in. "Hey, Shawn. Darren just called me. You doing the case?"

"Yes, if Dr. Farley doesn't mind."

"Have you scrubbed with him before?"

"Yes. In fact, he was the surgeon for my final case as a surgical technologist before I left for PA school."

"It'll be fine. He's very technical. Depending on his mood, he'll either be very quiet and focused, or he'll ask you lots of questions. Hopefully it's the latter."

Even though I had met him two other times during this rotation, he had no recollection of it. "Great to meet you, Shawn. Nice to have you here today. I hope you learn a lot. Our PAs are outstanding."

During the ninety-minute case, for the first seventy, I stood there, yawning, unable to see into the 3 cm incision, begging to be hazed. Someone, anyone, throw me a bone before my eyes roll up into my head and I pass out onto the floor.

"Shawn? Why are we doing a laminectomy on this gentleman?" Dr. Farley asked.

"Spinal stenosis."

"Yes, but why? Why do people need laminectomies?"

Okay, I was right, but he was looking for something more. "He's had progressive pain and neuropathic symptoms for over a year, not relieved by other conservative treatments."

Dr. Farley looked over his loupes (special magnifying lenses built into a pair of glasses) and focused on Brad, creating a brief stoppage in the action. "How do you know this?"

"I got here early and read the chart."

The tech handed Brad a needle driver and forceps as Dr. Farley asked me another question. "What is Brad going to sew up? Take a look in there."

"The muscle layer?"

"Not exactly. I will explain this to you in a way that leaves a lasting impression. When you are eating a steak, what part do you cut off because it's so tough that you can't possibly chew it?"

"It's not the fat. That's where the flavor comes from. I want that part in my mouth." Everyone laughed. "Must be the fascia?"

"Yes. The fascia. You have to put the fascia back together. Now, which fascia is Brad sewing up?"

Brad and I had just reviewed this during a case last week. "The big diamond-shaped one. Thoracolumbar? Lumbodorsal?"

"Yes. Lumbodorsal. Excellent."

Dr. Farley backed away from the patient, removed his gown, and advised Brad, "Close with Shawn." Farley motioned for me to take his spot. Answering a few questions earned me a place at the table (not the dinner table, although steak had been rumored to be on the menu).

"You've done some closing, right Shawn?" Brad asked.

"Only once, just before Christmas, during my GYN rotation. I can't do one-handed knots yet."

"That's okay. Let's alternate tying knots. You do them the way you're comfortable. Watch me do the single-handed ones. Eventually, you'll need to be able to do them left-handed and right-handed."

I've been in awe of anyone in the OR who could do that. It's such a mark of expertise.

While we were finishing up, the circulating nurse, Cyndi, said, "You know, it seems like everyone around here is hiring PAs. Dr. Hopedale, the chief of surgery, is even looking to hire a second one. I think for his new partner."

Upon leaving the PACU (post-anesthesia care unit), I headed to the locker room to change out of my scrubs. And who was standing there? None other than Bob, Dr. Hopedale's PA. "Hey, Bob?" I said. "I heard you guys are looking for another PA. Is that true?"

"Well, yeah. Um, who are you? You look very familiar."

"Oh, sorry. Shawn Roussin. I was a surg tech here for a while, but now I'm finishing up my PA program. You and I have spoken twice before about working with Dr. Hopedale."

"That's right. I remember now. We have a new partner in the practice, so it'll be mostly for him. You should talk with our office manager, Nora, as soon as possible. Do you know where the office is?"

"I do. I'll drop by tomorrow."

January 9, 2001, Tuesday.

[1 day since last entry]

Brad knew what I was up to, so when I requested to leave early, he endorsed it without reluctance. The only reluctance was on my part. Am I sure about pursuing this? Yes. Is this the optimal first job for me? Probably not. I shouldn't be specializing just yet. Though I loved the variety and thrill of the ER, working weekends, nights, and holidays—not so much. The long, high pressure, unpredictable hours of surgery? Also, not appealing. The market is getting saturated with PAs in this part of New England, so I'm feeling the need to be proactive and jump at any offer that presents itself. This could be a great one. Dr. Hopedale is triple board-certified in general, thoracic, and vascular surgery. His new partner is a general and colorectal surgeon, thus bringing some variety.

After changing into a suit, I headed over to Dr. Hopedale's office to inquire. "Hi, I'm Shawn Roussin. I'm a surgical technologist from Hillsborough Hospital who is about to complete a PA program. I have an appointment to speak with Nora about your new PA position."

"Oh, yes, Shawn. We heard you were coming in. Hang on. I think Nora is busy right now."

She left and disappeared down the hall. Seconds later, she snuck into my peripheral vision and got my attention. "Shawn, come on back. Dr. Hopedale is in his office and wants to chat with you."

Shit! I wasn't expecting that. I'm not prepared to meet with the chief of surgery—the most admirable, competent, and skilled surgeon I have ever seen. Am I about to get embarrassed by unanswerable questions from the deepest regions of medicine? I was merely one step through the doorframe when I saw his silhouette. He was standing in front of the window, adorning a white coat, arm raised as he spoke into a microcassette recorder. Sensing my presence, he clicked a button, turned, and presented his hand to me. While he reached over his majestic desk to meet mine halfway, I said, "Dr. Hopedale, thank you for having me. I know your time is valuable. I heard you are looking to hire a second PA for your practice."

"Yes, well normally I'd have Nora meet with all candidates first, but since she is busy, have a seat and let's start without her."

"This office is stunning." It was modern industrial with a twist of African aesthetics—beautiful warm wood, marble stone, and etched glass surrounded you. It felt nothing like a medical office.

"Yeah. We just had the entire suite renovated. It's my wife's creation. She's the boss who runs the show around here. I can't take credit for any of it. You might need to know that... You look kind of familiar. What's your background?"

"I've scrubbed many of your cases over at the Hillsborough."

"Right, right. I remember you now. What are you doing here? Vacation?"

"No. I'm with the neurosurgery group for an elective rotation. Each rotation is five weeks. I do ten of them over the course of a full year."

"When do you graduate?"

"May twenty-sixth. I have three more rotations in New York, so I'll only be in town for a few more weeks. That's why I came right over when I heard you were looking for someone."

"New York? Really? Where exactly?"

"RTC. Rocksville."

"You're kidding me? That's where I trained, but at the university. I was out there five years."

He started naming doctors, waiting to see if my face lit up with recognition, but it never did.

"Where did you do your surgical rotation?"

"I haven't completed it yet. That's my tenth and final rotation—at High Point Hospital."

"So, then how do you know you want to go into surgery?"

This is where the rubber would meet the road. I knew my answer here would be crucial. Lay it out for him in priority format. Be succinct and sincere. "I always knew that's where I'd end up. Nothing has changed that. My conviction has only grown stronger. Aside from developing skilled hands, I possess sound judgment and will always treat our patients as if they are the most important people in the room."

He nodded and cracked a grin. He leaned forward in his chair and clasped his hands together on the desk as if he was about to offer me the job, but I continued. "This is where my home is. I was born and raised here, and this is where I will always be."

"That is super, Shawn. It's quite the process getting anyone licensed with the state and privileged at the hospitals—especially fresh graduates, because they must pass their board exams first. If it goes perfectly, we're talking six to eight weeks. My practice just made this decision a week ago. The formal search was not set to start until the end of spring, but I've got to tell you, Shawn, this is great. You just thrusted your way to the top of a short list. Have you considered attempting to take your boards early? That would help."

"Yes, sir. The end of April. I'll pass them."

"Perfect. Here's my card." He began writing on the back and said, "This is Bob's cell number. You stay in touch with him as well as my office manager, Nora. Send her your cover letter and resume as soon as possible. Does Bob know you're here?"

"Yes, sir."

"Good. Call him so he can give you all the details about what our lives are like, expectations on a day-to-day basis, requirements for the state, etc. You get the picture. He works way too many hours. We need to get him some help. And get us that resume. I want it this week."

He stood, shook my hand again, and said, "Great seeing you. Thanks for coming in today. Please excuse me. If I don't get back to seeing my office patients, the staff will have my head. They're the team that holds us together. Gotta keep 'em happy."

He showed me to the lobby and off I went. *Holy shit!* He practically handed me the frigging job right there in his office. Is this what I want? I looked down at Bob's number. I wanted to make the call right then and there. *Don't seem too enthusiastic, Shawn. Give it a day, maybe two.*

I've got a feeling that Bob will hold the key to my decision.

I couldn't do it. I couldn't wait. After I ate a quick dinner and did some board review questions, I secluded myself in a bedroom, cleared the floor to allow myself space for nervous pacing, and made the call.

"Hello, Bob? This is Shawn Roussin."

"I was expecting your call. The big guy gave me the head's up."

I gave him my abbreviated bio again, and then he gave me a dissertation on a typical week in the life of Bob.

"Expect to work twelve-hour days. That's average. We cover two hospitals on opposite sides of the city. Each morning, prior to doing surgery or before office hours start—depending on the day—every patient is rounded on. Right now, I do all the morning rounds. The docs will see patients in the evening, but typically only the ones they operated on that day. Therefore, we need another PA. Hands down, we are the busiest surgical practice in the state. And now that we've added another surgeon, things have gotten a bit crazy, to say the least. One of them is almost always performing surgery somewhere, four to five days per week, and we need to be there to first-assist.

"Although our job is hospital-based, one of us will need to be in the office to perform post-op appointments, pre-op physicals, and dictate notes. This is because Dr. Hopedale has fifteen-minute appointments, and every single one of them gets double-booked, so think seven-and-a-half-minute surgical consultations for five to eight hours straight, two days per week.

"When you're not helping in the office, you're scrubbed into a case or rounding on all of our admitted patients. Right now, only the docs take call (carry a pager and phone for urgent overnight communications), but that could change. I have been asked to scrub out of a case, run down to the ER to consult on a patient, put out a fire, sometimes admit them to our service, then rush back up to finish the case, close the wounds, and wheel the patient to recovery to begin writing orders.

"Because there are so many general surgeons in town, night-call for them is about once per week. As PAs though, we're required to round on all admitted surgical patients every sixth weekend at both hospitals, which could be upwards of thirty, and let me tell you, those weekends can suck. Basically, we're responsible for writing and/or dictating every single note on every patient, every day. The surgeons don't touch pens, they only touch instruments. Any questions?"

What in bloody hell? "No, Bob. That was an outstanding summary. I didn't have time to create a list of questions, but thanks to you, I didn't need to."

I'm reeling. I'm shaking. I'm still pacing. But I'm excited. It's my job to lose now. It'll be a safe one though. I know these hospitals, the staff, the names, and where everything is. I have no kids. The commute would be long, as would the hours. It'll be high-pressure, fast-paced, and grueling, but I can do this. It's the right time in my life. My heart has been telling me to go into emergency medicine, but maybe my heart is wrong.

January 10, 2001, Wednesday.
[1 day since last entry]
This morning, I was in the ICU with Brad, and Dr. Hopedale walked in. "Hey, Shawn. How are you doing?" He turned to Brad, "Hey, what cases has Shawn assisted on?"

"He's done a couple of discectomies, a laminectomy or two, and a posterior lumbar interbody fusion."

Dr. Hopedale grabbed a loose piece of paper from the desk and handed it to me. "Write me three post-op orders for a discectomy. Anything. I don't care. The first three things that come to mind."

"We just did a T-twelve burst fracture and I'm about to write the orders. Can I just do that?"

"Yeah, sure. I don't care, just go. You've got one minute. Any three."

Dammit. Just yesterday, I was talking to Brad about wanting to focus more on post-op orders because my general surgery rotation was coming up and I wanted to be ready. I thought we hadn't spent enough time on that, and now I'm being put on the spot, timed, for the chief of surgery, the guy I may work for in a few months. *Shit.* This is part of my interview—right here in the ICU. I whipped out my pen and started writing: "Vitals every hour x 4 hours, then every 4 hours x 24 hours."

"Okay, stop." He swiped the paper out from under my hand, took one look at it, and threw it away. "That's good. You passed!"

What the hell was this guy talking about?

"You passed." He spun around and headed towards a patient's room. As he slid the glass door open, he smiled back at us. "I just needed to be sure that I could read your handwriting. If there is one thing I can't stand, it's terrible handwriting. You passed."

January 11, 2001, Thursday.
[1 day since last entry]
It didn't take long for Dr. Hopedale to start inquiring about me around the hospital. I showed up this afternoon and the first person who came up to me was Christine, one of the lead surgical technologists. She said, "Dr. Hopedale was asking about you during a case this morning."

"You're kidding? I just spoke to him less than twenty-four hours ago."

"Yup. He was telling everyone in the room that he met with you at his office earlier this week, and then put you through a quick handwriting test yesterday. Don't worry, I put in a good word for you. I think it would be an amazing first job for you. You'd be perfect."

Dr. Hopedale made an excellent point about the handwriting. Reading paper charts is brutal. I know electronic charts are coming, but it could be years before that's a reality. For now, the reality is that this might be the best job offer I receive.

I told her how much I appreciated the endorsement, but I was hesitant due to the extremely brutal hours, long commute, lack of predictability, and the fact that it was not primary care.

January 15, 2001, Monday.
[4 days since last entry]
I threw all etiquette out the window. I needed more information to help me decide about pursuing this expected job offer, so, with Brad's

blessing, I cornered Bob in the locker room to talk numbers. "Bob, as a new graduate in New Hampshire, working long hours in general surgery, what do you think my salary might look like with Dr. Hopedale?"

He glanced over his heavy brown plastic-framed glasses, then scanned the room for informants. "Dr. Hopedale does not like high numbers."

"The national average for new graduates across all specialties that work a mean of 45 hours per week is 58,000. If I'm going to be working upwards of 60, then 58,000 would be considered very low."

"Like I said, he doesn't like high numbers."

"Can you elaborate?"

"Let's just say that I'm not making that, and I've been with him for about three years."

Shit! Was he serious?

"Yeah, I've been wanting to sit down and talk to him about that… But don't just look at your starting salary. His practice puts together a nice benefits package, so consider the big picture. Plus, you'd get to learn under the best. There is a prestige factor that should not be overlooked."

"Okay, I guess. If the health insurance is great, I get three weeks paid vacation, a good continuing medical education fund, and all of my professional fees paid for, fifty-eight might be enough."

"You won't get three weeks, just so you're not surprised. Anyway, don't forget that you can't even apply for surgical privileges at Hillsborough Hospital until you have your New Hampshire medical license, and you can't apply for your license until you graduate and pass your boards. Did you say you were taking your boards early?"

"Yes. In April. No three weeks, huh?"

"No. You won't get three weeks' vacation until you've been with him for five years. And you won't get 58,000 either. No high numbers, remember that."

I need a job. I need money. I'm getting married in nine months. I'm way behind on my board review goals. I keep saying to myself that

I have time, but I don't. I have to take my boards early and I have to pass them on the first try. I have to have a job lined up and ready to start as soon as legally, contractually, and humanly possible.

January 17, 2001, Wednesday.

[2 days since last entry]

Brad and I walked out of a patient's room in the Hillsborough office and took one look at each other. We knew exactly what the other was thinking: *Those pants.* Until now, I've never seen anyone with pants so tight that they looked like they were painted on. This thirty-five-year-old woman was a knock-out. She knew it, and she was advertising it to the universe. Covering up the black pants were black go-go boots. The brushed-nickel hooks held laces all the way to the knee. Despite freezing temps, her pink crop-top exposed the bottom of her bra, and revealed her navel piercing, which matched her silver dangling earrings. Winged insect? Dragonflies, perhaps. She was modest enough (or cold enough) to be wearing a knee-length black leather trench coat. Keeping the black theme going was her suspiciously black hair color which provided a sharp contrast to her striking cobalt blue eyes.

Walking to Dr. Jackson's office, Brad whispered to me, "Are you wondering what is in her small paper bag? She kept it pretty close to her the entire time, guarding it like it was wads of cash from a drug deal."

"You saw that, too? Maybe she packed a lunch. I don't know. She didn't have a purse or anything with her."

"Dr. Jackson is gonna love this one."

We sat across from Jackson, and Brad let me present the case. I ended with, "The big question everyone wants to know is, what's in the bag?"

"Huh? Bag?"

Brad laughed. "You'll see. Oh, and the pants."

Dr. Jackson went into the exam room by himself, but spent much longer in there than he usually does. As he exited, we heard him say,

"We'll get you set up for those injections, but if the injections don't work, call us." Jackson headed back to his office to dictate his note while Brad and I were standing in the hallway near the checkout counter.

The young woman flew out of the room with her rolled-up paper bag tucked under her arm, frantic. She said, "Can you guys help me? I'm on limited time. I have to get to the airport to pick up my boyfriend."

I decided to be the brave one. "I see you brought a bagged lunch to your appointment. If you tell us what's for lunch, we might help you." That caused a massive blush. She giggled and covered her eyes with her free hand.

"That's what I sort of need help with."

"Your lunch? Do you need help eating it? It's almost lunch time. I'm sure the office is hungry and wouldn't mind an appetizer."

"Oh, it's not lunch. You can't eat it. Do you really want to know what's in it?"

"Nope! Now I don't. None of my business. Your face told me everything I need to know."

"I'll put it to you this way. Show me where your bathroom is. I need to do a little Superman phone booth change."

Brad then tried to rescue me. "Wait, what? You mean that you're going to change into what's in that paper bag?"

"Uh-huh. It's a dress. To surprise my boyfriend."

"A dress? In that bag? No. You can't fit a dress into that bag. No way."

"Well, there is, and I'm running out of time. I have to change here, right now." And with that, she ran past us and vanished into the waiting area bathroom.

I looked at Brad. "We shouldn't be here when she comes out."

He laughed and said, "Ha! You're right. We shouldn't."

When Superwoman barged out of the phone booth, the office went silent. Transformed from the dark of night, to the white of a New England snow, the silky spaghetti-strapped dress, clung to her cleavage. Hugging her waistline and barely masking her glutes, it exposed four feet of leg down to her white heels. "What do you think? Do you like it? If you were my boyfriend, what would you do to me?"

"What do we think?" I said. "I think you should get to the airport. I hope you make it past security. I think you're going to get frisked." And with that, we turned and hightailed it out of sight.

January 18, 2001, Thursday.

[1 day since last entry]

While rounding at Green Mountain Medical Center (GMMC), I had mentioned to Darren that I had seen an ad in one of the PA journals that the GMMC emergency department was looking for a full-time PA. Armed with that information, once we completed the note on our final patient, Darren says, "We've got a few minutes, follow me."

We roamed into the ER's waiting area, where he flashed his badge at the front desk, and asked if Stephanie was in. After getting confirmation that she was, we were allowed to go see her.

"Who's Stephanie?" I asked Darren.

"She is one of the full-time ER physician assistants. I've never met her myself, but she's the only name I know of down here. I thought we'd introduce ourselves and you might have an impromptu interview."

Darren found the charge nurse and asked where Stephanie was. She directed us to a small office just down the hall. Arriving at an open door, Darren leaned in and asked, "Are you Stephanie?" After her acknowledgement, he introduced himself. "I'm Darren, from neurosurgery. We haven't met. And this is Shawn Roussin, a PA student from Portsmouth, who is rotating with us. He's graduating in May and heard this ER is looking for a PA. If that is still true, can he have a few minutes of your time?"

We shook hands. "A student?" she asked. "Well, this ER has a history of avoiding recent graduates because we have the busiest ER in the state. We need someone who can hit the ground running and function with a great deal of autonomy."

Disappointed before I even had the chance to plead my case, I said, "I understand. My interest in emergency medicine sparked during my ER rotation at Daniel Webster Hospital last summer. I was even on the brink of doing an ER residency there through Alderson Broaddus University, but it fell through a few weeks ago when the hospital refused to pay the minimum student stipend. I don't believe all six ER doctors were completely on board with the idea. Anyway, that's probably the real reason it got nixed."

"I've heard of that residency. I doubt this hospital would go for something like that, either."

"Well, can I at least get my resume into the hands of the right people?"

"Of course." She ripped off the next yellow Post-it note, wrote a name and address on it, and handed it to me. "This is where it goes. We're struggling to fill it, so, you never know. Get it to us as soon as you can."

I thanked her for her time and stuck the Post-it note to an index card in my chest pocket. As we left the ER, I couldn't have thanked Darren enough.

January 19, 2001, Friday.
[1 day since last entry]
Being a student means facing potential mockery, and when these incidents occur, they can be unnerving, embarrassing, and generate animosity. How you respond and cope will build the foundation for which future medical decision-making disputes are handled. I now recognize that some past reactions of mine that were emotionally driven could've been conducted with more class and professionalism. Colossal fatigue and fierce overtaxing will push people to an edge. As you teeter on that boundary, advancing a single inch can cause collapse. It's risky. Sometimes you'll fall into the safety net. Oftentimes, you'll suffer a near-death experience. I need to be better at recognizing the danger and retreating. This usually means keeping quiet and cutting

my losses. There's a fine line between sticking up for yourself and burning the bridge you're standing under.

Brad and I were at one of the offices with Dr. Jackson. A seventy-eight-year-old man had come in with six months of worsening back pain and left leg numbness. Brad sent me in alone. Through my review of systems, the patient mentioned that he had been having severe intermittent dizzy spells for the past week. He denied headaches or any visual disturbances. As part of my exam, I listened to his carotids, and I'll be damned if he didn't have a loud right-sided bruit (a vibrating sound that denotes turbulence). Strokes come from two places: your heart and your carotids. I wasn't saying he was stroking out, but I wondered if this was the source of his dizziness.

I told Brad about it and he advised me to bring it to Dr. Jackson's attention.

Since neurosurgeons have no need for stethoscopes, Dr. Jackson had to borrow mine when the time came. "Shawn tells me he may have heard some abnormal sounds within the arteries of your neck, so I'm going to take a listen like he did, okay?" Regretfully, I hadn't mentioned this to the patient. I was looking for confirmation from a doctor before causing any alarm.

As I had done, Dr. Jackson advised that the patient hold their breath during auscultation (listening with a stethoscope). "Well. Everything sounds fine here." And he got up and walked out of the exam room. I followed him out and practically chased him down the hall. He was laughing. "No bruit there!"

Brad overheard it and looked over at me as I trailed behind Dr. Jackson. I rolled my eyes and shook my head out of frustration, which I know must have appeared arrogant.

I took a seat across from Dr. Jackson in his office. "He has a bruit. You really didn't hear anything?"

"Shawn, it's okay. You probably just heard him breathing. It's a common mistake that new students make."

"No, no, no. I always have them hold their breath, just like you did."

"Well, maybe he didn't hear you and was still shallow breathing, or maybe you were just hearing his heartbeat radiating into the carotid. That is quite common too."

"He wasn't breathing. I swear to you. It was like the strongest bruit I have ever heard."

"The strongest one ever? How long have you been doing this?" Still laughing. "When you hear a bruit, you'll know it, and apparently you haven't heard one yet. It's okay. You're a student. You're not supposed to pick up on these things."

The patient had a bruit.

January 22, 2001, Monday.
[3 days since last entry]
Although the GMMC emergency department lead wasn't very promising, it ignited a fire under my ass this weekend. I put together fourteen cover letters and resumes for every emergency room within fifty miles of Portsmouth. Those went into the mail today. I also tracked down the names and addresses of more than two dozen general surgeons and sent them the same, even though none of them were advertising open positions. The goal was to get my name out there and circulating. I'll do follow-up calls with each of them every few weeks.

Although the job search took up the bulk of my free time this weekend, I managed to complete four practice board exams. I'm still not caught up, but I've been content with my average scores on them.

I know that once I leave New Hampshire this time, I may not be back until after graduation, so I'm trying to spend every spare moment with family and friends—especially Karen. I don't want to leave her, but while preparing for the boards, it may end up being the best thing for me.

January 29, 2001, Monday.
[7 days since last entry]
I received an unexpected call from Brad on Friday night. He told me he ran into Bob and Dr. Hopedale and they were wondering how

much longer I was going to be in town because they wanted to talk to me again. Brad told me to call Dr. Hopedale's cell around 2:00 pm on Saturday.

"Hey, Shawn. Thanks for calling. I heard you're leaving next week. My partner, Dr. Driscoll, needs to meet you before you go. It's a formality thing. Can you swing by the OR on Monday to meet him, answer a few questions?"

So, today I went to the pre-op area at the time he thought would work best, but Dr. Driscoll hadn't arrived. Dr. Hopedale strolled in and told me he had just seen him in the recovery room, so he'd be over any minute. I asked where his next patient was, and a nurse directed me to room 8. Devising a way to look as impressive as possible, I walked right in and introduced myself to his patient. I must have chatted with her for a good twenty minutes when the curtain flung open and Dr. Driscoll poked his head in. "Give me thirty seconds."

Another ten minutes of great conversation and he pops in again, "Another twenty seconds."

Close to another five minutes ticks away and he leans in again, "Shawn? Come with me."

I excused myself and rushed out. Driscoll had his hand extended. We shook. "Nice to meet you. Let's walk."

Leaving the surgical floor, we began roaming the halls. He did all the talking. "Dr. Hopedale thinks you're the guy. He is obviously well-respected around here and gets what he wants—he's the chief, after all. But I'm the head of the endoscopic department and the trauma service. I trained at the best surgical program in the country, Chicago. He may have twenty-five years of experience, but I'm on the cutting edge. I will know things he doesn't."

"You'll be with me the first few months so I can get you trained how I want. I need things to go smoothly every second of every day and you will be crucial to that. I can't tolerate inefficiencies. I know ninety-nine percent of everything that I need to in order for our days to go perfectly. If it doesn't go perfectly, my demeanor will change and everyone around me will know it, including you.

"Basically, I don't want to be here, you know, in the hospital, any longer than I have to each day. I've got this new girlfriend and things are going really well. Eighty-hour workweeks piss me off, especially when they only need to be fifty to sixty. I'm done with eighty. I want to be busy. I want to be moving all day, but only with a purpose. We get shit done and we go home to our lives. When stupid unavoidable things happen that fuck with my ability to get home, I'm not happy. That drives me up a wall. Does this all make sense?"

"Absolutely. I'm with you."

"Good. You're the fourth candidate we've had come in. Two others were students too. This is not the position for a new graduate, so I was skeptical when Dr. Hopedale showed me your resume, but in my eyes, you have the OR experience—which is huge. You're also a presence. I wish you weren't six inches taller than me. If you're good, and you will be if you're with me, and you act confident, no one will fuck with you. If they do, I'll have your back."

This dude was cocky as shit. I wasn't sure how to process it all. It excited me, but was also intimidating. I never want to become that person: conceited, egotistical, abrasive, and perhaps overconfident. I'll need to be the counterweight: humble, approachable, unpretentious, and respectful. He was charismatic and funny, though. We hit it off well.

After a lap or two, we arrived back at the pre-op area where Dr. Hopedale had remained seated. "How'd things go?" he asked Dr. Driscoll.

"I agree. This is our guy," he said, slapping my back convincingly.

"Great, great. Okay, Shawn, do we have your New York address? If not, we need it. My office will mail you an offer by next week. Call me after you've reviewed it with your fiancée."

Throughout the entire ride home, I'm thinking, "*Well, I guess I'm starting my career in surgery.*"

I pulled into the dry cleaner to pick up my pressed shirts before the move back to New York, and who did I run into but Dr. Ed from my ER rotation this past summer. He would have been the MD overseeing my ER residency through Alderson Broaddus.

"Hey, Ed. What are you doing in my neck of the woods?"

"Oh, hey, Shawn. Your neck? I think you're in mine. What are you doing back in New Hampshire?"

"A neurosurgery elective."

"Oh, cool. Are you still interested in coming to work for us?"

"Absolutely. I kind of left the ball in your court and hadn't heard anything."

"I know, I know. It went on the back burner because we hired a new doc. Plus, I figured it was too late for you. I apologize for not getting back to you, but if you're still interested in doing it, I can go to the team and begin making another push. Maybe we can shoot for next year."

"Of course I am. That'd be great. I loved emergency medicine and the whole team you had over there, but I have to be completely honest, I just left my third interview with the chief of surgery at Hillsborough Hospital. He literally told me an hour ago he's mailing me an offer next week."

"You're kidding me? Wow, that's great news—and so soon! You don't even graduate until May, right? That's unheard of, man. Way to go!"

"But, seriously, I love the ER. I'm even applying for an open position at Green Mountain Medical Center, but was told that they're not granting interviews to new graduates, so I doubt anything will come of that. Last week I mailed out a letter and resume to every ER around here. Those envelopes probably haven't even been opened yet."

"As a new grad, it's going to be especially tough landing that first job. Your experience is in surgery, so you're going to have the best chance with a surgical position. If I could give you some advice: Don't wait too long. Secure a position by the end of April. People graduate in May. In June, docs finish their residency training. All of them will be job-hunting. The smart ones are starting now."

"That's what I was thinking."

"Well, congrats on the upcoming job offer. Go grab a year or two of experience and get back to us. You never know."

That sounded like an endorsement. It was also exceptionally sound advice, delivered sincerely by someone trustworthy like Dr. Ed.

In three days, I will pack the Accord to the top of the windows and make the several-hour trek back to Rocksville. I don't know when I will see family, friends, or Karen again. This rotation was the break I needed. I took advantage of it, but now the devil is coming to collect. Boards are approaching soon, and I can't keep ignoring the intense preparation required to succeed.

22

ROTATION #8— ORTHOPEDICS

February 5, 2001, Monday.

[7 days since last entry]

I'm sitting in the parking lot at High Point Hospital in Rocksville, New York, after a typical sleepless night before the first day of a new rotation. My seasonal affective disorder has shifted into high gear. Because of my experience during the OB/GYN rotation, my dread has been on full-tilt since I started my drive to get back out here.

Fortunately, I'm staying with Chris and Carolyn again, so I have the comfort of familiarity. They have been kind enough to open their home to me when I've needed them. They've provided me a room three times, and I might need them again. I decorated my room with everything that reminds me of home, mostly pics of Karen and me.

Karen and I had an amazing five weeks together, and for the first time we can say that we made tremendous progress on the wedding plans. We booked our DJ and photographer. All the table centerpieces are done and we've narrowed down the short list of honeymoon destinations. There is a good chance I won't see her for about four months. We may try to plan a long-weekend rendezvous, much like we did in Cooperstown last fall, but now with the board exam date lurking out there, that may not be possible. It's officially scheduled for April 28th. I'd aimed for a mid-May exam, but this was the best I could do.

I've been told this rotation will be 95% surgery. This has both advantages and disadvantages. The operating room is my refuge, but, as a PA student, I'm lowest on the totem pole and will have to compete with the medical students and residents for scrub time. Regular office work and treating patients with musculoskeletal complaints would be necessary for me to become proficient in joint exams. Since that kind of experience doesn't look like it will be provided, my goal now is to become better at writing post-op orders, especially since my final rotation, arguably the most challenging of all, is general surgery and I want to be at the top of my game for that one.

Surprise! I'm bored as hell again. My own damned fault. I was just too timid, and that cost me. As I said this morning, it's the competition factor. I lacked the necessary fight. I've got to be more assertive and unrelenting, otherwise I'll be left standing in the corner, forced into observational status, while everyone around me gets their cake and eats it too. Fuck that. Time is running out. Tomorrow, everyone will ask, "Who the hell is this cat and where did he come from?"

February 6, 2001, Tuesday.

[1 day since last entry]

What a difference a day makes. I spent another night festering in misery and depression, but when I rolled over at 5:00 am, turned off my alarm, flicked on the light, and saw Karen's face staring back at me from the nightstand, I knew what I had to do. Yesterday morning, all I wanted to do was sleep for the next four months, wake up in Karen's arms the day after graduation, and drive home with her. But today?

I met Patrick, my preceptor, at 6:30 so we could round on a few patients. As we were doing so, we ran into Dr. Reed, one of the orthopedic surgeons. Patrick asked if I could observe and possibly assist with his four cases today. Before Dr. Reed could get out his first word, Patrick was quick to add that I had a lot of scrubbing experience. Dr. Reed seemed less than thrilled, but agreed. I had overheard him talking to a lot of colleagues and residents at rounds the day before, and let's just say he came off as…pretentious.

Patrick warned me, "During the first case, suck up to him. Tell him how great he is, and lay it on thick, but in a non-condescending way. If you do, he may invite you to scrub the next one." I didn't want to play along. I'm sick of these games, but I also didn't want to stand in the corner of the operating room for the next five weeks. So, I put on my best ass-kissing face and we all headed down to the locker room to change into scrubs.

As we were changing, Dr. Reed, acting as if I'm deaf or invisible, confirms with Patrick, "Wait, did you say he had OR experience?"

Out of turn, I chimed in. "Yes. A thousand cases as a scrub tech."

Now acknowledging my presence, and appalled that I had the gall to answer a question not directed towards me, he said, "Oh, great, great. You should be a nice extra set of hands today, then."

"Whatever I can do to help."

"Okay, good," he said as he left. Patrick and I followed Dr. Reed into the OR and helped with positioning the anesthetized patient for their shoulder decompression and rotator cuff repair. Dr. Reed announced, "This is Patrick's student. He's experienced. Let's get him a gown and gloves."

Observation status averted. While gowning, I leaned over to the scrub tech. "Hi. I'm Shawn, Patrick's PA student. I've been an OR tech for a few years. You can yell at me and slap my hands whenever you need to."

She laughed, but whispered back, "I won't slap you. You're about to be abused by Dr. Reed, and I'm just glad he has you to focus on, not me."

My heart sank a bit. Great, so he's one of *those* guys? That's fine. "Do you mind if I help you drape and get the field set up?" I asked her.

No sooner did she agree, when the interrogation started by Dr. Reed. "Shawn, to educate everyone in the room who may not know, please name the three rotator cuff muscles."

Baffled, because I know there are four, I turned to him. He didn't look up. Okay, I'll play along and see what happens. "There are four rotator cuff muscles," I said with conviction. "They are the supraspinatus, infraspinatus, subscapularis, and teres minor."

"Oh, Shawn thinks there are four. I guess he's old school. Well, the teres minor is falling out of favor, but I'll give that one to you. What does the teres minor do? Where does it come from and where does it go?"

"Well, although it helps with rotation, it's more of a stabilizer. It arises from the scapula with its attachment point on the greater tubercle of the humerus."

If these questions get any harder, I'm in trouble.

"Yes. Yes. That is correct."

With the patient ready, he called for the scalpel and made his first incision. This created a brief suspension of Orthopedic Jeopardy. When we got back from commercial break, he invited me to look into one incision. "What's my finger on?"

"I believe that is the deltoid muscle."

"Yes. What are the functions of the deltoid?"

"It is the strongest of the flexor and abductor muscles, but also aids with rotational movements."

"Yes. That's right. Good. Does it adduct?"

"Hmm. I would say no, but since you phrased it how you did, the answer is probably yes."

"That's okay. Difficult question. It does, but it's a weak adductor. Tougher question now, the deltoid is innervated by...?"

"That'd be the axillary nerve."

"I need to make these harder. Not all residents make it this far. What dermatome overlies the deltoid area? If a patient comes to your office with neck pain and numbness over their deltoid region after falling off of a ladder, what level of the spine is their injury most likely located?"

This guy doesn't know that I did an independent study with Dr. Doolittle, extracting the entire central nervous system from a cadaver. "C-four," I announced.

"That's right! That's right!"

He couldn't stump me. For the rest of the day, he was treating me like his right-hand man. "Here. Put your finger on this. Do you feel that? That's a bone spur. Shawn, get in here. Come look. You've got to see this." It never ended. It was one of the best days I had ever had in an operating room. My drive, motivation, and commitment during the previous six years had prepared me for that moment, and I was rewarded.

By mid-afternoon, we were about to finish our fourth and final case. "Well," Dr. Reed said, "there are three incisions and three of us. What do you say we each take one, close 'em up, and get the hell out of here? Are you game, Shawn?" He dabbed my incision with a sponge. "That's the fascia. Get a running Vicryl in there. You know how to close, right?"

"Yup. I'm all set." I held my hand out, and the tech slapped that needle driver right into my palm, producing the perfect whack.

"I figured you did. Then do a running subcuticular stitch. Staples for the skin. It's not a race, but don't make me look bad by finishing before me. And whatever you do, be sure your closure doesn't look better than mine."

Despite finishing last, my work looked just as good as his. Since he was in a jovial mood, I kept the one-liners going, "I sure hope my wound stays closed long enough for the patient to make it over to the recovery room." The entire cast of the operating room broke out in laughter.

Dr. Reed made my day when he said, "It will. I watched your every move. You can scrub with me anytime, Shawn."

He appreciated me. I felt horrible that I had assumed he was an arrogant prick. Maybe he can be, but it just goes to show that you can't always take someone else's word on things like that.

February 9, 2001, Friday.

[3 days since last entry]

I've given residents a bad rap at times. We're in similar boats, contending for knowledge and experience, but if I'm being truthful, most have been helpful. Since one of my goals for this rotation was to get better at writing post-op orders, I devised a plan earlier in the week to follow the residents to the recovery room after a case, stand behind them, look over their shoulders, and copy all their orders verbatim. Every resident has their own preference cards for post-op pain control, diet advancement, and medication selection for nonprescription drugs like acetaminophen and stool softeners, depending on the complexity of the procedure and expected length of stay in the hospital. After a couple of days of taking notes, it was time to begin bootlicking and applying my new knowledge.

Today, I arrived at the surgical suite early and scoped out all the cases on the schedule to see which residents would be present for each, and which procedures they'd be performing. From that information, I mapped out a plan of attack. I made a request to be with Dr. Susan, a fourth-year resident, for the first couple of surgeries. As had often been the case, I became the designated retractor holder. Susan and her attending were great, though. They capitalized on every teaching moment, and the pimping was fair. As soon as we completed the first case, I rushed over to the PACU, grabbed the patient's chart, and began feverishly writing the post-op orders. Two chairs away, Dr.

Susan began dictating her procedure note while the details were fresh in her mind, a common practice with most surgeons.

I knew I'd only have a few minutes. When Susan completed her dictation, she stood up and began scanning the area for the chart. I had just slid my pen back into my chest pocket when she approached. "Shawn? Is that the chart? I need to write the post-op orders."

"It is, but I just completed them for you."

"What? They're done? You can write orders? I thought you were a student."

"I can write them, but they can't be executed without a co-signature," I said. "I always write a big S after the PA. Take a look. You can change or add anything you want, then sign beneath me."

Dr. Susan ran her finger down the two pages as she scanned, her lips moving as she proofread. "Super! Nothing wrong with these. Thanks so much."

I repeated this for the next two cases, then went back up to the floors to round on those patients before signing out for the day. I wanted to see if Dr. Susan had made any changes to my work, but she hadn't; her signature was there on each of my post-op orders and notes.

I scooted down to the main orthopedic office where everyone has lockers and desks, and Dr. Susan was there at a table, eating grapes, with two open books, one on either side of her. "Hey, Shawn. Thank you for all your help today. I've never had a student write my post-op orders before. I had no idea they could. Saving me those extra five minutes allowed me to grab a snack and a few sips of coffee, and that meant a lot to me, so, thanks again."

"You're welcome. I'm happy to assist. I was trying to take some initiative and create some learning opportunities for myself."

"Well, any time you want to scrub on our cases, just give me a heads-up. I'll run it past the attending, and we'll get you in there, okay?"

"Much appreciated. Thank you."

On a small couch in the corner, between two sets of four battleship-gray lockers, was Dr. Robert, a third-year resident. He was packing up for the day. I had already assisted (stood beside him doing nothing) on a couple of knee scopes this week. He overheard us and joined in. "Shawn, have you looked at tomorrow's schedule yet?"

"I haven't. I usually arrive early to look at it and come up with a plan for my day."

Reaching into the pocket of his white coat, he pulled out a full-sized piece of paper that was folded in half. He handed it to me. "There you go," he said. "I've circled my cases. Let me know if you're interested in any. Susan shouldn't get too angry. She's in clinic tomorrow, not the OR." He smiled.

Dr. Robert had four cases, including a total knee replacement. "I'll spend the entire day with you, if you don't mind," I said.

"You got it. Meet me right here at six in the morning."

Sweet! The residents are now fighting over me. I wasn't expecting that.

This rotation just got a bit more interesting.

February 10, 2001, Saturday.

[1 day since last entry]

The fantastic week doesn't erase the deep sadness of being away from Karen. I needed to get out and let loose. Dan and Bethany and one of her friends, whose boyfriend canceled on her at the last minute, decided we'd go to a local nightclub. I was going to be the fifth wheel, but now, only the fourth. I drove to the club separately from the three of them and had spaced out two drinks before I left. We didn't arrive at the club until 10:45 pm, upon which I bought the first round for everyone. Bethany's friend had her drink down in minutes and before we knew it, she had summoned a waitress over to order a round of cocktails called slippery nipples. Sipping time was over and the liquid was connecting with my synapses. Dan led Bethany to the dance floor, and we all followed. We secured some open space next to three girls, all dancing with each other. One song in and I turned to Dan, "That blonde in the white snakeskin boots is checking me out. Can you verify?" I played dumb during the next medley, but every time I caught her eye, they were already glued to mine.

Dan moonwalked over to me, grabbed the back of my neck, and screamed into my ear, "Verified! Oh, and if you turn around…"

Boom! As I did, the blonde grabbed my hips and the grinding began. She pulled me in close and released her breath on my neck. It was hot and sweet. She smelled like an expensive Cosmopolitan perfume. Whenever she'd whip her hair around, wisps of it would get caught on her pink lip gloss and she'd set it free with one of her fingernails. She followed this by biting her lip and looking down at her cleavage, then up at me, and then down below my waistline, inviting me to take a more invested stare. But she didn't know that this was one investment property I was not permitted to enter. I shouldn't even be on the same street. And I certainly shouldn't be ringing the doorbell.

The sexual tension was rapidly rising with the blood alcohol level, when suddenly this six-foot-seven, two-hundred-and-eighty-pound bouncer, busting out of his red T-shirt, ripped through us to go break up a fight. It was the only thing that could release me from her clench. She lunged back onto me and I said, "I wouldn't mess with that guy. I'm pretty sure he could kick both of our asses, even if he were hogtied and face down in manure."

"Would you look at that. He talks."

Those were my first words to her all night. To be fair, she hadn't exactly said anything to me, either. Her hands and eyes did all the talking. My silence had been purposeful. I didn't want to get to know her for fear that I might actually like her.

By now, everyone was dripping with sweat. Dan and Bethany slipped back to our table, and this woman's two friends have vanished. After a couple more tunes, this babe backs her ass up into me, grabs my wrists and forces them onto her inner thighs. Her skirt lifts as she extends her head onto my shoulder. Now that she has my hands where she wants them, she slides one of hers between us, onto my little friend, which you could've hung a wet beach towel from. She's licking the salt from my neck. Backing away now would leave me exposed. The pack of remaining patrons is getting a show, and we're the headliner.

Every beat attracts more attention towards us. I couldn't find my friends. I needed help to get out of this. There is no way to signal anyone, send out an SOS, nothing. But God was watching, and his voice, sounding much like the DJ, announced the last mix of the night. I've never been so relieved to hear the thunderous beat of a track that was not a ballad. That would have led to making-out and my beach towel post ending up under the front of her skirt. The alcohol was metabolizing, so clearer heads were prevailing. When the lights came up, she gave me a friendly hug, then kissed my cheek. As she pulled away, she said, "I'm Haley. I didn't get your name."

"Shawn."

"And what are you doing here tonight, Shawn?"

"Inappropriate things with a beautiful girl named Haley. And you?"

"Me? I am doing very appropriate things with a hot guy named Shawn. What do you do by day, big guy?"

"I'm a senior at RTC."

"I'm a senior at Montgomery Community College, studying nursing."

Ahhhh, friggin great! Of course, you are. Couldn't be marketing, or economics, or English literature. Nope, had to be in healthcare. Perfect. Okay. I need to lie. Just lie. Go ahead. Make something up, but not in healthcare. Don't create a connection. Don't do it, Roussin. "No kidding? I'm doing my physician assistant internship right now." *No! Roussin, you idiot!*

Intrigued, and now blushing, she said, "Well then. I think I need to see you again, and soon. My friends and I come here a lot. How about we meet right back here three weeks from tonight?"

"Three weeks from tonight? Here? On this dance floor?"

"Yes, but don't bring any friends, and neither will I, because I think we'll be leaving early. Will I see you then?"

"Yes."

We did not exchange numbers or emails, and nothing was written on a bar napkin or a palm. It was a verbal contract: a location on a specific night, with explicit instructions.

But it ain't gonna happen.

February 11, 2001, Sunday.

[1 day since last entry]

Once I mitigated a mild hangover, my first order of business was to call Dan. He picked up after three rings, which was three rings too late for me. Laced with sarcasm in his best New York Italian accent, "Hey there, rock star, how you doin'?"

"Nothing happened, bro. Nothing. Seriously, Dan. You've got to believe me. Dan, c'mon, man."

"I don't care if it did. She was smoking hot, dude. Besides, she was clearly the aggressor."

"No, Dan! Nothing happened. I didn't get her number, nothing. I have no way of contacting her even if I wanted, but I don't want to. That's the truth. And you have to tell Bethany that nothing happened. What if she and Karen talk? I can't tell Karen what happened. You've gotta believe me!"

"I believe that absolutely no one else at the club saw your raging boner. And certainly no one saw her grappling with it, so I don't think you have anything to worry about."

Dan was laughing his ass off and laying it on thick.

"Dan? Bud? I feel like shit. I'm an asshole for letting that go on as long as I did, but nothing happened. That was three drinks, two shots, and one poor decision away from lifelong regret. I was hoping you'd come save me."

"Ha! Save you? From getting naked? With her? Um. Then I might be the one living with regret." Dan is one of the funniest sons-ofbitches I know, and he was not taking it easy on me. I appreciated the humor, but what I needed at the club was an air-sea rescue, or a baseball bat up the side of my head. I got neither. All I have now is this crushing guilt.

"Listen to me, Dan. She told me to meet her back there in three weeks, to come alone, and we'd leave early. That's what she said. I'm not going."

"No shit? Oh, man. Yeah, you can't go. You know exactly what will happen the next time she sees you."

"I know, Dan. I know. I'm not going."

"I trust you. And don't worry about Bethany."

February 12, 2001, Monday.

[1 day since last entry]

I know it has only been thirty-six hours, but I have not found the cure for guilt.

Right before the last case of the day, I popped my head into the operating room where the nurse and anesthesiologist had just wheeled in our patient. A fully gowned OR tech, a robust Black woman, looked up at me and said, "And who do we have here?"

"Oh, hi. I'm Shawn, Patrick's PA student."

"Hey, everyone! Look who's here. It's Shawn, Patrick's PA student."

The circulating nurse, who was assisting the patient onto the OR table, turned to look at me. "Shawn? So you're the one we've heard about."

"Crap. What did I do? Is my name atop of some secret dry erase board, denoting that I am the lead demerit-getter around this joint already?" The anesthesiologist and Dr. Robert erupted in laughter, nearly blowing their masks off.

The OR tech said, "No, no. It's all good. We heard you know your stuff, that's all, son. You know your instruments, how to do counts, how to drape, set up Mayo stands. Hell, we even heard you're closing wounds already, and you've only been here a week. Man, people are talking 'bout you. Now, what size gloves do you need? Go scrub and get your butt in here."

February 13, 2001, Tuesday.
[1 day since last entry]
Dr. Solomon, whom I was with all day, refuses resident coverage for his service (all patients admitted under his name). That just means that the staff PAs assist in all his surgical cases and round on all his patients. To get familiarized with my patients, even though I may never see them again, I find their chart in the pre-op area and read the last orthopedic office note, as well as their pre-op clearance note. Since I'll be writing post-op orders, I also review each patient's allergies. Our hip replacement patient had penicillin and Compazine listed on her chart.

After the surgery, we took down the drapes, the patient was extubated, and while coming back to consciousness she announced she was about to get sick. The nurse raised the head of the bed and put an emesis basin under her chin. The young-appearing anesthesiologist, likely a resident, had a fourth-year medical student with him. "What do you want to give her for nausea?" he asked her.

The med student announced, "Compazine, five milligrams, IV."

"Sounds good."

As he drew it up and headed for the IV port, what was happening suddenly registered with me. I reached out and grabbed the anesthesiologist's wrist. "Whoa, whoa, whoa! Wait, wait."

The room fell into a state of shock. Aside from the dry heaving in the background, you could hear a pin drop. Technically, I just committed an assault. I should not have grabbed his arm, but it was instinct.

"Isn't she allergic to Compazine?" I whispered, knowing the patient was inches away.

He turned to the patient's chart, flipped a page, and gasped. "Oh, shit! She is."

The nurse to my left gave me two quick taps on my shoulder and when I glanced over at her, she gave a single nod. I looked over at the med student. She removed her mask, released a puff of air, placed her palm on her forehead, and walked away without a word.

In recovery, I just hung in the shadows, waiting for a brief window where I could swoop in and get my hands on the patient's chart. I needed to see what was listed as her reaction to Compazine. Dr. Solomon closed it and left it on the counter. I saw my opening. I only needed a second. There it was: anaphylaxis—the worst possible allergic reaction; it could have been life-threatening. I returned to the shadows. Three times that anesthesiology resident walked past me and never said a word, nor did he even make eye contact with me. I suppose he could have me written up, but he knew he messed up. Writing me up could actually put his career at risk. I can hear the attorney now: "Mr. Resident, I see you have filed a complaint against Shawn A. Roussin, physician assistant student—for assault. Could you elaborate as to the nature of this offense?"

"Why yes, judge. This student prevented me from killing my patient."

"Case dismissed." Gavel down.

Egos have no place in medicine. I hope to God I never develop one.

February 14, 2001, Wednesday.

[1 day since last entry]

At the conclusion of our last conversation, Karen and I had arranged tonight's call for Valentine's Day purposes. So, at promptly 8:00 pm, the cell phone sitting on my chest rang out as I lay on the bed reading about growth plate fractures. Despite anticipating the call, I was startled nonetheless.

My first words, "I miss you."

"Aww. I miss you too, babe. But, hey, I've got a bit of a bone to pick with you."

"Me? What did I do?" Then the lightbulb flipped on in my brain.

"Last week, I took a few pics during our snowstorm and finally finished the film that has been in my camera since at least Christmas. Today, I picked up those pictures. You wouldn't have any idea how a bunch of photos of you holding babies ended up on my camera, would you?"

She seemed entertained by them, and I didn't hear her loading a sniper rifle. "Oh, those silly things? Yeah, the ladies in the pediatric office put me up to it. They thought it would be funny since they knew of my baby fever and your baby chills."

"Oh, really? They put you up to it? You know I'm not buying that for a second, Mr. Roussin."

She knows me too well. It was all my idea.

"And just so you know, as I sat in my car thumbing through them, I smiled at each one and maybe even became a little choked up," she said.

"You? Choked up? Now I know you're lying."

"I did, Shawn. In those pics, I saw such joy on your face, but also admiration on the faces of those kids. I have never felt so connected to you, knowing you are my man, and one day you are going to be an amazing father to our children."

"So, you liked my little prank?"

"No, I loved it."

February 15, 2001, Thursday.

[1 day since last entry]

Today, I scrubbed with the absolute worst surgeon I have ever seen, and for that reason, I will just call him Dr. Slaughter. By the end of the day, I was asking serious questions. People were forthcoming, but spoke to me off the record. Apparently, he was originally from a different hospital here in Rocksville, but they revoked all his surgical privileges. Eyewitnesses corroborated stories of him bullying residents in front of patients and staff members, and blaming every surgical complication on them.

Patients wrote letters to the board of directors and the head of the hospital's residency program. There is an ongoing legal battle, yet somehow, they granted him privileges at this hospital. He's not allowed to interact with any residents or use them for coverage, so this falls on the in-house orthopedic PAs.

Fifteen minutes into the first case, knowing none of this, I said to myself, "I have to get out of here. I can't have my name on any chart associated with this hack. Do I fake getting sick?"

I know RTC has liability insurance for me, but I don't care. I want out. This idiot doesn't know what the hell he is doing. He's careless, indecisive, and impatient. I'm told that he purposefully leaves his pager in the car; no one can ever reach him when they need him. He's delinquent on operative reports. Other surgeons exclude him from the call schedule because they refuse to let him see their patients. In the middle of an arthroscopy, with a Black surgical technologist, he literally said, "Christ, why is it so hard to get good help around here, especially white help?" My fists balled up, and I had to stop myself from rendering him unconscious. Pretty sure that is unlawful.

I had six cases with Dr. Slaughter today. Six! There won't be a seventh. Ethically, I can't. I need to speak with Nadine or Bailey, and it can't wait. Patrick, my preceptor, just went out on disability, so there is only one other PA, a nurse practitioner, and me covering all of ortho at this time. I don't think I'm getting out of this.

After the disturbing day ended, I went back to the ortho office. Dr. Robert (the third-year resident), was grabbing a bite to eat. "Hey, how'd your day go?" His sarcasm was clear.

"I'm never scrubbing with that inept racist again."

He replied, "You don't know the half of it."

"I actually think that I do. It doesn't seem to be a big secret around here."

"Didn't take you long to figure him out, huh? Let's just say that there are twenty-eight surgical residents across town who want him dead. Eventually, he'll get what he deserves. Do your best to avoid spending a single second in his presence. And whatever you do, if you are scrubbed with him, watch your hands. He has stabbed multiple techs with dirty needles and loves throwing instruments. My advice: Just stand there. Don't move, touch anything, or say anything unless spoken to."

February 20, 2001, Tuesday.
[5 days since last entry]
Today was another site-visit day. This was my fourth one, and I was convinced that it was my best. Bailey and I found an empty conference room where we sat across from each other. I handed her a copy of my presentation and I kept mine on the table in front of me for reference.

"Okay, Shawn, whenever you're ready, just take it away."

I scooted to the edge of my chair and pulled my copy towards me. I slid the paper clip off and set it aside. Before I could finish the second sentence, Bailey stood up, reached across the table, grabbed my presentation, and flipped it upside-down. "Oh, stop reading! You don't need this, Shawn. You know your patient, right? Just talk to me, tell me about her."

"But, Bailey, I don't know if I can do that. I wrote this more than a week ago and have only reviewed it once since."

"Don't give me that. Just try it."

Turns out, she was right. I fluently blazed through it without interruption or stuttering. I couldn't believe what I had just done. When my mouth finally closed, I looked up at her and she proudly beamed from ear to ear, nodded, slapped the desk multiple times and said, "See? You knew your patient. You knew what you were talking about. It was all in there, well organized. You trusted yourself and look what happened."

It was the first time I felt like I was talking to her as a colleague, not a faculty member. It was as if I had completed some rite of passage.

"Thank you, Bailey. I needed that affirmation. Something weird has been happening. I don't know if it's unique to me or if it's an expectation for everyone, but I feel ready. It's hitting me, like, just in the last several days. I can't explain it. Things are making sense. They're clicking. I'm ready for the next step, but I'm still conscious of my boundaries and limitations. I've reached a level of solace that I've never experienced before, but I promise you, I will *not* be resting on that."

"Good. Remember that. And you're not unique, but I think you are the first in your class to arrive there."

Ever since my in-patient rotation, I've felt like my relationship with Bailey has been strained. I've been walking on eggshells around the entire faculty, always feeling one misstep away from dismissal. Now I feel like I have repaired all of that. I consider today to be another defining moment in my training.

March 8, 2001, Thursday.

[16 days since last entry]

It has been over two weeks. Sorry. Today is my last day at ortho. It has been going so smoothly, especially since I managed to completely avoid any interactions with Dr. Slaughter. I think I emphasize the negative things more than the positive. I guess I won't know if that statement holds true until I go back, listen to these tapes, and analyze the scorecard. Maybe I've been off-base, so I want to spend my last entry talking about the two residents that I spent the most time with: Dr. Susan and Dr. Robert. They never treated me as a subordinate. Perhaps it would've been different if this was my first rotation as a PA student. I'm an entirely different person now than I was at the end of last spring. I'd like to think that I didn't receive any special treatment, and that these two are just great, kind-hearted human beings who would've done the same for any other student on their service, no matter their level of experience.

Everyone knew, especially these two, that I couldn't tie one-handed knots with either hand, let alone my dominant one. They also knew about the likelihood that I was about to accept a job offer in surgery. One early afternoon, I entered the ortho office where both of them were deep into their textbooks reading during their lunchbreak. I had already eaten in the cafeteria, but was searching for a free coffee. A hot pot was always sitting in the office—even though its age was questionable—so I snuck in and poured a mug.

"Hey, Shawn. How's that knot-tying going?" Dr. Robert asked.

"It ain't. I don't know. I need to get some paracord or something. You guys tie so frickin' fast that I never have time to lock down how you do it. You make it look so easy."

"This is your last week here, right?" Dr. Robert asked.

"Yup, and it has been awesome. I can't thank you both enough. You always treated me as your equal and made me feel welcomed as a true part of the team."

Susan closed her book and stood up. "Okay. Today you're learning one-handed knot tying. Lefty, righty. Let's go. Rob? You got your stuff?"

Dr. Robert pushed aside his lunch and walked over to a locker. He reached on top of it and pulled down a coffee can. As he walked back to the table, he turned the can over and dumped out some instruments and several small spools of suturing material.

Dr. Susan grabbed her grapefruit, wedged it into a coffee cup so that half the sphere was still protruding, and set it in front of me. "This is your patient's skin."

For the next thirty minutes, they sat on either side of me and methodically taught me how to tie one-handed knots. By the time I had performed about a hundred of them with each hand, I was tying them as quickly and artfully as them.

"You got it, man! Look at you. Okay. Time to increase the level of difficulty," Dr. Robert said as he grabbed the coffee tin, which I had just assumed was a container for supplies. He made me look inside. The can was a prop, and secured to the bottom was a small hook. "Now your job is to tie knots onto that hook with one hand, like you're deep inside an opened abdomen."

"What's the schedule for the afternoon?" I asked.

"We have no more cases today, but we've got the call-pager, so you can just tag along with us. Maybe we'll get some ER consults or an emergency case."

"Hmm. Okay, um, can I just stay and tie knots?"

They looked at each other and shrugged. Then Dr. Susan said, "I'll make a deal with you: you stay and tie knots on that hook until the entire spool of suture is gone, then you can go home. Leave the can on top of Rob's locker. I want to see it tomorrow."

It was dark by the time I secured the final knot. I had early symptoms of carpal tunnel syndrome, but managed to pack up my things and head home for a late dinner.

The following morning, right before rounds, when most of the teams were back in the ortho office, Dr. Robert grabbed the coffee can from atop his locker, looked inside, laughed and nodded. He then walked over to me and said, "This is perfect. You want another challenge? Find yourself a similar can, but maybe not as deep. You'll need to find some suture packs. Since I know the inventory supervisor who disposes expired sutures, I'll get you some before you leave. Now, throw a raw chicken thigh in the can, leaving the skin on. Put on a pair of latex gloves that are way too small or way too big and get your gloves coated with a bit of olive oil. Grab your needle driver and forceps and start putting stitches into the skin of that chicken thigh. Don't tear the skin. Don't drop an instrument. When you think you're getting good at that, stop looking into the can when tying the knots. Do them blindly. Master that before your first day on the job."

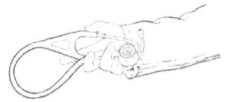

I'm sitting in my car now, having just walked out of High Point Hospital. I'll be back in five weeks to do my general surgery rotation. The ortho team said they wanted to take me out for dinner and drinks as a sincere thank you for making their lives easier and for "doing such a great job." I don't know if that will happen, but it's a gracious gesture. I could use a night like that. Not like the night I met Haley, which, by the way, didn't involve meeting up with her at the club last Saturday.

I should dedicate tonight to prepping for tomorrow's Recall Day orthopedic exam, but I'm exhausted. I'm sick of the darkness. It's always dark. It's dark when I wake up. It's dark when I arrive at the hospital, and it's dark when I leave. This seasonal affective shit has a tight clutch on me, and like the only cure for eclampsia is giving birth, I think the only cure for my SAD is going to be graduating, or maybe passing the boards. Speaking of that, our faculty told us that tomorrow the entire class will take a 150-question mock board exam in the afternoon. They deliberately withheld this surprise from us until a couple of days ago because they didn't want any of us preparing for it.

I'm looking forward to it. What I'm *not* looking forward to is finding a place to stay during my next rotation. I've been with Chris and Carolyn three times during these eight rotations. They said they would welcome me five times, but never back-to-back, so I'll have less than forty-eight hours to move my Honda full of stuff to a new location—somewhere within driving distance of Glenwood Hospital, where my psych rotation is located. If I can't, I may be living out of my car indefinitely. That could push me over the edge, and I could end up being admitted to the very psych unit to which I am assigned. Nothing like diving right into your work!

23

ROTATION #9— PSYCHIATRY

March 10, 2001, Saturday.

[2 days since last entry]

Both exams went fine. I'm assuming that I passed the ortho one, otherwise they would've found me to arrange a remediation date. I earned a 91 on the mock board exam. Taylor had mentioned that the class average had been 82 since they initiated this practice a couple of years ago. I believed her because the questions seemed rather simple. I can't fathom the national boards will be on this level. The faculty clarified that their exam does not predict success on the actual board exam.

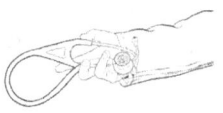

Holy crap! What have I done? I can't believe where I'm living. A room became available in a large six-bedroom home in a shady suburb of

Rocksville. I heard about this place from classmates. Other PA students will be there with me for the next five weeks, so I won't be alone in the house with strangers. Apparently, the owner lives there, and he is this thirty-something-year-old sex addict. Those who have rented rooms from him have said that ear plugs are required. Well, if nothing else, trying to study there should be entertaining.

Not quite ghetto, and not exactly Slumlordville, this place is downright disgusting. It smells like a mix of cheap stale beer, two-week-old trash, and swamp-ass. The living room contains an oversized ping-pong table covered in half-empty red Solo cups. Every step you take, as your feet lift off the floor, sounds like you're peeling masking tape off a cardboard box. What minimal furnishings were scattered about undoubtedly came from the town dump. Sweat-stained pieces of moth-eaten foam represented sofa cushions. The armrests were tattered, torn, and smeared with cigarette burns. It was all set against a backdrop of assaulted sheetrock and mismatched peeling wallpaper. Amongst those injuries to the walls, were phone numbers and pornographic poems written in various inks.

In the kitchen, for which the owner designated me a single cupboard, was a dark green 50-gallon garbage can with 100-gallons of trash pouring out of it. I suspected there was a counter, but it was not visible, thanks to heaps of dirty dishes piled at least a foot high in places. I was informed that I had been given a section of the fridge, shared with six others, but upon opening the door, I discovered it was already crammed full. An uncapped milk container had fallen onto its side into a small puddle. Next to it was an immovable jar of jam stuck to the shelf, lidless, of course. Despite knowing that my tetanus status was up-to-date, I dared not attempt rearranging any of the fuzzy objects to make room for my essentials. This was my prize for being the last sucker to move in.

Then I remembered that Karen was coming out next weekend. *No!* I can't bring her here. I need to talk to Chris. Maybe he and his wife, Carolyn, will show some mercy and let us crash there for the weekend.

March 12, 2001, Monday.

[2 days since last entry]

I can endure anything for five weeks, right? Living in this hellhole is going to test that theory. I've been fortunate, for sure. Chris and Carolyn have been wonderful. I've stayed with them for three rotations, been home for three, with Barbara once, and the other time was with three other female classmates in a four-bedroom apartment just off campus, so I made it to rotation nine before my first questionable living arrangement.

In the first hour of my first day at Glenwood Hospital, I asked a favor of my preceptor, Dr. Lyles. "My fiancée is coming into town from New Hampshire this Friday afternoon. I know it's a terrible look to ask if I could leave early, but I haven't seen her in almost six weeks. I'd be happy to make up any time that I miss."

"Oh, Shawn, don't worry about it. Of course you can. Around here, mental health is everything. Your happiness is important to us. In order to take care of people and make them happy, you need to be happy as well. How early is early? 11 am?"

"Oh, no. I was thinking probably about 3 pm." Not knowing him well, I didn't care if he was being facetious. I was caring less and less about these rotations, and more and more about passing the boards. Plus, I wanted every possible second with Karen this weekend.

"That's fine. No problem. Whatever makes you happy. We want to make sure that everyone is happy here."

I think he's fucking with me. He's just laying it on too thick, but again, I don't care.

I had heard that this rotation was a joke, so I am biased going into it. Arrival is at 8:30. It takes about thirty minutes to get the morning report from the overnight staff. During that time, all the students are seated in a semicircle behind that day's psychiatrist, who sits at a pair of old conjoined wooden school desks which have a recessed groove to place your writing utensil, preventing it from rolling to the floor. Each desk had the carved initials of past couples and partially removed graffiti. In our group, there was also a social worker and the charge nurse.

Once the report was completed, we started rounds, but at this facility they were conducted in a nontraditional manner. To prevent the group from just wandering around the psych ward, staff delivered each patient to us in the abandoned conference room. The questioning was almost identical for all patients. "So, how are you doing? How do you think the medications are working? Do you want to harm yourself? Do you want to harm others?" This would sometimes open up another line of interrogation. "Do you feel depressed? Are you afraid to interact with others? How are you sleeping? How are you eating? Do you want to die? Have you thought about killing yourself? Are you still thinking about killing other people? Do you hear voices or see things that aren't really there?"

If any of these questions are answered in the affirmative, the probing algorithm flows even farther downriver. When the personal interviews are finished, there isn't much for us students to do. Once the psychiatrist leaves to write their notes, we usually find a quiet area (not easy on a psych unit) to do whatever we want. For me, that's board review questions.

Today, we got out later than expected, just after 4:00 pm. Studying for boards for two or three hours daily at this rotation site would be the perfect scenario.

March 13, 2001, Tuesday.

[1 day since last entry]

Esther is a seventy-six-year-old woman, weighing all of eighty pounds and not topping five feet tall. Her eyebrows are painted on, and they don't match her blue hair. Rheumatoid arthritis had aged her knuckles to look more like her knock-knees. Similar to yesterday, Dr. Lyles asked the same series of opening questions. She'd select one of us from the semicircle, stare into their eyes, and concoct the most senseless, bizarre answer you'd ever heard.

"Esther? How is your mood today?" Dr. Lyles asked.

No response as she scanned her audience.

"Esther?" he repeated.

In an angry, suspicious whisper she said, "You're trying to get me."

"Oh, no, Esther. We are not trying to get you."

The patient turned to me. "I remember you. Are you trying to get me?"

Defending myself, I kindly responded, "No, Esther. I would never do that. My name is Shawn. I'm on the team here that is trying to help you."

With a voice resembling Linda Blair's from *The Exorcist*, Esther said, "I'm not confused. I know who you are. You better hope I don't get you first."

Splendid! Death threats on my second day, and from a waist-high, anorexic senior citizen speaking in tongues, no less. Didn't take long to make friends here. Turns out, she has baseline dementia, but it has been progressing rapidly for about two months. We spoke to her about having ECT (electroconvulsive therapy) later this week since it worked well for her during a prior admission, although it only seemed to help for a few weeks. It's an unconventional treatment for depression that has been refractory to medications.

"Shocks?" she said. "I knew you were going to hurt me. What if I did that to you?"

"It doesn't hurt. You've had them in the past and they helped," Dr. Lyles tried to explain.

She rose from her chair, looked to the heavens, reached into her mouth, and pulled out her false teeth. She shook them violently and drool began whipping through the air.

Dr. Lyles and the entire team of residents, nurses, social workers, and ancillary staff in the room all reacted like it was a Gallagher show, looking for a sheet of plastic to hold up as a shield. "If I go for shocks, they must take out my teeth. Those shocks hurt my mouth. If they don't, I will use my teeth to bite their faces off when they are sleeping."

Those were her last words for the day. She answered no more questions, just sat and stared right through us. I hope I wake up tomorrow morning with my face still attached.

March 14, 2001, Wednesday.
[1 day since last entry]
Cheyenne is a forty-three-year-old obese Native American woman who has been on the unit since late last week. On Monday, when the team met with her, she was alluding to hearing voices, but struggled to form her own words. Yesterday, she came across as normal. This morning, she refused to leave her room, so the team had to go to her. Barefoot and wearing loosely fitted hospital clothing, she stood in the middle of her room swaying back and forth and slowly turning clockwise in a tight circle. Occasionally, she would reach for the air high above her head, close her fist, and pull it back to her chest. Unresponsive to questions, Cheyenne would only click her tongue off the roof of her mouth. Since she wasn't being disruptive and we weren't getting anywhere, we headed back to the main interviewing room to meet with the next patient.

Cheyenne's mother, with whom she lived, came by every day around lunchtime to see her and to check in with the team on her daughter's progress. When I read the notes in her chart yesterday, I learned that the mother had been pumping up Cheyenne with an immense number of herbal supplements for several weeks leading up to her admission. At around 2:00 pm today, Dr. Lyles and the team had our meeting with her mother in the conference room where we see the patients each day, and it was damn near gut-busting.

"I know y'all don't wanna hear it again, but you need to be giving Cheyenne her medicines." One by one, she retrieved over a dozen bottles from her purse and lined them up on the wooden desk, followed by at least twenty pages of articles that looked to be clipped from various magazines you'd see in the grocery store checkout line.

"I read all of those after you dropped them off to us last week. I'm sorry, but the writer of these is a quack," Dr. Lyles told her.

"A quack? Oh, really? A quack? If you think he's a quack, then you're not a good doctor. They brainwashed you at doctor school. Maybe you need some of these here bottles."

"You can believe whatever you want to believe and that's fine, but this guy has no basis for his conclusions. He's not a doctor, has no credentials, and as far as I could tell, he's just clever at marketing. He's a quack." Dr. Lyles remained calm and spoke in a monotone, matter-of-fact manner.

Cheyenne's mom wasn't having it. "You're gonna give her these meds to make her better or I'm fixing to pull her outta here real fast."

"We absolutely will not be giving her any of these non-FDA-approved supplements during her stay here with us, especially since the team is convinced that these may be the cause of her behavior. We don't recommend these as doctors. If we did, we'd be putting our professional licenses at risk. There are no scientific studies to back up any of their claims. Your daughter is here because you have been coercing her to take these."

Mom's eyes were bloodshot. She slammed her fist on the desk and stood up so hastily that her chair flipped over. The back rest hit the floor with such force that it cracked into several pieces. If there had been a secret hand signal, code word, or emergency button to alert security to an inevitable altercation, this would have been a good time to use it. As she crammed each of those bottles back into her purse, she kicked her fallen chair across the room. One bottle fell to the floor, the lid opened, and dozens of clear capsules filled with green shavings rolled under our seats. Cheyenne's mother was not leaving without them, so she threw herself to the floor and frantically began collecting the pills, not even taking the time to place them back into the bottle. She just crammed them into her coat pockets. Once satisfied that she had retrieved all of them, she stormed off toward the stairwell.

Apparently, no one gave that hand signal.

My classmate Liesl, who was also assigned to this rotation, and I found our secluded study corner and began completing our daily write-ups. After about thirty minutes, I had just moved on to reviewing my practice board questions when an orderly flew around the corner. He said, "Hey, have you seen Cheyenne? She's missing."

Liesl and I dropped our pens and looked at each other. "No, not in an hour," she said. Missing? How does one go missing up here? It's a locked ward."

"I don't know. Someone must have let her out. We need all hands on deck to find her. Can you help us?"

"Of course. What do you need us to do?" I said.

"Start searching rooms. Behind furniture, closets, under beds. Anywhere a person can fit."

It didn't make sense for Liesl and me to team up, so we went in separate directions. We knew that Cheyenne was here somewhere. She had to be. You need a key to get out. The only possibility is that she overpowered someone entering, such as a janitor or food service worker. With the entire unit on the prowl, it only took minutes to conduct a thorough combing. She wasn't to be found.

With all available search staff back at the main desk, security was made privy to the situation. One of the guards instructed us to branch off the ward and begin exploring the hospital. I scrambled to the closest set of stairs, bolted down to the ground floor, and exited the first set of glass doors I came to. If Cheyenne wanted to escape, she could have done it by now. This was only my third day here. Long-term employees have difficulty finding their way around the building. I had no chance. I'd surely get lost, and by nightfall security would send out search units for me.

I figured the patient's mother must have been connected to the disappearance. I wondered if she came in a car. *The parking garage!* Across the street from the hospital's main entrance was a parking garage for patients and visitors. I situated myself at the exit. As each car paused at the gate, I focused through the windows, waved at the occupants, and scoped the interior for our fugitive. After inspecting the first twenty vehicles, my index of suspicion was waning, so I headed back up to the ward. The moment I entered the unit, I heard a commotion two rooms down from the nurses' station, in the room of Cheyenne's neighbor. As I ran to the scene, someone at the main desk, tending to the phone, alerted me. "They found her!"

Arriving on scene, staffers were on the defensive. Cheyenne was heaving anything she could get her hands on. With each throw, she'd scream out, "Mommy! Help me! Mommy! They're trying to kill me." Tactfully, security attempted to surround her, and I occupied what measly space there was between Cheyenne and the door. Once the security guard had closed within an arm's length, she made a run for it. As elusive as a greased pig, yet as powerful as a grizzly, we were no match for her. She divided us with shoulder checks, then spun away from our grasps like Barry Sanders.

Cheyenne sprinted down the hall trying to open every locked door. Unsuccessful, she hurdled over the nurses' station counter and picked up a phone. Without punching any numbers, she began pleading with the dial tone, "Mommy! It's me, Cheyenne! Come get me, Mommy! They're murdering me! Help!"

With her back turned, two security guards seized the opportunity and tackled Cheyenne to the ground. Face down, they both lay on top of her. A young male social worker named Roscoe tried to pin down Cheyenne's shoulders while attempting to calm her with words. Silas, a staff PA, accompanied by a male nurse who was an obvious Olympic weightlifter, each took an arm. I was now the only person not physically engaged in this violent encounter, but that was about to change because Cheyenne was winning.

"You! Get on her right leg!" I don't even know who said it, but I knew the command was directed at me. I sprawled out on the floor, placed my armpit on the back of her calf, and grabbed her ankle with both hands.

The Olympic nurse was stunned. "She's too strong. We just need to keep her from hurting herself and let her burn out."

The security team member who was laying across Cheyenne's butt and facing her legs had a plan. "Hey! Each of you, drive your knees into the back of hers, and pull her foot towards you. Cross her ankles. We need to hog-tie her so we can lift her onto a gurney and get her back to a room. Got it?"

Following orders, I knelt on the back of her knee and tried to bend her leg. Nothing. Wouldn't budge. My partner wasn't having any luck, either. I gave up when the blood vessels in my brain started swelling, but the Olympian on the left leg wasn't as reluctant to throw in the towel at first. When he eventually gave up, he shouted, "What the fuck is she on? Holy fuck! He's right. Keep her secure until she tires herself out. We might be here for a while. Can we give her Vitamin H?" This was code for: haloperidol—an injectable antipsychotic medication often given for severe agitation.

"I suppose we could," Silas replied, "but I think she's weakening."

Outside in the hallway, two nurses wheeled a gurney to the door of the office. One by one, each of us began loosening our grips to assess her response. She was done. Still muttering for her mommy, the fight was over. The two security guards lifted Cheyenne to her feet, led her to the gurney, and laid her down. I noticed the four-point restraints, but they would not get used today—at least not on Cheyenne.

March 15, 2001, Thursday.

[1 day since last entry]

There's something about the three o'clock hour. As I was settling in for some board review questions before being dismissed for the afternoon, the intercom system shot off. "Code gray! Code gray! Nurses' station. All personnel report." It was only my fourth day at this rotation, but I already knew that "code gray" meant a cage match was about to be unleashed by a patient who was out for blood.

Since I'm included in "all personnel," I jumped up and ran to the nurses' station. First to arrive, I witnessed a patient (not Cheyenne) standing on the counter, fending off a couple of nurses with a phone receiver. When she wasn't using it to strike staffers, she was yelling into it, "They're poisoning me, Mommy! They're gonna kill me! They want me to die." Everyone around here wants their mommy.

Silas was the second to arrive, just moments after me. I had him by six inches and about eighty pounds, but he was solid. Still flailing her arms and being combative, I turned to Silas and said, "We've got to do something. One staffer is down, bloodied in the corner. Do I have your permission to tackle her?"

"Permission granted. I'm right behind you."

As the patient searched for another weapon, she turned her back to me, so I pounced. Down we went. Silas wrapped up her legs when we struck the floor. In the same location, twenty-four hours later, here we are. Her strength, like that of a silverback gorilla, was impossible to match. Lying on my back, I had her arms secured in a bear hug. If security hadn't shown up when they did, she would have broken my clutches and gained the upper hand. It's plausible that I could have left the psychiatric ward in a body bag. But I evaded death today. Or at least an ER visit. This place is wild. People do this every day? Oh, HELL no!

If I survive my short day tomorrow, I'll get to see Karen. The key is escaping by 3:00. That's "code gray" hour.

March 19, 2001, Monday.
[4 days since last entry]
On Friday afternoon, when Karen pulled into Chris and Carolyn's driveway, I flew outside and raced to her car. Before she had the ignition off, I was prying the door open. She beat me to the seatbelt, so I held my hand out for her to grab. I yanked her out of the bucket seat and embraced her. Her hair, freshly dyed my favorite color—a deep auburn red, smelled like coconut. An itch started in the back of my throat, so I distracted myself by kissing her. It was the only way to hold back the tears.

"Leave your stuff here. I'll get it later. Come inside," I said. Neither Chris nor his wife was home yet. We dashed up the stairs to my room and collapsed on the bed where we spooned for hours, falling asleep under the winter covers. I'm not sure when my eyes opened, but it was getting dark and I could hear someone downstairs. Karen was motionless, breathing with romantic content. "Don't leave. Don't go back home," I whispered.

She grinned, cracked open her green eyes, and turned to face me. "I'll be okay."

"Well, I know *you'll* be okay. I was thinking about *me*," I said sarcastically. "It feels way too good having you here."

"Shawn, you're fine. You've got this. You've made it this far, right?"

"I know, I know, but I wish we had done this differently. I'm so unhappy, alone, and freaking out about the boards. This rotation is dismal, and the next one is the granddaddy of them all."

"Babe. I'm here now. Let's just have a great weekend. Monday morning will be here before we know it."

And in the blink of an eye, Monday arrived, and she was driving away. I don't know when I'll see her again. The next time will probably be at the White Coat Ceremony in mid-May. That's two months away. It's too long.

I couldn't sleep last night. I was overcome with this tragic tightness in my chest. My alarm clock was unnecessary. I didn't shower. I skipped breakfast and didn't pack a lunch. Fuck the tie today. There's no point in brushing my teeth since I won't be seen today without a coffee in my hand. The only thing worse than morning breath is morning breath laced with cheap coffee, but I don't care anymore.

As soon as Liesl saw me, she ran right over and said, "How was your weekend, Shawn? I bet it was awesome."

"It was. We had a blast. Thanks."

"You don't look like you did. Are you okay?"

"Nope. I think I feel worse now than I did last week."

She gave me a big hug. "Don't worry. You're almost there. Everyone in our class is feeling the same."

"I know. Karen tells me the same thing, but it doesn't make it any easier. I am five weeks and one day from the board exam, but I have no ambition to study. Time is slipping away from me. I should just reschedule for after graduation."

"Wait. Don't you have a job lined up? Isn't that why you're taking them so early? And I thought you said you need to earn a couple of paychecks before you and Karen get married."

"No, Liesl, you're right. You're one hundred percent right. That was the plan, but I don't know if I can do it. I need the feeling of Karen being here, without Karen actually being here."

March 22, 2001, Thursday.

[3 days since last entry]

Diego, a forty-five-year-old Hispanic male, wants to kill his girlfriend. One of the first lines in his chart is a direct quote: "I want to strangle her with my bare hands and look into her eyes as she dies." Yet, after meeting with him each day this week, I have found him to be extremely likable. He is genuine, articulate, calm, and rational (aside from the murder part).

During our daily meeting with Diego last Friday, Dr. Lyles asked him if he had questions.

"I don't have any questions, but I do have a special request."

Dr. Lyles seemed concerned. "Sure, Diego. What is it?"

"I like hot rod magazines. If you have any, or know of anyone who does, can you bring them in for me? I love hot rods. Looking at them and reading about them will relax me. I think they will help me keep calm and allow me to fall asleep better."

That was an odd request. Dr. Lyles nodded, "Okay, Diego. We'll all see what we can do," he said as he surveyed the room to affirm that we had heard his request.

The social worker said she'd look around the unit, even other parts of the hospital, as well as visit the gift shop to see if she could find something.

On Sunday, the day before Karen left, she and I were out doing some grocery shopping at Wegmans. As usual, Weggies was crazy busy. Right after getting in line, my eyes scanned across the handful of magazines next to the candy bars and gum. "Oh, shit! I forgot something. Wait here. I'll be right back." Bobbing and weaving through the foot traffic and rubber-coated wire carts, I found the aisle with a sign hanging from the rafters that included "Greeting Cards, Books, Magazines." I grabbed the first hot rod magazine that I saw and scrambled back to the checkout line.

On Monday, not wanting anyone to know I had this gift for him, I waited until after we completed rounds and all the patients had finished their lunches. Instead of jumping right into my board review questions, I began roaming the unit. I spotted Diego and approached him. "Diego? Hey, I'm Shawn, one of the students. Last week you asked us if we could bring in hot rod magazines. I was at the grocery store yesterday and picked this up for you."

I pulled the rolled-up magazine out of my pocket—a space typically reserved for my stethoscope—and handed it to him. "I don't know if you're supposed to have this, and I don't want to get in trouble, so let this be our little secret, okay?"

"Wow! I can't believe you did this. Thank you, thank you, thank you. This is great."

"I hope you enjoy it. I like cars, too," I said. "My uncle Johnny has an old purple Ford Roadster that he built himself. I think it is from the nineteen-thirties. And my stepfather, Norm, is building an old C-cab van. Do you have a favorite car?"

"Oh, man! This is so cool. I can't believe you did this for me. Thank you so much. I just like all cars. I don't have any favorites. Do you?"

"My favorite car from the '50s is the '56 Chevy Nomad. I love sport wagons. From the '60s? Definitely a '68 Ford Mustang Fastback. My dad had a '69 Dodge Charger when I was born. That may have been the first car that I ever rode in as a baby. I'd take one of those in a heartbeat too."

"Oh, yeah, man. Those are all great cars. I just still can't believe you got me a magazine!"

"Remember, Diego, this is a secret. Keep it hidden in your room somewhere."

Mentally ill patients, or maybe just the homicidal ones, are apparently not very trustworthy with keeping things classified. The following day during the team's meeting with Diego, he said, "Hey, Shawn. Can you stop by my room today? I have something for you to show my appreciation."

Everybody else looked at me, intrigued. I smiled and said, "It's nothing. I just brought him a hot rod magazine like he had requested."

"You had hot rod magazines?" Liesl asked.

Eagerly, Diego broke our pact. "No, he bought me one at the grocery store."

"Sorry. I hope it's okay. I didn't break any rules, did I?" I'm about crapping my pants, knowing the hospital is as strict as hell with potentially dangerous items in here, even though he already has his weapon of choice at the ends of his arms—called hands.

Dr. Lyles weighed in. "I think a magazine is fine. Did you enjoy it, Diego?"

"Yes, of course. I'm going to read it again tonight."

"Well, good. That was very nice of Shawn. Thank you," said Dr. Lyles.

Later on, I approached a nurse and asked if he could let me into Diego's room. He agreed, but had to accompany me. When we entered, Diego's face brightened. "Oh, good, you're here! I made something for you in the craft room last night." From the top of his dresser, he removed a mosaic-tiled coaster that was perched upon a small metal stand. He gave it to me along with a handmade card. "Don't read it in front of me, please." He reached out to offer me his hand. I grabbed it and pulled him in for a man-hug. "Man, you the best. You the best, brother." He wept.

"I hope you find peace," I said. "You're a good man. And... I go shopping every Sunday. Not that I want you to still be here next Monday, but if you are, I'll grab you another magazine."

March 23, 2001, Friday.

[1 day since last entry]

It's a damn good thing coffee is legal, although in the quantities I've been consuming the stuff, it might not be. I think it started in the middle of winter, just after the first of the year, when my seasonal affective disorder began kicking in. I was home in New Hampshire, had long commutes to multiple hospitals, and it was always dark. I had begun ramping up studying for the boards. Prior to PA school, I drank coffee twice per week, and only in the morning. As each year clicked by, I added another cup per day. This year, with each rotation, I'd add yet another. Since this is rotation nine, that's nine cups per day.

During the third week of my last rotation, it wasn't uncommon for me to go days without scrubbing a case, and the ortho service never had more than four patients admitted at any given time. I tried to take advantage of this situation by going to the hospital library with my board review materials, but I would often find myself dozing off—sometimes for an hour, multiple times per day—despite drinking more than eight cups of coffee by mid-afternoon. My tendency to fall asleep extended to lectures, grand rounds, and even lunch.

As soon as I arrived home, I'd put on some coffee, sit down while it brewed, and the next thing I know, I'd be out again for another hour. Later in the evening, I'd doze off for five or ten minutes between each board review question.

This psychiatry rotation has not helped. For the first few hours every single day, the team would sit in their chairs as staff marched in the admitted patients, one after the other, for their daily conversation between them and Dr. Lyles. I'm falling asleep during those too. The only time I'm not on the edge of another nap is when WrestleMania breaks out or when I'm running around Rocksville, searching for escaped patients.

Of course, the real answer for my severe fatigue is an undiagnosed medical condition, like iron deficient anemia from a bleeding ulcer, but what do I know?

March 28, 2001, Wednesday.
[5 days since last entry]
While we were sitting in morning rounds awaiting the next patient to be brought to us, someone I didn't recognize entered and ushered out all the employees. The students were told to stay put. Five minutes later, all the hospital staff returned. Many looked upset, angry, or in shock.

Dr. Lyles let us in on the secret, something that was going to make the headlines on every news station in the city, maybe all across New York State. Glenwood Hospital would close its doors for good in 90 days. More than 2,000 employees would lose their jobs. My first thought was the RTC faculty. Nadine and Bailey had spent the previous months securing rotations for next year's incoming seniors. There are twenty-seven students, and at ten rotations each, that's 270 individual rotations. Around 60% of rotations occur at this hospital, which is RTC's primary affiliation. That's roughly one hundred and sixty new rotations that RTC has to scramble to arrange in the next seven weeks. Impossible! I can't comprehend the magnitude of this looming crisis. I thought about all the upcoming seniors. I know most of them. How will they react when they find out? They've worked hard and anticipated this experience for years. Their entire year is now questionable, potentially in complete disarray. And then there are all the employees. Their livelihoods, careers, security, now shattered. The patients? Thankfully, this hospital is not in a remote area. The Rocksville healthcare system will absorb them, but not without some disruption. There will be a massive change in the atmosphere here over the next few weeks. It doesn't appear as though they will be accepting any more psych admissions. Today, we have eighteen on the unit. Once these current patients are discharged, that's it. What a disaster.

March 30, 2001, Friday.
[2 days since last entry]
The ship is sinking fast. The fear and worry are palpable. We discharged two patients yesterday and six more today. That's a record since I've

been here, and word has it, it's unprecedented. Concerned staff believe once we get to zero, the unit will close, long before the ninety days have concluded. The nursing director is demanding patients be discharged as soon as possible. "All patients must go. We have to get them out of here."

Every news outlet in the city led with the closing of the hospital. The ER is empty. Who would want to come to a compromised hospital? Now there is a rumor floating around that the ER will lock its doors in two weeks. Since all psych admissions come from the ER, if no ER, then no psych patients.

I left the hospital early and called Nadine to see how she was doing. I wanted her and the other RTC faculty to have had time to process the news.

"Hey, Nadine. It's Shawn. How are you holding up?"

"Thanks for calling, Shawn. We're okay."

"Don't you and Bailey still do some shifts at Glenwood?"

"Yes, but very few."

"Do you still have the juniors' radiology class at the hospital?"

"We sure do, but we can work around that. No big deal."

"And your H and P class? That was over there, too, right?"

"Yes, but that's also an easy fix," said Nadine.

"My thoughts are with you, Helen, Bailey, Taylor, RTC, and the soon-to-be rotating students. I want to do something. I need to help. What can I do? Name it."

"Pass your boards. That is what you can do. I appreciate you thinking about all of us, but it is our job to figure this out. Your job right now is to pass the board exam. Don't let this affect you. Don't let this derail you. Keep reading, keep studying, and go kick ass on that test. The higher your mark on the exam, the better we look."

"For four years, Nadine, you have been helping us. I know there probably isn't much any of us can do, but I promise you that if you reach out to me, I will be there."

"That is very kind of you. I have a job to do, and so do you."

In what is likely the worst week in the history of the RTC physician assistant program, Nadine has but one message for me, "Pass your boards." It fills me with pride knowing that our faculty will take control and prevail, as they always do.

April 1, 2001, Sunday.

[2 days since last entry]

If there is one thing that will aid in making your depression and loneliness worse, it's listening to a forty-eight-hour sex show. This was only the second weekend I had stayed in my rented room. I was told to expect raging parties every Friday and Saturday night, and the second weekend didn't disappoint. That first Friday, there were several dozen people, multiple kegs, and the loudest music the windows could withstand. I locked the door to my room, wedged a chair up against the doorknob, put in useless earplugs, and kept the light in my room as dim as possible. Was it shocking that none of the staggering, vomiting, obnoxious partygoers seemed to care that I was right above them, preparing for my board exams later this month? No.

This Friday night was different. The party only seemed to take place in Ronnie's room, adjacent to mine. He's the homeowner, and I had only met him the day I moved in. I shook his hand, gave him cash, and hadn't seen him again until two nights ago.

As you get to the top of the curved staircase there is a long hallway with wide pine floors, distressed from decades of neglect. My room was first on the left. At the end of the hall, which had no working lights, was the second-floor bathroom. This was used by Ronnie, two guys renting space on the third floor, and me. To access that bathroom, you had to walk past my bedroom and then Ronnie's.

After I left the hospital Friday afternoon, I went to the RTC gym for about an hour, then stopped to get some food to bring back to my room. After I ate, I used the bathroom. As I was heading back to my room, Ronnie crested the stairs and was heading down the hall towards his room. He was leading a woman by the hand who had long, straight, dark hair parted on the side, bangs shielding half her face. Slung over her neck was a raggedy denim bag, frayed like her excessively long boot-cut jeans. The hems dragged behind her heels, creating a train of long white threads. As the two of them passed through the light cast from my room and into the hall, I noted her white, lacy top that hung off her shoulders, revealing several silver necklaces and what seemed to be a butterfly tattoo on her chest. I hugged the wall as a courtesy to let them through. The sweet delicate notes of wildflowers greeted my face as they passed. After the obligatory thank you nod, they continued on their way. I kept my door open, but heard Ronnie's close. Before I could sit at my makeshift desk and take the first bite of my steak bomb sandwich, their music came on and indistinguishable conversation and laughter emanated through the wall. By the time I had taken my last bite, our shared wall was being beaten and there was the rhythmic creaking of a metallic box spring, interwoven with unpredictable skin-on-skin slapping sounds. Every phrase the woman released from her throat was, "Fuck me!" "Oh, my God!" "Yes. Harder!" Or the demanding, "Don't you fucking stop!" And let me tell you, Ronnie didn't.

I don't know what the hell this guy was on, but this went on for hours. It's not like she ever gave up, either. She had to have orgasmed upwards of two to three dozen times. Just after midnight, and her thirty-seventh explosion, Ronnie's door opened and I assumed he was entering the bathroom, but his footsteps were coming my way. Stopping at my door, wearing only silky red boxers, and hair soaked, he tapped my doorframe to get my attention since I was pretending to study. "Sorry. I forgot your name," he muttered.

Faking a startle reflex, "Oh, hey! Um, Shawn."

"You want some of that?" he asked, looking down the hall.

Seriously, dude? You just fucked her for over three hours.

"I can't do much more. My second pill is wearing off and my dick hurts. She's fucking incredible though. She'll let you do anything. I'm telling you, man. Do you want me to have her come down to you?"

"While I appreciate the offer, I'm engaged, and I need to focus on a huge test I have coming up in a few weeks. I can't help you tonight. Or her."

"Suit yourself. Maybe tomorrow night?"

"Huh? Tomorrow?"

"Yeah. Tomorrow night. I don't know who it'll be yet. Maybe someone who likes two dicks. Then I'll really need your help."

Letting out an evil laugh, he returned down the dark hallway. I closed my door and inserted my earplugs thinking that I'd better make plans to be far away from this house on Saturday evening.

Last night, I successfully stayed up past my bedtime, which is not easy or advisable. It was a dreary day in Rocksville with winter clinging to life. I had fallen behind on my board review, so I found a corner of the RTC library and set up base camp for the day. The whore house was quiet when I'd left just before noon. I packed enough food and water to last me until dark, with a plan to conquer one hundred questions in the heavily weighted specialties. The board exam will focus on general medicine, but within those hundreds of multiple-choice questions, one can expect a higher volume related to the cardiovascular system versus ophthalmology (no offense to ophthalmologists).

Achieving success as the sun went to rest, I walked back to the Honda, threw my tote in the backseat, and grabbed my gym bag. Since I had been following an all-American student diet for years, especially during this internship, I would attempt to offset that with occasional light workouts. The RTC Student Life Center gym was notoriously uncrowded on Saturday nights, and I was already on campus, so, why not pretend that I care about my health for an hour or two?

After becoming a sweaty mess, I made it back to my temporary locker to discover that I had forgotten my towel. I really did not want to shower back at the brothel, especially since I had no idea what I'd be walking into once I set foot in there. I also did not want to prepare a meal in that kitchen if there was a house party going on, so I scraped for a few bucks in my belongings and grabbed the cheapest pre-made sandwich I could find at Weggies.

Returning to my room, it shocked me to find a couple of housemates in the living area, watching a hockey game. No party? That's odd.

I grabbed a water bottle and napkins from the kitchen, then headed upstairs to my room. I could hear muffled electronica music through the wall to Ronnie's room. Since the bathroom wasn't in use, before I ate, I seized the opportunity to shower. When I surfaced from the shower with just a towel around my waist, Ronnie's door was open and the music abruptly faded to a whisper. Facing me, leaning against Ronnie's doorframe, was a pint-sized, fit, Asian woman in her early twenties. Half of her silhouette glowed purple from the light emitting out of Ronnie's room. I scanned her miraculous body and became rock hard as if I had just encountered Medusa.

"Oh, good. You like?" she questioned, as she glanced into the room to get Ronnie's approval.

"Um, hey. You, umm, don't have a top on."

Giggling, she wet her middle finger. Her nails were professionally lacquered in a glossy powder blue. After biting her lower lip, that finger began circling one of her nipples, leaving a glistening trail. They were pierced with tiny chrome barbells and already erect.

"So, you're Shawn?"

"I am. And you're missing some clothes. Wow…" She was wearing black underwear, or should I say a triangular piece of fabric the size of a guitar pick that was attached to her hips by floss.

"I'm Fuyuko."

The same glistening finger now shamelessly dipped behind the guitar pick. Her knees buckled slightly as she arched her back.

"Fuyuko? What does that mean?"

"It means 'winter child.' It means I am very cold, but you are making me hot."

If she was that cold, some clothing would've been helpful. She was an arm's distance away from me. I had the chance to escape to my room, but

I was still shocked by the situation unfolding. That's when she reached out and forced two fingers between my towel and hip. As she tugged, I covered her hand with mine and secured it. When she pulled harder, instead of the towel releasing, her body lunged against mine. I could feel her barbells pressed against my abdomen and she began licking my chest. Still attempting to render me completely naked, her other hand crept up the back of my leg and she sunk it into my flesh. As she bit my nipple, she forced me up against the hallway wall. It was now going to be more difficult to escape and possibly require a minor act of violence.

"I'm gonna get this towel off, Shawn, and then I'm going to drag you by your balls into this room and you will do whatever I tell you to do for the rest of the night. How does that sound?"

Trying to act naïve, I said, "But Ronnie is in there."

One of her eyebrows peaked, "Oh, he's got stuff to help. Whatever you need. C'mon. You won't regret it. I promise."

"I'm sure I'd have a great time. You are absolutely stunning, but I promise you, I would regret it. Please, put down my cock and let me go."

Aghast, she released her grip. Stepping back, she made a final unsuccessful tug at the towel. I heard footsteps coming up the stairs, so I ran to my room. Fuyuko yelled, "Come back anytime tonight!" Then Ronnie's door closed.

I've never faced temptation like that. I have to get out of here. There is only one more weekend to survive without getting murdered, contracting a disease, being slipped a date-rape drug, or worse yet, breaking my vow to Karen, then it'll be on to general surgery, the final rotation.

April 4, 2001, Wednesday.

[3 days since last entry]

People get better. I hadn't seen a lot of that while here, but they do. Kassie, a forty-year-old bipolar, schizophrenic woman, has been on this psych unit for twenty-six days. Prior to her admission, she decided to stop taking her meds and almost immediately decompensated. Amusing to observe, yet frustrating to manage, Kassie was in constant motion. She'd cross her legs, uncross them; fold her arms, unfold them; stand up, sit down, stand up again; walk around the room; touch and adjust every object, picture frame, and article of clothing. She'd leave mid-conversation with the treatment team, roam the halls, still talking, then stroll back into the room like she'd never left.

During each interaction, Kassie would always repeat the same theme, "I've got to get out of here. It's not safe. The air is making me sick. It's contaminated. There's no sunlight. There's nothing to do. I can't exercise. Everybody smokes. They give me rotten food." With her brain on repeat, as you might imagine, she could not effectively participate in group therapy sessions.

She was a magnet to windows. She'd never be far from one, lips up against any crack where she felt a draft, trying to inhale "clean air." When she was unable to find any doses of unpolluted oxygen to breathe, you could recognize Kassie by the veil of towels that shrouded her face, held over her mouth and nose as an elaborate, archaic filtration system.

Glenwood Hospital had a problem on their hands. Over two years ago, Kassie's condition worsened, and she was admitted here for five months while the doctors determined the perfect combination of medications, allowing her to function as a nondisabled individual in society. Monday was day twenty-four of this admission in a hospital that is closing soon. *What is going to happen to Kassie?* The team of social workers, the few that remain, have been attempting to secure a bed for her at the Rocksville Psychiatric Center (RPC), but until this week, she had been resistant. You would think the constant threat of being transferred from this facility, where she does nothing but complain, would motivate her, but it hadn't. RPC has a beautifully landscaped courtyard, a gymnasium, an indoor pool, and an enormous cafeteria. It sounded more like an all-inclusive vacation resort when compared to the shithole I had been living in the past few weeks. If she doesn't take a spot over there, I will.

With her parents' encouragement, Kassie agreed to the transfer once a bed opened up. Although this was a sign of a breakthrough, the ink on those transfer papers was still wet when Kassie shocked us all.

Late last week, she was placed in a partial hospitalization program to improve the chances of RPC accepting her. During one of the group sessions, Kassie asked to speak to the group of patients. She rose and clasped her hands in front of her chest. "I have learned to ask myself, 'What is the best choice? Is this a healthy choice for me and no one else? Will my decision make my life, and the lives of the ones that I care about, better?' Dr. Lyles gave me this advice every day and I believe that if each of you takes that same advice, and uses it every time you face a decision, you will get better."

And with that, she sat down. Liesl and I looked at each other and then we looked over at the social worker, who was in utter disbelief, and we knew at that moment, Kassie was going home. Three hours later, in a meeting with both of her parents, the social worker and staff nurse handed her discharge papers, Kassie hugged and thanked all of us, including Liesl and me, and we escorted her down to the lobby.

It was beautiful to witness someone so dysfunctional, disabled, fearful, and paranoid, walk out of here with dignity and hope.

April 7, 2001, Saturday.
[3 days since last entry]
The news of the day isn't that I miraculously avoided getting my nipples bit off last night, but rather that Dr. Hopedale had left me a voicemail while I was at the gym this afternoon. "Shawn. It's Dr. Hopedale. We've completed the interviewing process and I would like to offer you the position. Please call me on Monday afternoon."

Holy shit! This is real. This is actually happening. I have a job!

April 9, 2001, Monday.
[2 days since last entry]
Today was the mother of all fucked-up days. It was the most bizarre one I've had since starting rotations over ten months ago. Fasten your seatbelt, pull it tight, and hang on. I'll do my best to recap the events of the last eight hours.

Dr. Lyles is gone. He's been gone since last Friday. Earlier that week, Dr. Lyles had made the announcement of his resignation. Then, last Monday, we all showed up and there was a new guy sitting in the treatment room with us ready to start interviewing the remaining patients. Apparently, that doctor was just a placeholder for a week until the hospital could hire a rent-a-doc, which I believe they call a locum. Sure enough, the new psychiatrist, Dr. Franklin, showed up impressively late today, and as soon as he arrived on the unit, he asked where he could get a cup of coffee. *Dude, you're late. You missed your opportunity to grab a cup of joe.* But someone led him down to the café anyway.

As we waited for our new leader to return with his coffee and take the only empty seat in the room behind the wooden desks, we learned that the semi-retired Dr. Franklin had driven up from Naples, Florida, and had practiced psychiatry for thirty years after spending the first twenty years of his career in internal medicine. Yes, the math is concerning. That puts him over eighty years old, although his shuffling gate indicates he could be on the other side of ninety. Maybe that's why he is missing. Perhaps he just wandered off. After forty-five minutes, our head nurse wondered out loud, "It doesn't make sense to overhead page him, does it? If he's lost, he won't know where to go anyway. I'll go down to the lobby and start looking around. Stay here."

Not long after she left, the head nurse and Dr. Franklin both entered the treatment room. The latter tried to justify his disappearance. "I was just waiting for someone to come get me," he said. He took his throne, and the rounds that typically start around 8:30 am began at 9:45 am.

Dr. Franklin didn't seem quite ready. Instead, he began entertaining us with stories of his decorated fifty-year career. "My best friend in medical school invented the SOAP note. The S means subjective. That's what the patient tells you. The O is the objective, or what you observe by watching and examining the patient. The A is your assessment. This is where you create your differential diagnosis and defend it. The P is the plan. That should be self-explanatory."

No one said anything. An odd feeling flooded the room. *Did he just give us a lecture on SOAP notes?* Looking proud of himself, as the rest of us sat dazed and confused, a social worker finally brought the first patient to us.

Sitting in silence for another minute, Dr. Franklin eventually formulated his first inquisition. "I see you're on a medicine, ten milligrams. Do you like it?"

What? Do they like it? And how does the patient know what medicine he is talking about?

The patient looked at him as if unsure of what to say. "Um, well, I guess?"

"Okay, well I also see that you are on a medication for depression. That makes two medications. Do you like that one, too?"

"I don't know. Sure?"

Where is he going with this? Who asks patients if they like their meds?

"Good. Patients normally stay admitted three days. That's how long they stay. I don't know how they do it here, but medicine should make you better in three days, so, after three days, if you're better, we will send you home."

And with that, he called for the next patient. You know what he asked of them? Correct. "How do you like your medicines?" Between each new patient visit, Dr. Franklin would launch into stories of his long and award-winning career, mentioning past patients by their full names. Even when the next patient sat down in front of him, he wouldn't cut a story short, but rather kept rambling through to conclusion.

By the time we reached the fifth patient, it was almost lunchtime and we still had six more to interview. At least he kept entertaining us with his dumb line of questions and narcissistic tales.

The next patient was Phil. He had been admitted and discharged multiple times in the past few months. Our social worker pointed this out to Dr. Franklin as Phil was led into the room.

"So, I hear that you've been here before. The last time they discharged you, what street did you go to?"

"What street?" Phil appeared as flabbergasted as the rest of us.

"Yes. You walked out of the hospital and went down what street?"

Arbitrarily pointing behind Dr. Franklin, Phil said, "Marshall Avenue."

"No, not what avenue. I asked what street."

If I were a defense attorney, this is where I'd stand and object, "Irrelevant line of questioning, your honor."

Since Phil said he liked his meds, and he hadn't yet been there three days, they returned him to his room. It was 12:20 and we hadn't yet seen half of the patients on the unit. Normally we'd be wrapping up by this point, after having seen upwards of twenty.

Mercifully, the head nurse suggested we break for lunch. With everyone in agreement, we all knew we had a crisis on our hands. After receiving directions to the cafeteria, Dr. Franklin was the first to leave the ward. Confirming he had left, the treatment team convened at the nurses' station. I had wondered why one of the social workers had left in the middle of the second patient's interview. She had marched over to human resources and had an emergency meeting with two quality assurance team members. They had been waiting for us to break for lunch so they could meet with the entire team to hear our concerns.

When one of them asked for my take, I gave it to them straight. "I'm a student. This is my fifth and final week here. I can assure you that I know more about psychiatry than this guy does. He may have been a decorated doctor at some point, but there's something not right about him now. Maybe he has dementia or something. I know everyone around here will be losing their job soon, so it's a moot point, but whoever vetted this guy needs to be fired today. It's inconceivable that someone talked to this man and concluded he could care for patients." Then I thought, "*Shit, what if that person is standing right in front of me?*"

After everyone else had chimed in with similar assessments ('A' is for assessment, you know), someone from the quality assurance team announced, "Okay. He's not to see any more patients. When he comes back from lunch, if he can find his way back, we'll be waiting for him."

It was about 1:30 when Dr. Franklin returned to the unit. We were all still hanging around the nurses' station, finishing up our lunches, having no clue what our afternoon would look like, but had surmised that no more patient care would occur. After all, we were about to have our rent-a-doc sent back to Florida after only a half day's work.

Down the hallway, Dr. Franklin emerged from a small, private office and began making his way over to us. He had the beginnings of tears in his eyes. My heart sank as I realized that all of his belongings were right beside me. I could not have positioned myself any more poorly. Despite feeling awful, I knew he shouldn't still be practicing medicine. He may have once been a renowned psychiatrist in Florida, but those days were over. Perhaps he couldn't bring himself to abandon his life's work. Was he married? Widowed? Did he have kids? Had most of his friends and lifelong colleagues retired, or worse, passed on?

I could feel his presence standing behind me. I became avoidant, refusing to turn around. Liesl was off to my left, acting similarly. Statuesque, she stared at the book in front of her, breathing nervously.

To anyone willing to engage, Dr. Franklin asked, "Heart to heart, tell me, do I have dementia?"

None of us there were qualified to label him with that diagnosis, but we were all thinking it. No one answered him.

It felt like an eternity had passed, then he reached over my shoulder to collect his personal possessions. Clearing his throat to get my attention, "Excuse me. Would you mind if I asked you a couple of questions?"

Of course I minded. Why me? What did I do to deserve this?

I replied, "Um, sure. I guess. What can I help you with, Dr. Franklin?"

He pulled up a chair and we both swiveled around to speak face-to-face. I leaned back, placed my elbows on the armrests, and folded my hands over my belt buckle. *Please, God, let this be brief.*

"How long have you worked here?" he asked.

"Oh, I'm not employed here. I'm a physician assistant student, as is Liesl." I know she's thinking, *What the hell, Shawn? Don't drag me into this.*

"A physician assistant? What is that, exactly?"

Yup. That's what I thought. I gave him the CliffsNotes version, knowing it wasn't the true reason for his interrogation.

"It's my first day here, you know? I'm wondering," he said, "when you meet with patients, because it's different wherever you go, what am I supposed to do?"

I guess I should not have been surprised by his question, but I was. I asked for some clarification, somewhat sarcastically, "What are you supposed to do? Is that what you're asking me?"

"Yes. What am I expected to do with patients?"

My mind is blowing up. If I could compose an answer, would he even comprehend it, and will this satisfy him enough to walk away? That is the goal: get him to leave, preferably without security.

"It is the job of the full treatment team surrounding you each day to listen to the patient during your interview, observe their behavior, review social work notes, med lists, and nursing notes, then assess whether the current treatment plan is working. If it is not, you—the psychiatrist—have the ultimate authority to change that plan. It's kind of like a SOAP note."

"Ah. A SOAP note. Yes, hey, my best friend invented those back when I was in medical school."

"Oh, wow! I think you had said that earlier today."

"I did? Sorry. How come I never got a chance to ask questions?"

"You had a chance. Remember? You asked the patients if they liked their meds."

Nothing seemed to be registering. The light bulb was off. It's not even screwed in.

"It's important that they like their meds," he reiterated. "Three days on meds and they can go home, but only if they like them. Why didn't anyone ever give me a chart, or a med sheet? I always look at the med sheet."

We always set the full chart of each patient on his desk, right in front of him, but he ignored them. He never recorded notes. In fact, I never saw him with a pen.

"I think if I just could've had more time to ask questions, everything would have worked out better. Oh, and been given a med sheet. I always look at the med sheet. Can I get some note cards? If I had note cards, I could take some notes—maybe just write down their meds. That could help me when I see patients this afternoon."

That's when the quality assurance team came to my rescue. "Dr. Franklin? Remember, you're not going to see any patients this afternoon. We just talked about this. Please get the rest of your things and walk with us. Is there someone you need to call before we escort you down?"

"Oh, right. No. I guess I'll just head back to Florida now."

And with that, Dr. Franklin was gone.

No more patients were interviewed for the rest of the day, giving me the freedom to call Dr. Hopedale as he had requested. He again offered me the position and told me to call Bob, his current PA, and his office manager, Nora, so she could get the formal written offer out to me for review, and if necessary, to negotiate any revisions. He urged me to get started on the reams of paperwork, applications, and forms required for state licensure and hospital credentialing. Although he recommended I take the health insurance offered, I declined, so he said he'd make it up in salary.

Later, I called Bob. He told me that another new PA graduate in town had recently been hired and it took her ten weeks to get her license and credentials. So we needed to get the ball rolling in hopes of getting me started by mid-August.

Boards are in a couple of weeks. Finding out whether I pass them could take three weeks. I can't even apply for my New Hampshire PA license until I pass them and graduate. This is all happening so fast, but it's really happening. Someone pinch me. No, hit me with a Louisville Slugger!

24

ROTATION #10—
SURGERY

April 16, 2001, Monday.

[7 days since last entry]

Before I tell you about the first day at what they call the "mother of all rotations," let me recap the last few days. Recall Day went fine. I scored just well enough on the psychiatry exam to maintain the A grade my preceptor had awarded me. I've been attempting to prioritize my learning experience over my grades, but during my last rotation, 99% of my focus was on the boards.

Earlier in the week, I had run into Ronnie and asked him when he needed me out of my room. Since he didn't have a new tenant lined up, he told me I could stay through the weekend if I needed to. Wanting to give Chris and his wife the full weekend without my imposition, I stayed in the ghetto house until yesterday morning without further incident. There was still wild sex on the other side of the drywall every night, but I somehow managed to get enough sleep to maintain a basic level of sanity. Each morning for five weeks, I expected to walk out to my car and find it up on blocks, the tires missing, and the entire interior stripped out, but it never happened. And never have I been so grateful to be back in Chris and Carolyn's home.

If today is any indication, this rotation will be terribly disappointing. I didn't scrub a single case. I met Hillary, my preceptor at Rocksville General Hospital, at about dawn and tagged along as she completed her morning rounds. I wasted no time in telling her about the general surgery job offer back in New Hampshire. That prompted her to ask if I had taken my boards. It was the perfect segue for me to introduce some of my thoughts and ask her a favor.

"I take my boards in less than two weeks, so, as I am sure you can relate, I'm on edge, overtired, and hyper-focused on them right now."

"As you should be."

"So, if I'm spacey and slow to the punch, that'll be why."

Hillary seemed to understand.

"If I give the impression of not wanting to be here and appear eager to leave, please don't take offense or let it impact your motivation to provide me with an excellent experience. Once I get through these first two weeks, whatever shortcomings you may have perceived from me, I will make up during the final three weeks, I promise you."

"Listen. I get it. No worries."

We chatted a lot about what the next five weeks would hopefully look like. She warned me that some days would be slower than others and that there would be time for reading every day. "You'll have to compete for scrub time with the medical students and residents. Take every opportunity to establish good connections with the doctors. They have to feel you out, especially the fresh faces they don't recognize, but I'll be an advocate for you. I'm on your side. If we have to do some manipulating to get you at the surgical field, we will."

Around 8:30, Hillary finished her rounding and we went to review the day's surgical schedule. "Damn. There's not a lot going on here today. Is it school vacation week? Ugh! This is crazy. Well, there is a TRAM-flap (a type of breast reconstruction surgery) set to start at 11:45. Why don't you read at the library and come back by 11:30? Jules, one of my colleagues, is assigned to that case. I'll introduce you to her and see if we can get you in on that one."

After three hours in the library, I arrived back at the office for 11:20, thinking I was early. Jules and Hillary were already there. As soon as I walked in, Jules jumped up, "Shawn? We gotta go. You don't even have scrubs on yet. Follow me."

Surprised by the sudden urgency, Jules led me to the male locker room telling me she'd wait in the surgical lounge, but to change quickly. There had to have been forty lockers in there along with twenty docs, residents, and med students, all immersed in technical conversations, darting around, and changing. In under a minute, I opened every locker that didn't have a lock through the handle. Every one of them was nearly full. The one with the least amount of stuff became mine. I was about to share storage space with a complete stranger, hoping they would be understanding and not steal my shit.

Before I had my tie loosened, I heard Jules pounding on the door, "Shawn! Let's go! We gotta move!" I stripped, balled up everything I was wearing, tossed my clothes on top of whatever was sitting at the bottom of the locker, and threw on the first pair of sage-colored scrubs I could find. They were so tight that my forearm veins began popping. Leaving my shoes untied, I charged out to the lounge. It was a struggle to breathe in the medium top, hugging my extra-large frame. The bottoms were like yoga pants, providing me with a deep wedgy and male camel toe. Jules was already jogging out to the operating rooms, so I started my sprint. We began browsing through the windows above each scrub sink to investigate where I'd have the best chance of participating.

Jules began calling out, "Room one is an anal fistula. That should be over before it even starts, and there are already three guys huddled around that asshole…" She burst out laughing. "Over here we have an open abdominal case, but there are already five scrubbed in. Room three is empty, but an eye case is going in there next. Nothing to see here," she punned. "Room four is ortho. Five? Gyno with four scrubbed in for a vaginal hysterectomy." (That's a surgeon accompanied by three students, each doing nothing but holding a retractor for an hour and a half.) "Shit, and there is nothing in six or seven right now. Damn, it's slow."

"I thought we were going to be doing a TRAM-flap at 11:45?"

"Oh, right. That got canceled. The patient drank coffee this morning. Okay, well, I know Hillary is doing an abdominal fistula closure on an admitted patient. That's an add-on case, so it'll go once the scheduled cases are done. I'm thinking at around one or two."

"I'm up for anything. Just get me in a room. I can handle whatever comes my way."

"Why don't you head down to the library and read about abdominal fistulas? Keep checking back on Hillary's case. If I see her first, I'll let her know the plan."

So, back to the library I went. Shortly thereafter, around 1:00-ish, I was back to lurking and pacing at the scrub sinks. Hillary arrived about thirty minutes later and informed me that the fistula closure was canceled due to the patient experiencing a cardiac event or pulmonary embolus. However, she had encountered a urologist on one of the floors who requested her assistance with a varicocele, and she accepted.

"I'm so sorry, Shawn. Go read about varicoceles and be back here at 2:30." (Varicoceles are varicose veins within the spermatic cord.)

Guess where I headed… Back to the library. There's not much you can read about varicoceles, but I was going to be ready for anything the urologist—or Hillary—might quiz me on. At 2:15 pm, I ran back to the lounge and Hillary was having a late lunch. "Are you ready for the big hydrocele?" she asked. (Hydrocele is a fluid filled sac around the testicle.)

"Hydrocele? You said varicocele, didn't you?"

"Did I? I don't think so, but that's okay, the case isn't going until 3:00, so you have time to go read about hydroceles."

Guess where I headed... So far, everything that I have done today, I could have done at home. I wouldn't have received the same cardiovascular StairMaster workout, but I could've completed the seven hours of reading.

I don't think I had re-opened the same urology text in the library when Hillary floated in and whispered, "Hey, you ready?"

Without putting the book back, we headed for the stairs. "But I didn't read a single word about hydroceles."

"Don't worry, neither did I," she joked (since these cases are easy and she's probably assisted on hundreds of them).

In the final corridor before reaching the surgical lounge, a young woman wearing the short white coat of a medical student was standing outside of a small meeting room as we approached. "Are you guys here for my presentation?"

Hillary stopped in her tracks. "Presentation?"

"Yes. Five other medical students and I are giving a presentation on burns. It starts in five minutes. Come on in if you're not busy."

Oh, I'm busy. I'm very busy. It's 3:00 and I'm about to scrub on a hydrocele, or, in other words, stand around in a surgical gown and answer questions from people with way more experience than me.

"Shawn, I think you'd get much more out of this presentation than watching a hydrocele removal."

I wanted to say, "Fuck that! It's my damn surgery rotation. Get me in an OR. This is bullshit." But I didn't. I played nice in the sandbox. I was going to need a huge favor soon, and Hillary would be the one to either grant it or deny it, so burns it was.

At least I wasn't heading back to the library.

April 18, 2001, Wednesday.

[2 days since last entry]

Third day on the surgery rotation, and third day without sleep. The board anxiety is crushing me. The weight is unbearable. It may have been a monumental mistake scheduling it in the middle of my surgery rotation. I should have waited until after graduation or scheduled it at the very end of my psych rotation. I'm getting out of bed at 5:00 am and getting to the hospital by 6:00, so I can round on the patients assigned to Hillary. Twelve hours later, I'm heading home. After I eat, I hit the books for at least six hours. Even though I wilt into my bed at midnight, I just stare at the ceiling, feeling guilty about not continuing my preparations. I purposefully waited until a couple of weeks before sitting for the boards to begin focusing on cardiovascular material so it would be as fresh as possible. That could prove to be an error as well. I procrastinated and now I'm struggling to catch up. On top of that, this dumbass decided to stop drinking coffee seven days ago. Cold turkey. The withdrawal headaches have been debilitating. I've been alternating maximum doses of ibuprofen and acetaminophen every two hours since Saturday. At this rate, I'll have liver cirrhosis and be on dialysis by graduation.

Our program's faculty posted grades after the last Recall Day. I calculated my overall GPA for all four years at 3.58. To graduate with high honors, one needs a 3.60. You can do the math. I regret discovering this. Now I can't let go of it. One of my goals upon arriving at RTC was to graduate with high honors. I believed it to be out of reach. There is only one grade remaining in my entire RTC career. I suspect an A for this rotation would push me over the top, but my focus has to be on the boards right now. Hillary knows this. I told her I probably wouldn't look very devoted during my first two weeks, but that I'd overachieve during my final three. And now that I know I'm 0.02 points away from high honors, I have to do whatever it takes to earn them, starting today.

April 19, 2001, Thursday.
[1 day since last entry]
Commence the brown-nosing. I don't like losing. Dangle that 0.02-point carrot in front of me and I will chase that vegetable to the end of the earth.

The PAs on the surgery service will visit patients several hours after their operations and write what they call post-op notes. If the surgery is mid-afternoon or later, the on-call PA or resident will see the patient and write the note. Knowing this, as soon as morning rounds were over, I meticulously studied the OR schedule, recorded the surgeries assigned to Hillary and Jules, wrote down the patients' names, and devised a plan to write all the post-op notes before Hillary or Jules would have a chance to.

Prior to lunch, Hillary and I had completed our two cases. As we were heading to the recovery room, I noticed Jules still scrubbed in on her second case. I confiscated the chart before Hillary could seize it and I began the post-op admission orders. When Hillary came over to where I was sitting, I asked, "Have you post-opped the first patient yet?"

"No, I haven't."

"Okay. I will head over there, but from now on, I'll complete them all. I'll do Jules's too. I'll check on all our patients before leaving the hospital each day."

Hillary now appeared confused. "I thought you said you were leaving early every day to prioritize the boards?"

"I'll be fine. Caring for patients is more important." I hurried upstairs and came across our first post-op patient. I swiftly penned a note and stumbled upon Jules's first post-op patient. I located the chart and didn't see a note, so I took care of that one too.

Arriving back down to recovery, I found Jules. I said, "Hey, I did the post-op on your first patient. He's doing great, already sitting in a chair and sipping on clears. Before I leave for the day, I'll see this one too." I verified the name and noted the room she'd be going to. "You have another case after lunch, right? I'll post-op them too. I know it probably won't be until much later this afternoon."

At around 5:00 pm, I trekked back up to the surgical floor to do the last post-op note. Upon opening the chart to the progress notes section, I saw there was a pale-yellow Post-it note addressed to me. It said, 'Shawn, 7:30 am colectomy tomorrow. You and me.' It was signed by Hillary.

I think she was testing me to see if I was actually going to stay late, post-op the patient, and find her message. *Hell, yeah!* I'll be first at the scrub sink by 7:00 am. I won't be pushed aside by any med student or resident for this one.

April 20, 2001, Friday.

[1 day since last entry]

Hillary and I had forgotten that I was taking my H&P practical competency exams at another hospital at 11:20 am, but I was able to reach her by cell last night. She still had me scrub the case, but I ended up having to leave just prior to the case being completed.

While I had Hillary on the phone, I decided it was a good time to ask her for that favor. The weekend after the boards, I wanted either that Monday or Friday off so I could travel home to be with Karen. Since I had only seen her once since Christmas and my birthday is May 5th, I wanted to celebrate and take a much needed mental health break. I made sure she understood that my effort, dedication, and commitment to the rotation would be absurdly impressive upon my return.

"Sure. I'm fine with that," she said. "Whatever day you want. Just let me know next week. I know these boards have been stressing you out. You deserve a day. No worries."

Well, that was easy—almost weirdly so. Now, the big question: how do I ask Nadine and Bailey? Although I am heading over there now to take the competencies, this would not be the best time. I'm not particularly anxious about taking these unofficial oral boards. I've invested more than an adequate amount of time over the past two years, so I don't expect any stumbling. No matter what the scenario requires, I know I can confidently perform all the physical exams in the allotted time.

I just ran back out to my car. Is anybody looking this way? If I scream, will anyone hear? It appears to be safe.

"Fuck!"

I failed. I fucking failed! How is that possible? This is not happening right now. What am I going to do? I'm so stupid! Holy shit! My exams were flawless, but I performed the wrong ones based on the scenario. I just went down the wrong clinical pathway. Well, not entirely, but just enough. The secondary exam components that I conducted weren't weighted as heavily as the primary ones. And I didn't do a set of vitals! Are you fucking kidding me, Roussin? They're called vitals for a reason, you moron! What's going to happen to me now? Am I done? Was this it? Do I pack my shit? Am I allowed to go to my rotation on Monday? What the hell is going on? How? I can't believe this.

Okay, think, Shawn. What happened? Let's replay this. Alex, my partner, played the sixty-five-year-old man who was an alcoholic with right upper quadrant pain, pale stools, and tea-colored urine. Upon reading the clinical scenario, Nadine asked me if I was ready. After I nodded, she said, "You have ten minutes to complete the appropriate clinical exams. You may begin."

I took a deep breath. I looked down at the index card with the handwritten details. *Shit.* I was trembling. I couldn't hold the card still. *Dammit!* Another deep breath. Relax. *Okay, GI exam. Definitely the GI exam. Gallstones? Pancreatitis? Cirrhosis? The alcohol thing? Think: liver. Encephalopathy? Yes. That's where my brain took me. Thank you, ICU rotation. Neuro exam? Yes, of course. What else? Esophageal varices, an ulcer? The alcohol thing again. Of course. That has to be what they're looking for. A rectal exam? Absolutely. Guaiac that stool* (a chemical test to check for the microscopic presence of blood). *This guy could have a GI bleed. That's it! I've got it: GI, rectal, and neuro exams.* I even had over a minute to spare. I nailed it!

Not so fast... After they reviewed Alex's passing score (who went first), Nadine informed me I had failed. "First, Shawn, you did not collect any vital signs. Had you done so, you would've learned that his blood pressure was seventy-eight over forty-eight and his heart was irregularly irregular—a sign of atrial fibrillation. That should've prompted you to do a full cardiac exam, which, of course, as we have taught, is always performed in conjunction with a lung exam. The secondary exams for this patient were, in fact, GI, rectal, neuro, skin (for jaundice), and eyes (scleral icterus). You performed three of the five secondary exams, but did not do the two primary exams, and that is the reason for the failure."

I turned and shot out of the room. The hall was lined with fellow students awaiting their turns. I couldn't make eye contact as I sped by, but I could feel their empathy. They had to have known. My pride was dragging behind me, clinging to dear life.

It's official. I'm incompetent. Surely this is foreshadowing for my boards, if I even take them now.

Not knowing what to do, I drove across town to RTC and went to Nadine's office. I sat on the floor outside of her door, waiting, hoping she would eventually show up. About three hours later, she appeared from around the corner. It was evident from her expression that she was expecting to find me sitting there. I stood up and she unlocked her door, motioning me in.

"You okay?" she asked.

"No, not really. Am I done? Is this it? I'm so sorry that I failed you and everyone here."

"What? Shawn, no. You're not done. Next week, for those who didn't perform up to standards, we have a remediation day arranged. No one knows about it. Tonight, I was going to call each of the students who didn't pass, and schedule them for their make-up exam. We couldn't tell you up front about a remediation process, otherwise, some of you may not have taken this competency seriously, right? If y'all thought today was your only shot at passing, you'd be sure to prepare like your life depended on it. But you should expect the remediation competency to be more difficult. We're even going to allow twenty minutes per student."

"I just can't believe I failed. I was so ready. We all were. The pressure got to me. It's a weird way to perform. I thought my years of experience on stage would have helped."

"I think the stakes are a bit different, wouldn't you agree?" Nadine asked.

I had to laugh. "Just a bit. So, can we pick a time for me to retake them now?"

"Don't you take your boards soon?"

"Yes, at the end of next week."

"That should be your sole focus. After you take them, come find me. We'll work on a time."

The walk back to my Honda was long. What if I don't pass the boards? What will I tell Karen? I'm sure my job offer would be rescinded. What if I fail the next H&P competency? You know what? I don't deserve high honors. I'm an embarrassment. What a waste. I'm just going to go pack my shit and drive home.

When I got to Chris's, his wife was in the kitchen preparing dinner. I walked past Chris who was on the couch, reading. He said, "You okay, bud?"

I knew he knew. Word travels fast. "I guess? I don't know. Not really. I'll figure this out. I always do. I'm probably going home."

"Home? What do you mean?"

"I don't know," I said. "I'm probably done. I gave it my best. I had a good run, but I think I've been fooling myself. The weight was too great and today I crumpled under it. What's going to happen when it's an actual patient?"

Whatever utensil that Carolyn was using hit the bottom of the stainless-steel sink, and she marched into the living room. "Done? Leaving? Right now?"

Chris jumped off the couch and confronted me. I was hoping he was going to lay me out cold with a right hook and knock some sense into me, but the adults in the room began using their reasoning skills. "Did you get kicked out?" he said.

"No."

"You're sure?"

"Yes. I just came from Nadine's office. They're gonna schedule make-up exams for those that failed."

"Great! When is yours?"

"Don't know. Nadine told me to not worry about it until after I take my boards."

"That's awesome! Okay, see? You're gonna be fine. You're not done. We've all failed exams before, but we're still here. Dude, listen. Six years you've been at this dream, right? Six years! You're one week from the national board exam. You're three weeks from the coating ceremony. In four weeks, we graduate. You have a job. You're getting married. You're not quitting. You're going to keep fighting like you have been every day for six years! Do you hear me?"

I exhaled and nodded, and Chris pulled me into one of those manly half-hugs. Carolyn, in her tomato-sauce-stained apron, rubbed the middle of our backs with each of her hands. "You boys got this. Believe in yourselves. Last push. You're only a couple of weeks away."

Each of us was a bit tearful as the huddle broke. I fled upstairs to the bathroom and after splashing water onto my face, I looked into the mirror and performed the Stuart Smalley Daily Affirmation as seen on Saturday Night Live. "I deserve good things. I'm entitled to my share of happiness. I refuse to beat myself up. I am an attractive person. I am fun to be with. I'm going to help people, because I'm good enough, I'm smart enough, and doggone it, people like me."

Laughing at myself and feeling some adjudication, I headed to my room. Contemplating my escape plan, I sat on my bed pondering how to pack my belongings without being detected. I knelt down on the carpet and began pulling out the few items of mine that were hidden under the bed. The first was a small metal lockbox where I kept valuables like cash, some important documents, and the completed microcassettes from this project. In my jacket pocket, I found the key to unlock it and also grabbed the recorder.

I located cassette #1, side A, and popped it into the player. I listened to my voice for forty-five minutes. My very first entry from almost two years ago echoed from my chest as I lay in state, motionless on the comforter. And when the final sentence trailed off, I pressed "stop," hit "rewind," and knew what I had to do next.

I grabbed my hit list (a final tabulation of the most important items I had wanted to study), a highlighter, a black pen, a blue pen, and a red pen.

I had eight days. A setback is a set-up for a comeback, and here I come.

April 22, 2001, Sunday.

[2 days since last entry]

I made a couple of calls today. I should've called Karen Friday night because it was a big day for her. She called me three times, but I didn't pick up. That was very selfish of me, but being a jerk, I assumed her news was good and could wait. I'm an awful human being and should've returned her call yesterday, but I was still basking in my misery. Hitting rock bottom, I just needed time in my own head.

Karen did not get the job that she really wanted. After her second interview, she was feeling confident, but it wasn't in the cards for her. It was difficult to hear her break down over the phone. Normally a rock like her Marine father, Peter, she is usually devoid of displaying sad emotions. That's the polar opposite of me. Hearing her weep made my problems appear trivial and I was helpless. I needed to be there, but I couldn't. I should've answered her call Friday night and driven home. That's what a real man would've done. That's what any decent husband would've done. I am such a worthless failure. When she asked me about my H&P competencies, I lied. Maybe that was my good-husband moment? Lying was protecting her. Lying was the noble path. This meant that if I earned my redemption by passing the remediation, I could not share that glory with her unless I first entered a confessional. If I fail the boards and my H&P remediation competencies, I won't need a confessional. I'll need a half-dozen pallbearers.

April 23, 2001, Monday.
[1 day since last entry]
My informal, improvised, twelve-step recovery program is going well. I'm so grateful for friends like Chris and his wife, Carolyn, and Dan and his girlfriend, Bethany. My daily affirmations are dissipating my anguish. I'm coming to terms with my mistakes and formulating a game plan to mitigate them. My life fell out of balance and I couldn't reposition the weights to correct it before they collapsed on top of me. I needed this weekend to dig out of the rubble. Drawing on more than six years of inspiration and grueling work, thinking about my family and Karen, and acknowledging the remarkable patient experiences over the last year, I have arrived here. It all comes down to this week. I can fold and walk away or I can climb out of this crater, throw off my short, stained white coat, rip open my shirt, display the superhero emblem on my chest, and slay the foe that's rising before me.

April 24, 2001, Tuesday.
[1 day since last entry]
Balance... Last night, Dan, Bethany, and I went to another Guster show. Of course, I felt guilty, but we had been planning this for two months and, frankly, it couldn't have come at a better time. It was hard getting to the hospital to round this morning after a three-hour nap, but I only had one case to scrub. Otherwise, I spent seven hours in the library studying. Hillary knows what's at stake. She's leaving me alone and getting me down to the library as much as she can. She told me to forget about the post-op notes until next week, and unless it's a really interesting surgical case where I can assist, she told me to stay away from the OR.

Tonight I finished my hit list, and tomorrow I'll begin thumbing through a cool book called *Pearls of Wisdom*. It's page after page of one-liners: facts, broken down into specialties. The studying is over. It's *Pearls* until Friday, the night before boards. I plan on having a glass of whiskey, watching a movie, and going to bed early.

April 26, 2001, Thursday. 2 days before the national board exam.
[2 days since last entry]
I stood at the scrub sink for my only case of the day. My mind was right. I was calm and at peace. I needed to clutch this feeling and keep anything or anyone from disrupting it. Hillary had already scrubbed and was inside the OR helping the surgical technologist complete the draping. Arriving at the sink next to me was a short 120-pound Indian gentleman who was feeling informative. "Excuse me, but you do know that your shirt is not tucked in, no?"

In my zone, I said, "Yup. I do know."

"Well, you better stop what you are doing and tuck in your shirt. You cannot do surgery with an untucked shirt."

"Oh, really? And why is that?" *Stay in the zone, Shawn.*

"That is bad technique. You will contaminate everything. Then what will we do?"

I said nothing and kept scrubbing. It quickly became awkward, but I refused to be broken.

"I can see you dislike my idea."

"Actually, I do like your idea. It is very reasonable, and I agree with you. Not having my shirt tucked in shows poor technique, so in the future I'll be sure that doesn't happen," I said. "I will be exceptionally cautious when drying off my hands and putting on my gown. If you feel like I'm about to contaminate some portion of the sterile field, please politely warn me."

"Very well then." And with that, he walked into the OR and I followed.

"Dr. Kumar. How are you this morning?" The OR team greeted him. *Oh, crap! He's the surgeon. This is about to get interesting.*

After we all settled in at the surgical field, Dr. Kumar asked for a scalpel. Then, as he was making the initial incision, he directed his concern to Hillary, "Your partner here has displayed improper technique by not having his shirt tucked in. If I see that again, I will dismiss him from my operating room."

With a solid pinch of sarcasm, Hillary came to my defense. She said, "My partner here is a surgical technologist who has scrubbed over a thousand cases and can close surgical wounds better than most of your residents. I would not worry about his untucked shirt, but it's your call."

"Very well then. We'll see about that. What is your partner's name?"

"My name is Shawn." I didn't let Hillary answer for me. "I'm a PA student."

"Okay, Shawn. Switch places with Hillary. You just became my first assistant. Can you handle it?"

"Yes, sir. Thank you, sir. Let's go."

I stayed in the zone.

April 27, 2001, Friday. 1 day before the national board exam.

[1 day since last entry]

One can only put in so many nineteen-hour days—twelve at the hospital and seven immersed in board prep—but tonight that ends. Fighting for that 0.02 has been taking a toll. Included in those seven hours of studying is reading about the following day's surgical cases, so when the pimping comes my way, I'm ready. History has proven that those who surround the surgical field and provide correct answers to the attending's questions get the honor and privilege of touching instruments, and maybe even tying a knot.

For the rest of this rotation, I was going to need to avoid Dr. Schultz, a fifth-year resident, who was about to be released out into the world and on her own. Today's rounds were led by her, but also in attendance were a second-year resident, three medical students, a respiratory therapist, a dietician, a social worker, Hillary, and Jules. I had been following three patients in recent days and was asked to present one of them to the group. It was not my best performance, proving again that regular restorative sleep is vital to having a sound mind and body.

As the entire entourage paraded into my patient's room, I nudged my way to the foot of the bed and faced the audience. Dr. Schultz opened the patient's chart on the adjustable, faux wooden over-the-bed table, which was the signal for me to begin.

I had made it fourteen seconds before I was interrupted. "Wait, did you say she had a Foley catheter?" Dr. Schultz asked, appearing disconcerted.

"Yes, and her urine output has been adequate," I said, trying to provide some clarification.

"Can you show me where it is?"

She just folded her arms. Never a good sign. I started lifting sheets around the edge of the mattress, knowing that it would be hung there, somewhere. With each section I looked under, I became more and more baffled, then frantic. *Shit. I didn't see one.*

"And after you locate her missing catheter, can you describe to the rest of us what 'adequate' means?"

"Um, sure. Her output has been greater than her input?" Dr. Schultz was now questioning everything that I said.

"Oh, good. We don't use actual numbers in medicine anymore? Got it. Let's move on. Which one of the three diets you listed her as being on is she actually on? This one should be easier for you, since numbers are not required as part of your answer."

What is she talking about? Three diets? "She's on a full clear-liquid diet."

The second-year resident, Dr. Manuel, perhaps trying to save me from myself, said, "No, no, no. She's only on sips."

I agreed with her. "Right. Clears. Sips of water."

Schultz's frustration was boiling over. "Well, is it a clear diet, full liquids, or sips? Pick one."

"I think she's on sips of full clears."

"You think she's on sips of full clears? Is she getting only sips of water, or is she on a clear diet?" Dr. Schultz continued to press.

"Wait a minute. Which one did I say she was on?" It's poor form for students to be the ones asking questions. "I'm pretty sure I said that she was on clears."

"Pretty sure? Like, pretty sure she has an invisible catheter, recording invisible urine, in pretend amounts? That kind of sure?"

"I said she was on clears, Dr. Schultz."

"Then my apologies. My mistake. I just misheard you. My fault. No worries. Please continue. You're on a roll. This is going so well. And by the way, Dr. Manuel—the other resident—disagrees with you."

"No, my apologies. I guess I mixed up the difference between sips and clear liquids."

Dr. Manuel chimed in. "She's on sips."

"Great, we have the diet under control. Shawn, can you finish this remarkably precise presentation in a way that makes more sense to us? I don't know, maybe construct it like a SOAP note. Do you know what a SOAP note is?"

By now, you know me extremely well, so you know what I wanted to say in that moment: "Why yes, Dr. Schultz, I do know what a SOAP note is. In fact, I recently met a psychiatrist whose best friend in medical school invented the SOAP note. The S means subjective. That's what the patient tells you. The O is the objective, or what you observe by watching and examining the patient. The A is your assessment. This is where you create your differential diagnosis and defend it. The P is the plan. That should be self-explanatory." But I didn't.

Hillary was amazing. Again, jumping in to defend her student, as we concluded rounds in the final patient's room, she said, "Dr. Schultz, Shawn is taking his national board exam tomorrow, so I know he has been under a lot of pressure and is functioning on very little sleep."

Everyone, except Schultz, wished me luck. Schultz, however, addressing every person in that room, said something that made perfect sense and will stay with me forever: "I don't care. You know who else doesn't care? The patient. Your patient deserves you to be perfect, every time, no matter if it's your kid's birthday, your grandmother died, it's Christmas Eve, or you're taking your boards. Am I clear?"

I took that advice, went home, and did precisely what I had promised I would not do, studied until midnight. If I can get one question closer to perfection, it might save a life.

April 28, 2001, Saturday. The national board exam.
[1 day since last entry]

It's over. I was expecting to feel this immense weight lifted, but I don't. Beyond my windshield, staring back at me, is the dimpled gray wall of the parking garage. Rising from my hood, as if projected onto the concrete, is a daydream of scrolling board questions. They frequently stop to hover, I question my answers, then it shifts to the next one. On that wall, I revisited and reanalyzed all 360 questions. They came in blocks of ninety, with one block being completely experimental (questions that wouldn't count, but would be used "for research purposes"). Students don't know which ninety they are. You are allotted ninety minutes per ninety-question block and can't leave the room until those ninety minutes are over.

I figured I was in trouble when I had to completely guess on the first eight questions. At that point, laughably, I figured I had little chance to pass, but the exam seemed to get easier. During the first ninety, I felt reasonably confident with two-thirds of my answers. That second batch was brutal. The script had flipped. I only felt confident on a third of them.

At that point, I was fatiguing, so I signed out and took lunch in my car, finishing it with a king-sized Snickers bar to give my brain some sugar, and even went for a drive with the windows down. I saved twenty of the sixty permitted minutes of break time in case I wanted it before the final ninety, and I was glad I did. I used every second. The 180 post-lunch questions were just about where I thought they'd be on the difficulty scale. I couldn't believe how many questions seemed verbatim from my *Pearls of Wisdom* book. If I pass, the odds of which might be as good as rolling snake eyes on a single throw of the dice, I'll be able to credit that hit list I focused on during the final two-week push.

The results will be mailed and should arrive in less than three weeks. I might wait until after my graduation party in June to open them.

Dammit! I don't feel any relief. What is wrong with me? This is crazy. I'm flat and numb. What do I do now? I didn't plan a party. I don't feel like calling anyone, but I suppose I have to. I'll be on the phone all night, repeating the same story. How about a celebratory whiskey? Nah. A half-gallon of ice cream? Meh. I just want to retreat to my room and sleep for two days. That's what I want.

Where's the relief? I deserve some fucking relief!

This is how I am going to feel until I open that envelope in three weeks, isn't it?

April 30, 2001, Monday.
[2 days since last entry]
The moment I saw Hillary, I noticed a big grin on her face. "So, how'd it go? You must be so relieved! Everyone always is," she said.

Lying through my teeth, I replied, "As expected. It was tough, but I think I did okay."

"When will you know?"

"A couple of weeks, they said. But, hey, I wanted to thank you again."

"For what?"

"Now that my focus is no longer on boards, I'm ready for anything you throw at me. And thank you for sticking up for me at rounds last week. You didn't need to do that, and it was probably risky for you. It didn't go unnoticed, so, thank you. And if it's still okay with you, I think I need to go home on Thursday night like we had discussed. I need to be sure RTC is okay with it. I haven't asked them yet."

"You got it. And if you choose not to say anything to them, your secret is safe with me."

"Thanks, but I will definitely clear it with them first."

When I made it home, I had to call Dan. He took the boards on the same day as I did. I wondered how he was feeling. I know I couldn't think straight yesterday. I fretted all day. Dan is always calm and level-headed. Whenever I've been standing on a cliff, this guy has talked me down. "So, Dan, what did you think?"

"I mean, I probably passed, but if I didn't, hey, it's only one test. I can take it again. How about you?"

"Well, bud, I'm in a bit of a predicament. As you're probably aware, I failed my H&P competencies."

"What? No way! You're frickin' lying. You did not. I was just telling a bunch of people last week how, if there is one person in our class who knows these exams inside and out, it's you."

"I know them. I just chose the wrong ones to perform. I took the scenario they gave me down a wrong path and couldn't get myself back on track. It would've helped if I'd remembered to gather a set of vitals. I'm such a dipshit. Nadine was so cool, though. I ran right over to her office afterwards and we chatted for a bit. I guess I'm not the only one. They're going to have a remediation day. But listen, I can't stop thinking about the boards. I was convinced by having them in my rearview that I'd have this massive weight lifted, but I feel exactly the same as I did the night before I took them."

"Really? I got into my car, cranked up Pondering Judd, and headed out to some jewelry stores to look at diamonds for Bethany. I felt great. Hey, it's one test. You can take it again if you don't pass. It's not the end of the world. You'll still get to go to the coating ceremony and graduate even if you don't pass your boards, although I'm sure you did. And now that you have the experience of the H&P competency, you'll crush that remediation."

I took one step back from the cliff.

"How's your surgery rotation going?" he asked.

"My preceptor, Hillary, has been amazing, but I requested leniency during the first two weeks because of the boards, so now I have to step up my game. I did some math after my grade came in for the ninth rotation. As it stands, I'm a fraction of a point away from graduating with high honors. An A on this rotation will get me there."

"Well then... Go get that A! Not that anyone will care twenty years from now."

I knew he was right, but my brain couldn't come to terms with it. If I failed my boards, but graduated with high honors, at least I'd have a consolation prize.

May 1, 2001, Tuesday.
[1 day since last entry]
The caseload was slow today, so I took the opportunity to get to a secluded area and call Nadine.

"Shawn! Oh, my God! You, Dan, and a couple of others took your boards this weekend, right? You must feel so relieved."

"Ha! Everyone keeps saying that, but it's not becoming any more believable. Nadine, I don't feel any relief at all. Am I the weird one?"

"Yes, but not for that reason. I'm sure you did great. You put in the time. You'll be rewarded. If not, you just take it again, but next time you'll know exactly what to expect."

"The irony here is that I'm calling to schedule my H&P competency remediation, you know, because I was rewarded last week for putting in all that time learning my physical exams over the last two years." We both got a chuckle out of that. Okay, maybe only *she* found it funny. "And the second reason I'm calling is because I have an enormous favor to ask of you. I need to go home this Thursday night."

She immediately thought the worst. "Is everything alright? Your family? Karen?"

"They're all fine, but I'm not alright, Nadine. Boards are done. I've only seen Karen once in four months. It's my birthday on Saturday. I need to go home. Three days is all I'm asking. Let me miss clinical this

Friday. Hillary and I have already discussed it, and she is completely supportive."

"Go!" she said.

"Seriously?"

"Go, Shawn! See your bride. Come back with renewed vigor. But I expect an A out of you for this one."

Oh, I'll get that A. I will graduate with High Honors.

May 7, 2001, Monday.

[6 days since last entry]

I drove home from New Hampshire last night feeling like a new man. This weekend with Karen, and seeing friends and family, could not have been more perfectly timed. There was no talk about "the exam," my failure at competencies, or my standing micrometers from high honors. Yes, the board results were still hanging over my head, but more like a butter knife than a freshly sharpened guillotine.

I have a massive decision to make when I arrive at work tomorrow. Dan called me about ten minutes ago to inform me he passed his boards. Since we took the exam on the same day, if his score was in, so was mine.

"Shawn, you have to call," Dan demanded. "Someone named Sue picked up. I gave her my social security number, date of birth, and confirmed my testing date and site. She said, 'Congratulations, Dan, you passed.' I just started running around the office and yelling, 'I passed! I passed! I passed the boards,' and I could not stop laughing. Everyone was cheering and shaking my hand. When I could finally breathe again, I confirmed Sue was the name of the person on the other end of the phone. 'It's Sue, right? Okay, Sue, listen. I have no kids, but I can promise you this: when I become a parent, I'm naming my firstborn Sue, or Susan, or Suzanne, whatever your name is. I don't care if it's a boy or a girl. Their name will be Sue. Thank you, thank you, thank you, thank you!' So, Shawn, you must call tomorrow. Get this over with. Do it."

"I'll sleep on it, Dan, even though now I won't actually sleep at all. But congrats, brother. I love you, man."

That solidified my decision. I will place the call tomorrow. I needed to know. Untreated insanity is costly for the soul and can arrest the heart. I was about to be robbed of a restful night of sleep, but closure could be hours away.

May 8, 2001, Tuesday.

[1 day since last entry]

While we were in the recovery room after our second case, I told Hillary that I needed to make a private call at some point.

"Is it your board results? It is, isn't it? So, you decided to call? Are you sure your results are ready?"

"It is, I did, and they are."

"Okay, let's go get lunch and head up to the office. I'll leave you alone and be sure no one walks in on you."

At lunchtime, when I got to the cafeteria check-out line with my tray, I had spilled a quarter of my water from shaking, and I still had my surgical beanie on, looking like I had just run a 10k in ninety-five-degree temps.

Hillary opened the door to the surgical PA's office for me. "We'll be down the hall in the lounge. No rush. If you need to take a walk after to clear your head, no worries. Come find us when you're ready."

The door closed behind me and I sat at one of the three desks. My back was to the door. I looked down at the large paper calendar where my elbows rested and found the empty box for today: May 8. An old-style burgundy phone was staring back at me. Connected to its receiver, which found its way into my hand, was a three-foot, tightly coiled cord. I took an index card out of my breast pocket and stared at the phone number. *No matter what happens, and no matter what they tell me—pass or fail—I'm going to be okay. This won't be the end of the world. I need to know. I can't live like this until after I graduate.*

Minutes lapsed before I found the courage to dial. I took three seconds between pressing each number. With the eleventh digit entered, I swallowed hard as the phone rang. My mouth became a desert.

There's still time to hang up and wait a bit longer. Maybe I'm not ready to hear this. Maybe there...

"Good afternoon. N-double-C-P-A. This is Bonnie. How can I help you?"

Hang up. Hang up. Hang up.

"Hi, Bonnie. I'm calling about the status of my national board exam."

I gave her my vitals: name, date of birth, social security number, date of exam. I could hear her clicking the keyboard as I rattled them off.

"Are you sitting down, Shawn?"

Oh, shit. I failed.

"I'm sitting." The lump in my throat swelled.

"Well, you may want to stand up and start celebrating. You passed!"

"I passed? I passed?!" I did stand up, like a bloodied and swollen Rocky Balboa, after triumphantly defeating the Russian, Ivan Drago, in Rocky IV. I just wanted to leap into someone's arms, and I would get my wish as the door busted open behind me. Hillary, Jules, and a half dozen medical students and residents, who I'm guessing had their ears to the door, fled in, surrounded me, began cheering, and hoisted me onto their shoulders.

The relief that I had been longing for since April 28th had arrived, and it was the most incredible feeling I had ever encountered.

Now, as for those 0.02 points? I've got nine days. I'm going to ride this high to the promised land. It should be easy, but I've still got one intimidating obstacle: the H&P competency remediation, which is in three days.

May 11, 2001, Friday.

[3 days since last entry]

Nadine and Bailey positioned themselves in the exam room, along with a classmate, acting as my patient. *No matter what, just do vitals first.* Hoping to break the tension in the room, "I'd like to announce that no matter what scenario is presented, I will be starting my exam by getting a set of vitals. Just an FYI." And it worked. I had put myself at ease. No one had to ask if I was ready. My chest was out and my chin was high.

"Shawn. Here is your scenario. Kelly is a twenty-nine-year-old female with no past medical history. She arrived in your office with right lower-quadrant pain, which she's had for a few hours. She has no appetite and feels a bit feverish and nauseous. She and her new husband have been trying to conceive, and she tells you she is about two weeks late for her menses. She had an inconclusive pregnancy test this past weekend. You have twenty minutes to complete the appropriate physical exam. Your time starts now."

They were setting me up to think appendicitis, but tossed in the ectopic pregnancy possibility. Upon collecting the vitals, I noted that her blood pressure was soft (low) and her heart rate was almost 130 (normal is between 60 and 100). Her temp was normal, making infection less likely. I performed an abdominal exam and learned that she had guarding and rebound (signs typical of a severe acute inflammatory or infectious process). Concerned for both ectopic pregnancy (in the fallopian tubes), or miscarriage, I talked through the GYN/pelvic exam, which was normal, aside from the deep pelvic tenderness. Because of the abnormal vitals, and having several minutes to spare, I completed a full cardiopulmonary exam as well. "I'm done. Can we call an ambulance for her now?"

My partner nodded in agreement, and Bailey and Nadine conferred for a moment, then Nadine announced, "That was perfection, Shawn. You missed nothing. It could not have been any better. Great job! This is how we knew you could perform. You're ready."

May 18, 2001, Friday. The final Recall Day.

[7 days since last entry]

Two dozen physician assistant students gathered in the College of Science at RTC, most to take their final written exams, a few to give their final oral patient presentations, and each with a clear sense of relief beaming from their faces. The day was purposefully cut short as final preparations for the Annual White Coat Ceremony still needed to be completed, and the faculty knew that everyone had family arriving in town today.

My final ten days with Hillary at Rocksville General Hospital went brilliantly. I was sure to be the first to arrive every morning, visit all our patients, write the notes and orders, and present them flawlessly at rounds. I fought and earned my way into the operating rooms, quickly proving to the residents and attendings that I was worthy of a front-row seat, not just being anointed as the prince of pulling retractors. I wrote a post-op note on every single patient assigned to our service and when the work was done for the day, I hung out with the evening residents. Whenever they would get paged, I'd ask if I could tag along hoping to run into a valuable learning experience. They were happy to have me. Based on the comments that Hillary wrote on my final evaluation, word of my dedication must have reached her, as she awarded me an A for the rotation.

Just before leaving campus, Nadine allowed us to go to her office one by one to get the scores on the exams we took that morning. I just needed to pass it to secure the 0.02 points, so when she showed me the 88, I knew it would put me over the top.

I have achieved the goals I set when I arrived four years ago. I passed my boards. I passed my H&P competencies. And I will graduate with high honors. What I wanted right now was a quiet moment in the atrium of the College of Science, to kneel, lean forward, and lay a sweet kiss onto the etched marble floor, but as I was making my way there, Dan flew by me towards the exit.

Something was wrong, terribly wrong. This was completely out of character for him, so I got into hot pursuit. Just past the courtyard and nearly into the parking lot, I caught him. "Dan! Hey, Dan! Dude. You alright, brother? What's up?"

"I'm not done."

"Huh? What the fuck are you talking about? You just passed your boards. You passed your H&P competencies. What do you mean?"

"Shawn. I have to retake my psych exam. I just found out I got a sixty-eight on it. I missed passing by one question. If I don't pass the remediation test, I have to redo my entire psychiatry rotation. With Glenwood Hospital closing any second now, who knows how long it might take to find me a place to redo it... Nadine said they'd still let me partake in the coating ceremony tomorrow and at least walk through graduation with our class, but I won't actually receive my degree. All because of one question. One damn question over four years could literally delay my degree by months. It'll certainly make job interviews awkward. One freakin' question. Can you believe it?"

"Dan, think about what you just said. One question. That's all that lies between you and this phenomenal accomplishment. That's it. I failed my competencies, remember? It's okay, man. You got this. You're gonna be fine. You just need to be one question better than before. That's it and you're done. Dude, don't let this cloud the ceremony tomorrow, or graduation next week, or celebrating with friends and family. You've earned this. We've all earned this day. We all deserve it."

I could see his eyes welling up, so I gave him a hug, including the customary three pats on the back just prior to separation, but this time Dan clung on for a few extra beats and I was fine with that.

25

THE GIFT

May 19, 2001, Saturday. The White Coat Ceremony.

[1 day since last entry]

The entire class had been told to arrive at the College of Science one hour before the start time to meet in a small auditorium next to the location of the ceremony. It was the most relaxed I had ever seen the faces of my classmates in four years. They looked glamorous as each of them strut to a seat in the first few rows. Many of the women had flawless make-up and hair that looked freshly cut and styled. They were almost unrecognizable without the pajama bottoms and oversized hoodies befitting of a young college student. The cleanly shaven men wore pressed shirts and creaseless, muted neckties. Accordingly, none of us wore jackets.

During Recall Day, I had made it a point to seek out Helen in confidence so that I could ask her if she'd allow me to address our class for about ten minutes during our private meeting. Before agreeing, she desperately tried to learn the reason behind my request, but I didn't give in.

After Bailey, Taylor, Nadine, and Helen delivered heartfelt final send-offs to us, each with similar themes that would be just what you'd expect for such a memorable occasion, Helen said, "Before we line up to head out, we still have some time. Would anyone like to stand and deliver any thoughts? After a silent pause, Helen shot me a glance and a nod of approval.

"I have a surprise announcement, if you don't mind," I said as I rose and picked up a small backpack. I made my way to the podium and said, "Two years ago, I approached four students in this room to see if they'd be interested in joining an exciting project. Thankfully, they agreed. Upon being accepted to RTC, I vowed to write a book about the experience of going through such a rigorous and demanding medical program. During our first two years, I paid very close attention to every single one of you, knowing that I would eventually settle on a few of you to be my accomplices. I could have picked any of you, but I was looking for very specific qualities. Diversity was important, but commitment and honesty were the most critical elements.

"For the last two years, these select classmates of yours—myself included—carried a microcassette recorder with them everywhere they went. Each of us were to push that Record button and relinquish our most personal thoughts and feelings, or relive a major event, milestone, or interaction on the journey. The mission had to be kept secret. If anyone were to learn that we were recording our most intimate thoughts, it would have irrevocably compromised the project. I needed the recordings to be raw, real, and unapologetic. One of our classmates that I chose was Alex. I have to commend Alex for something he did very early on during our junior year. He bowed out. Why? He expressed difficulty in being as candid as the project deserved. Honesty was the number-one aim. Although saddened by this, I was grateful for his integrity. That left me with three: Dan, Janelle, and Heather. I'd like to have each of them come up here and join me."

As the three made their way to stand by my side, I pulled three wooden plaques of the Declaration of Geneva from my backpack, each customized with their name. After saying a few more words about each of them, I thanked them for their continued commitment that would be necessary through this summer as they finished their final entries. "I don't have any timeline to complete this. It may be two years, or twenty. Who knows? What I do know is that in about five minutes we are going to march out there amongst our faculty, friends, and families, and receive the honor that we have been longing for since we stepped foot into Biology 101, four years ago... the full-length coat, baby!"

A cheer went up and we headed to the corridor. We lined up alphabetically behind the third-year students, who were patiently awaiting our arrival. Those poor souls were there to receive their short coats, just days from starting their first rotations. I recall the fearful look in their eyes and I can say that none of us envied their positions.

The atrium was filled with our loved ones. As the background music faded to zero, Helen addressed the crowd and asked that they welcome the class of 2002 to their reserved seats. A moderate applause filled the space as, one by one, the line of students disappeared in front of us. Once arriving at their chairs, they remained standing and turned their eyes back at us, awaiting our introduction.

Helen announced, "And now, without further ado—they've waited four long years to get to this moment—your next class of physician assistants. Let's hear it for the class of 2001." Thunderous applause rang out, bouncing off the industrial walls and marble floor, reverberating into the high ceilings several levels above, and then back down to us again.

When the crowd came into view before us, they were all standing, and not a single one without an enduring smile directed at their favorite new PA. Huddled together just feet from the tables that held the neatly organized and folded collection of white coats, I found Karen, my parents, my sister, both of my grandmothers, and my future in-laws. I shot them a wave, blew out a puff of air between my lips, and tapped my heart, perfectly content in savoring the moment.

Among four rows of six chairs, my seat was in the far back corner, out of view from most of my classmates. When the roar of the crowd began dissipating, I motioned to them with my arms, encouraging them to keep this ride going for another lap, and they obliged with a bit of laughter and another upheaval of cheering.

After inspiring comments by distinguished guests, the faculty rearranged their positions, forming a line next to the table of coats. Nadine, at the mic, looked right at our seated class, overflowing with anticipation. "This is it," she said. As the alphabet would have it, Dan was first. "Daniel Barney." Our section was not going to let anyone leave this ceremony with their hearing intact, so with each name called, the ovation remained on full-tilt, energetic and unruly.

As tradition would have it, after each graduating senior was summoned to the stage to have Helen slip on our coats, that senior, accompanied by Bailey, would help apply the short white coat onto a member of the upcoming class behind us.

Twenty seniors later, I rose from the back row, knowing my name was next. Nadine called into the mic, "Shawn A. Roussin." I never felt the marble beneath my feet. I was at Nadine's podium in a blink of an eye to give her a thankful embrace.

Helen, ready with my long white coat, invited me to insert my right arm. Once secured, I twirled to accept the left. After she hoisted it upon my shoulders, I turned back to her and gave her a bear hug of epic proportions. "Congratulations, Mr. Roussin. You're a physician assistant. How does that feel, huh?"

"Love you, Helen. You are amazing. This team is amazing. This place is amazing."

"You're our colleague now," Helen added. "Go do great things, Shawn. We trust that you will."

Trying to wipe more mascara from her cheeks, Bailey was next. "I'm not crying. You're crying," she said while trying to keep her cool.

"Bailey, there's only no crying in baseball, so you're allowed a few tears today."

Taylor, who had been shaking everyone's hand, was not getting out of this one. I pulled her towards me and compressed the air from her lungs. "Taylor. I couldn't have done this without you. Thank you for your hard work and dedication to our profession."

I observed the crowd in the mezzanine, the proud families, and the classmates who played a crucial role in my success. Upon arriving at my seat, the buzz was still Richter-scale-worthy as we watched our final classmate, Kristen, receive her coat.

Before Helen began her closing comments, she invited our class to stand on the three descending marble steps that lead to the atrium floor. Once positioned, the keynote speaker instructed us to open our programs to the "Declaration of Geneva" so we could recite this oath together.

The Geneva Declaration, originally adopted by the World Medical Association (WMA) in 1948, has been amended several times, and was intended as a contemporary successor to the 2,500-year-old Hippocratic Oath. Unlike the case of the Hippocratic Oath, the WMA calls the Geneva Declaration a "pledge."

In unison, we read:

*I solemnly pledge myself to consecrate my
life to the service of humanity;*

*I will give to my teachers the respect and
gratitude which is their due;*

I will practice my profession with conscience and dignity;

The health of my patient will be my first consideration;

*I will respect the secrets which are confided in
me, even after the patient has died;*

*I will maintain by all the means in my power, the honor
and the noble traditions of the medical profession;*

My colleagues will be my sisters and brothers;

*I will not permit considerations of age, disease or disability,
creed, ethnic origin, gender, nationality, political
affiliation, race, sexual orientation, or social standing
to intervene between my duty and my patient;*

*I will maintain the utmost respect for human life from
its beginning, even under threat, and I will not use my
medical knowledge contrary to the laws of humanity;*

I make these promises solemnly, freely and upon my honor.

Helen directed us to return to our seats. Once we were settled,
she began her closing comments. She knew to keep it succinct. Our
families were waiting to party and we had long coats to wear around
town (and maybe even to bed). Whatever Helen said, I'm sure it
was immeasurably moving, but during those final words, all that the
twenty-four of us could do was look down at our coats, adjust the
collars, caress the sleeves, try out the pockets, and rub our fingers over
our names that were embroidered in black cursive on the left chest.

Feeling the stitching of my name, I grazed the tip of an object
protruding from the pocket. A pen had been secured into its own
dedicated slot and I inquisitively slid it out. The barrel was coated in a
shimmery satin blue. A polished black ring divided its center. The clip
was glossy gold. I twisted the two ends a quarter turn which presented
the tip of the ink cartridge. It was now ready for writing. As I did this,
it drew my attention to the barrel again. I saw my name, Shawn A.
Roussin, PAC, engraved on it in gold block letters. It was the very first
time I had ever seen PAC after my name.

I turned to Heather on my right. "Oh, my God! These pens are awesome. Can you believe the faculty did that for us?"

Holding my pen out for her to acknowledge, she looked down into her chest pocket, felt around and patted her other pockets, but came up with nothing. "I don't have one." She turned to her right where Tracy had just stood up and was calculating a path to her family. "Tracy? Check your pockets. Do you have a pen?" Heather pointed to her empty pen slot. Tracy looked down, tapped the pocket, and said, "No, why?"

"Shawn had this gorgeous pen in his. Look."

I held it out for Tracy to admire. "Wow! It's beautiful. And your name? Shawn, I think that's a gift."

"Wait. What? But…" *Karen? Where's Karen?*

I left my position and rushed towards her, fully aware of her last location. Only steps away, she divided an older couple. "Sorry. Excuse me," she said as she weaved around three kids. "Sorry. Trying to get through." Nearly toppling my dad, she apologized to him. "Oh, sorry, Arthur!" After vaulting up two steps, she leapt into my arms. Her heels left the floor. "You did it, baby. You did it. You're a physician assistant."

"The pen." I pulled it out to show her.

"Yeah, I planted it in your coat before the ceremony started. Now you have something to use for your first official signature as a PA."

August 16, 2001, Thursday.

[Who cares how many days since my last entry?]

I met Dr. Driscoll in the surgical lounge at Hillsborough Hospital just after 7:00 am for my first official day at General Surgical Specialists of New England. After changing into scrubs to prepare for our 8:30 am inguinal hernia repair, I put on the white coat that I had received from RTC back in May.

I confirmed my pen was in its home, against my heart, right under my name, then Dr. Driscoll and I headed over to the ICU to check on a patient he had admitted over the weekend for a perforated diverticulum. He wrote the progress note, a few orders, and signed them both.

Since we still had a little time, we ran up to the sixth floor where he had another post-op patient from the previous week who was probably going home today. "Have you done discharge summaries before?"

"Only a few, but it was during my final rotation, so I'll be fine. Slow, but fine."

"Okay, because the PAs do all the DC summaries. Get them done as soon as possible. Don't let them pile up or they get on my ass about being delinquent."

"Got it."

Dr. Driscoll wrote the note and signed his orders.

The hernia procedure was swift and uncomplicated. Dr. Driscoll showed me how to do a buried subcuticular stitch using a dissolvable suture. He started it, I finished it. "Well, well, now. I can see you've operated a needle driver before. You're closing all of my surgical wounds from now on."

Dr. Driscoll was waiting for me in the recovery unit when we wheeled the patient over. He said, "Post-op orders: I have a standard template for certain procedures that we keep in this filing cabinet under my name. This guy had a hernia, and because he's older with some cardiac issues, he'll probably stay overnight. We'll see. Let's plan on that." He withdrew his order form from the folder and handed it to me. "Take a look. Fill it out as best as you can while I dictate my operative report, then I'll review it."

Most of it was completed already. Using a plain black pen that I found sitting on the counter, I circled a few things from an optional list and then wrote in the patient's regular meds.

When Dr. Driscoll finished, he wheeled his chair over to me. "Perfect. Just sign it and throw it in the orders tab of his chart."

He said, "Sign it."

I looked down at the thin black line positioned at the bottom of the sheet. I thought back to the days in high school when I would sit in English class and practice my autograph as Mrs. Myers would read excerpts from *Brave New World*, knowing one day I would sign the poster of my band, a copy of our latest album, or a groupie's chest. Or maybe I was preparing to sign the end of a Louisville Slugger, the sweet spot of an official Major League baseball, or my own Topps baseball card.

I'll never make it on to MTV. And you'll never see my Hall of Fame plaque hanging in Cooperstown. But that's okay. This autograph would be more important.

Dr. Driscoll interrupted my reminiscing, "Hey, you okay? You gonna sign? You need a pen?"

"I'm good. I've got a pen." I pulled out my gift, read my name in gold, and gave it a twist. "This is my first official signature as a PA."

"Do you want me to take a picture?"

"No, not necessary. I have a feeling this moment will stay with me forever."

Shawn A. Roussin, PAC   date

EPILOGUE

Three weeks after that first signature, I was in an exam room shadowing Dr. Driscoll when his phone started vibrating. He would normally do the respectful thing and allow it to go to voicemail, but since he was on call that day, he removed it from his belt and glanced down.

"My apologies. I have to take this."

After he shimmied out of the room, I grabbed the pre-op forms from the counter and picked up the interview where he had left off. Before I could finish asking the patient about his family history, the door flew open.

I hadn't known Dr. Driscoll that long, but it was long enough to read the terror on his face.

Still holding his phone to his ear, he waved me out. "Now!"

Leaving the room, I chased Driscoll through the maze of hallways, passed the kitchen, and into an empty office.

"We've got to get to New York," he announced. "It's almost nine o'clock now. Can you be back here by noon? Pack for a week, maybe two. Just the essentials."

"New York? What the hell are you talking about?"

"That was my sister. She's a cop in Florida. She's outside an elementary school where President Bush is. The secret service is buzzing like a nest of pissed-off yellowjackets. A plane hit a building in New York City. Report of a hijacking. Probably a terror attack. She's not sure. Couldn't say much more. New York needs us. Can you go?"

"Yes. I'll be ready, but what do we do right now? We have a waiting room filling with patients."

"Waiting room!" Driscoll ran to the check-in counter and found three of our staff at their usual stations, cluelessly calm. "Where's the TV remote?" he demanded.

Ginny spun her chair around. "It's next to the fax machine, in that white wicker basket. Why? What's up?"

Driscoll ignored her, snatched the remote, and slid open the frosted window above the counter. Pointing the remote towards the waiting room television, he began frantically scrolling through channels until he landed on live footage of smoke billowing out of the World Trade Center's North Tower.

The patients in the waiting room gathered closer, glued to the coverage. They all pulled out their phones. One came to the window, where we were all viewing the unthinkable video. "I'm leaving. I'll call to reschedule... or maybe not."

Ginny knew who it was. "No problem. We'll wait to hear from you."

The gentleman turned around, reached for the hand of his wife, and as the couple headed for the exit, Driscoll yelled, "Oh, shit!" Those that remained let out a chilling cry. The man and his wife froze as another passenger airliner vanished into the South Tower, raining fire and debris onto the streets below.

Driscoll unintentionally dropped the remote onto the hardwood floor (surgeons don't drop things). "We're at war," he whispered.

"And New York City is ground zero," I clarified. "So why the fuck are we going there?"

"Shawn, New York is going to need trauma surgeons. That's what I am."

"Well, New York may not be there by dinnertime."

"Damn. You might be right." He turned to Ginny, who was still staring at the TV. "Let's hold down the fort here and see how this plays out between now and lunch, but we may need to consider cancelling all appointments for the rest of the afternoon—hell, perhaps the entire week."

We marched back into exam room two, where our patient was engrossed in the book, *The Art of War*, seemingly oblivious to the matters of the world. "I hope everything is okay?" he asked.

"Just an emergency. We should be all clear now," Driscoll said reassuringly.

But we weren't.

While the patient was signing surgical consent forms, I heard a familiar, faint buzzing. Driscoll unsheathed his phone and excused himself again.

I walked our patient to the awaiting surgical scheduler then wove my way back to the unsecured bunker where covert phone calls were being conducted. Driscoll had just ended a conversation. "They hit the Pentagon."

"What?"

"Another plane. Shawn, we're under attack. And they have more."

"More? They?"

"Whoever is doing this. They probably have hundreds more planes in the air right now, ready to hit targets all over the country. I don't know. The White House? Other buildings? Sears Tower? The Capitol? If they can hit the fucking Pentagon, they can hit anything. I'm calling the boss. Hopefully he's out of surgery."

By "the boss," he meant Dr. Hopedale. He put the call on speaker.

"You've heard?" Driscoll asked.

"I figure I am about as up-to-date as the rest of us. How are things at the office?"

"A few have cancelled, but most are still on the schedule."

"Can you muddle through the rest of the morning without Shawn?"

"Of course."

"Okay, let's send Shawn across town to the Medical Center to get the rounding done. Bob and I have one case left and then we'll see all of our admitted patients over here. Let's check in at least hourly. Got it?"

"We got it. Let's roll," I confirmed, grabbing my keys to the Honda, unaware that it was about to be driven on its final voyage.

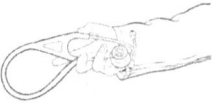

As I drove across town, I called Karen. "What are you hearing down there?" I asked. She had been working in a northern suburb of Boston, still close enough to see its skyline.

"They are leaving it up to the individual employee as to whether we want to go home. Some have spouses and family that work downtown, so those that do are tending to leave. It is my understanding that they are evacuating all high rises in the city. What about you?"

"We have a plan for the rest of the morning, but mostly going about the day as usual unless something changes. Let's try to talk again during lunch."

As I dashed through the hospital halls, nurses' stations were abandoned. Staff were crowding into patient rooms to gather around televisions, so I went about my work entirely unnoticed. That was, until I overheard a respiratory therapist reading the scrolling words at the bottom of the live feed. "All civilian aircraft ordered to land at nearest airport."

"No flights?" Removing my stethoscope from the patient's abdomen, I stood up and turned to the TV. "But I'm going on my honeymoon in a couple of weeks."

"I don't think anyone is going anywhere for a very long time," my patient softly muttered. Then her voice turned to shock. "Oh, my God! Look! One of them is falling."

The South Tower had collapsed onto its footprint. A plume of dust rose so high that only the antenna of the North Tower remained visible, and the cloud was so wide that it blanketed all of Manhattan within seconds.

I sped out of the room, wrote the most concise progress note of my fledgling career: "No complaints. Afebrile. Benign exam. Continue current care." I scribbled the same note in the charts of my other two patients then ran to the exit.

I turned left out of the physician parking lot and coasted down the hill to the stop sign. As I released the clutch to make my way onto Main Street, my dash lights lit up like a Christmas tree, and the Honda went dead. No matter how many times I turned the key and pumped the gas, I couldn't revive it. Punching the steering wheel and elbowing the driver's side door window also wouldn't ignite the engine. I sat in the middle of the road. New York was falling, DC was burning, and we were approaching Defcon 2. I looked up through my sunroof and saw the contrails of a plane—*the sky is full of bombs.*

Two physicians who were behind me and had witnessed the Honda's death pushed me to a safe place, where I broiled for an hour in the sun, awaiting the tow truck.

From the waiting area of the local dealership, Karen finally picked up my fifth call. "Everything alright? I wasn't expecting to hear from you for another hour or so."

"Not exactly. I mean, it's kind of hard to bitch about what I'm going through right now after watching people trying to avoid incineration by jumping from ninetieth-story windows."

"Are you serious? I can't get to a TV, not that I really want to if that is what they are showing. What's up on your end?"

"I don't think the Honda is going to make it. Just had to get towed to a nearby dealer. Said they can put a tech on it now but it might be hours before they have a diagnosis."

I stayed preoccupied with the television as the hours ticked by. Both towers on the ground, the Pentagon still on fire, and somewhere in Pennsylvania, a single hole in the ground was found smoldering.

The service department supervisor sat beside me, the lone person awaiting their fate in the waiting area. The news was bad.

He ran down the list of issues and gave me an estimate for the repairs. "I also took the liberty to check the Kelley Blue Book value of your Accord, and well, basically to fix this it'll cost you twice as much as your car is worth. If I can get the parts in the morning, I could have it done by Thursday afternoon."

"Go ahead. I don't have much choice. I just started my first job a month ago and I'm getting married in two and a half weeks. I'm not in any position to buy a new car right now."

He went back to his computer to start ordering parts and I called Karen back.

"Any chance you can come get me after you leave work?"

"I just left," she said. "What's the verdict?"

"Gonna cost about two thousand dollars more than the car is worth. That'll more than wipe out my second paycheck, which I haven't even received yet."

"Shawn, do I recall you saying a year ago that you were going to spend your first paycheck to upgrade your car?"

"Yeah, but I was just blowing smoke. We can't do that... the wedding, honeymoon, saving for a house."

"Do it," she said.

I've never heard her so sure of something (aside from that wedding proposal acceptance thing).

"Just do it. You've busted your ass for how many years, babe? You deserve it. Sure, the timing isn't exactly ideal, but to hell with it."

Wanting to strike while the iron was hot, and since the nuclear holocaust no longer seemed imminent, I recruited my dad to be my wingman for several test drives. The only fee for his advice was a steak dinner and a couple Miller Lites, so I couldn't go wrong. Over several days, we tortured the salespeople at multiple dealerships, but nothing excited me until I hopped behind the wheel of a Lexus GS400.

"Dad. I don't know. It feels too big. It's almost too comfy. As boring as the Acura TL was, at least it felt sporty."

"What did you think about the Audi A6?"

"I absolutely loved driving it, and the styling was attractive, but it won't be as reliable as an Acura or Lexus."

"Hey, take a left at the next light," my father instructed. "I think there is an old industrial complex down there. It's time to see how much 'sport' is buried in this beast."

Upon arriving at the abandoned lot, my dad began advising me of the items I needed to thoroughly "test."

"Check the acceleration from a dead stop. Does it drive perfectly straight with your hands off the wheel? Perform a slalom. Hear any noises from the front end? Is it smooth? Pound those brakes a few times. Solid? Any rubbing? What's the turn radius? How fast can you corner before the tires start sliding on the asphalt and begin squealing? These are the things you need to know."

It took a few cautious laps, but I eventually crossed off each exercise from the assignment.

"What do you think?" I asked my dad.

"Who, me? How am I supposed to know? I didn't drive it. Besides, it only matters what *you* think. It's your name on the loan."

"I want your opinion, Dad."

"Then pull over."

Once the Chinese fire drill concluded, my dad adjusted the seat, mirrors, and steering wheel.

"Is your seatbelt secured?" he asked me with a shitty grin. "When you test drive a vehicle, you drive it like you stole it. So, hang on. I'm going to pretend this is my '69 Charger for a minute."

I wished I'd had a five-point restraint. A helmet may have been nice too. The suicide handle got a thorough workout, and for some reason, I smelled urine.

Once the Space Mountain ride had finally ended, he gave his conclusion. "This is the one. If it were me, I'd buy this one. Should we go talk numbers?"

"Yes, but can we find a restroom first. I need to change my undies."

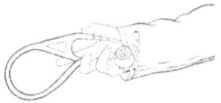

I returned home from the dealership with a pending agreement. Karen's brother and sister-in-law were joining us for dinner so we could put the finishing touches on our wedding festivities. Her brother asked me how the car shopping was going.

"Well, this afternoon I actually put a deal in place for a two-year-old Lexus."

"You mean you are not going with a BMW?" he asked. "When you drove ours this past summer, you absolutely loved it."

"You're right. I forgot about the BMW."

"You should at least drive one before making your final decision."

The following morning, Karen and I were at the BMW dealership and found two used bimmers that piqued my interest; a 528i and a 328i, both 4-door sedans. I assumed that the European racing green 5 Series would feel similar to the Lexus, so we took that one out for a spin. Before I was even out of the parking lot, I didn't like it, but still drove it the full length of the course.

As I pulled back in, I told Karen, "Well, the Lexus it is."

"But you didn't drive the little gold one." That was the 3 Series, a smaller version of the 528i.

"Babe, there is no way I'm going to fit into that thing."

"You're here, so just drive it. Hell, at least open it up and sit in it."

The salesman overheard the urging and pulled the keys to the 3 Series out of his pocket. He tossed them to me and attached the dealer plate. "I think you're gonna like this one. Same engine, but a lighter, more compact car. Have fun."

I followed the same route which included some highway, back roads, and stop-and-go traffic. This trial run was a tamer version of my father's *Drive it like you stole it*, but I was still giddy the entire time. When traffic was clear and no homes were in sight, I came to a dead stop in the middle of the road. "Hold on tight. My dad said I should do this to see if I wet myself." Clutching the wheel at ten and two, I took a deep breath in, held it, tucked my chin, and slammed the gas to the floor. A screech rang out, pine cones rattled off of several nearby trees, and birds scattered for cover. The RPMs still redlining, Karen reached over and grabbed my wrist on the shifter knob.

"Whoa! Whoa! Whoa! Holy shit, Shawn."

"Wooooo! Yes! You like?"

"I do! I do!"

"You wanna drive it?"

"Can I?"

"Of course, but you hate cars."

"I know. They suck. But that was fun. Give me a turn."

Rather than pulling back into the lot, I stopped in the breakdown lane just in front of the dealership. Karen and I traded positions. I assumed this would be like any other leisurely Sunday drive with an elderly woman at the controls, but I was pleasantly mistaken.

Following the same route, Karen initially drove conservatively, but as her trust in the ultimate driving machine grew, so did her courage. Stopping on the same stretch of pavement where I had just left my fresh artwork, Karen asked, "Okay, so now what do I do?"

"What do you do? Um, you make sure the coast is clear, you strangle the steering wheel, and push that pedal on the right all the way to the floor."

There was no countdown. She just pulled the trigger. "Like this?"

Our skulls snapped back and stuck to the headrests. Karen's face contorted as if her ponytail was pulled way too tight. One second in, she produced and evil grin. Three seconds in, she was giggling as if her pre-teen crush had just kissed her. A quarter-mile in and she's now laughing uncontrollably (because "cars suck"). Approaching the end to our drag way, I demanded that she select the only other pedal beneath her feet—the brake. Luckily, she takes direction well, or the back of that dump truck would have fed us brunch.

Recovering from my widow-maker, I asked, "So, what do you think?"

"I think if you don't buy this car, it'll be grounds for divorce."

"But we're not married."

"And if you don't bring this car home, you won't be married anytime soon, either."

I couldn't risk that she was bluffing, so moments later I did the only smart thing a future husband would do—I wrote the check.

Karen and I were married eleven days later, on September 29, 2001, in Rochester, New Hampshire, at the Governor's Inn. The weather that evening was perfect for the outdoor ceremony we had dreamt. In the tradition of doing nontraditional things, we expanded our wedding party to include a Man of Honor, as chosen by Karen, and a Best Woman, chosen by me. Karen selected her father, Peter, and with Karen's blessing, I named Kendra and Sadie.

Fortunately, flights were only grounded for four days after 9/11, so we were able to go to Cancun for our honeymoon. About a week into our ten-day adventure, Karen and I took the elevator down to the lobby to have an early breakfast before embarking on our deep-tank SCUBA certification. When we came around the corner, we saw the back of hundreds of frozen heads, all of them fixated on the wall of large televisions behind the bar. Operation Enduring Freedom was raining down on Afghanistan. Massive air strikes were relentlessly taking out Taliban and al-Qaeda forces, such that the video on the screens resembled a game of Space Invaders set to expert level.

I grabbed Karen's hand. "Now we really are at war," I said. "And we're in Mexico."

A couple that had stopped beside us, also in awe of the video game explosions, overheard me. "When are you supposed to fly out?" the woman asked.

"A couple of days. Why? Did they ground all flights again?"

"Not to my knowledge," her partner chimed in, "but that could change in a hurry."

"There are worse places to be stranded, right?" Karen added.

"True, but we both have jobs to get back to next week, although who knows what the country will look like by then."

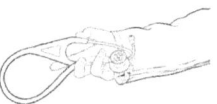

We returned to our homeland and our jobs on schedule to find every corner of our country carpeted in red, white, and blue. It felt like a great time to be American.

My concerns about the commute, long hours, unfair salary, minimal vacation time, and high stress were all validated. Those matters were conquerable, at least until we learned that we would be welcoming a son in early 2004. Ultimately, that was the real reason why I would resign from that first job, having not even been there a full two years.

No sooner had we confirmed the heartbeat on the sonogram, when Dr. Ed called from the Daniel Webster Hospital emergency department.

"Hey Shawn. How's that surgery job working out?"

"Why do you ask?"

"Our Express Care is thriving and we need another PA to help cover the expanded hours. You still interested in emergency medicine?"

"Yes. And your timing is impeccable. I am going to be a father. I need to get some of my life back."

"No kidding. Congrats. That's awesome. I'll have our manager call you to set up an initial meeting with the entire team."

Forty-eight hours after that interview, Dr. Otis, their medical director, called to offer me the job, but not without some trepidation. He made it clear that he had cast the deciding vote in my favor. Half of the doctors within the department had voiced their fears about hiring a provider without emergency experience. The other half fully supported me. Although their fears were justified, it was going to be an unwinnable battle for me from day one.

As Karen's belly expanded, we sank every penny into savings (except for the BMW payment). It was time to leave the confines of the in-laws and purchase a homestead of our own. After looking at about thirty properties, we settled down in historic Exeter.

In January of 2004, Carter arrived (named after my favorite character from the hit TV series, *ER*). But the new year also brought another bundle of joy in the form of the next elected medical director for the emergency department. This director had been on the side of Team: Must Have Experience at the time of my hiring.

It was nine months into the director's tenure when she called me into her office and closed the door. Carter had just begun taking his first steps. Karen and I had just paid our first property tax bill.

"Have a seat."

I had been waiting for this, but until it happens, you never know how you're going to react.

"We know you're in a tough spot, Shawn—new home, new baby— so we are empathetic to your situation, but the team has decided that the emergency department is not for you. Consider today to be your ninety-day notice. It's just not going to work out here."

The pleasure on her face was measurable. The alarm on mine was palpable. I had effectively just been fired.

I wasn't about to go back to surgery, and I hated the hours of the ER: every other weekend, half of the holidays, and half of the evenings. Not that it mattered—no ER was going to hire me now anyway. This medical director would make sure of that.

The ninety days flashed before my eyes as if it were ninety seconds. Despite my exhaustive job search, nothing transpired, so on day ninety-one, I was unemployed, at least as a PA. Anticipating the worst, and not wanting to default on my student loans or become homeless,

I had lined up several painting jobs—almost four months' worth—while I kept my eyes and ears peeled for the next opportunity.

"Babe. Pondering Judd is playing a show in Dover at a small club tonight. Mind if I go check it out?"

"Of course not. Say hi to the guys for me."

Brian, the bassist, who was an old high school friend, came to me with beer in hand during their first set break and asked me how I was doing.

"I'm actually looking for a job. Can you believe it?" I said.

"There is someone here tonight that you should meet. Her name is Michelle. She is the practice manager at a place in Barrington. Hang on. Let me go find her. I'll introduce you."

Brian located her on the far side of the bar and struck up a conversation. After a few minutes, he turned and waved me over.

"Brian tells me you're a PA," she asked.

"That's correct. I have a lot of surgical experience, and recently left a job in the Daniel Webster emergency department. I'm looking to get into primary care or urgent care."

"Here's my card. Call me Monday morning. I think I have a job for you."

"Tell me more."

"Half of the practice is a primary care office and the other half is a full-time urgent care that sees walk-in patients from 8:00 am to 8:00 pm, Monday through Friday, and 9:00 am to 3:00 pm on Saturdays. I have two full-time PAs that are going out on maternity leave at the same time in about two months and I have to find someone to work their hours for twelve weeks, maybe longer."

After two interviews over the next six days, I was offered the position. It was only per diem (as needed), but I was effectively full-time, working over sixty hours per week. The urgent care, one of the only facilities of its kind around, was thriving, so much so that when both Steph and Tara returned from their leaves, Michelle extended me an offer to stay on as a permanent employee.

In the middle of my five years at the Barrington Urgent Care, my daughter, Cecelia (CC) was born.

To make ends meet, I moonlighted at a local family practice, seeing only same-day acute visits, grabbed some shifts at the organization's emergency department, and landed a weekend urgent care gig right across the street from Fenway Park in Boston.

Despite the love and support of my wonderful wife and beautiful children, I was severely overworked and feeling increasingly empty.

One night, I confided in Karen, "It's time."

"Time?"

"Yes. I need music back in my life."

"I think you do too. I wondered when this day would come."

"Okay, but if I do get back into the music scene, I want a new drum set."

"Shawn, you've had the same set since you were thirteen. I think you deserve a new one."

The following weekend I brought home a five-piece DW Collector's Series kit wrapped in champagne sparkle. Within a few weeks, I connected with a local female singer-songwriter and eventually assembled a full band, Luscious Digs. We played in venues around New England for almost two years, then recorded a CD called Forever 29. Six weeks after the release party, two members fled for another project and we were never able to put the pieces back together.

Crushed, I never played drums again. And I was ready for another change.

In the spring of 2010, Tara and I were working side by side at the urgent care. She was about to forward me an offer.

"Have you ever thought about getting back into surgery?" she asked.

"I don't know. I have it pretty damn good here. I work three twelve-hour shifts, Tuesday through Thursday, so I can have a four-day weekend each week if I want it, even though I never take advantage of it with all of my other per diem jobs."

"What if someone paid you twenty-five percent more? Would that entice you?"

I stopped typing. "I'm listening, but it would have to be an absolutely perfect situation."

"Hear me out." Tara stood up and closed the door to our office. "You're going to get a call by the end of this week. I interviewed for a new PA position yesterday. It's working with the thoracic surgeon that covers Daniel Webster and Lilac City Hospitals. After listening to their pitch, I had to turn it down, but I told them I knew the guy who would be perfect... you. I gave them your contact info."

I couldn't pass it up, so back to surgery I went. Fast-paced, thrilling, demanding, and a massive pay increase, but it came at a price—taking seven days of call every other week. It was not sustainable. It was taking a toll on my marriage and my ability to be the father I wanted to be. I didn't want to leave, so I needed a way out.

Then along came an affiliation agreement between DWH (Daniel Webster Hospital) and MGH (Massachusetts General Hospital). Suddenly, thoracic surgeons from MGH were sitting in on our weekly multidisciplinary chest clinics. Soon after, one of them actually started operating at DWH, and I was being asked to assist. Less than a month later, Lilac City Hospital pulled out of Seacoast Thoracic Associates (the name of our practice), thus eliminating about a third of our patient referrals. The writing was on the wall—we were getting pushed out of business. The entire practice was eliminated a few months later, but during that time, at the urging of the Daniel Webster CEO, the head of the trauma service asked me if I would stay on to lead their new thoracic surgery program. "Let us know what it would take. Just name your number."

"They are giving me a blank check, Karen."

"What are you going to do?"

"I'm going to decline. I'm not taking on a larger, more stressful role. I'm done with surgery. I'm done with evenings, and weekends, and holidays. I'm done answering calls and pagers all night long. I've had it with chaos. I'm going into primary care; a job I'd promised I would never do."

Revising and polishing my resume, I blanketed the region with cover letters. I contacted every single person I knew who worked in the primary care setting.

Dr. Daniels, a colleague from the Barrington Urgent Care, was first to respond. He was working a per diem job in a family practice for a different organization.

"I took the liberty of forwarding your info to Angela, the practice manager who hired me many months ago," he told me.

With no experience in managing chronic diseases, Angela took a chance and offered me a full-time position in internal medicine at their Manchester office, about thirty-five minutes away.

It was like being a student all over again. The difference this time was that I retained my sanity. While they allowed me to ramp up slowly, I was allowed to have a life—the one I had missed out on for eleven years. I coached baseball, softball, and basketball. I was elected to the baseball league's board of directors and served for six years, becoming the Babe Ruth coordinator. I exercised regularly. I was hunting and fishing. And I relinquished every one of my moonlighting positions. But there was one thing left to do: come home.

At a baseball league bonfire at the conclusion of the 2016 season, I ran into Dr. Mike, a local family practitioner. I'd had a few conversations with him at games where he was watching his sons.

"You're Shawn, right? Aren't you a PA?" he asked.

"Yes, and yes."

"I never see your name on anything. Do you work around here?"

"No. I'm in Manchester. Internal medicine. Been there four years now, but I have been a PA for fifteen."

"Oh, really? That commute must get old."

"I guess. I'm very happy with my job, so I don't mind it too much."

"Do you live here in Exeter?"

"I do."

"What if you could have the same job, but practically in your backyard?"

"Go on. You have my attention."

"I know for a fact we have two open positions in primary care at the same address where I have my office." He pulled out a card from his wallet and wrote two names on the back. "Call Mackenzie or Lauren. I put their extensions on there. Tell them you spoke to me."

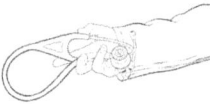

I got the job. On December 23, 2016, I finished my week of orientation. We were advised to dress formally on the final day because they'd be taking our official photos for the website. The only other time I have worn a tie since that day was the afternoon we took the shots for the cover of this book.

So, who am I now? I show up to the office casually dressed—never in a white coat. I walk into the exam rooms prepared. I use first names, or nicknames to greet my patients. I learn the name of everyone in the room. I always sit down, facing their direction. We always talk about things other than why they are here: "How did your son's baseball team do this season?" "Tell me about your fishing trip to Alaska." "Did you make it to North Carolina to meet your first grandchild this winter?" "Did you sell the Mustang and buy that travel trailer?"

Talking about life knocks down walls, creates open relationships and builds the trust needed to provide superior care. These are my patients. This is my community. And this is our home.

I don't know everything, nor will I ever pretend to. I have no problem pulling out my phone to check the top five adverse reactions to a medication that I don't have much experience prescribing.

If my patient doesn't understand something, I will grab one of my handheld dry erase boards and draw a picture of the lungs to show them where I think their pneumonia is, or the urinary tract to describe why kidney stone pain feels the way it does. Sometimes I create charts and graphs to compare their last three years of cholesterol numbers.

There is always time for questions. I want my patients to be comfortable with the plan; after all, this is *their* healthcare. This is *their* appointment time, not mine. In the end, they are in charge. They make the final call. If I think they are making a poor decision, I'll tell them why. If I agree with their decision, I'll show my support. If they don't want a vaccine that has been recommended by whatever governing body is endorsing it; it's their body—they get to decide what goes into it. By going on a cholesterol-lowering medication, this is how much you can reduce your ten-year risk of a cardiovascular event. Don't want to? Fine by me. Not sure you are ready to start a second blood pressure med? Here is what having uncontrolled hypertension will do to your body over the long term. But most importantly, I am going to talk to you about the ways you can address these things without taking a medication.

Unfortunately, this is where the medical establishment often falls flat on its face. Big Pharma, healthcare organizations, the FDA, and the government are not exactly in the business of disease prevention, despite what they appear to promote. There is no money in actual cures, right?

If physician assistant programs want to get serious about caring for patients in the most remarkable and honest way, their governing bodies, the NCCPA and the AAPA, need to make bold changes in the requirements for accrediting PA programs.

I took a full year of pharmacology, and I should have, but I didn't have a class dedicated to nutrition; after all, food is thy medicine and medicine is thy food—the most important drug of all. I took a ten-week pathophysiology course when I needed a full year. Orthopedics was a single unit that lasted about a week. How about an entire course on the art of exercise, or incorporating a series of functional medicine certifications? I can count on one hand how many times I've used information learned in my Algebra II course and still have five fingers left over to give you a high-five. Do you think patients receive any value when students are required to complete electives like Astronomy, Contemporary Art History, Gender Analytics and Equity, or Introduction to Ethnography?

It's encouraging that some healthcare organizations are at least appearing to prioritize patient-centered care, but because our system is deliberately broken and those with the power to create meaningful change simply continue to follow the money, you never know if tomorrow is the day when I ask the train to stop and let me off.

I signed up to learn medicine, and I did. But we can and should do better. How about we start putting the horse *in front of* the cart?

"Hi. My name is Shawn. I'm a physician assistant. It will be an honor to take care of you."

ACKNOWLEDGMENTS

My greatest thanks goes to Karen, my wife, for her love, support, and selflessness. Without her by my side, this memoir would not have been possible.

Thank you to my parents, who have patiently guided me through life with perfect balance, allowing me the freedom to find my way, while keeping me on a path that led me here.

To my in-laws, Peter and Barbara, who accepted me during a time in my life when the path was muddy and full of obstacles, yet loved me as your own.

To the greatest educator I have ever known, Dr. R. Doolittle. His dedication to his students is second to none. Always humble, grateful, and caring, your wisdom, humor, and mastery will be missed. Congratulations on your recent retirement.

To all the physicians who sacrificed so many years of their lives for the greater good of humanity, you have my utmost respect and admiration.

To the original Pondering Judd, who provided me some of my fondest memories: Marty, Steve, Blaise, and Eric. Marty signed a solo record deal in 2009 and released Razed and Reconstructed in 2010. A band by the same name then followed in 2012 and they released two additional LPs. In 2022, he formed North Village. This new project is about to release their debut album. But his most remarkable work comes through the Continuum Arts Collective, a 501(c)3 nonprofit that provides Maine and New Hampshire student artists and musicians with free musical instruments, art supplies, creative instruction, and experiences to flourish as creators. The CAC has served over 5000 students. Please consider visiting them at Continuumarts.org and making a donation.

To Kendra for setting me free. Kendra had moved to Oregon in 1999 where she attended law school, eventually becoming a public defender, legal aid attorney, and union organizer for non-profit law firms.

To Sadie for the ultimate inspiration, and the kiss goodnight. For several years after graduating college, Sadie worked at non-profits that provide wraparound services to individuals dealing with mental health challenges, addiction, and houselessness. She is now pursuing her Master of Social Work from Columbia University.

To my team of beta readers: Dan D., Jim A., PJ, Shelley, Julie V., Caitlin L., Kathy F.—an eclectic group who unselfishly volunteered their time to help bring this story to life. Their insight, life experiences, suggestions, and criticisms were invaluable in shaping this story. I am indebted to you.

Thanks to all of my preceptors. Your voices still provide me with pearls every day.

To my PA/NP students who continue to trust and inspire me.

Julie Blattberg, my first copy editor, whose expertise set the stage. Knowing when to reel me in, and when to let me swim on my own, your intelligence and candor left a lasting imprint on this work.

David Haviland, my final copy editor, whose brilliance, consistency, and craftsmanship to suggest the perfect word, all while wading through a sea of my dangling modifiers, poor use of italics, overuse of ellipses, and mixed-up tenses, finally guided me to type the final period of the final sentence on the final page. (He did not edit this paragraph).

Jim A., my very final proofreader. Just when I thought I was done, this guy meticulously x-rayed every molecule of ink with the vision of Superman. You're the best! To Julie V. and Erika P. for major contributions during the proofreading process. Just when I thought there was nothing left to find, this team uncovered a plethora of flaws that had escaped my final scrutiny. My apologies for overusing Oxford commas, hyphenated words, and em dashes. I owe you more than the loudest exclamation mark could ever scream.

Ed Moran, my photographer, who captured the face on the cover that has been described as warm, compassionate, and believable.

The team of BookBaby cover designers, who stuck with me through multiple "tear it up and throw it in the trash heap" iterations, tolerating one tiny tweak after another, until your brilliant masterpiece popped off the shelf and out of the screen.

Scene break art by Cecelia B. Roussin.

To the 2004 Boston Red Sox. I told you they'd do it, Buster. Rest in Peace.

And to all of those who I confided in, cried with, laughed with, sought advice from, and contributed to bringing this important work to publication.

Shawn A. Roussin is a practicing physician assistant in New Hampshire with over twenty years of experience. A national champion in the extemporaneous writing category for Health Occupation Students of America, Shawn vowed to write the book he had desperately needed to read prior to starting his career path —yet it did not exist.

Always on a quest to find the next delicious ninety proof bourbon, Shawn enjoys fly fishing, grilling the perfect steak, and belting out harmonies to his favorite tunes while in the shower.

Despite his passion for patient care, he'd relinquish all his medical knowledge to have the singing voice of a Grammy Award-winning vocalist for just one day.

SHAWNauthorROUSSIN.com

If you enjoyed this book, please consider leaving
an honest review at amazon.com

www.ingramcontent.com/pod-product-compliance
Lightning Source LLC
Chambersburg PA
CBHW061547120626
46550CB00004B/1402